Library of
Davidson College

Dr. Burney as Critic
and Historian of Music

Studies in Musicology, No. 62

George Buelow, Series Editor

Professor of Musicology
Indiana University

Other Titles in This Series

No. 36	*The Early French Parody Noël*	Adrienne F. Block
No. 57	*American Women Composers before 1870*	Judith Tick
No. 60	*Louis Pécour's 1700* Recueil de dances	Anne L. Witherell
No. 61	*The American Opera to 1790*	Patricia H. Virga
No. 63	*The Fertilizing Seed: Wagner's Concept of the Poetic Intent*	Frank W. Glass
No. 64	*The Secular Madrigals of Filippo di Monte, 1521-1603*	Brian Mann
No. 65	*The Rise of Instrumental Music and Concert Series in Paris, 1828-1871*	Jeffrey Cooper
No. 66	*The Crumhorn: Its History, Design, Repertory, and Technique*	Kenton Terry Meyer

Dr. Burney as Critic and Historian of Music

by
Kerry S. Grant

UMI RESEARCH PRESS
Ann Arbor, Michigan

Copyright © 1983
Kerry S. Grant
All rights reserved

Produced and distributed by
UMI Research Press
an imprint of
University Microfilms International
Ann Arbor, Michigan 48106

Library of Congress Cataloging in Publication Data

Grant, Kerry S. (Kerry Scott)
   Dr. Burney as critic and historian of music.

   (Studies in musicology ; no. 62)
   Revision of thesis (Ph.D.)–University of California at Berkeley, 1977.
   Bibliography: p.
   1. Burney, Charles, 1726-1814. 2. Music–History and criticism–18th century. I. Title. II. Series.
ML423.B9G7 1983   780'.92'4 [B]   82-15955
ISBN 0-8357-1375-X

To Kathy

Contents

Abbreviations and Cue Titles   *ix*

Preface and Acknowledgments   *xi*

1 Critic in Conflict   *1*

2 Burney's Style of Criticism   *17*

3 The Genesis of the *General History of Music*   *49*

4 The Debut of the Critic: The Continental Tours   *65*

5 Music to 1450: The Reluctant Historian   *95*

6 Sacred Music: The Domain of Counterpoint   *125*

7 Chamber Music: Burney the Progressive   *171*

8 Dramatic Music: Burney the Covert Conservative   *221*

9 Burney's Achievement as Critic and Historian of Music   *283*

Notes   *307*

Bibliography   *361*

Index   *371*

Abbreviations and Cue Titles

Correspondents

CB	Charles Burney, Mus.D.
CB Jr.	Charles Burney, D.D.
FB	Frances Burney.
TT	Thomas Twining.

Manuscript Collections

Berg   The Henry W. & Albert A. Berg Collection of English and American Literature, The New York Public Library.
B.M.   British Museum.
Osborn   The James Marshall and Marie-Louise Osborn Collection, Yale University Library.

Burney's Writings

"Memoirs"   Fragments of his "Memoirs" and related materials.
Memoirs   Madame d'Arblay, *Memoirs of Doctor Burney*, 3 vols. 1832.
Account   *An Account of the ... Commemoration of Handel*, 1785.
GHM   *A General History of Music*, ed. Frank Mercer, 2 vols., 1935.
MM   *Memoirs of Metastasio*, 3 vols., 1796.
C.   Articles contributed to *The Cyclopaedia; or, Universal Dictionary of Arts, Sciences, and Literature*, ed. Abraham Rees, 45 vols., 1802-20.
Tours   *Dr. Burney's Musical Tours in Europe*, ed. Percy A. Scholes, 2 vols., 1959.
MMM   *Music, Men and Manners in France and Italy 1770*, ed. H. Edmund Poole, 1969.
PSMFI   *The Present State of Music in France and Italy*, 2d ed., 1773.
PSMG   *The Present State of Music in Germany, The Netherlands and United Provinces*, 2d ed., 1775.

Tagebuch   *Carl Burney's der Musik Doctors Tagebuch einer musikalischen Reise,* 1772-73.

Other Works

GDB   Percy A. Scholes, *The Great Doctor Burney,* 2 vols., 1948.
Hemlow   Joyce Hemlow, *History of Fanny Burney,* 1958.
Lonsdale   Roger Lonsdale, *Dr. Charles Burney: A Literary Biography,* 1965.

Lacunae in the text, where the manuscript has been torn, deleted, or is illegible, are indicated by plus signs + +. Slash marks / / indicate an alternate choice of words in the manuscript. Conventional eighteenth-century abbreviations of "and," "could," "would," and such words have been expanded without note. The dates, attributions, and holders of manuscripts given in the notes are those recorded when the extracts were made from the documents. Continued research on the Burney family and the sale and exchange of manuscripts will doubtless change some of this data.

Preface and Acknowledgments

The heart of this study is the prose of Dr. Charles Burney. It is appropriate that one of music history's most gifted and eloquent writers should retain as much of the role of spokesman for his views as possible. The author's task has been to compile Burney's observations, public and private, from familiar, new, or just relatively unknown sources; to weigh and balance those that seem incomplete, confused, or contradictory; and, when necessary, to scrutinize them for their candor and veracity. No attempt has been made to correct the errors of fact or judgment in Burney's works; indeed, a far larger book than his *General History of Music* could be made by proofing his book and reproofing its author. Two hundred years of scholarship, much of it stemming from the *History,* have produced a chronicle of Burney's art far more accurate and comprehensive than his.

Burney's *History* is now more interesting for its viewpoint than for its utility, but time has not diminished his importance as an observer of his own age. Had he never published his tour journals and his history, our acquaintance with the eighteenth century would be impoverished not only in fact but in spirit. Few of Burney's readers have not become his friend and fellow traveler, visiting great and obscure musicians in France, Italy, Germany, and England through his vivid prose just as his contemporary readers did two centuries ago. His writings are a well-spring of fact and opinion from which few scholars of eighteenth-century musical life have not drawn. His critical assessments have carried great authority because they are manifestly those of an intelligent, musical, and perceptive judge. However, the confidence with which we instinctively embrace his judgments can be shown to be occasionally misplaced.

The genesis of this study was the discovery of a small but significant discrepancy between a passage in Burney's *History* and a parallel passage in a later source, the *Cyclopaedia*. Subsequent comparisons between the whole of the *History* and *Tours* with the encyclopedia articles suggested other topics for investigation and revealed that Burney's chronicle of musical life did not end in 1789 with the *History,* but extended well into the first decade of the nineteenth century. The large cache of manuscripts—only recently made accessible to the scholarly world, on which Roger Lonsdale based his magnificent biography of Burney—shed still more light on Burney's historical and critical writings, especially those about his own era. It is no exaggeration to say that the interest and significance to musical scholarship of the new evidence compelled the author to write this book.

The Burney papers, from which much of the evidence for this study is drawn, consist of more than 2,000 letters and manuscripts dispersed in various collections around the world. The three largest of these are the British Museum, the Berg Collection in the New York Public Library, and the James and Marie Osborn Collection in the Beinecke Library at Yale University. By far the richest of these holdings is the Osborn Collection. Most of the letters to and from Burney's musical acquaintances are preserved there, as well as six notebooks containing collections of materials and drafts of articles intended for inclusion in his *General History of Music* and the *Cyclopaedia*. Also deposited there are several notebooks and other materials such as his examples of Chinese music. The British Museum contains an immense collection of the papers of Burney's friends, associates and family, as well as the few surviving records of his musical colleagues, notably John Wall Callcott and Samuel Wesley. The eleven-volume collection of Burney's "Extracts from Various Musical Writers and Composers" with his annotations in the B.M. taken with the notebooks housed in the Osborn collection provide an intriguing insight into the critic's workshop. The Berg Collection houses a substantial number of Burney's letters, along with the fragments of the "Memoirs." Many fascinating observations about Burney and his time must await publication of the surviving correspondence by the Burney Project at McGill University, but much of the musically related material can be put to use in constructing a new reference with which to evaluate Burney's critical writings.

Burney's published works remain his most important legacy; as such they will take a central position in the analysis of his critical thought and in the evaluation of his contribution to the historiography of music. These include not only the *Tours* and *General History of Music*, but the lesser known *Memoirs of Metastasio*, the *Account of the Commemoration of Handel*, the reviews for the *Monthly Review*, and Burney's final great written achievement, the musical articles for Rees's *Cyclopaedia*.

With the opportunity to transform this study to book form came a great temptation to abridge the discussion of Burney's view of early music, especially the chapter on music before 1450. As Burney, I found "the authorities one is obliged to give in these matters for every *nothing* one says is ruination to all original thought, or connexion of matter: the whole will be shreds and patches..."; on reflection it seemed that only by following Burney through his laborious and difficult task could the reader fully appreciate his great

Preface and Acknowledgments xiii

achievement in making that portion of his work palatable and even occasionally entertaining. Moreover, though Burney's criticism of early music reveals little about the music under consideration, it is a remarkable mirror of the musical thought of his era.

A study of this kind is not possible without the generosity of the owners and curators of manuscripts. I owe a special debt to the late Dr. James Osborn for permitting me to work in his collection of Burney papers, and for providing copies of the most important documents. Dr. Stephen Parks, curator of the Osborn Collection, endured with unfaltering patience and courtesy numerous interruptions and requests for assistance during my weeks at Yale. His hospitality is warmly remembered.

I am grateful to the officials of the following libraries for permission to examine and quote materials in their custody: Yale University, New Haven; the Henry W. and Albert A. Berg Collection of the New York Public Library, Astor, Lenox and Tilden Foundations; the Folger Library, Washington; the Staats und Universitätbibliothek, Hamburg; the Royal Victoria and Albert Museum, London; the British Museum, London. I am also grateful to the staffs in other libraries, who courteously and promptly responded to my requests: the Herzog-August-Bibliothek, Wolfenbüttel; Staatsbibliothek der Stiftung Preussischer Kulturbesitz, Berlin; Deutsche Staatsbibliothek, Musikabteilung, Berlin; Bibliothèque Nationale, the Bibliothèque de l'Opéra, the Bibliothèque Nationale Department de la Musique, the Archives of the L'Institute de France, Paris; the Bodleian Library, Oxford; the Public Records Office, Norwich; and the Library of Congress, Washington. Financial assistance from the University of California, Berkeley, the Canada Council, McGill University, and the University of Oklahoma underwrote the completion of this work.

My debt to the community of scholars active in research on the Burney family cannot be adequately repaid by a mere list of names. Without exception they share the best of the generous and agreeable character of Dr. Burney. The basis of this study is the immense collection of manuscripts copied, gathered and catalogued at McGill University by Professor Joyce Hemlow. Her encouraging response to my first tentative inquiries into Burney research at McGill and her infectious enthusiasm were of great help at the outset of my research. I was privileged to use the transcriptions of Burney documents prepared by Professor Slava Klima and Professor Alvaro Ribiero. Both scholars have been very helpful, and my three years at McGill as a research associate with the Burney Project are fondly remembered.

I am grateful to Professor Vincent Duckles for his long-standing support and guidance. His expertise in historiography and English music and letters was of inestimable value. The suggestions made by Professor Daniel Heartz and his stimulating seminars on classical style and *opera seria* have done much to shape this work. His vigilance in reminding me that Burney's is not the only view of the history of music is acknowledged with gratitude. As iron sharpens iron, so the scholar, the scholar. Any blunt edges that remain result only from my flinching from the sharpening steel of scholastic rigor, not from any neglect on the part of my mentors.

Among my colleagues and friends, Professor Thomas Bauman merits particular recognition for his advice, assistance with German texts, and the confidence which his comprehensive knowledge of eighteenth-century German music and letters has lent to the discussion of Burney's work in that nation. I am indebted to Professor Mary Cyr for her interest in this work, and her helpful insights into French opera—this despite Burney's shabby treatment of the music of her favorite composer, Rameau.

There are a number of individuals whose contributions to this study need not be enumerated; they are aware of their part. Others need only know that their support and help was indispensable and is gratefully acknowledged. Among these are Bill and Mary Rainbolt, Professor Margaret Doody, Professor Allan Ross, and David Tegnell. Becky Jones prepared the manuscript with perseverance and good humor. Finally, I wish to record my profound gratitude to my wife, who waited, watched, helped, and understood. This book is dedicated to her with respect and deepest affection.

Kerry S. Grant
Norman, Oklahoma
July, 1982

1
Critic in Conflict

The life of Dr. Charles Burney (1726-1814), England's foremost critic and historian of music, seems to have been as effectively reconstructed as the passing of almost 200 years will permit. The standard biography for more than a century was the three-volume *Memoirs of Doctor Burney* (1832) written by Burney's devoted if misguided daughter Fanny. This intimate, but prolix and unreliable book was transformed into a valuable biography by Percy Scholes. Scholes's fine study, *The Great Doctor Burney* (1948), though superseded as a biography, remains valuable as one of the best summaries available of eighteenth-century musical life. The most recent biography is Roger Lonsdale's *Dr. Charles Burney: A Literary Biography* (1965). Drawing on a large collection of manuscripts unknown to Scholes, Lonsdale presents a new and sometimes disturbing chronicle of Burney's life and activities. In Lonsdale's book, Burney emerges a more vital and complex personality than earlier biographers suggest: he is a more human figure, ambitious, susceptible to the social and political forces around him, sometimes scheming, and even unscrupulous. Gone is the blurry shade of one of literature's and history's most charming characters: in its place is a clearly defined personality, one more in keeping with the image that Burney's published works project.

The new light which has illuminated Burney's life has reflected only dimly on his critical and historical work. The social tensions and conflicts that emerge in the restored biography had their effect on his scholarly activities. His driving ambition, almost inconceivable industry, and winsome personality were not always matched by uncompromising critical integrity. As he advanced in society from provincial musician to fashionable teacher and even further to recognition as a man of letters, he was compelled to consider ever more carefully the diverse sensibilities and tastes of his audience. Many of those whose tastes did not completely harmonize with his were men of position and influence; he was not unmindful of their prestige or their ability to enhance his career and social standing. Burney's extraordinary intelligence, wit, and unerring social instincts enabled him to write about the most sensitive and potentially contentious subjects in comparative safety by maintaining a delicate balance between veracity and concern for the taste of his readers. Indeed, he was so successful that it has required the evidence contained in his private papers to alert the modern reader to Burney's genuine views on a number of estranging issues.

Burney the social man proves to be so bound with Burney the critic that his biography and personal papers become crucial documents to the understanding of his published work. Unfortunately, Burney's biography, brilliantly though it has been reconstructed, is neither a complete nor accurate account of his life or thought. The reasons for its shortcomings are tied intimately to the history of the documents from which the biography was constructed. And though the tale is quite involved, it is worth the effort to trace the fate of Burney's *Nachlass* after his death in 1814.

In the dissolution of Burney's estate most of his vast collection of personal papers, including letters, memoranda, notebooks, and pocket diaries, were entrusted to his daughter Fanny Burney d'Arblay. She was the logical choice of all the heirs because she had helped her father with at least two preliminary examinations of his papers, first in 1796 and again from 1812 to 1814.[1] The extent of the collection she inherited is impossible to estimate, but it is clear from the catalog that Fanny drafted when she began her work—which she calls a "Register raisonné"—that a great deal has been lost.[2] In its totality it was a very full record indeed. Its comprehensiveness is indicated in Burney's comment to his son that he would have no difficulty in writing his autobiography, particularly for the years after 1760, because he had kept all of his pocket books and could tell him "where and how I spent every hour of my life."[3] After drafting the register, Fanny began a sorting task which was to occupy her for years, eliminating material of little interest or that which reflected negatively on her father or other members of the family. Gradually the collection shrank as she consigned the rejected material to the flames, marking the fate of the manuscripts in her special code in the margin of the register.

The most important part of the collection perhaps was Burney's own autobiography contained in twelve manuscript volumes. Though Fanny judged the work to be somewhat unpolished and uneven, it could serve as the basis for the biography which members of the family and others felt should be written in honor of her famous and distinguished father. She decided to augment his material with information from her own memory and diaries and from the extensive collection of his letters she had in her custody. She planned to supplement the biography with three volumes of letters. The presence of letters to Burney from such luminaries as Dr. Samuel Johnson, Horace Walpole, Edmund Burke, the Bluestocking Ladies, and others guaranteed a wide interest in the edition of letters as well as the biography.

Fanny conceived a biographical framework for her edition of the autobiographical "Memoirs" premised on the view that her father's chief ambition and achievement was to be accepted as a man of letters rather than as a mere musician. In setting forth this concept she wrote that her father was:

> a Man allowed throughout Europe to have risen to the head of his profession; and thence, *setting his profession aside,* to have been elevated to an intellectual rank in society, as a Man of Letters with the most eminent of his day.[4]

Her premise seems at odds with the evidence available to her. She surely could not be suggesting that Burney ever rose to the top of his profession as a composer or performer, and if she is insinuating that the publication of the *General History of Music* was the culmination of his career and that he then set music aside, the record belies her judgment: he continued as an active teacher even after the turn of the century. Whatever her rationale, she pursued her sorting task and the secondary task of editing the letters for publication in accordance with her literary theme. On December 9, 1820, her task complete, she wrote in her register: "These have been finally Examined, useful or peculiar memorandums Extracted, And the Rest have been Destroyed."

It was natural and appropriate for Fanny to review and sort her father's papers, and her father would certainly have given his sanction. Burney had been witness to the scramble to publish every scrap of Samuel Johnson's papers after his death, and joined with Metastasio in lamenting:

> "What right can men have to the possessions of others, without their consent? Is all idea of *meum* and *tuum* annihilated? These invaders must know, that every man says things in conversation and correspondence with friends, that he would not say to the whole world; and that such remarks on persons and things as are inoffensive in private, become injuries when published." And it is most certain, that there is no man, however candid and prudent, whose private opinions and conversations would not give pain to, and draw on him resentment of persons whom he would be sorry to offend.[5]

Unfortunately, Fanny did much more than merely remove the offensive, the unflattering, and the trivial. Guided solely by her own vision of her father's life, she selected the materials of interest to her and discarded the remainder. Fanny was certain that the popular reader would share her lack of interest in the day-to-day existence of a London musician. She was also alarmed at the great detail her father had given about the humble origins of her family. She did not share her father's pride in his early musical achievement nor in the professional activity which was prelude to and even accompaniment to his rise to recognition as a *littérateur* and peer to the notables of the Johnson Circle.

Though Fanny apparently began her memorial work with the intent of paying reasonable attention to Burney's musical activities—she promises a complete list of his compositions in volume I—she gradually lost sight of her intention and began shaping her own concept of her father's career.[6] Music intruded upon her theme, and as she worked on the "Memoirs" music faded from the foreground, becoming only counterpoint to her theme, and then disappeared altogether. Fanny acknowledges in the early pages of the "Memoirs" that it was Burney's musical abilities which distinguished him as a youth, providing the opportunity for the young man to travel to London, but she largely overlooks his purely musical accomplishments after the year 1751 when he was forced by illness to leave London. Her account of the King's Lynn years (1751-1769), for example, mentions his teaching only incidentally, and then only as a mechanism to explain his entrance into the homes of the influential. She completely neglects his tireless professional activities, which included organizing concerts and balls, giving recitals of sacred music, and composing trio sonatas, duets, and concertos as well as songs.[7] Rather than set forth a history of the life of a provincial music master, she provides sketches of the various personalities he met in that region.

Indeed, for the remainder of her biography, Fanny seldom places her father in the daily business of his profession. There are notable exceptions, such as her account of Burney's arrangement of Rousseau's *Le Devin du village*—which she mentions to explain Burney's close relationship with David Garrick—or his composition for the Oxford doctorate.[8] The extensive discussions in volume II of the *Memoirs* of the concerts held in the Burney home are also exceptional, but these accounts are not taken from Burney's own recollections. They are extracts from Fanny's own juvenile journal and serve to show Burney at the center of society, with fashionable guests visiting the Burney's to socialize with the best and most popular artists in London.

The surviving portions of Burney's literary estate are conclusive evidence that during her sorting Fanny Burney sought to systematically eliminate a large quantity of material dealing with music—in some cases by discarding the material, and in others by editorial markings calling for the deletion of material before publication of the rest of the document. One can gain an idea of what may have been the ratio of "musical" to "social" material in these papers from the specimens preserved in the Osborn and Berg Collections. These largely fragmentary records, most of which show the scars of Fanny's editing hand, exemplify her editorial method. Occasionally, amidst the hopelessly dense over-scribbling, one can read a provocative word or two referring to famous musicians involved with Burney, among them Haydn.

One fragment of Burney's diary records many of Haydn's activities during his stay in London. It is virtually certain that we would have almost a daily journal of Haydn's activities during his visit had the diary survived in its entirety. The passage is marked by Fanny to be omitted from whatever use she planned for the other information on the fragment:

> 2nd. of May. The admirable Haydn had a company at his benefit which did our country honour.

> 3rd. The Banti first appeared in Semiramide, but had no first man except the feeble Roselli, whose style, and taste were good, una poca voce.
> 8th. At the Honourable and Reverend Mr. Hamilton's concert there was an illustrious assemblage of great professors and masters. Haydn. Clementi, Cimadori, the Morichelli, Viotti, Yanovitz, Crosdil, and the Author who played the tenor himself. Miss Hamilton and Miss Hankey sung, and Miss Carey an *Elève* of Clementi played with uncommon neatness and expression.
> 15th. Paisiello's Te Deum and other pieces of Musica sacra were performed at the 6p. House. 3 great benefits this week, Barthelemon—Salomon and Giornavichi. (end fragment)[9]

It is impossible to accept Fanny's claim that she deleted this and similar material to make the *Memoirs* more attractive to the general reader. Haydn was the musical idol of England after his visits in the 1790s, and even the general reader would have greatly enjoyed the record of Burney's meetings with this famous musician.

Fanny's adaptation of her father's biography required the editing of all the documents to support her literary theme. She frequently struck out portions of letters written to Burney dealing with music. William Bewley's letters in particular are heavily edited, with most of his requests for music deleted, despite Fanny's reference in the *Memoirs* to his "passion for the art of music."[10]

Even those documents that interested her were subject to alteration. She often found that the literary style was not to her taste, or that the surviving record did not give as full and vivid a recreation of events as she would have liked. She embellished the record and did so primarily to aggrandize her father's social stature. Significantly, most of the surviving complete pages or groups of pages from the "Memoirs" consist of descriptions of and anecdotes about prominent men, reports of Burney's appearances at court, and other evidence of his social attainments. Often these same pages provide Fanny with an opportunity to inflate her own importance by unacknowledged tampering with the substance of Burney's narrative. Lonsdale, after a penetrating comparison of the surviving manuscripts with Fanny's *Memoirs,* notes a particularly disturbing passage and concludes, "Such falsification of a text offered as a direct quotation from her father's 'Memoirs' and [such instances] of Fanny's senile egotism may be taken as characteristic of her biography as a whole."[11] His conclusion about the reliability of Fanny's biography has important ramifications:

> It can be stated with confidence that hardly a single quotation from Burney's papers in her *Memoirs* escaped her interference; that, either through carelessness or design, simple factual information, especially dates, is often inaccurate; and that many episodes of Burney's life are blatantly misrepresented in her biography as a result of her idealistic simplification.[12]

Implicit in this judgment is the contingency that Fanny's editorial tamperings and selective destruction of documents were sufficiently pervasive to, in essence, direct any later investigation to a biographical construct in harmony with her own. Such has been the case in Lonsdale's book, which, brilliant though it is, presents a somewhat distorted view of Burney's life.

It was Fanny's perception that the "Memoirs" "could reflect no additional lustre" on her father's "bright literary character, but diminish its radiance" which is at the heart of her distortion of the autobiography. She differed with her father in her view of the interesting and important features of his life. Joyce Hemlow's assessment of what was removed from the "Memoirs" in Fanny's selective processing is telling:

> What seems to be lost besides curious vignettes of eighteenth-century life is detailed information about the musical and theatrical worlds, musicians and actors, together with amusing anecdotes, facts, and scenes relating to the Doctor's youth, which, as is frequently the case, remained more clearly etched in his aged memory than later events.[13]

In short, what has been lost is a collection of manuscripts which would have been, to students of the eighteenth century, what the diaries and letters of Samuel Pepys are to the investigators of the seventeenth century.

Fanny's tampering with Burney's biography and *Nachlass* presents, for the musicologist, a two-fold problem. First, fundamental misconceptions about the man lead to misinterpretation of his work. Second, the record, even as fully as it has now been reassembled, reveals much less about his historical and critical writings than Burney himself probably would have wished. He was a man with a sense of history, and he knew full well that scholars of later generations would mine his books for information about his era just as surely as he himself had prospected in the work of scholars of former generations and centuries. He planned to provide posterity with a lively, even controversial, account of his life and times. A note on the original manuscript cautions that the "Memoirs" "will be drawn up with too much sincerity and integrity to appear during the author's lifetime."[14] The surviving documents clearly show that much of the delicate material Burney was concealing from his contemporaries reflected directly, even dramatically, on his writings about music.

Even with his remarkable charm, Burney did not move effortlessly into the company of England's great literary and political figures. He worked hard to gain access to the wealthy and the influential. Like any ambitious man of his station, Burney required the assistance of those whom he called simply "the Great" in order to realize his aspirations. Whether the partiality of "the Great" was in the form of patronage or merely favorable notice, it was highly desirable. It was this partiality that Burney sought from the higher ranks of society, often with the same eagerness with which he might have sought a political appointment worth hundreds of pounds a year.

At its best, patronage freed great minds and talents to pursue their work without concern for their comfort; at its worst it corrupted both the giver and receiver. Samuel Johnson defined a patron of 1756 as "commonly a wretch who supports with insolence, and is paid with flattery." [15] Often no more favorably perceived, the hopeful beneficiary was commonly thought to be a man not only of lesser rank, but of mean talent: a sycophant who publicly courted, but privately despised and reviled, his benefactor. The widespread abuse of patronage in the first half of the eighteenth century cast an ignoble shadow over the practice. Patronage was still possible in the second half of the century, but, by the time Burney entered the stage as a hopeful, patron and applicant alike moved with caution and circumspection.

When Burney began his struggle to ascend into the world of the rich and powerful, he found that the essential task was to meet the right people, impress them with his talents and charm, please them with his manner, and hope for their benevolent interest in his position. His entrée into the families of high station was his profession of music master. Music was regarded as a necessary part of the training of a cultivated person, and a music master was a common sight in the homes of the titled and wealthy. Burney became one of London's most fashionable teachers, popular not only for his teaching ability, but for his grace, wit, and ingratiating manner. He was uncommonly well read for a musician and able to speak knowledgeably on a wide range of topics.

It was this unusual concurrence of musical talent and intellectual gifts that allowed Burney to move into the higher social circles. The transition in Burney's life was effected through the notice of a wealthy young gentleman, who challenged one of England's prominent instrument dealers to produce a musician who exemplified "mind and cultivation as well as finger and ear":[16] Burney was produced to win the wager. He found himself pulled out of his modest position of apprentice to Thomas Arne and cast into a new world, that of Fulke Greville. Greville was a gambler and high liver, but nonetheless a cultivated, well-traveled man who had been on the grand tour to France and Italy; he knew the manners of the court and higher circles as well as architecture, sculpture, painting, music, and poetry. Greville made Burney his almost constant companion and brought him into direct contract with "the Great" folk. Of this period Burney later wrote,

> I may be said to have been in the great world ever since I first went to Wilbury with Mr. Greville which is now near 60 years—and though only a musician, I was never sent to the 2nd table, nor was I gêne to the company with whom I had the honor of dining... [17]

During his time with Greville, Burney was to learn many lessons in living and wooing the great. None was so important as his heightened awareness of the feelings of the nobility and gentry about the music of George Frederic Handel.

Two remarkable half-page fragments from the "Memoirs" take us directly into the music room of Wilbury house, located on Greville's 3,000-acre estate in Wiltshire:

> In the Autumn of 1747, I went again with Mr. G[reville to] Wilbury; where I met with Mr. Crisp, a man of infinite taste in all the fine Arts, an excellent Scholar, and who having resided many years in Italy, and being possessed of a fine tenor voice, sung in as good taste as any professed opera singer with the same kind of voice, I ever heard. [I also met Mr. Boughton]... who played a good fiddle, and who had been a constant attendant at the Opera in Handel's time, being extremely partial to him and the old Italian School; the disputes and partialities of these two Gentlemen were of singular service to me:... Mr. Greville, of the same school and party as Crisp, made me a present of the two first books of Scarlatti's lessons... Mr. Boughton... to support his musical principles, and make head against Scarlatti, and the Italian School, made me a present of Handel's two books of Lessons; which obliged me to practice both, and to admire the merit of both in a total[ly] different way: Scarlatti fanciful, capricious, wild, and full of new effects and passages; Handel rich in regular harmony, masterly in design, original, and grand and new in the style of his youth, even in Italy. These were my exercises, and practice of a morning before the family was up; and my exhibitions of an evening, alternately, to the Abetters of the two schools.[18]

These fragments, which would be of mild historical interest in the life of most musicians, relate evidence vital to an understanding of Burney's life and work. He is, though only in his early twenties, keenly aware of the intensity of the advocates of the two schools of composition: the old school, that is, chiefly Handel and other musicians of what we may refer to for convenience (though without unqualified historical accuracy) as the composers of the baroque style; and the modern school, chiefly the Neapolitan composers whom we may label as practitioners of the pre- or emerging classical style (again without being concerned about the debate surrounding the use of such terms in recent years).

The intensity and complexity of this conflict of musical taste is difficult to relate concisely, because the issue was inseparably intertwined with politics for many of the partisans. Its roots lay in the intense conflict between Handel's royal patron, George II, and his eldest son Frederick, Prince of Wales. The prince, who opposed his father in every conceivable way, was able to gather impressive support from the opposition nobility, in part because of his substantial power of patronage. The prince was, of course, also being used by the opposition to further its political goals. On the musical front, the struggle emerged publicly in the form of an opera company, the Opera of the Nobility, which was set up against Handel's Royal Academy of Music, the opera patronized by the king and his supporters.[19]

In a curious turn of history, Handel became the public representation of the government of George II and his greatly disliked minister, Robert Walpole. Contemporary pamphlets intimately link Handel's operatic enterprises with the practice of Walpole's ministry. While it was possible that a too-fervent attack on the king on political grounds might appear treasonous, Handel, as a surrogate, could be vilified at pleasure. A preference for the opera of Handel came to be seen in the eyes of many as a sign of allegiance to the king. Support for the Opera of the Nobility (with its Neapolitan composers) could be seen as allegiance to the rebellious Prince of Wales.

The dissipation of the family argument with the death of Frederick in 1751, and even the death of Handel in 1759, did not end the intense conflict. Handel's music was to be preferred by all the kings of England throughout the century, and composers in competition with Handel, even men of vastly inferior talent, believed that they were constrained by the royal preference for his music. In truth, George III remained a supporter of Handel's music long after public favor (and the financial success that went with it) had shifted. But even without a following among the public, George III's devotion to Handel and that of the powerful nobility who followed the king in his allegiance exercised a marked influence on English society and did, in fact, affect the opportunities available to composers of a more modern stripe.

Burney could hardly have been unaware of this debate long before he went to Wilbury House with Greville in 1747. During his first years in London he played viola in Handel's oratorio orchestra and coached two of Handel's leading singers, Frasi and Guadagni, but at Wilbury he learned the fine art of accommodation. The lessons of his youth in the skillful conciliation of the Handel partisans were never to be forgotten. He became then, and would continue to be, a man intensely interested in pleasing all "men of taste" and position. He was evidently remarkably successful in conciliating all parties, for we find him moving freely around the royal family and their supporters throughout his life, despite his own strong commitment to the modern school. He was, moreover, successful in gaining some minor positions through patronage at the royal court.[20]

He was first enlisted as an "Extra Musician" in the King's Band. His name appears on the list in 1767, and he remains on it, drawing a salary until his death in 1814. Several years after this initial appointment he was promoted to "Musician in Ordinary to the King" at a salary of £ 40 per year. Very likely these positions involved little, if any, actual duty. Adam Carse, after studying the appointments made at this time, concluded that the Lord Chamberlain "appointed as nominal (yet salaried) members of the band his friends, or their butlers, valets and other servants, many of whom could not play upon an instrument."[21] These minor positions were comparatively easy to attain, and it is significant that both appointments came about through the influence of friends of families to whom Burney was music master, but Burney had greater ambition.

In 1779, when the post Master of the King's Band became vacant on the death of William Boyce, Burney was confident that the position and the £ 300 a year which went with it were to be his. He had a champion at court in Lord Hertford, the chamberlain, but a hitch developed in the necessary political procedure, and the king appointed John Stanley without ever so much as having heard Burney's name. Burney felt this failure keenly. He wrote to his son later that "despite the Notice and Countenance of the great, I still remain a drudge amid the smile of Wealth and Power."[22]

He failed in another bid for patronage at the court in 1782, this time as organist in the Queen's Band of Music. A letter of support for Burney's application for this position, written by Mrs. Thrale to an unknown recipient, is revealing in its candor about the relationship of merit and influence in attaining such an appointment. It says in part:

> If a consummate knowledge of the Theory of his Art, if Perfection in the practice of it; if the Knowledge of a Scholar, the elegance of a Gentleman, and the Conduct of an amiable inoffensive man can be urged as Claims—my dear Dr. Burney will not fail of Success—but all this will not shew him the way to Court Preferment; and what I torment you now for, is to put us in the Road.[25]

He suffered disappointment again in 1786 when he received a promise from a nobleman of an appointment as Master of the King's Band in Ireland which was not fulfilled.

Finally, later in 1786, he was sure his reward had come due. John Stanley died, and the post of Master of the King's Band was vacant once again. Word quickly reached Burney, who rushed to the home of a court officer to receive counsel on how to procure the coveted appointment. He was instructed to appear on the terrace at Windsor Court that evening in a spot where the royal family would pass during its promenade. He was assured that the king, seeing him there at just that time, would understand and would be far more pleased by this gesture than by direct application. The scene can be recaptured by quoting from Fanny Burney's account of her appearance with her father on the terrace:

> We stayed some time on the terrace...[my poor father] looked so [self] conscious and depressed that it pained me to see him. There is nothing I know so dejecting as solicitation... My dear father was not spoken to, though he had a bow every time the King passed him and a curtsey from the Queen. But it hurt him, and he thought it a very bad prognostic... We did not get home till past eleven o'clock. We were then informed that Lord Brudenel had called to say Mr. Parsons had a promise of the place from the Lord Chamberlain.[24]

In justice to poor Burney it must be stated that he was not merely building aerial castles in his anticipation of receiving this and other positions. Other documents from the period indicate that Burney was the accepted choice for the position, but in this, and each of the other unsuccessful instances mentioned, some small but crucial cog in the delicate mechanism of court politics slipped at the critical moment. Success or failure had little if anything to do with merit. If a passive but anxious appearance on a terrace was the most desirable method of gaining life-long security and position, it is small wonder that men would take extraordinary precautions to insure the continued favor of their friends and to win over those who were unfriendly or merely disinterested.

Burney's efforts to improve his situation through increased patronage during these years have important bearing on the interpretation of his critical and historical writings. It was during these years that he produced his most famous and influential books: the two travel journals giving his impressions of the present state of music in France, Italy, Germany, the Netherlands, and the Low Countries, his *Account of the Commemoration of Handel,* and most of his monumental *General History of Music.* There are indications throughout these works that Burney's ambition to gain patronage constrained the expression of his heartfelt convictions.

He sought widespread acceptance in part to make alliances which would assist him in his effort to advance socially, and because it was simply his nature. Though he had a reputation for being the most agreeable of men, Burney was privately torn by conflict, often afflicted with melancholy, and narrow-minded and jealous in pursuit of his profession. The very source of his fame, his writings on music, often threatened to undo his hard-won gains. The facets of Burney's conflict are many, but they emanate from a single source: his intense desire to be liked. This drive dominated not only his public behavior but his professional activities as well. He was disturbed to find so many "endless controversies" carried on by men who would rather dispute than give themselves over to the enjoyment of their art.

He had seen too many

> soi-disant connoisseurs listen to the most exquisite musical performance with the same *sans-froid* [i.e. sang-foid] as an anatomist attends to a dissection. It is all analysis, calculation, and parallel; they are to be wise, not pleased. Happy the people, however imperfect their Music, if it gives them pleasure![25]

Music, the giver of pleasure, was an unsuitable subject for contention, particularly for the polite audience at which Burney aimed his writings. Indeed, the concerns of the professional musician and music lover were properly quite different.

> It is certainly necessary for professors to study and make themselves well acquainted with the fundamental rules of their art; but I would advise true lovers to Music to listen more than talk, and give way to their feelings, not lose the pleasure which melody, harmony, and expression ought to give, in idle inquiries into the nature and accuracy of their auricular sensations.[26]

Burney rejected Addison's *bon mot* that a critic was "a man that is ever more attentive to what is absent than what is present," choosing instead to be guided by its converse. He resolved to praise whatever was good or worthy in music and to remain silent about the rest.[27]

He once explained his philosophy of criticism to William Crotch, a popular lecturer on music in London who raised the ire of modernists by comparing Handel to Haydn to the former's favor. Burney suggested to Crotch that he could have praised the beauties and merits of modern composers, and explained their success, then balanced that with an appreciation of music of the old style; by implying his preference, rather than engaging in captious criticism, he could have indicated his choice without irritating a substantial part of his audience. He counseled: "you may conciliate parties and not make enemies among real Connoisseurs" by avoiding "praising one Master at the expense of another." Burney was certain that if Crotch would follow his example he would "not find it impossible to please a whole audience."[28] The "pleasing of a whole audience" overstates only slightly Burney's own critical aim. When forthright criticism might threaten his relationships with men of influence, Burney could and did withhold his genuine thoughts from his readership.

Burney's social awareness constrained his criticism in another way as well: he considered it quite inappropriate to criticize living English musicians or foreigners active in England. His reputation as a frank, sometimes brutal critic, derives from his commentary on Continental and deceased English musicians. He states his practice as a rule in the *Cyclopaedia*.

> ... we have adhered as closely as possible to the rule of confining our remarks to the dead, of whom an opinion may be given without fear or offence, if unfavorable, or of exciting envy by eulogies...[29]

This precept was in effect during the years in which he wrote the *History,* as a letter contemporaneous with the last volume shows. The letter was written to François Barthélémon, who had urged Burney to include an assessment of his friend John Worgan in the *History*. Burney responded:

> ... The title of my Book, which is a *General* not a particular History, and in which it was never intended to display the abilities of the living, but of the dead the true and safe objects of History; and you must know the world too well not to be certain that the less I discuss the merit of the living the less likely I shall be to give offence. He must be a bold man, indeed, who ventures to appreciate the Compositions or criticize the performance of living Artists. A few indeed are so prominent that they cannot be overlooked without disappointing the reader; but those are chiefly foreigners; for of my acquaintance, friends, and Countrymen, with whom I wish to live in good terms, during the rest of my life, it would be extremely difficult, if not impossible, if I spoke at all, not to offend, by too much or too little praise.[30]

When compelled to evaluate the work of living professors, Burney "weighed and measured with the utmost delicacy and precaution every word" in order to "avoid giving pain to those who are constantly endeavoring to give pleasure to the public."³¹ His philanthropy was admirable, but there was also a more practical consideration. He knew that were he to show partiality, he would draw upon himself the "fury of a nest of hornets that would never cease to sting or allarm [sic] me the rest of my life."³² In the end Burney yielded to Barthélemon's plea, and his public and private writings about Worgan can serve as a model of the "utmost delicacy and precaution" which influenced his public utterances. The assessment in the *History* seems straightforward.

> About this time, MR. JOHN WORGAN, since Dr. Worgan, succeeded Mr. Gladwin in playing the organ at Vauxhall Gardens. He then studied the harmony and modulation of Palestrina, and organ fugues of Handel. And with an extempore prelude, alla Palestrina, and one of these fugues, he used every night to preface a concerto of Handel. By constant practice he became a very masterly and learned fughist on the organ, and, as a concerto player, a rival of Stanley. He was first taught by his brother, and afterwards Roseingrave, till getting acquainted with Geminiani, he swore by no other divinity. His organ playing, though more in the style of Handel than of any other school, is indeed learned and masterly, in a way quite his own. In his youth, he was impressed with a reverence for Domenico Scarlatti by old Roseingrave's account of his wonderful performance on the harpsichord, as well as by his lessons; and afterwards he became a great collector of his pieces, some of which he had been honoured with from Madrid by the author himself. He was the editor of twelve at one time and six at another, that are admirable, though few now have perseverance sufficient to vanquish their peculiar difficulties of execution. He is still in possession of many more, which he has always locked up as Sybil's leaves. Dr. Worgan has composed innumerable songs and concertos for Vauxhall, and several oratorios, in which the choruses are learned and masterly.³³

In sum, Burney evaluated Worgan as an organist and found him to be very masterly in the learned style and a first-rate concerto player. He had a unique style of playing, one that was thought closer to that of Handel than to any other composer. His compositions are listed without comment, except the oratorio choruses, which are found to be learned and masterly. The remainder of the information is essentially biographical; the overall assessment seems favorable and respectful though not enthusiastic.

Burney's private evaluation of Worgan was a good deal more colorful. It is found in a letter which predates the passage in the *History* by seven years:

> ...the *common* was what he wished to avoid...Demo; Scarlatti in his *rapid* lessons has worse things of this kind: yet even *he* would not in *slow* movements, I fancy hazard a similar passage to that of Worgan. I have not seen the Lessons whence you give it; but did you ever discover *real Genius* in W—'s compositions? I mean real enthusiastic ebullitions of Spirit, Grace, Dignity, Pathos? I own I never did: now all imitation of Geminiani; now of Scarlatti, now of Handel, or somebody else. All his endeavors at novelty are clumsy and awkward, like Mr. Vellum's pleasantry—"you'll excuse my being jocular, Mrs. Abigail."³⁴

It is unlikely that any critic would be quite so harsh on a composer in public, but the intent of Burney's criticism is apparent: Worgan was neither original nor tasteful in his compositions, an attitude which is at best only remotely implied in the *History*. Burney wrote another assessment of Worgan for the *Cyclopaedia* many years later. As he had died in 1790, Worgan was then "a fit subject for criticism." The article is an expanded form of the passage in the *History*, and states, in part, that Worgan's Vauxhall songs, "though sung into popularity by dint of repetition, had not attractive grace, or pleasing cast of melody."

> He composed several oratorios, in which the choruses are learned, and the accompaniments to his songs ingenious. The *cantilena* was original, it is true, but it was original awkwardness, and attempts at novelty without nature for his guide.[35]

The coincidence of this passage with that written ten years earlier exemplifies Burney's manner of benevolent critical deception, and this case should alert scholars who intend using Burney as a guide to English musical taste. It is by no means unique nor even the most egregious model. Other instances can be found in Burney's criticism of his early music master Thomas Arne and of Felice Giardini. In each case it is material in Burney's private papers that betrays the disparity in his public and private opinions. The surviving manuscripts become, then, an important key to much of Burney's work, especially that concerning his English contemporaries. However, even this material can be misleading. We are cautioned by Burney himself, who states in his biography of Metastasio:

> The civility between authors in private letters, is no more to be understood literally, than the humility of the great, when they say to a tradesman: "Your humble servant, Sir," Metastasio, fond of quiet, and unwilling to disquiet others, when consulted by authors, which from his great celebrity frequently happened, treated them with such candor and lenity, as were construed into approbation; all, indeed, that consulting authors usually want.[36]

This passage is directly applicable to Burney's letters to J.C. Walker, letters of infinite politeness, full of information about music; it is somewhat startling to find Burney complaining to Malone that Walker had been the bane of his existence for almost twenty years.

Samples drawn from other letters will suffice to caution against indiscriminate acceptance of evidence from Burney's correspondence. In response to a parcel of music given him to inspect by Dr. Henry Harrington, including his *Eloi Eloi*, a "sacred dirge," Burney writes a glowing letter which states in part:

> There is merit of various kinds in the *Eloi! Eloi!* of the + + ingenious, and venerable +dilettanti+ musician Dr. Harrington derived not only from clear, pure and simple harmony, reverential and affecting melody but from meditation and good sense, good +text+ and a high respect for the sacred subject... I have long wished, in Ecclesiastical

music where the words are important that performers of each part would pronounce every syllable together in prayer or supplication fugue and + + seem absolutely prohibi[ted] by propriety and Commonsense.

The plain counter Point of the dirge the melody is truly in the voice of +complaint+, of sorrow, and regret for lost liberty, possessions and former national happiness, and if sung with feeling, by cultivated voices must awaken sensibility, in every auditor whose ears and heart are well organized.[37]

Despite his fulsome praise, Burney did not like Harrington's style. Although he had enjoyed Harrington's catches and glees, his sacred music bored him. His displeasure with Harrington's change in style is evinced in a letter written just a few months later to Mrs. Waddington.

> Dr. Harington [sic], a learned and ingenious man, who has written and set several humorous catches and glees very successfully, seems now to have become *(entre nous)* a *Methodistical* musician, and to like nothing but *Salmodia*.[38]

The discussion of metrical psalmody in the *History* makes it quite clear that this is not a compliment.

Burney's manuscripts, then, must be used with as much circumspection as his published criticism. With an adequate knowledge of the whole of Burney's works, it is possible to avoid many misconceptions and to detect those sentiments expressed by the social, not the professional, man. In a critic of less importance than Charles Burney, many small compromises would be of little importance, but Burney's stature as a critic and as one of music's most often-quoted sources mandates careful consideration of his work.

2
Burney's Style of Criticism

Music criticism in England was in its infancy when Burney began his work. In his estimation the "first elements" of musical criticism were hardly known to the English public.[1] Only one critic, Charles Avison, in his *Essay on Musical Expression,* preceded Burney in instructing the public taste. Aside from Avison's *Essay,* there were, of course, many speculative books about the mimetic power of music, and elaborate discussions of the sister-arts relationships, but these were written by men of letters who often included music only as a necessary but inferior relative of the other arts. Burney the philosopher read and debated James Harris's *Three Treatises,* Daniel Webb's *Observations on the Correspondence between Poetry and Music,* and laughed at Dr. John Brown's *Dissertation on the Rise, Union, and Power, The Progressions, Separations and Corruptions of Poetry and Music:* Burney the musician and critic surveyed the vast literature of aesthetics and concluded, "We have not yet discovered what benefit lyric poetry or vocal music can derive from such discussions."[2] Avison, in contrast, provided a model which Burney could follow.

Avison's *Essay* was a milestone in English criticism, because of its insistence on the expressive, as opposed to the imitative, power of music. It "lent currency to the notion that the place to look for the meaning of music could be in men's responses to it."[3] By placing severe limitations on the power of music to imitate nature in the same sense that poetry and painting were expected to imitate nature, Avison's work began the separation of the aesthetics of music from its sister arts.

Since the imitation of nature was not pertinent to music, another basis for judgment had to be found: the new basis was expression. Avison acknowledged, however, that

> After all that has been said, or can be said, the Energy and Grace of Musical Expression is too delicate a Nature to be fixed by Words: it is a Matter of Taste, rather than of Reasoning, and is, therefore, much better understood by Example that Precept.[4]

His concept of expression is then a *je ne sais quoi,* and he never defines it except as a tautology with his definition of taste; nonetheless it serves him as an effective device for criticizing music. His use of expression as a critical precept has been aptly called "a wild card used to trump any opinion with which he disagrees."[5] Burney's critical view mirrors Avison's: one listens, tests his response to the music, and only later seeks to confirm by reason the judgment already formed by taste.

Burney's critical perspective permits a wide range of styles, and he is considerate of the sensibilities of those who disagree with him. He allows that "every hearer has a right to give way to his feelings, and to be pleased or dissatisfied without knowledge, experience, or the fiat of critics." This is no less than saying that the person who lacks an adequately formed taste has as much right to be pleased as the person with taste. There is, nonetheless, a superior taste or perhaps several superior tastes, and the purpose of the critic is "to instruct the ignorant lovers of Music how to listen, or to judge for themselves."[6]

In order to establish confidence in the impartiality of his judgment, especially with regard to recent musical history, which many of his readers knew first-hand, Burney included his "Essay on Musical Criticism" in volume three of the *History* "to explain and apologize" for his criticisms, and thus "prevent their being construed into pedantry and arrogance."[7] Burney distinguishes between the unskilled listener and the prudent critic: only one who has experience in singing or performing upon an instrument can be an accurate judge. What is easy on one instrument is difficult or impracticable on another; the uninformed listener, dazzled by arpeggios on the violin and harpsichord, may expect the same brilliance in execution from an oboist or flautist, and thus err in his criticism. There is, then, a clear distinction between a person of taste, who may judge from his own sensations, and the professional critic, who in addition to relying on taste, judges from sensations and reason sharpened by knowledge and experience. This difference gives Burney his authority over his readers: it is unlikely that many had his impressive experience as a keyboard player, violinist, composer for the theatre, chamber, and church, and coach of England's leading singers. Though seeming to give the reader authority for his own opinions, Burney establishes his superior qualifications, and invites the reader to elevate his taste by following the master's guidance. In his "Essay" Burney establishes a rational foundation for the confidence that readers of similar taste had in his judgment. He also asserts his authority over those who disagree with him, requiring them to attempt to show through reasoned demonstration the fallibility of his taste by a system at least as principled as his.

Burney's system (if such a subjective approach can be called systematic) distinguishes between kinds of enjoyment. The first, and most universally understood by persons of taste, could "transport the listener into regions of imagination beyond the reach of cold criticism." This was music infused with genius and passion. The second was music which, though it did not transport the hearer, was nonetheless "correct." Such music was not to be equated with affective music, but could provide a "tranquil pleasure, short of rapture, in which intellect and sensation were equally concerned."[8] In other words, one who has been transported, that is, "put into ecstasy and ravished with pleasure," need not question the merit of the music which created the sensations: it was by definition successful. Short of transport, reason and taste must judge.

Burney, like Avison, avers that taste is best taught by good example, rather than by "reasoning speculation,"[9] but certain principles can be applied in judging music. Chief among these is that "no one musical production can comprise the beauties of every species of composition." This principle is an important key to understanding Burney's critical writings. One must seek in his discussions the merits particular to each style of music—church, chamber, or theatre—under consideration.

Despite his reliance on taste, the most subjective of all critical precepts, as the supreme judge of music, Burney makes a valiant effort to construct a critical theory based on reason. Perceiving that it is not "unusual for disputants in the arts to reason without principles," he attempts to give "a clear and precise idea of the constituent parts of good composition, and of the principal excellencies of perfect execution."[10] He thus seeks to provide his criticism with as rational a basis as possible, in order to convince his readers that his own judgments are based on principles, not prejudice. The paradox in Burney's system is that taste remains the sole arbiter of its constituent elements: only taste can determine the proper balance of simplicity and learned contrivance, grace and insipid facility, or invention and propriety.

The greatest obstacle to the effective use of Burney's criticism is his use of descriptive, rather than technical, language. When he says a composition is full of fire, pathos, grace, taste, and propriety, we perceive that he is favorably impressed, but have no firm idea of just what musical substance or quality is referred to by these epithets. Burney faced the problem that has dogged music critics since pen was first put to paper: how to "act as a go-between, as a midwife, between the artist's perception and the beholder's recognition of it in the created thing."[11] What words are appropriate to this function has not yet been decided. Burney's vocabulary was probably as successful in describing music to his readers as any used by subsequent critics. Two centuries later Jacques Barzun commented that music criticism, "like that of the other arts, must be written for the layman; an educated layman, if possible, but a layman, and not a professor."[12] This Burney certainly achieved. However, because the language of today's layman differs from that of Burney's eighteenth-century audience, it is now necessary to apply eighteenth-century definitions to readings of Burney's criticism. The reader who does so will come away much better informed, but even so may be uncertain as to the utility of Burney's vocabulary since the same terms are used to describe music of widely varying styles.

Burney's "Essay on Musical Criticism" leaves no doubt that he views his critical vocabulary as being relatively precise. He writes of "decompounding" music (in an analogy to a chemical process) into its constituent ingredients, "melody, harmony, modulation, invention, grandeur, fire, pathos, taste, grace, and expression."[13] These are, by analogy at least, substantive elements, measurable and comparable. The various styles of music, like any compound, were made up of different elements and proportions. A composition was successful in its style when its proportions were in balance with the ideal standard for that genre. Burney's criticism is largely concerned with acquainting the reader with the balance of the qualities germane to the style of music under discussion. In a comparative sense, his criticism reveals his ranking of the music of his time, but it does not necessarily transmit a clear idea of the musical substance which was responsible for his decisions.

Burney would understand perfectly our present-day difficulty in evaluating his writings. As a historian, he was perplexed by the writings from earlier centuries, and cautioned his readers against taking them too literally.

> Nothing is more certain than that the best Music of the time, in all ages, has greatly delighted its hearers. But notwithstanding the great difference between that of one age and another, the same terms have been constantly used in describing it. However, from a *similitude* of description, we must not infer a similitude of the thing described. Words are vague and fallacious; and the exclamations, *admirable! fine! exquisite!* represent nothing fixed or certain. The utmost weight we ought to give them, is to suppose that the Music or Musician, upon which they were bestowed, was the *best within the knowledge of the writer*. This kind of merit is all comparative. No terms can be devised to express the last refinements, and even excesses of opera singing, more strong than those which Strada uses to describe the musical refinements of the sixteenth century. Yet, if examples of these refinements could now be heard, their dissimilitude would sufficiently prove the fallacy of verbal description.[14]

Despite the "fallacy of verbal description," historical writings are the substance of history for all periods prior to the advent of sound recordings. Vague as these writings sometimes are, used properly they reveal a great deal about music.

The examination of Burney's critical vocabulary is a thorny problem in a work of this size. His language is that of his own era, and cannot be thoroughly investigated without immersing oneself in eighteenth-century aesthetic theory, an immense literature filled with contradictory conclusions drawn from the same evidence. Beyond that, one need only compare present-day literature with that of the eighteenth century on the single term "taste" to realize the impossibility of clarifying even one concept. Consequently, discussion will be limited primarily to Burney's own definitions and critical vocabulary, leaving to more intrepid scholars the task of sorting out the attendant philosophical and aesthetic influences.

As early as 1935 Frank Mercer drew attention to the importance of appreciating the eighteenth-century meanings of Burney's critical terms. Calling the period an "age of frank speaking," he rightly noted that many of Burney's "so-called 'savage and harsh strictures' will not appear unfair" if consideration is given to usage common to his period.[15] To do so is not an easy task. The fluctuations of language are such that some words have since assumed a meaning more forceful than in Burney's day—words such as barbarous and licentious—and these must be divested of some of their acquired color. It is equally essential to discern the intended meaning of a word from among the various possibilities that were current in the eighteenth century. Although modern readers familiar with eighteenth-century criticism will generally understand Burney's intent, the numerous errors in interpretation of his critical works evident in scholarly studies indicate a need for guidance.

The term "barbarism" will serve as a case in point. Two clearly distinguishable definitions are possible: 1) want of culture, rudeness, roughness; 2) savageness. Johnson presents the following definitions:

BARBARISM.
1. A form of speech contrary to the purity of language.
2. Ignorance of arts; want of learning.
3. Brutality; savageness of manners; incivility.
4. Cruelty; hardness of heart.[16]

The various meanings derived from savageness can be excluded at once. The first and second definitions under "barbarism" seem appropriate to art criticism, but the differences in meaning between "a form of speech contrary to the purity of language" and "ignorance of arts; want of learning" are profound. Most often the context makes it clear that Burney uses the term to mean a breach of the rules of music, or as defined above, "an impurity of speech," certainly a far less emotional connotation than the modern reader, influenced by the second Latin definition of the word, would probably first consider.

A musical barbarism, then, is merely an offense against the purity of the rules of musical grammar. Burney specifies this usage when speaking of language, as when he calls the Plebian dialect barbarous, that is, in a language "different from pure Latin."[17] That being the case, it is perplexing to note that Burney's plates of Dr. John Blow's "errors" are called "Dr. Blow's Crudities," rather than his "barbarisms." This no doubt reflects Burney's emotional response to Blow's music. The manuscript of these plates bears an even more emphatic title, "Dr. Blow's Beastialities."[18] For less grievous offenses against the ear, the epithet "barbarous" sufficed.

Another term highly emotional for modern readers, but with an altogether different significance for Burney, is "licentious." In the *Cyclopaedia* he defines the concept.

> LICENCE, in *Music,* a seeming breach of rule. There are licences in harmony as well as melody. As the laws of counterpoint were at first arbitrary, and formed of narrow and contracted principles, they became subject to change at the caprice or taste of the composer, and at all times, the breach of an old rule by a great master became the establishment of a new one for a composer of inferior fame.
> If the effect be good, it is a licence, if bad, a fault.[19]

If the breaching of rules produces a good effect, it serves to advance the art, bringing into common usage techniques which violate old rules: these then become inviolate themselves. The absolute adherence to the canons of composition was viewed by Burney as an impediment to progress. Thus we read of Purcell's "new melodies, modulations, and happy licences."[20] Where Burney could find no merit in the error committed by a composer, the license was viewed as an unwarrantable barbarism. He thus criticized Monteverdi's numerous consecutive fifths and octaves as being "without the least necessity," because such "licences" did not produce "new and agreeable effects."[21] In "Dr. Blow's Crudities" he wished to "point out a few instances of his great, and to my conceptions, unwarrantable licentiousness, as a contrapuntist."[22]

Burney's use of a similarly colorful vocabulary in his discussion of contrapuntal music has resulted in widespread misunderstanding of his attitude toward the contrapuntal style. Far from being an enemy of counterpoint, as is frequently asserted, Burney placed great value on the study of counterpoint. His life-long preoccupation with counterpoint, beginning with his training at Chester, attests to this fact. Burney reported in his diary that when Arne heard young Burney's music in 1744, he remarked: "he was glad I had +retained+ this chronology of these studies, as I should be ashamed of them sometime hence if ever I learned counterpoint regularly."[23] There is every indication that Burney applied himself vigorously to the subject, and became a "regularly bred contrapuntist."

His music, though often uninspired, is correct, and many of his compositions include contrapuntal movements. The three early sets of trio sonatas are highly contrapuntal, and the last movement of his Opus 1, No. 6 (1748) is a *capriccio* on a four-note ground, with the violin parts "moving almost throughout in Canon."[24] His *Six Cornet Pieces* (1751) contains a final fugal movement, and his last large-scale keyboard publication was a set of *Preludes, Fugues and Interludes for the Organ, Alphabetically arranged in all the keys that are most perfectly in tune upon that Instrument...*(1787). At about the same time he published his very pleasing *XII Canzonetti a due voci in Canone* (1790) set to poetry by Metastasio. He wrote, in addition, a large number of fugues which were never published. His last will and testament mentions "A great number of Manuscript Fugues and pieces for the Organ, many of them composed so late as the Summer of 1791, to amuse me during confinement by indisposition..."[25] Burney was indisposed often during the last decades of his life as a result of rheumatic attacks. His claim to have spent this time composing fugues is well documented: in 1796, for example, he wrote to his sick son, "I wish you knew enough of musical composition to make canons, during bad nights—it was my specific for *oblivion of self* when opiates failed."[26] He described these canons to another correspondent as being "of the most complicated and difficult construction."[27]

It would undoubtedly confound Burney's critics to discover several of his most complicated and difficult constructions published as models of canonic writing in the very excellent company of Kirnberger, Marpurg, and C.P.E. Bach. A.F.C. Kollmann published three of Burney's canons, which were "transcribed from a collection of his manuscript canons, containing upwards of a hundred Canons in all varieties of intervals, and in various lengths and forms...(ex. 2.1)."[28] Here are Kollmann's keys for the solutions of these elaborate contrivances:

> Canon I...This Canon might have been expressed in one line...But to facilitate its resolution it is written in two lines like a double Canon. It is infinite, but calculated to conclude at the place marked with a pause, and with those notes of the replies which are expressed by small ones.
>
> Canon II. This aenigmatical Canon is explained underneath by *Dr. Burney's* own solution, which shews: that the notes with the tails turned upwards are the first part, those drawn downwards the second, and the middle line unison.
>
> Canon III...The first and third part of this Canon is in C, and the second in F, which is pointed out by the flat at the clef of the second line; and when turned upside down, the first and third line is in F, and the second in C. It must be performed as thus: first, all three performers sing the right way, with the same words; then the piece is turned upside down, and all three performers sing again one way, and with the same words, as it appears in the inversion; at last it is inverted again and sung like the first time, when the first and second part are continued as long as the third, by the small notes.[29]

Burney's writings attest to his admiration for contrapuntal music when used in the proper style. It was not to be tolerated in dramatic music, and only occasionally in chamber music,[30] but in the church it was the most appropriate style. However, the *study* of counterpoint was necessary for a composer in any style.

> Those who despise this seeming Gothic pedantry too much, resemble such half-bred scholars, as have expected to arrive at a consummate knowledge of the Roman Classics, without submitting to the drudgery of Grammar and Syntax. Indeed a great Composer has, perhaps, never existed since the invention of Counterpoint, who, at his moments of leisure, has not attempted to manifest superior learning and skill, in the production of Canons, and other difficult arrangements and combinations of sound; and who, if he suceeded, was not vain of his abilities. Before the cultivation of Dramatic Music, as Canon and fugue were universally studied and reverenced, they were brought to such a degree of perfection, as is wonderful; and though good taste has long banished them from the Theatre, yet the Church and Chamber still, occasionally, retain them, with great propriety; in the Church they preclude levity, and in the Chamber exercise ingenuity.[31]

24 Burney's Style of Criticism

Ex. 2.1. Burney's "Contrivances"

It is clear that Burney felt that contrapuntal studies were stimulating exercises for professors of music: they were not natural and elegant productions meant for a polite audience, but examples of musical science at its acme. "Scientific" music was not music of the sensations, but of the intellect, and it was scarcely polite to demonstrate so much science publicly.[32] Burney's attitude regarding the place of these compositions is best reflected in a passage in the *History*, which he indexed as "Reflexions on learned Music."

> But there are many avenues through which a musician may travel to the Temple of Fame; and he that pursues the track which the learned have marked out, will perhaps not find it the most circuitous and tedious; at least Theorists, who are the most likely to record the

adventures of passengers on that road will be the readiest to give him a cast. A learned and elaborate style conceals the want of genius and invention, more than the free and fanciful productions of the present times.[33]

Burney frequently describes the contrapuntal music of his time as "gothic," and the context usually makes it evident that he intends the term to be pejorative. He states, for example, that Scarlatti and Hasse "are distinguished by all lovers of Music who are able to separate original genius from froth and bombast, and taste, propriety, and exquisite sensibility from noise and Gothic barbarism." Elsewhere he writes that imagination had been "manacled by narrow rules formed on Gothic productions."

Fugues and canons of the sixteenth century, he says in the *History,* should be "preserved as venerable relics," like the Gothic buildings in which they were sung.[34] However, once melody was liberated by the establishment of a treble-dominated style in the seventeenth century, Gothic constructions were antithetic to taste, because the strict rules of fugue and canon fettered imagination. Burney considered the use of Gothic artifices, such as writing over a ground bass,[35] a lapse in taste or judgment.

Gothic in itself was not always a negative term. Burney's *Cyclopaedia* article on this term is in answer to Antonio Eximeno's comments in his *Dell' origene e della regole della musica* (1774).

> GOTHIC *Music.* When signor Eximeno calls fugues and canons Gothic compositions, he does not disgrace their structure any more than he would our cathedrals, by calling them Gothic buildings. Let fugues be banished from the theatre and private concerts, if he pleases, but let them remain in the church as a distinct species of composition, where they were first generated, and where they can never become vulgar or obsolete. The style is naturally grave, requires musical learning, and will, by the solemnity of the words and place of performance, continue to be reverenced and respected. It is allowed that variety is more wanted in music than in any other art, and by totally excommunicating canons and fugues from the church, the art would lose one capital source of variety, as well as ingenuity; and intelligent hearers be bereaved of a solemn style of music, to be heard no where else.[36]

Gothic compositions had their place in church, especially in England. Burney's usage also hearkens to the eighteenth-century use of Gothic as "a style or taste opposed to Classic." The term Gothic "exactly parallels and opposes the range of 'Classic,' which can denote a historical period, a particular style (symmetrical, cleanly articulated in design, harmonious and massive, simple, undecorated, un-Gothic, etc.), or any work of lasting value."[37]

When writing of "Gothic productions," Burney frequently associates the term "contrivance" with "scientific," "artificial," "laboured," and "learned." "Contrivance" has taken on a disparaging connotation in the minds of readers who have fastened on such passages as that describing the music of J.S. Bach. In this passage Burney suggests that Bach could have extended his fame by sacrificing "all unmeaning art and contrivance."[38] However, wherever contrapuntal music could be used with propriety, contrivance was properly admitted. He thus praised Josquin's mass *De beata virgine* because it "abounds with canons, fugues and imitations of admirable contrivance."[39] In a piece by Antoine Brumel, he found "the merit of harmony and contrivance."[40] In evaluating the state of English music to the middle of the sixteenth century, he found "our Counterpoint and Church Music arrived at a perfection with respect to art, contrivance, and correctness of harmony, about that time, which at least equalled the best of any country."[41] Of the collection *Pammelia* (1669) he wrote, "great musical science is manifested in the canons, and the harmony and contrivance of the rest are excellent."[42] Indeed, a lack of contrivance in a contrapuntal composition rendered it valueless. In a mass of Jean Mouton's composition, he found "no variety of measure of subject; nor is the want of melody compensated by richness of harmony, ingenuity of contrivance, or learning of modulation."[43] Similarly, music in general during the reign of Henry VIII he found "was not only deficient in Measure and Melody, but in design and contrivance."[44] Thus, throughout Burney's criticism it is evident that "artificial," that is, "made by art; not natural; or Artful; contrived with skill,"[45] is quite proper in connection with contrapuntal music.

"Contrivance," if modified by the adjective "laboured," ceases to be a positive term of criticism. Burney knew all imitative writing required great skill and effort, but when he characterizes a piece as "laboured," he seems invariably to refer to one of Johnson's definitions: that of "tiresome; not easy." The term is deprecatory, since the audience is aware only of the composer's labor which it hears without effect. Burney's idea of the merit of canon and fugue, the most labored of all compositions—written when they were no longer in favor, that is after 1600—is elucidated in a passage about Romano Micheli's *Musica vaga et artificiosa*.

> Those who still regard these contrivances with veneration, will find much entertainment in this book; but others, who seek for melody, grace, and modulation, will find in it nothing but toil and pedantry. And it must be owned, with due reverence for this species of musical science, that imagination is so manacled during the composition of these perpetual fugues, that elegant melody is always precluded, and, in general, harmony is rendered so meagre and imperfect, that in a canon of three of four parts, it is often reduced to a unison, octave, or insipid fourth.[46]

The seeker after "melody," "grace," and "modulation" would find it in the modern style. These epithets and a number of related terms dominate Burney's descriptions of the lighter "classic style," a style which had its roots in Naples in the early decades of the eighteenth century. Here he found "grace, fancy, feeling, and clearness," qualities which were to him "superiour to all other merits."[47] Each term is associated with a number of others that are related and represents, in fact, a descriptive category rather than a single term: thus fancy is associated with invention, imagination, and genius; grace is found in conjunction with ease, propriety, and natural; feeling with pathetic, fire, grandeur, spirit, force, and effect; and clearness with transparency, contrast, and the related foreign term *chiarezza*.

Since music had no model in nature to copy, Burney saw the musician as having "more to invent than the professor of any other art. Every passage, every combination, every motivo or subject, that has not been used before, is invention." There was apparently precious little invention; Burney averred that in many compositions a prototype could be found in every bar. Alternatively, some composers were so ambitious of being innovative "that the ear is teazed [sic] and disappointed by the constant struggle and labour to be unnatural." Burney does not provide an "infallible receipt for invention; all a master can do is to recommend to his disciples to avoid excesses of every kind: too easy and common, too hard and uncommon."[48] In other words, to avoid extremes (though we have not yet defined the terms), invention must be bound on the one hand by sufficient originality or genius and on the other by taste.

When sufficient invention is present, Burney allows the piece to have "character," which he sets forth in the *Cyclopaedia* as a technical term of music. Each movement should have a "distinct cast or character."

> Without some specific stamp or impression, to awaken in the hearer the idea of some passion, affection, or sensation, it is of no character, but resembles Shakespeare's "Fellow without mark of likelihood."
>
> It is but in modern times that this kind of stamp has been aimed at or expected. Neither Corelli nor Geminiani stamped the melodies of their movements with anything but a kind of wafer seal, regularly barred indeed. Pure and sweet harmony, masterly fugues, and pleasing effects are produced in most of their productions; but that innate and striking cast of melody, which is instantly felt, which distinguishes a movement from all others, and which, without learned modulation, studied combinations, or ingenious arrangement of the parts, seizes the attention, impresses itself on the hearer's memory, never to be effaced, is wanting.[49]

Burney credits Handel with having many movements of distinct character. Among the composers of more modern style, Pergolesi, Jommelli, Piccinni, and Sacchini produced "airs of character so frequently that it is now [ca. 1800] formed into a principal [sic] by men of genius."[50]

Works of imagination are, according to Burney, works of pure inspiration. Compositional forms, such as canon and fugue, rely on art and require great science but little imagination.[51] The fame of many keyboard players derived from the invention or fancy they demonstrated during extemporaneous playing. There was a mystique about the emotionalism and relatively free form of this kind of creation. Even rules of composition could be suspended to accommodate the inspiration of the moment. Burney says that in improvised performances "we have frequently heard great players produce passages and effects in fits of enthusiasm and inspiration, that have never appeared on paper. In these happy moments,

> Such sounds escape the daring artist's hand
> As meditation never could command;
> And though the slaves to rules may start,
> They penetrate and charm the feeling heart.[52]

The great extemporaneous players he knew by firsthand experience or reputation were Sebastian Bach, Handel, Louis Marchand, François Couperin, Joseph Kelway, John Stanley, John Worgan, and John Keeble. Several of these, presumably among the Englishmen, "played better extempore, than they could write with meditation."[53]

The enthusiasm of audiences for these extemporaneous performances was so great that independent efforts were made in Germany and England to construct a mechanical device to transcribe improvisations directly from the keyboard during performance. Burney remarks that "Such a contrivance has been long among the musical *desiderata* of the most important kind." To record the "floating sounds" created during the "extatic [sic] moments of enthusiasm" would be "giving permanence to ideas which reflection can never find, nor memory retain."[54]

Closely allied to the terms invention, fancy, and imagination is the term genius. Burney does not define "genius" in his writings. In the *Cyclopaedia* under that term, he merely makes reference to Rousseau's article noting that it contains "peculiar eloquence and enthusiasm." The term is prevalent in Burney's vocabulary, as it is in all critical writings of his time. He uses the term both in the common sense of "a man endowed with superior faculties,"[55] and in the specific sense of "a natural talent, or disposition to one thing more than another."[56] In his article on "Composer of Music" in the *Cyclopaedia,* largely a translation from Rousseau's *Dictionnaire* article, Burney includes this reflection on the French critic:

> All the science possible, without the inspirations of genius, is unable to command attention, and interest an audience, at all times, and in all places. They are only gifted men that possess such powers. What is meant here by genius, is not a whimsical and capricious imagination, that quits a flowery road to ramble in thickets, through briars and brambles; that to render harmony piquant, loads it with discords; and instead of grace and elegance, is labouring to surprise by extraneous modulation, and to divide the whole scale into half notes; true genius is that latent fire which inflames the composer, irresistibly forces him to write, and incessantly supplies him with new melodies, always agreeable, expressive, and natural, accompanied by a harmony pure, touching, and majestic, which embellishes melody, without overpowering it.[57]

Throughout his writings Burney maintains special regard for men of original genius, that is, those responsible for innovation in the art, among them

Josquin des Prez, Leonardo Vinci, C.P.E. Bach, and Joseph Haydn. The aspect of composition most dependent on genius, in Burney's view, was the conception of melody. "All the other parts require only art and labour in filling them up. But the principal melody depends on genius, and it is that alone which manifests invention."[58] Yet genius, however brilliant, was not sufficient to form a composer; study was required:

> A good painter, poet or musician, can never be made without education, study and models. Ingenious works have been produced by dint of genius, but never faultless. The awkwardness of self-teaching will always appear; and taste, elegance, grace, and often learning, will be wanting to render them perfect...[59]

Yet that "grace" by which the new style was made superior to the old was an attribute of nature, not study; Burney was of the opinion that it was "in vain for the composers to sit down with a resolution to compose a *graceful* movement; it must come unsought, and insensibly."[60] In his criticism, grace is most frequently used in descriptions of the works of Burney's favorite composers, those of the Neapolitan school. The term is almost invariably linked with the words "facility," "ease," and "simplicity." Johnson's definition of graceful, "Beautiful with dignity and Gracefully; Elegantly; with pleasing dignity," seems best to describe Burney's conception. When composers became too easy and simple by "pushing facility to an insipid excess," they "rendered opera music proverbially flimsy and frivolous."[61] Burney quotes with approval Marmontel's definition of grace as a "polish, a lacquer, a varnish, a gilding to every human action; without which we may be surprised and entertained, but never perfectly pleased."[62]

"Easy" is, of course, the opposite of difficult. The balance of the two characteristics was the subject of a lengthy reflection on critics of Jommelli's music.

> It is the *excess* only of learning and facility that is truly reprehensible by good taste and sound judgement; and *difficult* and *easy* are relative terms, which they can only define. To lovers of music who have heard much in various styles, little is new; as to others who have heard but little, all is new. The former want research and new effects, which, to the latter, old music can furnish. Palates accustomed to plain food find ragouts and *morceaux friands* too highly seasoned; while to those who have long been pampered with dainties, simplicity is insipid. How then is a composer or performer to please a mixed audience, but by avoiding too much complacence to the exclusive taste of either the learned, or the ignorant, the supercilious, or the simple?[63]

One of Johnson's definitions of "easy" is particularly apt to Burney's most frequent use of the term: "Unconstraint; freedom from harshness, forced behavior or conceits."[64]

"Natural," like "easy," is not always a term of approbation. Burney found, "It is very difficult to determine what is *natural* music." The difficulty arises because what one listener perceives as natural, another considers common or rustic. "When persons unacquainted with the refinements of the art talk about natural music, they mean only such strains as are common, and which by frequent hearing, they think they understand."[65] Burney's definition provides some guidelines:

> A melody or air is said to be natural, when it is smooth, easy, graceful, and sometimes when it is common. Harmony is said to be natural, when not loaded with discords, or deformed by extraneous modulation; but confined to the harmony of the key. Music is likewise said to be natural, when it is clear and free from confusion, neither of difficult intonation nor execution; neither too high nor too low; too quick or too slow; nor affectedly loaded with accidental flats and sharps.[66]

In the most literal sense, acording to Burney, "there is no such thing as natural Music; it is all a work of Art."[67] A useful example of Burney's use of this term in balance with the other attributes of good music is contained in his criticism of Michele Mortellari.

> His style, though very agreeable and in good taste, never reached the grand or sublime; but his single airs and cantatas abound in grace and elegance of a particular kind: there is so much facility in them, and they seem so natural, that it is difficult to imagine the melodies to be new; however, he is guilty of no common plagarism; for upon examination, we can only find, that he has robbed nature in sentimental expression.[68]

"Simplicity" is a frequent companion of "ease" and "natural" in Burney's prose. His most direct statement on this principle in music is made in an answer to remarks by Benjamin Stillingfleet in his translation of and commentary on Giuseppe Tartini's *Trattato* (1754). Stillingfleet suggests that the tunes in the *Beggar's Opera* "should be the standard of good melody, modulation and harmony."[69] Burney responds,

> Simplicity is a desireable thing in the arts; but let it be an elegant simplicity, free from vulgarity and barbarism. Why should people of refined ideas, and, if you will too, delicate taste, be governed by the ignorant and unpolished...[70]

In a different vein, he replies to the lovers of folk tunes, who felt that the ancient melodies were superior to modern compositions.

> Simplicity in melody, beyond a certain limit, is unworthy of the name that is bestowed upon it, and encroaches so much upon the rude and savage boundaries of uncouthness and rusticity, as to be wholly separated from proportion and grace, which should alone characterise [*sic*] what is truly simple in all the arts: for though they may be ennobled by the concealment of labour and pedantry, they are always degraded by an alliance with coarse and barbarous nature.[71]

Two brief extracts will further serve to illustrate Burney's use of simplicity in his criticism. In his article on Johann Adam Hiller, a composer of German singspiels, he attributes the popularity of Hiller's comic operas to his airs, which "were in general favour among the lovers of simplicity and unlearned music, thirty years ago."[72] These he sees as a conscious imitation of folk-like simplicity. By contrast, Giovanni Paisiello composed with elegant simplicity. Burney writes of Paisiello's *Le Trame per amore:*

> The music pleased me very much; it was full of fire and fancy, the ritornels abounding in new passages, and the vocal parts in elegant and simple melodies, such as might be remembered and carried away after the first hearing, or be performed in private by a small band, or even without any other instrument than a harpsichord.[73]

It is, then, the conjunction of elegance and simplicity which makes the difference. Music which is not too complex, but which retains cultivation and refinement, is art music. A vulgar simplicity of the kind to which Burney was so firmly opposed is characteristic of what is now referred to as folk music.

"Elegance," as has been evidenced, is usually linked with simplicity, ease, and grace. Burney's application of the term to Paisiello's music might be summed up by Johnson's definition of "elegant:" "Pleasing with minuter beauties." Similarly, Burney uses another term, "propriety," to express approval of Hasse's *Salve regina,* and his usage can best be explicated by turning to the definition familiar to eighteenth-century grammarians:

> Propriety of language denotes the selection of such words as the best usage has appropriated to those ideas, which we intend to express by them; in opposition to low expressions, and to words and phrases which would be less significant of the ideas we mean to convey. To preserve propriety in our words and phrases, we must avoid low expressions; supply words that are wanting; take care not to use the same word in different senses; avoid the injudicious use of technical phrases, equivocal or ambiguous words, unintelligible expressions, and all such words and phrases as are not adapted to our meaning.[74]

This meaning seems completely compatible with Burney's usage and fittingly expresses his very high regard for Hasse's music.

"Feeling," though Burney listed it third among the characteristics of the best modern Italian music, is actually the most important of all, for Burney, like Rousseau, believed that the "chief excellence of music was the expression of the passions and affection of the mind."[75]

> ...None of the fine arts can subsist, or give rapture, without *passion.* Hence mediocrity is more intolerable in them than in other inventions. Music without passion is as monotonous as the tolling of a bell...[76]

The other aspects of style are important only insofar as they contribute to the creation of music which can arouse the passions. Most of the composers

Burney mentions who possessed the attributes of style he valued most highly were composers of opera, among them Galuppi, Jommelli, Perez, and Piccinni. Serious opera had as its purpose the creation of emotional states in the audience which paralleled those of the characters in the drama. Beautiful singing, including elaborate divisions and virtuosity, had its role (though a secondary one) in delighting the audience and providing contrast, thereby heightening the effect of the pathetic aria, the most exalted form of aria.

Composer's efforts, then, were foremost to be directed to the transmission of passion and sentiment, above all consideration of artifice. Burney's definition of "opera," drawn from Rousseau, speaks with enthusiasm of the affective power of dramatic music.

> Opera, a dramatic and lyric representation, in which all the fine arts conspire to form a spectacle full of passion, and to excite, by the assistance of agreeable sensations, interest and illusion.
>
> The constituent parts of an opera are the poem, the music, and the decorations... and the whole ought to harmonize in order to move the heart...[77]

There is a close relationship between "feeling" and "pathetic," a similarity reflected by Johnson, who defines feeling as "to be affected by," and pathetic as "affecting the passions." So it is that Burney lists "pathos" as one of the ingredients of good music. His conception of "pathetic," music which he revealingly says is "so well known, as seemingly to need no explanation," is (after Rousseau) a kind of dramatic and theatrical music which tends to "move and paint the great passions, particularly those of grief and sorrow."[78] His enthusiasm for the pathetic style is reflected in his selection of an "admirable simile" from Abbé Morellet's essay "On Musical Expression and Imitation."

> A beautiful and pathetic air is the collection of a multitude of accents escaped from souls of sensibility, as the features of Venus have each excited separately, but never together. The sculptor and the musician unite these dispersed features, and give us pleasures which truth and nature never gave.[79]

Burney does not hesitate to call music "the language of passion." The pathetic style's expressivity derives from its frequent use of slow tempi (though Rousseau cites fast pathetic arias in the Italian style), more colorful harmony, and the liberal use of the appoggiatura. Indeed, "In pathetic strains, the soul of the melody may be said to reside in the appoggiaturas:"[80] those below the note he felt were "more tender and affecting than those above; which are however, more graceful and interesting."

Burney's own essay in the pathetic is his song *Constancy* (1753) (ex. 2.2). Written in a slow tempo and minor key, the melodic line is laden with ascending and descending appoggiaturas at both half and full cadences. The instrumental interlude in measure 12, which also serves as the postlude, is a virtual cascade of

Ex. 2.2. Burney: "Constancy"

When kill'd with Grief AMINTAS lyes
And you to mind shall call
The sighs that now unpity'd rise
The Tears that vainly fall
That welcome Hour that ends his Smart
Will then begin your Pain
For such a faithful tender Heart
Can never break can never break in vain

appoggiaturas. Melodic tritones heighten the evident distress of the lover on such evocative words as "unjustly" and "sigh." Leaps of a minor seventh and octave also increase the tension in the piece. In addition, the underlying harmony, rich in a variety of seventh chords, often in their most dissonant inversions, maintains and intensifies the tension, especially in the important phrase "and to revenge my slighted love." Throughout, a surprisingly varied harmonic vocabulary and tonal design effectively sustain the miniature drama and provide contrast. Even the deceptive resolution of the final phrase seems appropriately placed. The Neopolitan sixth chord at "will still love" (final time) shows Burney's operatic allegiance. In short, Burney has wrung every expressive turn from his text, and strengthened it with affective musical devices.

The most successful composers, if we are to believe contemporary reports, were able to draw tears from the audience at will. The most effective music was therefore the most affective. To create less was to be insipid, which in a dramatic composer was the greatest possible fault. The eighteenth-century definition of "insipid" is far more incisive than the modern; Johnson gives only two definitions: "1) Without taste; without power of affecting the organs of gust; and 2) without spirit; without pathos; flat; dull; heavy." Neither of these concepts could be tolerated in dramatic music.

The "expression" of true pathos depends upon the composer's ability to seize upon and translate into music that same passion with which the poet had infused his verse. Expression is carried principally by the melody. The melody shall "furnish musical inflections the most consonant to the sense of the words," using conjunct lines for soothing and sorrowful strains, and disjunct patterns for grief and passion. It is vain to attempt to enliven an inexpressive melody with expressive harmony, for it will only render the piece rude as well as inexpressive. Whatever the dramatic situation, the expression must not override the beauty of the music, for "there is no painting sentiment without giving it this secret charm [agreeable imitation] inseparable from it," nor is it possible to "touch the heart without pleasing the ear."[81] "Expression in *Music* is a quality by which a musician manifests his feeling, and executes with energy all the ideas with which he ought to impress the hearer, and all the sentiments which the composer intended to stress." And further:

> Nothing but the last degree of fury can permit the union of rapid measures and harsh chords. When the head is distracted ... this energetic and terrible confusion may be communicated to the mind of the spectator, and in a like manner make him lose his reason. But if the composer is not inflamed and sublime, he will only be coarse and cold.[82]

At the far end of the spectrum from the pathetic style is the sublime. Often linked with grandeur, sublime refers to an overwhelming sense of power and awe, reverence or lofty emotions through beauty, and vastness.[83] It is a term

Burney consistently affixes to his description of Handel's best oratorio choruses. The sublime effect can be associated with pieces of various styles, often those of great energy or "fire," as Burney puts it.

Along with the epithet "fire," we may consider the associated terms "spirit" and "force." Fire is defined by Johnson as "anything that inflames the passions." The inclusion of "fire" in a list that already includes "pathos" and "expression" stresses the importance of eliciting emotion in the auditor. When Rousseau speaks of a composer writing music for a character with a deranged mind, he considers the composition successful only if the audience feels the same distraction of their own passions.[84] "Force," according to Burney (after Rousseau), "implies energy, strength, loudness and intensity," although the fire must of course be controlled by taste. In the same general sense "spirit" is animation and fire in performance.

A piece which successfully communicates an emotion is frequently described as full of pleasing "effects." The term seems self-explanatory, but Burney, again translating Rousseau, gives a specific meaning of "effect" in music:

> To produce an effect, is to cause an agreeable and powerful impression in the ear and the mind of the hearer, by unusual musical combinations; so that the word *effect*, in music, means something uncommonly excellent; and effect is not only applied to a single passage, but to such whole movements or works, as are full or effects which produce sensations that appear superior to the means employed to excite them.
>
> Long practice and observation may teach a musical student how to discover passages of effect upon paper; but genius alone inspires them.[85]

One of the most important *desiderata* of good music was "clearness." This concept appears in the *Cyclopaedia* under a variety of different words, indicating the importance that Burney placed on it. In its various guises it is fundamentally the same as Rousseau's "Unity of Melody." The melody or air is the most expressive constituent of music, and all other elements, especially harmony and counterpoint, are to support the melody, not detract from it. Under *"chargé"* Burney writes, "This is said of Music when the subordinate parts are so loud and busy that the principal melody cannot be heard through them." The Italian *Caricato* conveys a similar meaning: it is "... applied to a song of which the accompaniments are too full, or to anything crowded or overcharged." The opposite term in Italian, *chiarezza,* is also defined in the *Cyclopaedia.* When Baldassare Galuppi gave Burney his definition of good music, he said, "vaghezza, chiarezza e buona modulazione." *Chiarezza,* or clarity, is placed in opposition to the style of accompaniments, such as those of Handel, containing contrapuntal activity which detracts from the melody. In its most primitive form *chiarezza* is embodied in a beautiful and effective melody over the simplest of non-melodic bass lines. "However numerous the parts, the principal, the best or most interesting melody should be respected, to whatever part it may be assigned." This clarity is desirable in all styles, but is essential in theatrical music.

> In productions for the church, where tranquillity and profound attention are supposed to reign, learning and complication are more likely to be understood than in a theatre, where the interest of the drama, the beauty of the poetry, the gestures of the actors, and the pomp of representation, all conspire to attract the attention of the audience from the labours of the musical composer. These considerations not only furnish an apology for a thin score in opera songs, but render it an object of praise. Clearness in dramatic music is so much more necessary than in that of the church or even chamber, as the objects that distract the attention of the audience are more numerous.[86]

Clarity was not limited strictly to homophonic music. It is "a favourite excellence with musicians in speaking of counterpoint: and in compositions of many different parts carrying out different designs, that clearness in their texture and arrangement, which enables the hearer to disentangle them... we think might with some degree of propriety be termed *transparency*."[87] By whatever name, in every style the listener is never to be so burdened with parts that he is unable to comprehend them, particularly when the composer is trying to be expressive.

Among the most important of Burney's requisites in composition is "contrast." One of the principal duties of an opera composer was to contrast the arias within an act. In all musical changes—slow to fast tempi, dynamic contrast, simple and elaborate accompaniments, variety in harmony—the emphasis must be upon producing agreeable effects, thereby sustaining the audience's interest. In the best modern compositions "*Contrast* in Melody, Harmony and Modulation keeps the attention perpetually awake, and gives different coloring to every phrase in a movement."[88] It also serves to win the favor of a diverse audience.

> ...What can a musician do, but court their favour alternately, by the contrasts of pathetic and cheerful, hard and easy, full harmony and solo, complication and simplicity?—and whoever goes to an oratorio, opera, or public concert, in the capital, will certainly be presented with all this variety.[89]

The three most significant musical characteristics on Burney's list, "melody," "harmony," and "modulation," are also the most difficult to define from his critical writings because they pervade the discussions of music of such diverse styles. Yet, useful insights scattered throughout Burney's works can shed some light on a few of his judgments.

The most nebulous of the requisites of composition is good "melody," the soul of a composition, but also the element which could least be taught or described.

With respect to melody, its flights will ever be so wild and capricious, as to elude all laws, or require a new code every year; it is as subject to change as the surface of the sea, or the fluctuating images of an active mind.[90]

Despite his diffidence, Burney makes a real effort to chronicle changing fashion in melody (a progression which will be followed in the chapter on dramatic music). Burney saw dramatic composition at the forefront of the process of refinement in music, especially melody, for "it was on the stage that she [melody] studied public opinion, and acquired the approbation of persons of sensibility, taste and discernment."[91] What little Burney does say about the specifics of good melody pertains to rhythm and phrasing. Each bar of an air should be well accented, and the period well phrased. He told Ebeling that good music had "its accents, its phrases, and its periods, all capable of being as strongly marked by the performer as those of Rhetoric or Poetry by an Orator."[92] He insists that the only graceful and natural phrase or period is an "equal number of bars; as 2, 4, 8, 12, or 16." An uneven period, built on units of 5, 7, 9, 15 or 17, is "lame and ungraceful."[93] He believed as late as 1800 that it should be a precept "for all young students of composition who aspire at grace" to write evenly phrased periods. A breach of regular phrasing is allowable to express sudden "gusts of passion or surprise" in opera, or, in comic opera, to produce a "grotesque or humorous effect." In these circumstances "phrases are frequently broken with success; but never, where either grace or energy is required."[94] This opinion, which seems curious given the frequent irregular phrasing practiced by Italian opera composers, not to mention Haydn's sprightly irregular phrases, was echoed by Thomas Busby in 1811, who defined "Phrases Manquées" as "Certain imperfect passages, or phrases, sometimes introduced by injudicious composers, by which the melody is maimed, and the expression destroyed or weakened."[95]

In melody, it was the divisions which went most rapidly out of fashion, therefore Burney uses them as a guide to age and taste. He urged great care in the use of divisions, for when used to excess he found them as great a vice as fugues and canons in dramatic music.[96] Judiciously used, they had the ability of expression beyond mere words. Critics of divisions called them "capricious, unmeaning and trivial." In defense of divisions, Burney asserted that "when the heart is much moved and affected, the voice can more easily find sounds to express passions than the mind can furnish words." This rationale did not apply to the imitation of words such as fall, round, twist, and other literal representations, which Burney felt were reprehensible, although they were used by his greatest heroes, even Hasse.

The term "harmony" in the eighteenth century is sometimes ambiguous, as it was often used in reference to counterpoint. In this sense, Burney's attitudes have already been explored under the several terms "contrivance," "scientific," "learned," and "Gothic." Burney was insistent on the mastery of the rules of harmony by a composer, and disagreed openly with Rousseau, who allowed the title "composer" to "The inventor or compiler of a high part." On the contrary, Burney asserted, "if the author of the melody is incapable of cloathing [sic] it with harmony, he is no *composer*." Fortunately, the rules of harmony and modulation are more fixed than those of melody.

Burney's basic rule for harmonizing the diatonic scale is the French "Règle de l'Octave." He specifies that this is for gradually ascending lines only; when the bass skips, common chords are satisfactory. This very restrained harmonic vocabulary is, of course, merely a guide for students; it is not the ideal of composition. Burney's own harmonic palate is not so limited, as his song "Constancy" attests. The harmony of the song, rich in seventh chords, is heightened by diminished seventh chords, a chord recommended by Rousseau in "enforcing the effect of certain passages." The diminished seventh chord is particularly characteristic of the pathetic style. Burney gives an "Example of the Pathetic Genus, in which are expressed its successions in the Cromatic [sic] Scale ascending and descending." The genus consists of diminished seventh chords, except for an initial suspension and cadence formula (ex. 2.3).

Burney's criticism of harmony and modulation discriminates between natural and extraneous. He defines a "natural modulation" as one which remains within the diatonic structure of the key. Specifically, he gives the following formula for "the natural and usual modulation" in the course of a movement of considerable length:

> MAJOR: I - V - ii - vi - iii - I - IV - I
> MINOR: i - III - VI/iv - VI - III - i
> or
> (i - V (old-fashioned)

These constitute the natural points of modulation; extraneous modulations lead to a tonality which is not a diatonic member of the key, or to the key of the leading tone. Busby defined extraneous modulation as "forsaking the natural course of the diatonic intervals, digress[ing] into abstruse and chromatic evolutions of melody and harmony."[97] The term "extraneous modulation" also appears in William Shield's *Introduction to Harmony* (1790), a treatise which Burney reviewed very favorably in the *Monthly Review*. Shield gives a plate of extraneous modulations, of which he says, "the uneducated ever must listen attentively to many such extraneous modulations as the following, before it can relish the beauties of modern music."[98] Shield's extraneous modulations pass from C major to every non-diatonic member of the chromatic scale in both major and minor form. As Shield's statement indicates, "extraneous" is not a pejorative term: it is merely descriptive.

Burney was not reluctant in his use of extraneous harmonies in his keyboard music. His early sonatas, reminiscent of Domenico Scarlatti's style—

Ex. 2.3. "The Pathetic Genus"

though not of his control and judgment—strive toward varied and unusual harmony.[99] The first two excerpts of example 2.4 are from his early sonatas. Example 2.4a is the final twelve measures of the first movement of the first sonata. The sudden digression to the parallel minor [a minor] followed by an F major chord [♭VI] in A major is highly colorful, and certainly "extraneous." The descending series of diminished intervals and major thirds similarly add color to this cadential extension from the G minor Andantino of the fifth sonata (ex. 2.4b). The final example (ex. 2.4c) is from the allegro of Burney's third accompanied sonata. The deceptive resolution of the V of V to B♭ major (m. 8) is striking in its early occurrence in the movement, especially since the diminished seventh chord following resolves immediately back to the V^7 of V.

There seem to have been very few extraneous modulations which were unpleasant to Burney, providing they did not pass too quickly. Even a modulation to the leading tone in Purcell's anthem *O God, Thou Art My God* passes uncensored. He says of the last movement in B♭ major, "the harmony... is piquant, and the modulation agreeable, though the close in A is very extraneous."[100] When extraneous modulations become too rapid or too extreme, the context of his criticism clarifies his usage of the term: "In this production... there is a manifest struggle at extraneous modulations and new effects, perhaps too much at the expence of facility and grace."[101]

The suitability of an extraneous modulation was measured by taste. Rousseau allowed extraneous modulations in slow tempi, where "the mind may have leisure to disentangle the dischords, and follow the rapid chain of modulation."[102] Regardless of tempo, according to Rousseau, it was the composer's responsibility to "render present and sensible the chain of modulation throughout... in order that no interval or trait of melody shall be heard, without feeling at the same time its relation with the whole."[103] Although Burney translated Rousseau's article on modulation for the *Cyclopaedia,* he was not as restrictive in his view of harmony and modulation as was Rousseau. He termed Rousseau's characterization of harmony as "a Gothic and barbarous invention" one of his paradoxes, and stated, "In music, melody and harmony have distinct and peculiar beauties; but after being heard together, nothing can compensate for their separation."[104]

As a teacher of dilettantes Burney followed the conservative, fundamental theories of harmony and modulation, even publishing his own summary of the rules on a thorough bass card.[105] But as a music lover and composer, he argued against the pedantic restrictions imposed by the rules of composition. He noted, for example, that despite the prohibition against two common chords descending diatonically, the progression could be found in Corelli's twelfth solo in a progression from D minor to C major, and in Pergolesi's *Stabat Mater* from F to E♭ major. These, despite the license in the progressions, he found pleasing, though uncommon. How, he queries, is a *tiro* to reconcile these contradictions? The answer is found in sense, not reason. "Whatever melody or

Ex. 2.4. Extraneous Harmonies in Burney's Keyboard Music.

Ex. 2.4a

Ex. 2.4b

Ex. 2.4c

harmony has been found, or may be found, that is grateful and pleasing to the ear, may surely be admitted in practice, though not consonant to mathematical demonstration or the speculations of mere theorists."[106] This attitude is not surprising considering Burney's reverence for Domenico Scarlatti, Emanuel Bach, and Haydn. These composers were at the forefront of the style of their time. Conservative musicians censured their licenses, but modernists, like Burney, saw in them the advancement of the art before their very eyes. As

Burney explained, "Em. Bach used to be censured for his extraneous modulations, crudities and difficulties; but like the hard words of Dr. Johnson, to which the public by degrees became reconciled, every German composer takes the same liberties now [1789] as Bach, and every English writer uses Johnson's language with impunity."[107] Only through familiarity were these licenses adopted, and initially only by the elite of music lovers.

> The extraneous, and seemingly forced and affected modulation of the German composers of the present age, is only too much for us because we have heard too little. Novelty has been acquired, and attention excited more by learned modulation in Germany than by new and difficult melody in Italy. We dislike both, perhaps only because we are not gradually arrived at them; and difficult and easy, and new and old, depend on the reading, hearing and knowledge of the critic.[108]

It is important to note that the collective "us" does not include Burney or many other professional musicians. Burney's writings are consciously and continually directed to the taste of his audience, and many of his statements which seem to reflect his own ignorance or prejudice in reality reflect the state of the English audience. Thus, he notes that the latest, most refined music "is only understood and felt by such as can quit the plains of simplicity, penetrate the mazes of art and contrivance, climb mountains, dive into dells, or cross the seas in search of extraneous and exotic beauties with which the monotonous melody of popular Music has not yet been embellished."[109]

The compositional form most suited for "extraneous and exotic beauties" was the *capriccio*, particularly the free *capriccio*, which was little else but a written form of the style popular with extemporaneous players.[110] What was shocking in a written composition was often the most effective in the extemporaneous style. Shield specifies that to modulate into the "extremest key" in the shortest manner was consequently the most "agreeably surprising manner."[111] Burney enjoyed the freedom and skill which the best musicians exhibited in this kind of performance, in which "the variety to a man of science is unbounded."[112] The greatest fault in these pieces was want of invention, not breach of rules.

> ... it is above all in preluding and giving way to the imagination, that great masters, exempt from the extreme subserviency to rules which the eyes of critics require in written music, display those talents of invention and execution which ravish all hearers far beyond the written labours of meditation and study.[113]

The great arbiter of all the essential ingredients of good composition was, of course, taste. Burney's definition, adapted from Rousseau, justly calls the word "the most easily felt and the most difficult to explain; it would not be what it is if it could be defined; for it judges of objects beyond the reach of judgment, and serves in a manner as a magnifying glass to the reason."[114] Three distinct meanings of taste are evident in Burney's usage: "Taste in judging, taste in composing, and taste in performance...which should be separately defined and discriminated."[115] Unfortunately, Burney never wrote the three definitions that are needed, but his usage can be clarified by an examination of his remarks on the three types of taste.

For the composer, taste legislated the balance between dull simplicity and wildness in melody. It was particularly important in controlling genius. "Genius creates but taste selects. Genius is often lavish and redundant, and in want of a severe critic to prevent him from the abuse of his riches." Burney's accord with this excerpt from Rousseau's definition is evident in his criticism. The effect of composition was not dependent upon taste, "Since many great things may be achieved without taste; but it is taste that renders them interesting."

Beyond controlling the composer's genius, taste led him to the proper expression of lyric poetry.[116]

> It is taste which enables a vocal composer to seize and express the ideas of the poet; it is taste which guides the performer to the true expression of the composer's ideas; it is taste which furnishes both with whatever can embellish and enrich the subject; and it is taste which enables the hearer to feel all these perfections. Taste is, however, not mere sensibility. A cold heart may have much taste; and a man transported with things truly spirited and impassioned, is little touched by grace and elegance. It seems as if taste attached itself to minute refinements, and sensibility to grand and sublime effects.[117]

Despite his apparent belief in taste as a *je ne sais quoi,* Burney believed that taste could be improved. Residence in Italy, or study with a master of composition, could not alleviate want of taste, but it could improve taste, and a "discriminating ear" was sufficient to allow exposure to fine music to polish and refine taste.[118]

For the performer, taste related to the inspired and original performance of music:

> ...the adding, diminishing, or changing a melody, or passage, with judgment and propriety, and in such a manner as to *improve* it; if this were rendered an invariable rule in what is commonly called gracing, the passages, in compositions of the first class, would seldom be changed.[119]

The Italian singers flocking to London used gracing as a device to gain fame. Many fine singers appeared, but those like Pacchierotti, who combined a pleasing voice with imagination and taste, achieved the greatest success. An evaluation of the favorite singers of the 1780s in the *History* reveals the place of taste in singing, as well as Burney's habit of praising merit and ignoring defects.

> In discriminating the several excellencies of these great performers, I should, without hesitation, say, that *Pacchierotti's* voice was naturally sweet and touching; that he had a fine

shake, an exquisite taste, great fancy, and a divine expression in pathetic songs. That *Rubinelli's* voice was full, majestic and steady; besides the accuracy of his intonations, that he was parsimonious and judicious in his graces. And that *Marchesi*'s voice was elegant and flexible; that he was grand in recitative, and unbounded in fancy and embellishments.[120]

Among the requisites of good performance listed in the "Essay on Musical Criticism," most relate to attention to rhythm, tempo and phrasing. Three—energy, spirit, and expression—reflect the insistence on affect which marks Burney's criticism. "Expression" for the performer, like the composer, means achieving a perfect unity with the expressive intent of the poet. The performer must bring to life the fire, pathos, and grace that the poet and composer alike had labored to capture. Gerard defined the power of expression as consisting "perhaps entirely in a capacity of setting objects in such a light that they may affect others with the same ideas, associations, and feelings, with which the artist is affected."[121] This same unity of affect is stressed by Burney.

> He [the performer] should express every thing as completely as if he were at once the poet, composer, actor, and singer, and he will then have all the animation which it is possible for him to give to the work which he has to execute.
>
> In this manner he will naturally embellish with taste and delicacy airs that are only elegant and graceful; with spirit and fire, such as are animated and gay; with sighs, the tender and pathetic; and with all the agitation of forte and piano, such as are expressive of rage and fury... Wherever sober ornaments, judiciously applied, manifest the abilities and facility of the singer, without disguising and injuring the melody, the expression will be sweet, agreeable, and animated; the ear will be delighted, and the heart affected; nature and art will at once concur in pleasing the hearer, and there will reign such a concidence between the words and the music, that the whole will seem to proceed from one delicious language, which can say everything, and always please.[122]

There were, then, two ways to achieve success: dazzle with brilliance and virtuosity, or affect the passions. The latter was considered the greater achievement.

The most perfect music, according to Burney, was produced by a balance of the requisites of good music in its style. Church music admits more learning than that of the chamber or theater; grace, elegance, and taste are dominant in the theater; and the chamber style is a confluence of all styles, neither so sublime as the theatrical nor as patently learned as the church style. Taste is to dictate choice, but there will always be a struggle between the polarities of too little and too much. Burney's observations on pedantry versus innovation can serve as a model of his view of this struggle.

> It is difficult to determine which is most injurious to Music, or the greatest impediment to its improvement, the pedantry which draws us back to useless and exploded customs, or wanton and licentious innovation, which quits the true and fundamental principles of the art, in order to pursue visionary schemes of reformation and singularity. Good Music is ever to be

> found between these two extremes; and though Pedantry takes hold of one hand, in order to draw her back to rusticity or exploded learning; and innovation seizes the other to drag her from the right path, into the company of caprice, affectation, and singularity; she pursues her slow and steady course towards taste, elegance, simplicity, and invention, under the guidance of Judgment and Science.[123]

In the same way, simplicity is opposed to rusticity, elegance and ease to insipidity, contrivance to simplicity, and genius to taste and judgment. The ideal composition would be judged as having the nexus of all the elements of composition, which are themselves in proper balance with one another.

A person who claimed taste in judging music needed the requisites of a good critic: "...extensive knowledge, long experience," and a "liberal, enlarged and candid mind." The critic needed to be open to all styles of composition, at least in their proper setting, and have "none of the narrow partialities of such as can see but a small angle of the art." Burney's evaluation of the prince of Wales, later George IV, will serve as a model.

> ... He is an excellent critic; has an enlarged taste admiring whatever is good in its kind, of whatever age or country the composers or performers may be; without being however, insensible to the superior genius and learning necessary to some kind of music more than others.[124]

Many readers today will be tempted to condemn Burney as a critic by his own standards. His own "narrow partialities" seem all too apparent. The immense chapter on Italian opera in England, for example, has been regarded as a monument to his own narrow view of music history.

Modern readers judge Burney from a greatly expanded vantage of music history, one which, as Burney stipulates, can "see all angles of the arts." Such objectivity may produce its own blind spots. Our view of eighteenth-century music has been clouded for years by a kind of egalitarian approach, where the tiny keyboard piece is treated as if it were no less important than an immense work such as an opera or oratorio. The key to changing styles (one hesitates to say advancing styles) is, as Burney recognized, opera and related forms of vocal music. Even the symphony had its beginnings in the theater, and only later developed as an independent form. A non-discriminating historical objectivity produces as many misimpressions as does narrow prejudice. In many cases objectivity is as narrow a prejudice as a critic can manifest. By insisting on the importance of music which has little or no impact on musical style as a whole, the main line of history, however exclusive it may be, is obscured. Both approaches, the objective and the highly subjective, reveal their own truths, but neither is an ideal method.

The abandonment of progressive theories of history has left Burney very vulnerable. He was, without doubt, a believer in progress. In his notebook he wrote, "In all the arts Improvement and perfection have been progressive: one artist standing on the shoulders of another is able to see further than his predecessors."[125] The preface to his *History* also speaks of the progressive improvement of the art, recording explicitly that "every art is progressive."[126]

Burney was more objective than these passages imply. Perhaps it was his perception of the beauties of the music he studied as a historian which raised conflicts with his fundamental belief in progress; whatever the case, he insists in the *History* that music must be judged only by values consistent with its conception.

> In speaking, therefore, of a Musician of past times, as it has been my constant rule to compare him with his contemporaries; so in describing the music in general of remote ages of the world, it has been my wish that the reader should mount up to each particular period of which I write...[127]

This notion occurs several times—too frequently to be dismissed as a fanciful or insincere remark. Burney wrote of sixteenth-century music, "It does not, however, appear just and fair to slight old compositions, though a totally different style at present prevails. *History* does not imply constant perfection."[128] There seems to be no reconciling this paradox. Burney's progressive sense dominates, but he struggles with it occasionally in order to trace history from as unprejudiced a view as possible. In part, it is his concept of taste which ties him to the progressive concept of art. Taste was evanescent: so much so that he compared taste in music to a ploughed field, which changed crops each year, leaving behind only scattered remnants of last year's crops among the weeds.[129] As taste changed, so did the fate of old music and musicians.

> What a fluctuating art is music, and how transient the fame of its professors! since we may be certain, that the works of him who now enjoys the highest reputation, will be for ever plunged into oblivion, at the latest in a period of 25 years; or appear as ridiculous to our children, as our ancient music now does to us.[130]

Burney maintained no notion of his era being the "golden age." Music had reached great refinement and perfection, but he had no illusions about a decline in the art. Even in his final years, when he was enjoying exquisite pleasure from the music of Haydn, Mozart, and Paisiello, and was prophesying great things from the young Beethoven, he viewed it all as only a passing excellence, soon to be superceded by new music and taste.

To the modern scholar, the challenge in using Burney's criticism is to "mount up" to the conditions under which his work was produced, conditions not only of time and place, but language as well. Burney's view of history is a personal, not universal, one. In making his judgments about music he stipulates that "Mine is but an individual opinion."[131] It is the opinion of a highly educated, and within clearly defined limits, perceptive critic. His blind spots seem to us to be enormous, but these spots threaten the modern scholar only if he or she fails to consider them in evaluating Burney's views.

3
The Genesis of
The *General History of Music*

The confusion over precisely when Burney conceived the idea of writing a history of music has not been resolved. Fanny dates her father's interest in writing a history of music from 1769. However, in a letter dated 27 May 1770, Burney describes his project as "an undertaking... for which I have been some time collecting materials."[1] Elsewhere his papers prompt other estimates. In 1788 he describes the *History* as having been thirty years in meditation and twenty in writing and printing, suggesting a date ca. 1758 for its conception.[2] But in a letter written in 1807 he wrote that he "began to meditate a General History of Music" after taking his doctorate at Oxford in June, 1769, thus seeming to confirm Fanny's statement in the *Memoirs*.[3] Whatever the case, Burney's extraordinary abilities were evident long before he received the Oxford doctorate, and it is perhaps his lifelong practice of reading and self-improvement which obfuscates the specific time when he began the labors on his *History*. The materialization of his interest in music history into a substantial project is described by Fanny in her inimitable style:

> A wish, and a design, energetic though vague, of composing some considerable work on his own art, had long roved in his thoughts, and flattered his fancy, and he now began seriously to concentrate his meditations, and to arrange his schemes to that single point. And the result of these cogitations, when no longer left wild to desultory wanderings, produced his enlightened and scientific plan for a General History of Music.[4]

Until quite recently the best source for acquiring an idea of Burney's plan was a letter to the Reverend William Mason of 27 May 1770, described by Fanny as containing "the opening view of the plan and tour." While Burney's letter to Mason is in no way the "scientific plan" which Fanny mentions, it does provide considerable insight into some aspects of his conception of his *History*. In it he cites Giorgi Vasari's *Le Vite de' più eccelenti architetti, pittori, et scultori italiani* (1550), declaring that he can "see no reason why the life of an eminent musician should not afford as much entertainment as that of a Painter." In reviewing Vasari's *Vite* he found that only one life, that of Leonardo da Vinci, could furnish "such great and interesting events, as the biography of Farinelli could afford to the lovers of music." It is evident from this letter that interesting events presented in an agreeable style were to have precedence over learning in his *History*. This is not to suggest that he underestimated the breadth of scholarship required of one who would write a general history of music. On the contrary, he told Mason that "The prospect widens as I advance... I find it connected with Religion, History, Poetry, Painting, Sculpture, public Exhibitions, and private life."[5]

Though he was overwhelmed with information, he found very little of any real use in the books written by earlier musical scholars. Indeed, he discovered that the existing books about music were "such faithful copies of each other, that by reading two or three, you have the substance of as many hundred." The literature on the history of music was so redundant and inaccurate that Burney resolved to set aside old authorities. His *History* was to be an original work, drawn from his own experience with modern music and first-hand investigation of the surviving records of antiquity. He therefore resolved to "fly to Italy" to allay his "thirst of knowledge at the pure source." On this journey he envisioned consulting public libraries to learn more of the "rise and progress of Music since Guido's time," and to "endeavour, by hearing and conversing with the most eminent professors to inform myself of its present state."

Judging from this letter, Burney had not yet drafted his "scientific plan." Had it been prepared, he most certainly would have sent a copy of it to demonstrate the seriousness of his purpose and to enlist Mason's cooperation. The letter is only a prospectus for his tour. Burney's plan for his *History* was a carefully wrought, very detailed prospectus, a fact evinced not only by Fanny's reference to a "scientific plan," but also by the numerous references to the plan in his published Continental travel journals.[6]

Despite its importance, no copy of the *Plan* remains among the Burney papers. It is no small wonder that the *Plan* has been so elusive: in August, 1773, Burney sent a copy to Twining for evaluation, but cautioned, "I must beg of you to return it to me as I have no other copy." His copy seems irretrievably lost; however, recovery of a copy of the Italian translation of the *Plan* in the papers of Padre Martini can at last lay to rest speculation regarding its contents. The *Plan*, copied in Padre Martini's own hand with some corrections and elaborations in Burney's handwriting, was discovered, along with a partial catalogue of Burney's library, by Vincent Duckles in the Civico Museo Bibligrafico Musicale.[7] It is a definitive and concise statement of purpose: the scientific plan to which Fanny referred.

> General plan of Doctor Charles Burney's
> history of music, with a catalogue of his
> musical library.

English School

John Tally
William Bird
Thomas Morley
Dr. Lawes
Dr. Blow
Henry Purcel
Dr. Crofts
Dr. Green
Dr. Boyce pronounced Boiss

General Plan of Doctor Charles Burney's
History of Music.

The author proposes to give as clear a picture of the music of ancient Greece as can be gathered from the best writers on the subject as well as information on the construction and use of their instruments with drawings of the same taken from the bas-reliefs of Kircher, Gruter, Monfaucon, Bianchini, etc., and with illustrations extracted from the ancient poets, historians, and philosophers. In realizing this part of the work, one can expect little new of note except in the realm of conjecture, where the author believes one who has studied and practiced the musical arts may have the prerogatives of a true antiquarian—at least, should the occasion actually arise, to conjecture, but only that which is practicable or at least possible.

The author believes that his work should be concentrated principally on the history of the present system of musical practice from the time of Guido d'Arezzo, who was the inventor of music in the eleventh century, up to the present. This part will cover the discoveries and refinements made in both vocal and instrumental music up to the time of publication. Here one will also find enumerated the most eminent and celebrated composers, the singers and instrumentalists of every time and country known to us, from the most authoritative sources, including a literary portrait of all their merits. There will be a chronological account of the principal books relative to the subject of music, in all languages, with translations of extracts therefrom.

And since posterity may be as curious about the music of the present day as we are concerning that of our predecessors (if indeed the writer of this history may be permitted to flatter himself that he has something to pass on to posterity), it would be well to give some musical examples of the best compositions of every type taken from the works of the greatest and most notable masters living today, thus enabling our successors to make a competent judgment of the state of music in approximately the middle of the eighteenth century.

A separate chapter of this work will contain the latest discoveries and advances in music.

Another chapter will be devoted to desiderata.

Titles of some other chapters
1.
Concerning the music of the Hebrews, its use in religious ceremonies; with a dissertation on the harp of David.

2.
Concerning ancient Greek and Roman music, considered in its martial uses as well as its lyric and theatrical usages.

3.
Concerning the music of the church, and its first introduction in the divine service; and here will be treated, beginning at their sources, Ambrosian chants and Gregorian chants, or *Cantus Firmus*.

4.
Concerning sacred drama, or oratorio, and its history.

5.
Concerning theatrical music, or opera.

6.
Various ancient and modern systems will be laid out and examined, such as those of Pythagoras, Aristosseno, Ptolomy, Boethius, Guido d'Arezzo, Briennio, Rameau, Tartini, etc.

7.
Concerning the national music of Italy, Germany, France, England, Scotland, Ireland, Wales, Russia, Portugal, Spain, Africa, Asia, and America.

8.
Once again will be attempted the history of several modern instruments—that is to say, of the organ, the clavicembalo, the violin, etc., with their refinements with regard to both their construction and their use.

> The author has been pursuing the above plan for the formulation of a history of music for some time. But not having found the satisfaction he had expected in the great quantity of books that he had consulted, and having become tired of and disgusted with continually reading and rereading the same things in the works of different authors,* in hopes, therefore, of stamping on his work some marks of originality, or at least of novelty, he determined to allay his thirst for the science of music at the true source by undertaking a voyage to Italy, from whence the rest of Europe has obtained not only all of the most celebrated composers and performers, but also all of the ideas concerning what is elegant and of the finest taste in the art of music. He resolved to go there in order to hear with his own ears, and to see with his own eyes; and, if possible, to hear and see nothing but music, unless drawn by a desire to profit from the council of men of learning and to converse with men of taste, hoping to have the honor of the former as well as of the latter.
> Indeed he might have amused himself agreeably enough in examining pictures, statues, and buildings, copy inscriptions, etc.
> But as he could not afford time for all this, without neglecting the chief business of his journey, he determined not to allow himself to be distracted from his established intention of other curiosities or research.[8]

The breadth of Burney's prospectus is astonishing, particularly in light of the current state of musical scholarship. It is understandable that upon first reading the *Plan,* Jean-Jacques Rousseau "cried out every moment 'ma foi, c'est vaste!' "

The salient feature of the opening of the *Plan* is its rationalism. Skeptical of the accounts of the wondrous powers of ancient music, Burney was prepared to offer a realistic history of the music of antiquity. The subject of the music of the ancients was not one with which Burney was sympathetic. In his letter to Mason he reservedly stated, "Something must of course be said about the ancient music." His lack of enthusiasm for the subject led him to consider not discussing ancient music in his *History* at all. He told Twining that he originally

> set off with a determination to begin at the 11th. century when Guido is said to have invented the scale which is still in use, but by reading a great number of fogram musical Authors, they

have so far Contaminated my Ideas as to incline me to dip into all the dark and unfathomable Stuff concerning Greek Modes and Hebrew Psalmody about which we know nearly as much, as of the Musical System used by the Inhabitants of the Planet Saturn. Something must perhaps be said; but my Say will be more to laugh at what others have written, perhaps, than to offer anything of my own Concerning them. The History of *Counterpoint* is certainly all that concerns a History of music—and this with a little Biography concerning Composers and performers will be chiefly attended to in the Course of my work.[9]

The discussion of ancient music was, then, a matter of necessity and form, rather than a reflection of genuine and voluntary interest. Once underway though, Burney was not disinterested, for he found that "it was impossible to read a great number of books upon the subject, without meeting with conjectures, and it was not easy to peruse these without forming others of my own."[10] Nevertheless, this section of his *History* was to be the section of least interest to the author, and the one which ultimately caused him the greatest difficulty.

The second paragraph of the *Plan* betrays Burney's progressive view of music history. He saw the history of music as beginning with a pre-history, the music of the ancients, followed by the true business of his book, the history of the evolution of music from a primitive and barbarous state to the state of perfection evident in his own time. His intention was to trace "the discoveries and refinements" of vocal and instrumental music and the merits of the performers throughout musical history. As Burney saw performers as being in a constant state of evolution—each new generation building on the taste and technical attainment of the last—this part of the *History* would be progressive as well. His readers might expect a "deep and well-digested treatise on the theory and practice of music"; however, he saw his principal task as "the collecting into one point of the most interesting circumstances relative to its practice and professors."[11]

As to the science of music, the *Plan* promises "a chronological account of the principal books...in all languages, with translations of extracts therefrom," as well as an examination of the principal theoretical systems ancient and modern, numbering no fewer than eight. Such a promise seems another instance of Burney's sense of responsibility to his readers and to the tradition of musical scholarship overiding his own interests. He did not perceive the science of music, particularly its history, to be a necessary or even desirable field of knowledge for most of his readership. The general reader might be interested in some insights into composition, but calculations, conjecture, and speculative investigations in acoustics were hardly proper topics for a dilettante.[12] Since one of Burney's objectives was to improve the taste of his readership, he was clearly concerned that praising treatises which taught composition in styles long abandoned might be harmful. He might occasionally acknowlege that a book was good in its time, but he was primarily concerned with warning his readers away from books which might instruct them in a false or superannuated taste.[13]

It is noteworthy that Burney refers to his plan to provide a history of music of his own time as a service to posterity. His rummaging in the literature of former writers instilled in him an appreciation of the value of books to future historians. His desire to serve the authors of later eras was tempered by his keen social sense, but Twining urged him on in this part of his work, proclaiming:

> These articles on the most recent music and books will be useful and interesting, not only now, but as long as your book exists; nay, they will give a *crescendo* to the value of it; and future inquirers and historians will bless the man who had a regard, so rare, of the curiosity and the indolence of posterity.[14]

The prospect of evaluating living musicians in other countries may not have seemed too threatening, but he was aware from the beginning of the dangers inherent in reviewing composers, performers, and theorists living in England.

The list of chapter titles in the *Plan* contains one startling subject: in chapter 7 Burney proposes an investigation of the national music (i.e., folk music) of most of the known world. The inclusion of this subject is surprising not only because national music has a negligible place in the published *History*, but also because in 1770 such a proposal was well in advance of its time. Ethnomusicological research was not an area of specialized study in the eighteenth century: what little was known about the music of non-European countries came largely from the reports of explorers, missionaries, and diplomats. Even the study of indigenous folk art was the province of the traveler to remote parts of countries where "civilization" had least affected the inhabitants, and where folk art was more or less untainted.

Voyage journals with musical information were not new in the eighteenth century. Jean de Levy's *Histoire d'un voyage fait en la terre du Brésil* (1585) contains descriptions of instruments, ceremonial music, methods of singing, and dancing. Many other voyages explored such countries as Mexico, Abyssinia, the Caribby-Islands, Russia, Persia, Lapland, the island of Faeores, Siam, the Isthmus of America, the Congo, Paraguay, Japan, Chili, Peru, Africa, and China. For all of the regions, some musical information was provided in the published journals.

One other source of information was the missionary movement, particularly that of the Jesuits. The Jesuit Jean Baptiste du Halde published his *Description géographique, historique, chronologique, politique, et physique de l'empire de la Chine et de la Tartarie Chinoise* in 1735, and provided "the main source of information on that country for Europeans until the late Eighteenth Century."[15] Other missions in different areas provided similar information.

The travel journal or "voyage" was a very popular form of literature throughout the eighteenth century, and Burney was numbered among the enthusiastic readers of this type of book. His library contained many of the reports of these "voyages," and he was, thus, not without a considerable body of information about national music, albeit of a very unsystematic and often unreliable kind. Despite the number of precursors who dealt with related topics, Burney's all-inclusive proposal for national music remains impressive. A decade would pass before a source would treat national music on such a broad basis.[16]

The philosophy of historical progressivism was pre-eminent in writings about the history of music at this time, and even the music of a culture as refined and ancient as that of the Chinese was regarded as being frozen into an early stage of its development, a development which, left to run its course, would lead to a system of music like that of eighteenth-century Europe. For the musician, a strong motive to study other cultures was the desire to discover the nature of the music of the ancients. The search for excellence in the arts through a rediscovery of Classical models was a failure in music. Only a few disputed fragments of ancient music existed, and little or nothing in these suggested the music which had been so glorified by mythology and the ancient writers. It was felt by some writers that the folk music of uncivilized cultures closely resembled that of the ancients.[18] Burney was interested in more than the supposed resemblance of national music to ancient music. As the record of his encounters with national music on his tours reflects, his interest lay also in defining and classifying the ethnic music of the countries listed in his plan.

There is one facet of Burney's conception of his *History* which the *Plan* does not treat: the nature of the audience for which it was to be written. Although the breadth of his prospectus would lead to expectations of a formidable and scholarly work, he originally had a very different audience in mind. He wished to have his book"so divested of Pedantry and Jargon that every Miss, who plays *o' top the Spinet* could make it her manual."[19] He planned to "Compensate for this total neglect of Erudition" by the inclusion of anecdotes, and he beseeched Twining to "pray send me all you can about the Shoe Buckles, Slippers, or whatever concerns have occasioned in the Fact of great men."

Burney's intention for his *History* in 1773 seems thus at odds with the formidable and comprehensive *Plan* that he prepared for the tour of 1770. The difference can best be explained as yet another result of his sensitivity to his audience. From the outset his was not to be a book meant to seem learned like those of his predecessors; it was designed to make the *reader* seem learned by providing a pleasant and entertaining approach to the history of music, the literature of which had, up to that time, been dominated by theoretical and speculative works of a kind that would defeat any but the most erudite and specialized readers. Burney found that his subject had been "so often deformed by unskilled writers, that many readers, even among those that love and understand music, are afraid of it." He did not wish to be approached with "awe and reverence" for his depth and erudition, but to bring on a "familiar acquaintance" with his readers "by talking in common language of what has hitherto worn the face of gloom and mystery," and been too much "sicklied o'er with the pale cast of thought." If he was to err in the balance of pedantry and entertainment, he would "rather be pronounced trivial than tiresome."[20]

A search for the models which inspired Burney's conception of his history of music would be widespread. Vasari's *Vite* has already been mentioned, and there were doubtless other models in literature and cultural histories. Setting aside general literature, it seems fruitless to search for a model in early musical writers, though at least twenty-five works treating the general history of music preceded the publication of the first volume of Burney's *History* in 1776:[21] Twenty-three works were in existence prior to his announced intention to write the book. Of these, nineteen appear in Burney's private library.[22] None of them, however, seems to be a prototype of Burney's massive undertaking. Perhaps the idea of using a "dissertation" in his first volume was taken from the *Storia della musica* of Padre Martini, but little else resembles the earlier work in content or design. Indeed, Burney claimed a certain novelty for his work, noting of earlier histories that he had "seldom imitated their arrangements and never servilely copied their opinions."[23] There were, nonetheless, a number of histories of music in a variety of languages available to Burney's readers, and he felt obliged to justify the need for yet another history. In the preface to the *History* he mentions seven earlier histories of music in French, German, and Italian. He reviews Bonnet's *Histoire de la musique* (1715), and criticizes it for being "written on a very narrow plan," and he is equally critical of the second volume which contained "nothing more than exclusive eulogiums of Lulli, and illiberal censures of every species of Italian music." He was equally severe with Charles Henri de Blainville's *Histoire générale, critique et philologique de la musique* (1767), calling it "nominally a *General History of Music,* yet notwithstanding the splendid promises in the title, the *historical, critical* and *philogical* parts of this work are comprised in less than half a thin quarto."[24] For the remaining five authors he provides no critical comment, stating only that the histories of Martini and Marpurg are not yet finished, and that Martin Gerbert's *Di cantu et musica sacra a prima ecclesiae aetate usque ad praeseuns tempus* (1774) deals only with church music; thus much is left to be done. Burney's later writings can, however, provide some useful indication of his opinion of these authors, as well as other writers whose work preceded his own efforts.

The earliest general history with which Burney was familiar was Domenico Pietro Cerone's *El Melopeo,* which appeared thirteen years after

Calvisius's *Exercitationes musicae duae* (1600), the book which Warren Allen regarded as the first general history.[25] Burney considered Cerone's *El Melopeo* to be "the most ample, correct and useful *musical* treatise that appeared in any country during the sevnteenth century."[26] It is curious that he does not mention its historical content in his extended critique, although he gives the number of pages and a description of its extensive treatment of counterpoint. The book was written in Spanish, a language with which Burney seems not to have been familiar. He found some way to unlock its secrets though, for Cerone's work is used as an authority in the *General History*.[27]

The only acquaintance which Burney seems to have had with Michael Praetorious's *Syntagma Musicum* (1615) is through the description of it given in Johann Gottfried Walther's *Musicalisches Lexicon*.[28] In contrast, he was well acquainted with Mersenne's *Traité de l'harmonie universelle* (1627), a work of considerable merit, in which "through all the partiality to his country, want of taste, and method, there are so many curious researches and ingenious and philosophical experiments, which have been of the greatest use to subsequent writers, particularly Kircher, as render the book extremely valuable."[29]

Burney's view of Kircher's own *Musurgia universalis* (1650) changed dramatically over the years. In 1781 he wrote that Kircher's work "contains much curious and useful information for such as know how to sift truth from error and usefulness from futility."[30] Many years later he reviewed the book again, this time castigating the author for being:

> always careless of what he asserted, credulous, and inaccurate; collecting, without choice or discernment, whatever he found relative to the subject upon which he was writing; and adopting whatever was offered to him, true or false, provided it contained anything marvellous.
>
> His *Musurgia*... is a large book; but a much larger might be composed in pointing out its errors and absurdities.[31]

The review ends with the lines from the *History* given above, but in its new context it seems hollow praise indeed.

The *Historische Beschreibung der edlen Sing-und Klingkunst* (1690) of Wolfgang Printz[32] was even in Burney's day so rare that he claimed to have never seen a copy of it, despite many years of effort on his own part, as well as that of many of his friends, to obtain one. He regarded Printz's work as the "first, in modern times," and though he knew only the extracts printed in Marpurg's writings, he determined that its plan and arrangement seemed to be good.

Burney had great difficulty also in acquiring Giovanni Bontempi's *Historia musica* (1695); once having obtained a copy, he found that he had expected to be "in possession of a greater treasure than on examination it proved to be."[33] The book seems to have typified the kind of writing on music of which Burney was most critical:[34]

> For with great parade of his learning, science, and acquaintance with the Greek *theorists,* that are come down to us, he leaves us in as utter darkness concerning the *practice* of ancient music as ever; and, to say the truth, he has furnished us with but little information concerning the modern of his own time, with which, however, as a contrapuntist, he seems to have been well acquainted. Indeed, by the frequent use he makes of scientific terms, his book, when casually opened, has more the appearance of a dry mathematical treatise than the history of an elegant art.[35]

Although Sébastian de Brossard's *Dictionnaire de musique* is not strictly a general history of music, Warren Allen has included it in his bibliography. The inclusion of lexicographic works in such a list would have met with Burney's approval. He acknowledged his gratitude to Brossard's work for opening many subjects of inquiry, for giving sources of information, and for providing a list of writers on music, both ancient and modern. He also defended Brossard against the charge by Jean-Jacques Rousseau that his dictionary was nothing but an Italian dictionary with a French title, noting that in 1702 [*sic*] the "musical technica" of the French language was "insufficient, alone to furnish a book."

The brief opinion of Jacques Bonnet's *Histoire de la musique* (1715) given in the preface of the *History* is the only review of it in that work. In the *Cyclopaedia,* however, Burney considerably enlarged the attack. The *Histoire* was begun by Bonnet's uncle, Pierre Bourdelot, who amassed a large body of material. Upon his death it passed to Pierre Bonnet-Bourdelot, who continued the work until his death in 1708. Thereafter, his brother Jacques organized the material and wrote the first volume of the work. According to Burney, the remaining three volumes were actually written by a physician named Frencuse, who:

> ...instead of a continuation of the history of music, has given us nothing but a violent philippic against the abbé Raguenet, for daring to draw a parallel between the music of France and Italy, and a censure of all the most illustrious Italians of the seventeenth century, such as Carissimi, Luigi Rossi, Scarlatti, and Corelli; and setting up Lulli against them all...[36]

As for Bonnet himself, Burney concludes that "he was no musician, and equally unable to explain the theory of the ancients and the practice of the moderns; so that his work is totally devoid of taste, order, and useful information."

It is curious that the first English contribution to a general history of music, Alexander Malcolm's *Treatise of Musick, Speculative, Practical and Historical* (1721) should receive such scant mention in Burney's *History.* It is listed in the "Chronological List of the principal Books published on the Subject of Music in England, during the present Century," found in the appendix, but it is not reviewed in the text, nor does it appear to have been used as a source anywhere in the four-volume work. The presence of the book in the 1770 catalogue of Burney's library attests to his familiarity with it during the writing of the *History*.[37] The critical notice of the work in the *Cyclopaedia* reveals that he found Malcolm's literary style distasteful, but felt the author had "drawn from the purest sources of information concerning ancient music," and did not seem ignorant of the modern. He gave Malcolm particular credit for being one of the first writers on music to doubt the existence of music in parts among the ancients, a doubt which Burney entertained. Despite these merits, Malcolm's work had little if any influence on Burney's historical writing, for he notes that he had not looked in the book "for nearly half a century."

Although it was not published until the middle of the nineteenth century, Roger North's *Memoires of Musick* deserves mention here, because the manuscript (completed around 1728) was available after the author's death in 1734, and Burney made ample use of it during the preparation of his own book. The *Memoires* had never been published, so Burney did not review it for the *Cyclopaedia*, but he did praise North as a "dilettante musician of considerable taste and knowledge...judgment and discrimination," and noted that the *Memoires* had been of great use in reconstructing the history of English secular music.[38] Beyond this assessment, Burney's high estimation of North's work is evident by the extensive citations from his work in the *History*.

Of all the publications Burney reviewed in his *History*, *The Monthly Review*, and the *Cyclopaedia*, no other received the unqualified praise given to Johann Gottfried Walther's *musikalisches Lexicon oder musickalische Bibliothek* (1732):

> Of all the books which we have consulted for information concerning musicians and their works, we have never met with more satisfaction than from this *Lexicon;* which...is so ample and accurate, that we have been seldom disappointed, and never led into error by it. This little volume contains, not only the technica of ancient and modern music, but biography, as far as names, dates, and works of almost every eminent musician that has existed in ancient and modern times...[39]

Burney's extensive citations from Walther throughout the *History* attests to the sincerity of his statement.

There is a definite change in the tone and content of Burney's reviews of critical publications written after the first third of the eighteenth century. In his criticism of early musical writings he was evaluating the publications about music and musicians with which he was relatively unfamiliar. But the writers of the middle portion of the century were discussing the music of Burney's own age. These writers often advocated music recent enough to be remembered, but old enough to be regarded with some disdain by those of more modern taste.

One such writer with superannuated taste was Johann Mattheson. Burney's notice of this author in the *History* is brief and to the point: "Mattheson, with all his pedantry and want of taste, was the first popular writer on the subject of Music in Germany; the rest were scientifically dry and didactic; but as taste improved both in Music and literature, better writers sprung up."[40] In his amplified criticism in the *Cyclopaedia,* Burney attributes Mattheson's want of taste to the fact that though he had "ceased to play and compose, he continued to write musical treatises, of which the names are now hardly to be found." Although Burney owned three of Mattheson's books, they do not appear to have been used extensively in his work.[41]

In contrast, Burney regarded the work of Frederick Marpurg, a contemporary of Mattheson, as both useful and full of good taste. He was in Burney's view the "first German theorist who could patiently be read by persons of taste, so addicted were former writers to prolixity and pedantry." Marpurg's *Historisch-Kritische Beyträge zur Aufnahme der Musik* was his principal contribution to the history of his art. Unfortunately, the main part of Burney's review of Marpurg's *oeuvre* is a very favorable notice of his *Abhandlung von der Fuge* (1753).[42] Of Marpurg's historical writings, Burney provides only the titles, but the ample citations from these books in the *History* attest to their value in his work. In the final line of his review, Burney declares that as a writer on musical subjects, Marpurg "surpassed all his predecessors and contemporaries in the German language, in clearness, elegance, and extensive acquaintance with the history and rules of the art."[43] It is thus rather surprising to find a quite contradictory assessment of this author in a letter written years earlier by Burney to the translator of his *Present State of Music in France and Italy* into the German language. Here Burney states that Marpurg's

> critische Einlictung in die Gaschicte etc. of Music [*sic*] affords me very few materials for my Work, which I have not repeatedly found in others. He is too short even as far as he has gone. It seems to me rather an INDEX of a complete general History, than the work itself, and his severe decisions concerning the modern Italians, I can by no means subscribe to; namely that they are *elende componisten:* and particularly that Galuppi ist ein schlechter componist. M. Marpurg must have decided without sufficient information concerning the works of modern Composers, or must be governed by prejudice.[44]

Perhaps Burney, after spending years on his own work, more fully appreciated Marpurg, or perhaps he had grown more aware of the need to consider historical writings in the light of the era and milieu in which they were written.

Chronologically, the next historical effort to appear before the European public was Padre Martini's three-volume *Storia della musica* (1757, 1770, and 1781). Despite the early publication date of Martini's first volume, Burney states in his tour journal that he had been unable to procure a copy, and did not lay eyes on one until he arrived in Italy in 1770. He was barely able to obtain a copy prior to meeting the author, who was then in the process of putting the second volume to press. Though Martini's *Storia* could not have served as a model for Burney's *Plan,* two volumes were available to him during his work on his own first volume.

Burney and Martini became friends during the several days in which Burney visited Bologna, and later were correspondents about musical matters. This friendship, as well as Burney's great respect for the knowledge and the massive collection of materials of the padre, seem to exert an effect on the tone of his review of the *Storia*. The lengthy article in the *Cyclopaedia* examines each volume in detail, with many complimentary comments. Nevertheless, the undertone of the article is one of less-than-full satisfaction with the work. Burney laments, for example, that "the first volume of this elaborate work only contains 61 pages of history, which advance no further in the progress of the art, than what the sacred writings have told us... The rest of the volume is filled with dissertations." Of the second volume, Burney writes that although thirteen years have elapsed between the publication of the first and second volume, the "learned and laborious author has advanced but a little way in the history even of ancient music." The third volume, which appeared in 1781, disappointed Burney, especially since it was the last volume that Martini published before he died. Burney had looked forward with expectation to the time when Martini would advance beyond the music of the ancients, because "in writing the history of ancient Grecian and Roman music, he had no other means of information than those of which others were in possession."

Although Burney was able to make extensive use of Martini's volumes in his *History,* the Italian scholar's work in ancient music seems to have been merely the best writing about a subject in which Burney had no genuine interest. Had it not been the work of a friend and internationally famous scholar, it would probably have received much harsher treatment at Burney's hands. The last paragraph of Burney's notice seems sufficient evidence of the care with which Burney expressed his view of Martini's work:

> The style has been said to be dry and prolix. It is indeed enlivened by no extraneous matter or ingenious reflections; but each page is replete with information on the subject in question: and the notes abound in curious passages from scarce books. The road through which the good father leads us, if not strewed with flowers, is not barren, but frequently affords a glimpse, at least, of incipient cultivation, which excites a wish and eagerness to advance out of twilight, into regions where the sun of science shines with more luster, to which, alas! the author did not live to lead us.[45]

In a less guarded moment, Burney confessed "that the History of the good Padre Martini so replete with learned authorities is what his Countrymen frequently call it, a *seccatura*."[46]

John Brown's *Dissertation on the Rise, Union, and Power, the Progressions, Separations, and Corruptions of Poetry and Music* (1763) was sufficiently regarded outside of England to be translated into German in 1769, and into Italian in 1772. Burney, however, was quite unimpressed.[47] Brown typified to Burney all those who had neither taste nor feeling for music, but who persisted in writing about it; especially that of the ancients. Burney wrote that these "profound critics," including Dr. Brown, were among the most learned men, but "being out of the way of good music, and good performers of the present times, [they] have formed a romantic idea of ancient music upon the exaggerated accounts of its effects, which they have read in old authors."[48] Indeed, Burney regarded Brown's work as negligible—so much so that he did not bother to contribute a discussion of this work to the *Cyclopaedia*. The anonymous contributor of the article concluded that "this dissertation, though ingenious and critical, advanced fanciful principles, and manifested a degree of credulity with respect to the supposed effect of certain public institutions among the ancients, which gave rise to a variety of strictures."[49]

If Burney generally ignored Brown's *Dissertation*, he was not so generous with Charles Henri de Blainville's *Histoire générale, critique et philologique de la musique* (1767). His review of all of Blainville's work, including the *Histoire*, is brief and brutal: "They are compilations without taste, which teach nothing new to those who know anything about music already; and not enough to those who know nothing."[50]

A French author who did inform Burney, and much of the rest of musical Europe, was Jean-Jacques Rousseau. The more than thirty quotations from Rousseau's works on topics ranging from the notation of ancient music to the state of opera in France stand in evidence of his influence on Burney's *History*. But his impact was far more decisive than this tabulation suggests. The aesthetic advanced by Rousseau in his *Lettre sur la musique française* (1753) was the very foundation of Burney's critical philosophy of dramatic composition. As late as 1814 he continued to call the *Lettre* "the best piece of musical criticism that has ever been produced in any modern language."[51] He particularly praised Rousseau's *Dictionnaire de musique* (1767) for its usefulness to historiographers, noting that, without promising anything more than an explanation of terms, it afforded "not only amusement, but more *historical information* relative to the art, than perhaps any book of the size that is extant."[52]

Burney fully subscribed to Rousseau's theory of the "Unity of Melody," with all of its implications. However, partial though he was to Rousseau as a man and a critic, he did not subscribe to all of his theories. He deplored his support of Blainville's theory of a new mode, and rejected Rousseau's new system of notation. He was also willing to weigh the opinion of other authors when they were in conflict with Rousseau's concepts. Finding Padre Martini and Rousseau in conflict over the use of the *tierce de Picardie*,[53] Burney, while agreeing with Rousseau that the raised third in dramatic music and song was deplorable, sided with Martini's authority because

> The learned author of the *Saggio di Contrappunto*, who was so perfectly acquainted with all the beauties and effects of Choral Music, is certainly more to be relied on in whatever concerns it, than the animated author of the *Dictionaire* [sic] *de Musique;* who, with the most refined taste and exalted views with respect to Dramatic Compositions, had neither time nor opportunity sufficiently to explore the mysteries of *Canto Firmo,* or to become a very profound contrapuntist.[54]

Although the *Plan* makes no mention of specific composers or schools, there is no doubt that during the evolution of the prospectus for his *History* Burney was strongly influenced by Rousseau's views of dramatic music. The "heroes of his *History*" were to be those of the French writer: the Neapolitan School and its stylistic descendants, the most famous of whom was Hasse.[55] Burney could claim that he took little of form and less of content from earlier historical writings, but the influence of Rousseau's writings strongly affected his perception of all kinds of music.

Two other important publications treating the history of music appeared prior to the first volume of Burney's work: Antonio Eximeno's *Del origen y reglas de la musica, con la histoire de su progreso, decadencia, y restauracion,* and Martin Gerbert's *Di cantu et musica sacra a prima ecclesiae aetate usage ad praesens tempus.* Both works appeared in 1774, and thus could not have influenced the genesis of the *Plan.* However, inasmuch as they were available for consultation during the writing of the *History,* they belong in the survey of Burney's attitude toward the musical-historical writings that preceded his own.

Though he was attracted to the "strength and eloquence" of Eximeno's literary style, Burney had little regard for the content of his treatise.[56] He recognized the author's "shrewdness and accuracy" in pointing out difficulties and imperfections in the theory and practice of music, but strongly criticized him because his own resources and experience were "totally insufficient to the task of correcting the old system, or forming a new one that is more perfect." As always, the most important criterion which Burney used in judging the book was the quality of the examples given by the author as models of perfection. Those given by Eximeno he found "below contempt," and from this Burney concluded that Eximeno had "more eloquence of language than science in music," an opinion he amplified by noting that his reasoning was both "ingenious and specious," even when his data was false."[57]

In contrast, it was the sound, painstaking scholarship of the *Di Cantu et musica sacre* of Martin Gerbert that attracted Burney to this work. In 1763, Gerbert published a "plan" for his own history which Burney read with such approval that he resolved to visit him during his tour of Germany and the Netherlands. Unfortunately, fire destroyed most of the priest's papers, and when the news reached Burney he cancelled the intended visit. However, sometime between 1773 and 1775, "by means of a German gentleman of great merit and learning, resident in London," the two historians began a correspondence, one which Burney said afforded him great pleasure in "the opportunity it gave me of shewing my zeal, for satisfying his enquiries in the best manner I was able."[58]

It is unclear as to whether Gerbert was of any service to Burney through their correspondence, but it is certain that Gerbert's history was of considerable use to Burney during his work on the origins of counterpoint, and the formation of the timetable. No fewer than five of the illustrations from these chapters are taken, with proper acknowledgment, from the plates in Gerbert's book. Beyond the obvious admiration which Burney had for the author's erudition, it is difficult to construct his assessment of this work from the published sources. Gerbert's authority is cited a dozen times in the *History*, but all of these citations are for opinions of the origins of counterpoint and the modern rhythmic system. Gerbert is not used as a source in the discussion of music after 1450, although his work extended far beyond that date. Burney's enthusiasm for the Abbot's writings was, in part, restrained by the nature of the music about which he wrote. Although he admired Gerbert's treatment of plain chant, he wrote that it:

> ...remain[s] more curious than useful. For to acquire a clear conception of [its] import would lead to no useful or amusing knowledge; as the chant or plainsong is genrally so rude, uncouth, and unamusing that it would furnish a very inadequate reward for the labour of deciphering it.[59]

Burney's rejection of chant underscores his motivation in originally deciding to begin the *History* with the advent of counterpoint.

In light of such sentiments it sometimes seems perplexing that Burney ever undertook the writing of a history of music. Not by any means an antiquarian, or even a whole-hearted admirer of the music of any age but his own, he was far more at home in the role of critic than historian. When he began his historiographical work he did not know the books of all the historians who preceded him.[60] Yet a great many were familiar to the author, and most occupied a place in his library in 1770.[61] Each made some contribution to Burney's emerging idea of what was needed to fill the "chasm" in English literature, and many had some influence in shaping the *Plan for the General History of Music*. With the *Plan* before him, the genesis of the *History* was well underway, and Burney prepared to set off on his research journeys to advance its development.

4
The Debut of the Critic: The Continental Tours

There is no evidence that Burney planned to publish a journal of his travels prior to his journey, but it was when he packed pen and pocketbook to record his travels that he began his career as a critic of music.[1] When he set out on his tour in 1770, his musical skills and taste were already well formed. He was a modernist and strong supporter of Italian music, with an aesthetic of operatic criticism based on the authority of Rousseau and the *Encyclopédists*. He was also a composer of solid, if modest talents, a performer of considerable ability, and had the distinction of the title "Doctor of Music" appended to his name. Although not normally listed as requisite for a historian, his apparently irresistible, ingratiating social manner was also a valuable asset in the pursuit of his goals. Once having gained admittance by way of his carefully collected cachet of letters of introduction, he appears unfailingly to have captivated the most illustrious men of continental Europe, enlisting their support for his project. The surviving correspondence from his acquaintances made during his first tour, including letters from the pens of Jean-Jacques Rousseau, Jean Baptiste Suard, Jean Monnet, the Baron d'Holbach, Denis Diderot, and Padre Martini, attests to his success. The *Tours* record many other successful encounters of shorter duration with numerous musicians, scholars, and royalty.

The fascinating details of Burney's *Tours* are far too well known to require summation once again. The *Tours* are unquestioned classics of musical literature, and even Burney's least appreciative critics allow that they are "full of interest."[2] Had the *Tours* been his only literary production, they would be sufficient for Burney to rank as the most quoted musical source from the eighteenth century.[3]

The value of Burney's Continental excursions to the eventual production of his *History of Music* is evidenced in page after page of the *Tours*. The principal libraries opened their collections to his perusal, the leading scholars and critics of Europe proudly made their private collections available to the visiting scholar, and a great many copyists and booksellers enjoyed profitable encounters with the musical traveler. Local artists, too, profited from the many sketches that would become the plates that decorate the first volume of Burney's *History*.

As soon as Burney returned from each of his journeys, he began preparing his diaries for publication. Since it was his intention to use their publication to prepare an audience for his *History,* it is not surprising that he took care to make them palatable to the same polite audience he had in mind when drafting his *Plan*. He later chided Mrs. Crewe for not having read his *Tours* because she feared she would "meet with the Jargon of hard words and the unintelligible Giberish of affected Science with which Books on the subject of music are usually crammed..." He assured her, "there is nothing more difficult to understand in the Books which I have hitherto published, than in the adventures of Giles Gingergread, or the history of Good two shoes." None of his readers, he claimed, "had ever complained of not understanding me."[4]

Upon publication, Burney's first tour, his *Present State of Music in France and Italy,* became a critical and popular success.[5] It is futile, however, to turn to the contemporary English reviews in order to determine the degree to which Burney's critical judgments are singular, or more reflective of general opinion. The two most important and extensive reviews, those of the *Critical Review* and *Monthly Review,* were carefully manipulated by Burney: they were given into the hands of long-trusted friends whom Burney could be assured shared common opinions and musical taste.[6] The critique in the *Monthly Review*[7] was written by William Bewley, described in the *Memoirs* as "A man for whom Mr. Burney felt the most enlightened friendship that the sympathetic magnetism of similar tastes, humours, and feelings, could inspire."[8] Bewley's review, consisting largely of extracts from the book itself, is very favorable,[9] and Bewley concludes with a favorable estimation of Burney's competence to undertake the writing of a general history of music.

Samuel Crisp, "a critic of the clearest acumen,"[10] and another writer with whom Burney enjoyed "a sympathy of taste"[11] in music, wrote the critique which appeared in the *Critical Review.*[12] As was then fashionable, the review consists largely of extracts from the book, but Crisp does make one substantial criticism of Burney's publication, noting that, "the impartiality we profess obliges us to take notice of the severity with which he treats French national music."[13] He acknowledges that Burney's attitude reflects fashionable views, "especially since the publication of Rousseau's letter on that subject," but goes on to say that "in a man of Dr. Burney's general knowledge of the art, and who is to give us a fair and impartial account of the music of all nations, we cannot but wonder, his enthusiasm in favour of a different stile [*sic*], should have hurried him into bitterness and invective against the French." In contrast to Burney, Crisp does not agree that "our relish must be confined to one stile only," and, borrowing an analogy from the sister art of painting, queries: "May we not be charmed with the grace and sublimity of Raphael and Corregio, and yet receive pleasure from Rembrandt or Teniers?" Noting that Burney had written that "the French music has undergone very little alteration since Lulli's time," he cites Joseph Addison's opinion that "French music is now perfect in its kind," and that the "music of the French is, indeed, very properly adapted to their pronunciation and accent."

To stengthen further his defense of French music, Crisp draws on the authority of Geminiani, "whose taste, we suppose, no one will dispute," and who was "an avowed favourer of French music, and professed to have profited much from his study and imitation of it."[14] Crisp is quite willing to "let the Italian have preference, which it seems fairly entitled to," but, he queries, "must the French therefore in contradiction to the general feelings of a whole nation, be anathematised without remorse?" In closing, he reiterates his earlier position that it was fashion that led Burney to his harsh strictures against the music of the French, for "Mode carries all before it; and music, like everything else, must be content to swim with the tide." Nonetheless, he concludes by proclaiming that the *Tour* is "highly entertaining, full of taste, judgment, and erudition; and that no one appears to be more capable of executing with success, the great work he proposes of a *General History of Music,* than himself."

It must have been particularly galling to Burney to have Crisp draw upon the authority of Addison and Geminiani in opposition to his own. Burney did not respect Addison as a critic of music, for though Addison "had visited Italy, and was ambitious of being thought a judge of Music, [one] discovers, whenever he mentions the subject, a total want of sensibility, as well as knowledge in the art."[15] As for Geminiani, Burney wrote that he was "as a Critic, *jamais de bonne Foi,* changing his opinions according to his Interest, as often as Caprice. One day he would set up French Music against all other—the next, English—Scots—Irish, anything but the best Compositions of Handel and Italy."[16] Nonetheless, it must be acknowledged by even the most sympathetic reader that Burney's relentless attack on French vocal music reflects an intolerance that can seemingly only be explained by prejudice, particularly in a critic of such international tastes.

It may seem paradoxical that Burney arranged for a review that is so sharply critical of his treatment of French music, but he not only arranged for the review, he read it prior to publication, and urged its author "to soften the attack on *my* attack of French Music." To Crisp's credit, if the review was softened, the critic's reservations are nonetheless clearly evident. Burney rightly observes that Crisp is accusing him of "*Injustice* and *prejudice,* two terrible Qualities in an Historian."[17]

Crisp correctly identifies the shaping influence of Rousseau's *Lettre sur la Musique.* Burney was enamored of the *Lettre* and worked on its translation during his residence at King's Lynn. More than a decade passed between Burney's initial exposure to the *Lettre* and his first opportunity to hear French music on its native soil.[18] This occurred in the early summer of 1764, when he took one of his daughters to a Parisian boarding school, and during the following summer when he returned to retrieve his daughter.[19] It is to these two visits that Burney refers in the *Tours* when he states that "it would have been both arrogant and unjust" to attempt an assessment of the art of music in France on the basis of the few weeks spent there during 1770. But during the earlier visits he "frequented very much its public places," and claimed to have "collected the works of the best composers, and the writings of the best authors on the subject of music, in that kingdom for the past twenty years."[20] He was, he felt, fully capable of judging French music fairly.

The influence of Rousseau's *Lettre* is evident throughout his *Tour*. He betrays his dislike of the French style very early in the book when he remarks that:

> Those who visit Italy for the sake of painting, sculpture or architecture, do well to see what those arts afford in France first; as they become so dainty afterwards, that they can bear to look at but few things which that kingdom affords; and as I expected to have the same prejudices, or feelings at my return, about their music, I endeavored to give it a fair hearing first...[21]

This claim of impartiality is of course nonsense, for Burney's taste was well established by his many years of activity in London, the satellite capital of Italian opera. Burney, then, seems to have been very much in the situation of the Armenian in Rousseau's *Lettre* who, once having heard an Italian air, could not from that moment be induced to listen to any French air.[22] Burney's veneration for Rousseau was such that, even though he had attained an audience with the illustrious writer during his Paris sojourn, he could not bring himself to open a direct correspondence. Instead he sought permission to do so through the intervention of Pierre Gui, telling him that:

> Rousseau will be, so to speak, the hero of this History and moreover, I will strongly say to the public that among the many thousands of books which have been written on this subject, his Lettre sur la Musique Francaise and his Dictionnaire de Musique are almost the only ones that one can read without disgust. One can acknowledge that he has done more good for music than all other writers together, in what concerns good taste and the refinement of his art.[23]

Burney rightly claimed that "many of the first persons in France, for genius and taste," joined with Rousseau in his distaste for French music, among them Suard, Diderot, and d'Alembert.[24] Paris in 1770 abounded with those who preferred music in the Italian style. The "Querelle des Bouffons" of the 1750s, pitting the native French art against the Italian style then being exemplified at the Opera by an Italian *buffa* troupe, had divided musical society into two camps: one fervently defended the national heritage, and the other, led by the *Encyclopédists,* vociferously advocated the Italian style. The degree to which Burney was in critical accord with the philosophes is recorded in his journal: reflecting on his initial encounter with Diderot, Burney writes that they "embraced with each other as cordially as if acquaintances of long standing—indeed his writing made him *mine* a long time ago—1st Vol *Encyclopédie* 1751."[25] He later referred to Diderot as one of "the three principal heros of my *Journal*," the other two being Rousseau and Padre Martini.[26]

Nonetheless, Burney felt compelled to beg the indulgence of his French associates when he sent them his *Present State of Music in France and Italy.* He wrote to Diderot that it grieved him "to treat with such seeming severity the Music of a Country which I respect as much as France." His strictures, he reiterates, were directed chiefly against the music of the serious opera and the *Concert Spirituel,* where, according to his feelings—from which he claimed that he would "constantly and honestly speak"—he found the expression of the music "vicious and unnatural—the melody dry and uninteresting—and the measure unmarked." He carefully noted that, "it is not such music as I had the pleasure to hear Mademoiselle Diderot perform, that I condemn—and upon that, as well as upon your admirable writings, I form my judgments of your taste in Music."[27]

In a letter accompanying his gift to the Baron d'Holbach, he stated that he solicitiously hoped that his

> Friends at Paris who think much in the same way as myself as to French singing in the old serious Opera stile, will pardon some severities and sarcasms which have escaped me in speaking of it... I respect the French Nation for a thousand good and great Quality's in its inhabitants—and I love with a Cordial affection many Individuals for their personal merit and amiable Characters; but I am at war with vice wherever I find it.[28]

His letter to Suard is more cautious than those to his other French associates, and he seems to have had some doubts that Suard would concur in all his judgments. He expresses the hope that "I shall be pardoned some severe strictures which have escaped me relative to your old Music and old Expression." Though he acknowledges that Suard is "a Good French-Man," for which reason he is embarrassed that he should see the *Tour,* he recognizes that Suard is also a "Citizen of the World, a Friend to mankind and an Illustrious and Liberal defender of truth." If the "first persons in the literary world did not love and adopt Italia's music," Burney remarks, he would not have "dared to give way to my feelings. As it is, those seem the best patriots among you who wish to get rid of what disgraces you so much in the opinion of your neighbors." His letter expresses the wish, echoed in his letters to his other

French friends, that Suard and his friend the Abbé Arnaud will not hesitate to inform him if their views differ from his, and that "it will grieve me to think differently from two such excellent Judges of every part of Science, of Taste and of human nature."[29]

Burney was more sure of Rousseau's reception of his work. He told him forthrightly that he had written about the music of France "with much frankness, and you will see sir a very faithful narration of all that I have felt. ... The French will not be flattered."[30]

Despite the severity of his remarks against French music, Burney planned a translation of the *Tour* into French, for "though the former part does not flatter" the French, "the latter [the Italian portion of the journal] may assure them."[31] He offered to submit the translation to Diderot for correction, assured that though he knew Diderot to be "so good a Patriot as to be tender of your Country's honour in things of importance—yet your judgment and your taste will I trust befriend my opinions in the present case."[32] Burney acknowledges that the book will require revision in translation, because "I speak of many things as an English Man who writes meerly [sic] for Englishmen to Read." The revisions would apparently not include any of his "Musical Principales as to Expression, Effects, accompaniments, Lyric Poetry, etc." which he was prepared to stand by unless proven erroneous.[33]

If Burney had any genuine anxiety about the reception of his book by his French benefactors, he was soon reassured by favorable responses. Diderot wrote that he had "read it with all possible satisfaction. I have traveled with you and that means travelling in good company."[34] D'Holbach assured him that he need have no fear "that your kind of thinking of French music is displeasing to the people that you frequented in Paris. People of taste are everywhere of the same religion... For me I have read your book with a great deal of Pleasure."[35]

Although Burney's book came into French hands very quickly, by way of his gifts to his Parisian friends, the French critical press seems to have taken very little notice of his work. He made a particular effort to have his book announced by the French press, entreating Suard to use his influence to secure announcements in any journals he had "concern in." But if Suard did champion Burney's work, he did so without apparent results.[36]

A survey of contemporary periodic criticism yields only one published review.[37] The *Journal de musique* did not mention the *Tour* until 1773, when it printed a short notice of its publication; not until 1777 did two substantial extracts, translated into French, appear.[38] This is rather surprising, since the editor of the *Journal* at this time was Nicholas Framery, a writer who had protested Burney's treatment of French music in a letter in which he gave, according to Burney, "a long feeble and dull defence of it."[39] It seems probable that had the *Journal* not ceased publication in 1777 in the midst of publishing the *Tour* extracts, Framery would have published his defense of the French style in that periodical. Other Frenchmen apparently objected and made their sentiments known to Burney: Fanny records that in June, 1773, Burney read to Garrick "an Answer he is preparing to some complaints made by French writers, concerning his censure of their Music."[40]

There seem to have been no letters of complaint from the prominent Italian musicians and men of letters who befriended Burney on his journey, and no indignant visits from the numerous Italian musicians resident in London.[41] His cordial correspondence with Padre Martini, and the unending flow of Italian musicians to Burney's London home, are testimony to the acceptance of his work in their country. He did receive some observations and corrections to his work from Giuseppe Baretti, a language teacher in London, who had published his own account of Italy for the English reader in 1768. Burney recorded some of these observations in a manuscript entitled "Errata to the Ital. Tour," and his corrections and comments thereon provide insight into the preparation of *The Present State of Music in France and Italy*.[42] For example, in response to Baretti's objection to his remarks about Italian poets and philosophers, he wrote, "This part was written before I set out for that country, and was founded on the small number of great names in the arts and sciences that had reached England compared with those in Music." The *Errata* also reveals that a footnote about the Gondelieri occupying the boxes at the opera, which was suppressed in the second edition, was not based on personal observation, but was taken from an anecdote supplied by Sir James Wright. Regarding another correction, Burney wrote, "This information I did not invent, but was told in Venice what I have written." It is clear from these and many other similar remarks in the *Errata* that not all of Burney's observations can be assumed to be the result of first-hand investigation, even when no other source is mentioned.[43]

Burney's response to several other suggestions reveals that though he was willing to accommodate his critics on nonmusical subjects, he was not as receptive to suggestions that he alter some of his musical comments. He retorted to one of Baretti's objections, "I *think* not—I must stand or fall by my own feelings and opinions about Musical Matters—others I am always ready to relinquish." If this statement can be trusted, the musician can rely on Burney's critical judgments in at least the first edition of the *Italian Tour*, but some caution should be exercised in accepting statements of a general nature.

Burney was held in higher regard in Italy than many other travelers who had published their tour journals. The author of the *Sbozza del commercio di Amsterdam, (1782)* described Burney as "the only traveler who had not abused the Italians."[44] Actually, Burney "abused" the natives of Italy far more than this Italian author knew, and he certainly would not have been as satisfied had he seen Burney's journal in its entirety. The journal, which Burney kept while on his travels, contained not only his reports of many musical personalities, concerts, church organs, and so forth, it also contained complaints about the ignorance and poverty of the people, the poor roads,[45] Gothic architecture,[46] and the poor state of the Italian spoken theatre,[47] not to mention the numerous complaints he made about the extortion to which the foreign traveler was constantly subjected. Because published reports from travelers on the Grand Tour were so numerous, Burney feared that there would be little interest generated by yet another general account, and he resolved to limit his published narrative to musical matters, a decision ratified by most of his friends and advisors.[48]

He used his very practical decision to advantage, claiming in the preface to the journal that he had determined, "To hear with my *own* ears, and to see with my *own* eyes; and, if possible, to *hear* and *see* nothing but *music.*"Of course, he saw and heard a good deal more than music, and recorded everything in his pocket books, despite his claim in the preface that to have amused himself agreeably in "examining pictures, statues, and buildings" would have taken more time than he could afford "without neglecting the chief business of my journey."[49] Amuse himself he did, and the very entertaining observations of "general interest" were copied into separate notebooks, which although not published during his lifetime, were intended to be part of his "Memoirs." Sometime later Burney revised his rough copy in preparation for publication. The fair copy of the journal passed through different hands, and was eventually purchased by the earliest Burney scholar, Percy Scholes, who used it as the basis for his edition of *Dr. Burney's Musical Tours in Europe.*[50] Although Scholes noted some variants between this manuscript and another housed in the British Museum, he concluded that the two sources "can be considered identical." E.H. Poole, upon his examination, came to a very different conclusion. He found that they "bristle with dissimilarities, many of them merely verbal, some substantial and important."[51] Consequently, Poole published this version under the title *Music, Men and Manners in France and Italy 1770.*[52]

The student of literary style and the reader who enjoys Burney at his outspoken best will derive a great deal of pleasure from perusing this source. It is easy to see why Scholes was misled, for the verbal variants are certainly the most obvious. However, there are substantial differences between the two versions of great interest to the musical reader: among these are some lengthy, detailed descriptions of performers, and several interesting comments on performance practice which were omitted or altered significantly in the original published version.[53] Those interested in Burney as a performer will discover that he deleted from his fair copy of the manuscript numerous references to his performances on keyboard instruments at the *accademia* he attended on his trip. Several of these are very apologetic.[54] In Florence, for example, he was called upon to perform at an evening of music also attended by both the famous violinist and student of Tartini, Pietro Nardini, and the English violin prodigy, Thomas Linley Jr.. Burney reported that the audience "pretended to be pleased, but I was by no means pleased with myself, and came home very sulky."[55] Perhaps as a result of his disappointment, expressed on several occasions, or merely out of modesty, he suppressed nearly all of the references to his performances on the Continent. Deleted also from the published version are some greatly expanded discussions of Burney's activities in libraries housing important music collections.[56]

Several intriguing alterations in Burney's text bear upon the candor of his published book. One concerns his opinion of Handel's music. In the rough copy of his journal he remarked of Handel's sacred choruses, "He [Handel] had the merit of adding to the noise and confusion of so many different parts as many different instruments." When published in the *Present State of Music,* the passage appeared in a form rather more favorable to Handel, "Handel had the merit of adding to the harmony of so many different vocal parts as many instrumental."[57] Among other alterations, a number of reviews of harpsichord and pianoforte performers were omitted from the published edition. One description which he did not omit was a very flattering account of the performance of Diderot's seventeen-year-old daughter, whom Burney described as "a great performer on the harpsichord." He printed his description of her playing very much as he had originally written it, but deleted the observation that in performance she was "not quite correct in time."[58] In the *Tour* she appears quite flawless, an appreciation which drew a thankful but somewhat skeptical reaction from her father.[59] Other variants reflect broader issues: when Burney drafted a list of the greatest dramatic composers in Italy, he originally stated, "according to my idea of their merit they would be in the following order: Hasse—Jomelli—Galuppi—Piccini—Sacchini, etc." But when he prepared his journal for publication, Hasse was removed from the list, presumably because he was not an Italian. He was, nonetheless, to Burney and to many others the greatest master of Italian dramatic composition.

As interesting as the many variants, additions, and deletions are, there is very little that is new in this source which sheds light on Burney's critical thought. The impression that one has of the traveler as a critic of music in the new source is not substantially altered from that gained from the better-known sources, although the vital nature of the man becomes more apparent.

Burney published a revised and somewhat expanded second edition of the *Italian Tour.* Generally the revisions are insubstantial,[60] but one of the more extensive additions, an appreciation of François Philidor, is disturbing in its implications. Philidor's name did not appear at all in the *Present State of Music,* but in the portion of his journal which he did not print, Burney wrote of Philidor's *Le Maréchal ferrant,* "I detest that mixture of old French Vaudevilles with Philidor's Italian plunder."[61] In June, 1771, Philidor arrived in London with a letter of introduction from Diderot, and befriended Burney, who helped the Frenchman with his translation of his book on chess. Perhaps as a result of their personal relationship, a very favorable statement appeared in the second edition:

> The French are much indebted to M. Philidor, for being among the first to betray them into a toleration of Italian music, by adopting French words to it, and afterwards by imitating the Italian style in several comic operas, which have had great success, particularly, *Le Marechal Ferrant, Le Bucheron, Le Sorcier,* and *Tom Jones*. He likewise composed a serious opera, called *Ernelinde,* which is much admired by the lovers of Italian melody, but the frequenters of the great opera house of Paris are not yet sufficiently weaned from Lulli and Romeau [*sic*] to give great encouragement to such attempts.[62]

This evaluation, in sharp contradiction to the spontaneous remarks expressed in his journal, raises doubts about Burney's avowed willingness to "stand or fall" by his own feelings and opinions about "musical matters." Virtually all other additions to the second edition are non-musical, enlarging upon descriptions of buildings, cities, and festivals.[63]

Despite the existence of the first and second published English editions, the two versions of Burney's general account, and an annotated German translation, after almost 200 years we do not yet have a definitive edition incorporating the material from all of these sources.

Burney's *Italian Tour* was not translated into French or Italian until the nineteenth century, with the exception of excerpts in the *Journal de musique*.[64] In contrast, a complete edition of the *Present State of Music in France and Italy* appeared in German only one year after its publication in England.[65]

Shortly after its publication, Burney's Italian journal caught the attention of Cristoph Daniel Ebeling of Hamburg. It impressed him so favorably that he sought to correspond with the author. Ebeling, a man of letters, and an extremely well informed dilettante in music, wrote expressing his hope that in Burney's forthcoming "Universal history of music" the natives of his country would not be "entirely forgotten amongst the Italian, English and French musicians."[66] It is not surprising that Burney's book came to Ebeling's attention so soon after its publication. Among Germans, and North Germans especially, there was widespread interest in foreign publications in literature and the arts. Genuine intellectual curiosity certainly motivated many readers, but fashion, too, provided an impetus:

> Every well bred person will apply himself to some branch of foreign literature, especially french, and as now is the fashion english and italian... Every Review (we have at least now *thirty* for different parts of our litterature, some british and french, Bibliotheques, some Universal reviews, besides more than twenty weekly Reviews) is full of criticism's *over* english and other foreign books. We know allways very early when there is published some foreign book of value, and even alak! Germany very early is overflowed with the bad ones.[67]

Motivated he confesses by "a little shade of Patriotism and the desire to serve a man that he esteems for his writings," he urges Burney to undertake a musical voyage through Germany. He argues that, though the "good musical fashion seems to now decline with us," Germany has provided some musicians of the first rank to all of Europe, and even to Italy herself, and if only for this reason is worthy of Burney's attention. He acknowledges that opera had recently declined in excellence, but he provides a long list of worthy German composers and still-splendid opera companies, in the hope of persuading Burney to undertake another tour. Despite these patriotic expressions, Ebeling was quite as Italianate in his taste as was Burney, so much so that he later undertook the translation of the *Italian Tour* into German.

It is not clear just when Ebeling began his translation, or whether he sought Burney's permission to proceed, for the correspondence between the two men has not survived in its entirety. Ebeling's letter of 4 June 1772, notifying Burney that "the translation of your journey is now in a fair way," is the first surviving reference to the translation. Uncertain, too, is the precise date of publication. The book had been projected for publication before Easter, but was delayed.

The late publication of the *Tagebuch* was a minor disappointment to author and translator alike. Ebeling reports that he received an amicable complaint from Burney about the delay in publication, who felt his forthcoming trip through Germany would be easier if German musicians, theorists, and critics had already made his acquaintance through his book. The work *Carl Burney's der Musik Doctors Tagebuch einer Musikalischen Reisen* was in press prior to Burney's departure from England in July, for he carried with him a few loose sheets from the German translation; it was released sometime between July and October.[68] Burney was very pleasantly surprised by the favorable notice that his book received in Germany; he wrote to James Gray that "the Germans have already done my little Book the Honour to translate it, and contrary to my expectations have been very civil to it in their Journals."[69]

Ebeling's translation is faithful to the original, and the translator generally fulfilled his pledge in the *Vorrede* not to impress his own personality on the book by the addition of numerous footnotes.[70] Fewer than forty footnotes are added to the 303 pages of text, most of them very brief. The notes expand the information supplied by Burney, filling in the complete titles of books and operas, matching arias with their operas, suggesting additional reading on related subjects, and providing similar information.[71] In one footnote Ebeling takes the opportunity to direct the reader's attention to Burney's recent addition of *La Musica che si canta la annualmente nelle funzioni della Settimana Santa nella Cappella Pontificia* (one of the first historical editions), which contains music by Allegri, Bai, and Palestrina.[72] There were, of necessity, some corrections given in the footnotes, but they were kept to a minimum, providing the reader with only the necessary information, and containing no remarks critical of the author.[73] The corrections were handled with restraint, which was prudent, since in one case the editor subsequently found it necessary to correct his "correction" in the *Vorrede,* after the bulk of the book had been printed.[74]

There is a marked change in the tone and length of the footnotes to the last fifty-six pages of the *Tagebuch.* The heavy-handed proselytizing found in these notes evinces a drastic shift in editorial policy which was caused by a change in translators during the final stage of the work. In the *Vorrede* Ebeling apologizes to the reader for the delay in publication and gratefully acknowledges the assistance of his friend Johann Christoph Bode, who "in his kindness even translated some of the pages himself." Bode seems to have been less in accord with Burney's views than was Ebeling, to whom Burney entrusted the translating of his book. Bode was also much less concerned about not impressing his own personality on the book, and certainly less considerate of Burney's sensibilities. Responding to Burney's criticism of J.J.L. de la Lande's comments on opera in his *Voyage en Italie,*[75] for example, the annotator begins: "In these footnotes against Mr. de la Lande Mr. Burney seems to reveal himself almost too much as the Englishman and composer."[76] This sentence is the first instance of even a veiled criticism of Burney's diary, and certainly the first personal attack. Burney had objected to la Lande's criticism that in Italy:

> There was scarce any machinery in the operas, a lack of rich dress, fewer and less able actors, fewer choruses and those that are heard are too light, and the union of song and dance was neglected.

To all of these complaints Burney answered that a real lover of music would respond "so much the better."[77] The translator's remarks challenge Burney's Italian-dominated aesthetic, and are reflective of upheavals taking place in operatic style. In this sense the translator is more *au courant* in his taste than Burney, and his exaggeratedly rational response to Burney's comments are intended to place Burney in a disadvantageous light. However, it was not, as Bode implies, Burney's wish to deny the sister arts any role whatever in opera. His criticisms were directed specifically to la Lande's advocacy of French over Italian opera.

As the lengthy note develops, it becomes clear that the translator, very much like the author, is using the book to expound his own aesthetic position. While Bode's argument focuses on la Lande and Burney, it appears that he is less interested in defending French serious opera than lobbying for a general improvement of the art, but not one necessarily based on French models. He is, in fact, advocating a series of views quite typical of those of North-German critics at this time.[78] Bode's comments become increasingly more obtrusive. When Burney states, for example, that the "rapidity in the minuets of all modern overtures renders them ungraceful in an opera, but in a church they are indecent,"[79] the annotator exploits the opportunity to object to the inclusion of the minuet in all instrumental forms. This is another typically North-German view which held that the lightness of the dance made it too different from the other movements of the symphony.[80] This, of course, has nothing to do with Burney's objection to the excesses in tempo in church performance.

In similar manner the translator seizes on the author's criticism of Matteo Colista's manner of playing fugues on the organ to present a lengthy defense of the instrument and the form.[81] Misconstruing Burney's comments as an attack on the fugue, he assures his readers that he has on more than one occasion heard fugues, fantasies, and preludes on the organ which greatly moved him. Any defects which Burney found in this style must therefore be attributed to Colista's manner of playing and his registration. He asserts that there is more than one way to the heart: one need not descend to the easy taste of an Italian keyboard sonata or an opera aria, as the playing of Bach, Krebs, and Sack (among others) has proved. Here and elsewhere the translator uses his editorial position to lodge complaints against the composers of "light music"—those who want only to dazzle, not to move the heart.[82]

Despite these intrusions, Burney had reason to be pleased with the German rendering of his work. Ebeling writes favorably of the author and his forthcoming *General History of Music* in the *Vorrede,* and he even appends a translation of the Preface from the edition of the music for the Pope's Chapel to give readers a specimen of Burney's historical writing.[83] If Burney did note the few adversely critical remarks contained in the translator's notes to the last part of his book, he could certainly be mollified by the closing lines of the preface, which credit him with zeal, insight, good taste, and a lack of prejudice.[84]

Burney's *Tour* attracted the notice of German periodical writers, both in its English and translated forms. This was probably due to the efforts of the publisher J.C. Bode, for the early announcements of the book invariably mention the forthcoming translation.[85] The *Jenaische Zeitungen,* noting the publication of Burney's book in England, found that there was much curious and interesting information about more than just music, but withheld its full review until the translation appeared.[86] The writer of the review of the German edition shared the Italianate tastes of Burney and Ebeling, agreeing completely with Burney that the closer Burney got to Italy, the more interesting his book became. He specifically cited the discussion of Tartini as being of great interest, particularly to those who were so lucky as to be taught by students of the students of Tartini, and who, by dint of these lessons, maintained good taste in their performance. He praised Burney's enthusiasm for Galuppi, and recommended, in a rather singular manner, Galuppi's definition of good music:[87]

> The reviewer recommends Galuppi's definition of good music to all composers who try only too willingly to flatter the ears of their listeners with the wings of the wind or the rattling of a rattlesnake, and who believe that every composition absurd enough to contain nothing singable is very original.[88]

His concluding phrase could not have been more flattering to the traveling historian:

> To quote more samples is not possible due to lack of space, but we hope that the present example of the contents of this valuable work, which arouses an extraordinarily strong desire for Mr. Burney's *History of Music* will be sufficient in recommending it to every expert and friend of music who will not only read but study it.[89]

The favorable critical reception of his *Italian Tour* in Germany did much to direct Burney's attention to the musical literature of that nation. It is apparent that at this point in his career he knew very little of the impressive contributions of German historians and critics. German publications have no place in the catalogue of books appended to his *Plan,* and he appears to have paid little or no attention to them until his meeting with the Baron d'Holbach in Paris, who promised to procure for him "several scarce and necessary books in German."[90] D'Holbach's offering arrived sometime around June, 1772, and was augmented by a large parcel shipped by Ebeling from Hamburg. It is surprising that despite Burney's great interest in practical music he did not own C.P.E. Bach's *Versuch über die wahre Art das Klavier zu spielen* (1752). The *Versuch* arrived in Ebeling's shipment, along with works on the theory of music and its history, such as Johann Mattheson's *Grundlage einer Ehrenpforte* (1740), and his *Lebenslauff von G.F. Handel* (1761), Johann Adolph Scheibe's *Der critische Musikus* (1737-1746), Friedrich Marpurg's *Kritische Briefe* (1759-64), and Johann Adam Hiller's *Nachrichten und Anmerkungen die Musik betreffend* (1766-70).

If Burney's knowledge of German writers was insufficient, he was well acquainted with German music. As early as 1771 he wrote to Ebeling that he did not hesitate to give it as his opinion that the Germans were the "first people in Europe at present both for the Composition and performance of *Instrumental music.*" He also asserted that for "many years" he had received great delight from the compositions of "Abel, Schobert, Echard, Eichner, Fischer, Wagenseil, Schwindel, Hayden [sic] etc.," and expressed respect for the "great industry" and thoroughness of the Germans in all the arts and sciences.[91]

Burney's German correspondents were very helpful to the industrious scholar in supplying him with "a great quantity of excellent music by the best composers," and works on the theory and history of music. Burney's growing awareness of the state of music in Germany, his increasing knowledge of the important German historical and critical writings, and Ebeling's entreaty for a

The Continental Tours   79

fair appraisal of German music in his *History* were sufficient to spur him into venturing on yet another musical tour. Despite the great quantity of material he had assembled, he concluded that "These Books...and the great number of German compositions I am now possessed of, are so far from repressing my Curiosity after the Musical Productions of the Germans that they excite a fresh desire to see and hear more."[92] In preparation for this tour, Burney collected the all-important portfolio of letters of introduction to musicians, gentlemen, and English representatives at the German courts who had sufficient influence to help him gain admission to the same level of society that he had penetrated on his journey to France and Italy.[93]

There can have been no doubt in Burney's mind that his second tour would give rise to a new *Present State of Music* for the countries he would visit: his new publication was in press only four months after his return. Once again, he took special care to ensure favorable reviews of his book. He called upon William Bewley to write the critique for the *Monthly Review,* and most probably Samuel Crisp to produce the article for the *Critical Review.*[94] It was apparently quite unnecessary for him to manipulate the reviews: the several notices over which he had no influence are as laudatory as those he suborned. The *Gentleman's Magazine* said in part:

> In this and the former publication [the *Italian Tour*], Dr. Burney has given such undoubted proofs of his abilities for the execution of the work that has been the chief object of his travels, as must raise an eager desire in the public for the completion of it. Every comparison that can be drawn between the importance of the Doctor's pursuit and the labour and expence of it, will not fail to do him honour.... The narrative, which is written with ease and elegance, abounds with such lively descriptions and just observations as may be expected from a traveler of taste and discernment, and is enriched with interesting anecdotes of the characters and fortunes of several persons known in the polite and learned world.[95]

The foreign press also noted the appearance of the *German Tour.* French periodicals, which had virtually ignored the publication of the diary of his journey through their country, reported the publication of his new work,[96] and even commented favorably upon it, despite the inclusion of several biting comments about French music in the first part of the book:

> If we cannot determine the degree of perfection which the author of this voyage possesses in the art on which he writes, we venture nevertheless to assert that one will find him a man well versed in the sciences and arts in general, an amateur distinguished by taste and by enthusiasm for the art which he has studied, a writer agreeable, free, and impartial, who dispenses justice to talents and virtues without regard to position, circumstances of birth, and all that which is only accessory.[97]

In Germany, the reviews noted the appearance of the English publication, but since the German publication was announced almost immediately withheld their criticism until the translation arrived in the bookstalls.[98] There was apparently a good deal of interest in Burney's work, not only among his friends in Hamburg, but throughout Germany. Interest ran so high that Ebeling and Bode were compelled to announce their translation immediately in a successful attempt to suppress a translation which had been announced in Leipzig. To further their translation, they advertised it as "the work of two friends of the author."[99]

When Burney's *Present State of Music in Germany, the Netherlands and the United Provinces* actually reached Germany, however, enthusiastic anticipation turned to zealous outrage. Ebeling headed his written response to the *Tour* a "declaration of war."[100] The reaction of Ebeling, Bode, and other Germans associated with the translation of the *Tour* bears careful examination, since their version is the only edition published in German. It has had, therefore, a considerable effect on the shaping of Burney's reputation in Germany, not only among his contemporaries, but among modern scholars as well.[101]

Ironically, it was not Burney's musical judgments, but his general remarks which provoked the greatest hostility among the Germans. In particular, there was the startling assertion by "an accurate observer of human nature" that "if innate genius exists, Germany certainly is not the seat of it; though it must be allowed to be that of perseverance and application."[102] Ebeling and all "true Germans" were quite furious at this and other "interspersed remarks against German genius." Friedrich Klopstock, the prominent poet, refused to read the book when he came across this sentence, and Ebeling contended "so every honest and true son of Germany will do and must do." His remarks were not only accurate but prophetic. The deprecation of German genius seriously compromised the author's reputation in Germany throughout the eighteenth century and beyond. Contemporary reviewers were indignant, and later writers, such as Johann Reichardt, Christian Schubart, and Johann Forkel, all made their own contribution to the Teutonic invective lavished on Burney, each in turn further denigrating his reputation. He undoubtedly would have fared far worse in Germany had his friends in Hamburg not intervened. In the preparation of the translation, Burney's rather unflattering evaluation of German poets was deleted, marked only with a note commenting on its absolute uselessness.[103] As it was, the remarks on German genius and literature which remained succeeded in alienating in Germany that class of reader to which Burney successfully appealed in England—the gentlemen of taste and position who were lovers of music, but not necessarily musicians themselves. He might be forgiven for differences of taste, or occasional errors of fact, but no native reader could allow the wholesale exclusion of all Germans from that exalted class "genius."

The two parts of Burney's work that most inflamed his critics were not his own, though he must bear the responsibility of publishing them. The anonymous critic who penned the remark on German genius and whom

Ebeling so fervently wished revealed was Louis Devisme, the English ambassador at the Bavarian Court, who was then living in Munich.[104] As the pages of the *Tour* attest, Devisme was of inestimable help to Burney on his journey. Nonetheless, it was he who was responsible for the greatest single blunder in the three-volume *Tours*.

Devisme also penned another observation which, if it failed to irritate contemporary critics, has since subjected Burney to ridicule: the judgment that Wolfgang Mozart, in 1772, was "one further example of early Fruit, which is more extraordinary than excellent."[105] Both of the above judgments Burney acknowledged to be the work of another writer, but he displayed less candor in his observations on German poets. These, which he says are "the general opinion there of men of taste and learning," are taken practically verbatim from a letter written by one Dr. J. Mumssen of Hamburg.[106] There are likely other examples of similar "lifting" from letters which have not survived, or which have simply escaped detection.[107] It was Burney's frequent practice to copy extracts from his own letters to be used in his published works, so it is perhaps not surprising that on occasion he followed a similar practice with those he received.[108] His choice of Devisme's letter for quotation was to cause him difficulty for years.

Burney was deeply distressed by the vituperative response of his German associates to his work. He extended considerable editorial latitude to the translators, urging them to "make my Book as palatable to your Countrymen and friends as you can."[109] As to the remark on German genius, he claimed to have "utterly forgot it was in my book." He was not about to reveal the name of his source, as Ebeling demanded—Devisme was, after all, still a British representative in Germany—but he assured his Hamburg friend that he would "give up the Passage with all my Heart in a 2nd edition." He requested that the offending matter be omitted from the translation, but if it was to be included, it was to receive no mercy: "brand it—and shew all the Patriotic indignation against it that you please, but spare the author, or rather the retailer of it...throw it upon inadvertance, not Malevolence or prejudice."[110]

Ebeling informed him that the editors would make selective deletions, correct some errors without comment, and add notes, but would not "omit a single of your judgments or phrases concerning music." It must have been small consolation to Burney to have Ebeling's assurance that "Even when I did not know the author personally, it would be his book I attacked, not his person."

In the end, Ebeling's promises of stern but fair treatment did not come to much; overcome by business commitments and poor health, he relinquished his part in the translation to J.C. Bode. Bode shared Ebeling's patriotic outrage, but not his depth of friendship for Burney, nor his willingness to convert Burney's work into an acceptable form for the German public without exposing the author. He begins the third volume with a foreword announcing

Ebeling's surrender of his part of the translation in a statement which explicitly sets forth his view of Burney's journal:

> It seemes to me that his judgement often was biased and often too hastily written down; and although I am not a musician, and convinced that I do not want to be partial by any means, I may appear so anyway to some readers in the few footnotes. I ask them to consider that I am a sincere lover of music and I am a German, and that a certain degree of partiality toward the fatherland is at least excusable.[111]

In fact, the negative reaction to Burney's work was based far more on nationalism, at this time a powerful force in German literature and the arts, than on a basic disagreement with Burney's musical judgments. There was a national hostility directed not only towards Burney's writings, but those of most English authors writing about Germany.

> ... Is it false that our critics shewed us so many ridiculous faults in your good authors as soon as they wrote about Germany? Men transformed into Towns and vice versa. Even your excellent authors Hume, Robertson, Harte, etc. are guilty of enormous blunders when they write about Germany. How many tales, judgements and remarks are notoriously false... Let any Englishman (that we know now) write about Germany and I will be hanged if I do not find a hundred faults.[112]

Bode was determined that Burney's errors would be mercilessly exposed. He organized a "small group of men... to correct the author throughout the text, but lack of time, illness [presumably Ebeling's] and distractions thwarted this activity, forcing him to limit the corrections." Not only had Bode attempted to assemble this group, but he also planned to encourage citizens of the cities Burney visited to submit their own essays which he offered to print after Burney's discussion of their city. He was deterred only by the delay which would have been caused by waiting for so many respondents. Bode informs the reader that he has made alterations in some of Burney's geographical descriptions. He assures them, however, that he has not tampered with Burney's musical judgments, not because he agrees with them, but "since Mr. Burney wants to write a general history of music, it is good that we Germans know beforehand, how such a history will turn out for us, so that our later amazement will not be too great."

The most apparent alterations in Bode's edition are the large number of omissions. Most are made without any indication to the reader, and several are extensive. As Bode states, most of the large deletions are descriptions of German towns and countrysides,—places, according to the editor, already well known to the German reader. Many of Burney's complaints about poor roads, bad food, and expensive chaises were removed "not by any means because they are exaggerated every time, but because people have read them so often already and do not expect them in a musical journey."[113] Bode also excluded Burney's description when more thorough reports of the same attraction were available. Thus, the account of the astronomical machine at Ludwigsburg is omitted, and the reader is referred to the *Beschreibung einer astronomischen Maschine welche sich in der öffentlichen Bibliothek zu Ludwigsburg befindet.*[114] Likewise, Burney's lengthy report of the Elector's art gallery at Dresden, one of the most famed collections in Europe, was omitted in favor of a reference to the catalog by Heineken.[115]

There are also deletions of politically sensitive material. The discussion of Ludwigsburg is heavily edited. Gone are such remarks as: "The Duke of Wurtemberg has been accused of indulging his passion for music to such excess as to ruin both his country and people," and "His passion for music and shews [*sic*] seems as strong as that of the Emperor Nero was formerly. It is perhaps, upon such occasions as these, that music becomes a vice, and hurtful to society; for that nation, of which half the subjects are stage-players."[116] Similarly critical comments on the Prussian Court were eliminated or reworded to avoid the banning of the book by the official censors. Several references to the religious tensions between German Roman Catholics and Lutherans were also omitted, either to avoid the censors, or to avoid offending the readers of either denomination.[117]

Bode was faithful to his promise not to alter, or omit, Burney's musical discussions, with one important exception—a passage which alludes to Emanuel Bach's being unhappy in Berlin because the reigning taste was so old-fashioned. The remark is removed without comment. Ebeling wrote Burney that Bach "denied that he was misplaced at Berlin as you think he was." It is unlikely, however, that Burney invented this idea. Burney's personal regard for Bach, and his foreknowledge that his book would be translated in Hamburg, make it improbable that he would falsify this account. More plausible is the possibility that Bach found the passage all too truthful, and requested that the editor, a close personal friend, suppress the passage. It was perhaps concern about angering Frederick the Great, or his friends and colleagues in the capital, which motivated Bach to request the suppression of this passage.

None of the deletions made by the editors can be construed as adversely affecting the book or its author. Indeed, if Ebeling can be believed, they were made in some measure to protect the author. "I wished You had not interspersed some of your un-musical reflections, some of them being quite false, and some not wholly true. It will hurt your credit when Germans read it." He even promised that "Some little faults I shall correct without mentioning it."[118]

Under Bode's direction, however, no such grace was extended. The footnotes are unevenly distributed in the two volumes—volume I has fewer than a score in 303 pages, while the second volume is littered with more than five dozen in 268 pages. The imbalance resulted from Bode's aforementioned expectation of collecting notes from his group of collaborators and correspondents, to be placed in the addenda. Failing in this, he greatly expanded his annotations in the last volume. The footnotes to the second volume are brief and generally innocuous, while many of those in the third volume range from sarcastic to opprobrious. For example, the charge is leveled several times that Burney does not understand German sufficiently to be able to formulate critical opinions.[119]

Perhaps the most curious feature of the German edition is its gradual transformation from an annotated translation to a work which conveys as much or more of the translator's personality as that of the author. The translator's vocation of publisher leads him to include a number of surprisingly extraneous notes detailing the number of fonts of type necessary for publishing German books,[120] the occurence of Gothic letters in English ornamented lettering,[121] and remarks on music printing.[122] Burney's belief that Friedrich Marpurg's "musical writings may justly be said to surpass in number and utility, those of any one author who has treated the subject" draws a rebuttal from Bode in which he recounts in detail his visit to Mattheson. Mattheson, according to Bode, claimed that he had written one volume for each of his seventy-two years of age, and had as many more in manuscript, a point which could have been made without recounting Bode's personal experience.[123] A score of pages later Bode inserts a lengthy account of a visit to Franz Benda "without paying too much attention as to whether this is the most fitting place to air my heart's feelings," with no point whatever except of using this opportunity to publish a lengthy encomium of the famous violinist.[124]

In the latter part of his work, Bode's intervention goes so far as listing the guests at a dinner party (whom Burney described only as well-bred persons).

> These were no other than Dr. Unser, known everywhere for his books on medicine, his wife (also known for her writings) and her brother, Mr. Ziegler. But such things a traveler, with only music and its goals in his soul, can forget without meriting blame for it.[125]

As he nears the end of his work, Bode begins inserting accounts of numerous musicians not even mentioned in Burney's tour,[126] and inserts an extensive biography of Johann Gottfried Müthel, whom Burney spoke of briefly but with praise.[127]

Bode did not hesitate to challenge Burney's qualifications to undertake a history of music. Burney's "astonishment" that the "German language, in spite of all its clashing consonants and gutturals, is better calculated for music than the French," is to Bode "incomprehensible" in a person aspiring to write a general history of music.[128] Certainly, he asserts, Burney should have known the published operas of Hiller, Fleischer, Schweizer, Neefe, Reichardt, and Wolf before he left England. "If one judges by this musical scientist all Englishmen," states the annotator, "one may think they are of the opinion that a German musician is not worth a great deal, who does not come to the Queen of cities, London."[129] He also viewed Burney's distaste for mathematical calculations in music with disdain, calling it a curious opinion for one who was a Doctor of Music.[130]

The diarist is also attacked for his thoughtless opinions, which Bode instances with Burney's remark that there was little opportunity to demonstrate "fancy" in the "German full manner of playing the organ."[131] He also complains that Burney did not always travel to areas where he might best have gathered the needed information.[132] He believed that Burney made stylistic judgments when he was unprepared to do so and was particularly critical of his treatment of the early German operas of K.H. Graun.

> Has the author really seen some of Graun's German operas? This would be necessary because he wrote all of these before he was in Italy, and they have much more melody, expression and novelty, than one can find in many of the arias of his newer operas.[133]

Not surprisingly, Burney's denial of original genius to Graun, who he says formed his style on Vinci, draws a lengthy retort from the translator. He characterizes opinions like Burney's as the work of "overly hasty critics."[134] Similarly, Burney's criticism of J. Gottlieb Graun's symphonies as being "to[o] like those of Lully," draws a response which clearly demonstrates the fundamental differences between the tastes of Burney and his translator. Bode's retort concludes with a wistful challenge of Burney's taste which, from a historical perspective, can perhaps illustrate the relative sagacity of the two critics, and show how limited the North Germans could be when confronted by the differing aesthetic of Austro-Bohemian instrumental music. "If only a Burney the Second were to travel in the year 1783, how would the heroes of Burney the First, for instance Haydn and so forth, be discredited."[135] Bode was generally annoyed with Burney's treatment of the entire Berlin school of composers and critics. He attacks Burney's observation that Berlin is years behind in its musical taste largely because of the musical despotism of Frederick the Great.[136] It is perhaps also indicative of the translator's attitude toward the Berlin School, and Frederick the Great in particular, that though sweeping cuts were made in Burney's "general" narrative, his extensive and enthusiastic description of Berlin and Potsdam, including Sans Souci, remained intact. There is little chance that this deference to Berlin was politically motivated; more likely, it expressed the close intellectual relationship felt between the Hamburg literati and the Berlin School. Emanuel Bach and Lessing had both worked in Berlin, and Bode himself had visited there as well as corresponding with Nicolai, the prominent Berlin publisher.

One of the fundamental aesthetic differences between Burney and his German critics was their respective views on old music. Burney had explained in a footnote that,

> When I use the epithets *old* and *new*, I mean neither as a term of reproach, or stigma, but merely to tell the reader in what style a piece is conceived, or written; and he will suppose it to be better or worse as he pleases.[137]

But this critical principle is belied throughout by Burney's expressed preferences. Ebeling felt that,

> Every musical Piece which was good and really affecting every unprejudiced heart, must be always so and in every time. So nothing can be bad Music now, which was good music for 40 years. New improvements in instruments can make new music preferable to old one, [*sic*] but genius is absolutely *operatalis* as good as new one...[138]

For his part, Bode had a contributor preparing an essay "About the stupidity of those who look down on old music because it is old," but this was not forthcoming in time for publication.[139] Nonetheless, Bode repeatedly voices his rancor at Burney's intolerant and selective modernism, particularly in his defense of Mattheson,[140] whose deafness late in life, he notes, accounted for his adherence to an older style of composition.[141] Bode also defends Quantz against the same charge—though his stylistic conservatism arose from different circumstances—and all of the Berlin School from Burney's reiterated comments on their compositional and critical conservatism, noting that there were important people of progressive taste in Berlin and at the Court itself.[142]

In his final footnote Bode surveys Burney's work, and he concludes:

> Here comes finally our Debit and Credit; and we poor Germans should know by now how things stand with us, considering, that we probably are using only half of our two cardinal virtues—patience—and are sufficiently pedantic to ask our bookkeeper, who is not under oath, whether he has counted up everything correctly. Seriously: if one reflects again on what one has read and how much credit Mr. Burney gave to our German musical masters' originality, to Hasse, Gluck, Bach, Vanhall, Hofman, Schwanberger, Benda, Muthel, Handel, etc., the thought should occur to one that this final judgement originates less in a cold-blooded consideration of grounds for and against a whole nation, but rather in a graciously playful, lovely symmetry of the four words: Patience, Profundity, Prolixity, and Pedantry, all of which start so nicely with a P. If anybody should find that this footnote contains too harsh a blame, I ask him to consider that it is written at a time when judgement is passed on a whole nation and on an art in which this nation has produced the most admirable masters for all the other nations, and it is judged in four words just as cavalierly spoken as if a young dandy were to pass judgement on his tailor, who made him a suit not to his taste. For the rest, I do not fail to appreciate in the least all the good in Mr. Burney, especially his warm sensitive heart which seldom abandons him except in cases of national prejudice and when evil circumstances have put him in a bad mood![143]

Bode's accusation of flippancy in the matter of the four P's is not justified. There is nothing contradictory to these sentiments to be found in any of Burney's manuscripts or published writings, and a good deal is present to support them. Though Burney listed *patience* and *profundity* as the musical virtues of the people of Germany, these were not qualities which he valued highly, except (for the latter) in church compositions.[144] As to the vices of Germans, *prolixity* and *pedantry,* Burney found both qualities in abundance in German music, as well as in critical and historical writings. His complaints about lengthy compositions and the "laboured contrivances" of German organ music are sufficient evidence of the sincerity of his remarks against German music, and his attitude toward the critics and historians appears in a number of letters between Burney and those who made translations from German sources for him.

Shortly after he returned from his German tour, for example, he wrote to Fountaine,

> ... Don't be nice at all about your future Translations—you may imagine that such long winded Gentry as these Germans must be sparingly used in my Work, which I shall wish to have *read.*[145]

It seemed to Burney that German writers consistently published all that they could "possibly scrape together," so much so that he was in "wonder they do not begin every Book they write by the *Alphabet,* and a few easy rules of orthography."

Among the other German writers who joined the outcry against Burney, the most vocal of a very outspoken group was Johann Friedrich Reichardt. His *Briefe eines aufmerksamen Reisenden die Musik betreffend* (1774 and 1776)[146] contains a searing attack on Burney's *Tour.* The author is criticized for lacking a fine and correct feeling for music, foundation and experience in composition, and knowledge of the music of the great German masters. Reichardt, too, is especially incensed about the remarks on German genius, and, like Bode, points out Burney's professed admiration for Hasse, Emanuel Bach, Gluck, and Handel, among others, as seemingly contradictory to Burney's (actually Devisme's) judgment. Like Bode also, Reichardt is annoyed by Burney's nonmusical essays on architecture, traveling conditions, and art—precisely the material that contributed to the success of the *German Tour* in England.[147] Johann Nikolaus Forkel also joined the battle. His lengthy and informed review of the first volume of Burney's *History* is prefixed by a critique of the *German Tour,* which is even less flattering that Reichardt's.[148] Like Reichardt, he also claims that national prejudice and a general hostility to the German people are evident, but more than this, Forkel asserts that Burney failed in his mission for lack of an indispensable necessity: "real musical knowledge." This want of "true, thorough musical knowledge" has led Burney to so many false conclusions, that he believes the publication of the *History* is more to be feared than wished.

Lest the reader think the reviewer himself is prejudiced, Forkel cites several examples to support his view. One, Burney's remark that the "full-voiced" manner of organ playing stifles imagination, draws a vicious rebuttal from Forkel:

> Can anybody have more dilettantish ideas about the innermost being of art than our musical historian, who, after all, is a Doctor of Music? Is not a single one of these instances enough to render all the other judgments of the author in musical matters suspicious to connoisseurs?[149]

This and the several other examples he provides, Forkel assures his readers, are indicative of the caliber of judgments and opinions to be found throughout the book. "What kind of general history of music," he queries, "do our readers believe they can expect from a man who has such a judgment in musical things?"[150]

There were other reviews, but the remarks of Bode, Reichardt, and Forkel have exercised the greatest influence over German readers. Burney never publicly responded to this triumvirate of Teutonic critics, but he was aware of their work. Some unpublished pages from his notebooks regarding J.C. Bode contain his response to his German critics, and reveal some intriguing aspects of his relationships with these prominent men. The article is apparently taken in part from a letter to a German associate.

> This coarse, vulgar, and clumsy writer [J.C. Bode], who not only assumed the character of a translator of English into German with little knowledge of either language; but set up for a critic in music, a subject concerning which he is so ignorant that he had never heard of the Italian term *appoggiatura,* and doubted whether any such word had existence, except in the account of the Present State of Music in Germany.
> When we think a book worth translating in England we seldom try to put the reader out of humour with the author. But in order to shew his critical acumen herr Bode lets nothing pass uncensured. That Mr. Reichardt attacked me in a very hostile manner was much more natural; I had censured the Berlin School, it was self-defense and patriotism in him to defend it vi et armi. But M. Forkel many years after in reviewing the first volume of my History treated me with a degree of determined severity and bitterness which I certainly had never experienced elsewhere, and which I do not think the greatest scoundrel and blockhead of my country ever met with from our most sour and vindictive reviewers. But to condemn foreign books and check their sale at circulation is not only a gratification of spleen to such writers, but enables them at some distance of time to use the materials as their own property. This M. Forkel does dayly in all his almanacs and other compilations. My name has never been used but when my writings are condemned. The honesty of your countrymen used to be proverbial; but Master Forkel will invalidate the praise. All the three Gentlemen from whom I have had such obligations, in order kindly to give me an opportunity of returning them, have all condescended to ask favour of me. M. Bode wished me to distinguish him from all my friends during the time of printing the first volume of my History by sending him the fair sheets as fast as printed, that he might be the first to translate and abuse it. M. Reichardt when he was in England in 1785 applied to me of all people to furnish him with letters of recommendation to my friends at Paris, a request with which I complied, wondering at the same time how it could possibly be made. But I was still more surprised the other day at a very civil and even humble letter from M. Forkel accompanied with a present of the first volume of what he calls *His* History of Music. Now my dear Sir, before I proceed in my

account of this book let me ask you whether you have seen it? And if you have, whether the frontispiece was the only thing that reminded you of the first volume of that very History of Music which he has so harshly treated in his Music Library? You understand English better than I German: now *is* it only in the titles of the Chapters that these books are alike? Or are the citations, conjectures, and reflexions [sic] the same? If you have not read, my friend and follower, Mr. Forkel, I wish you would, and collate the two Histories in order to set me right if I am mistaken in imagining I see an unfair use made of my property. But this present is intended to produce twins in return: for M. Forkel does me the honour to long to be in possession of so *valuable* a work as that History of which he has formerly so (benignly) reviewed the first volume. Nay more, he is impatient for the sequel of which I have lately announced the publication in the course of next winter. Ought I not to be very proud of such a correspondent and of his condescension and partiality. 2 huge volumes in 4to, however ill the material may be selected and digested, will doubtless be convenient repositories for compilers of musical magazines and almanacs—but, as heretofore they must first blast the character of the work, destroy all curiosity in the public to see it in the original, and take special care when it is plundered, to conceal and disguise the theft.[151]

Burney's comparative forgiveness of Reichardt is noteworthy, since it was his criticism which most mercilessly and analytically attacked Burney's qualifications as a musician and critic. It is perhaps the personal association of the two men during Reichardt's London sojourn that accounts for Burney's forgiveness. Forkel, and certainly Bode, were equally motivated by patriotic considerations, on a national if not local basis, but they did not receive the same indulgence. For his part, Burney openly acknowledged his error regarding the innate genius of the German people, and altered the passage in the second edition of his work. While he sustains his contention that it was *cultivation,* that is study, and not *nature* which accounted for the abundance of Bohemian musicians, the phrase about innate genius is deleted altogether. Rather than reverse his prior position, Burney included a phrase which seems to explain his motivation for including such a remark in the first place.

> ...The Bohemians may as well be called a learned people, because they can read, as superior musicians because they can play upon instruments, since the study of both are equally made by them essential parts of common education.[152]

The above retraction Scholes calls "not *quite* so handsome as it looks." In fact, Burney was contrite about the German genius remark, and acknowledged it to be unfair. Despite his recantation, his critical position regarding the national character of their music did not change, but was thereafter expressed with greater care for the sensibilities of the German populace, a position altogether wise for a subject of a Hanoverian king. An unpublished essay in his notes on German music for the *History* contains his most concise statement on German music. Though labeled as an afterthought, "This for the first fifty years of the VXIII century," the similarity of the views expressed here with those of the *German Tour* demonstrates that his opinion was relevant to many contemporary musicians as well.

> The Germans are always complaining of the miserable want of Learning among the Modern Italian Composers. Italiäner sind heutiges tages elende Componisten says Marpurg. But for heavens sake! does all musical merit consist in heaping parts upon the Ear by extraneous Modulations? Handel, Hasse, Gluck, Gasman, J.C. Bach, etc., have succeeded in Italy and the rest of Europe, but in proportion to their Imitation of the Italian style and manner of setting words and the rest of the Germans have but too frequently sacrificed Fancy, Taste and Facility, to learned Crudities with which Pedants only can be pleased, and which dry drudgery only can +execute+ Music in such Hands ceases to give delight to the +generality+ of Mankind as much as Painting when it represents a Figure made up of mere Bones and Muscles instead of the mature +Fulness+ Grace, and perfection which arises from the Glow of Health and +expression+ of the Passions. It is not sufficient to fill the Ears with mere sounds: music is expected now to paint images, to awaken ideas, and to carry sensations to the Mind. By [making] Harmony subservient to Melody we have acquired Grace, Invention, and Passion.[153]

Considering the harshness of the criticism he received, Burney made surprisingly few changes in the second edition of his book in order to placate his critics. He did add one paragraph praising a few uncommonly good German inns, although this single statement did little to balance the severe censures of German accommodations which remain unaltered throughout the rest of the work,[154] and it is similarly doubtful that the substitution in the description of the countryside around Ens of "a very disagreeable country" for "an ugly country" would be satisfactory to many concerned readers.[155]

One substantial addition which should have partially appeased his critics clarifies his view that the relationship between genius and cultivation depends upon musical training.

> ... From the musical establishments, in this city [Dresden], as well as from those in other places, a musical spirit is universally diffused throughout the empire, both in the protestant and catholic states, for which it is not difficult to account; if it be considered that the musical genius of each inhabitant, from the highest to the lowest order of the people, has a fair trial, and an opportunity of expanding. Hence the great number of performers and critics, as well as lovers of art, in this country.[156]

Another new paragraph noting the various accomplishments of the different geographic and political entities of Germany may have been addressed to critics such as Bode, who had remarked that Burney did not even know what a German was, and Ebeling, who complained:

> I believe there is a general mistake that You believe our Nation is to be considered as one people. No Sir, history and Geography will acquaint You that we are composed of different clans or even little nations quite different from one another in dialects, customs, notwithstanding many of them have been altered by administration, mixture with foreigners, transmigrating, etc., but allways say the Germans in genere. You should say the Bavarians, Upper Saxons, lower Saxons, etc.[157]

Ebeling had also questioned some of Burney's musical opinions, and it is noteworthy that though he generally stood firm on his musical judgments, he did accept Ebeling's suggestions. Thus Marpurg's compositions, described as "correct and pleasing" in the first edition, are only "correct" in the second.[158] Johann Friedrich Agricola's compositions Burney originally found "very masterly," but upon reflection and Ebeling's suggestion, he reports in the second edition that they had only "great merit."[159] More noteworthy to the musicologist accustomed to accepting Burney's first-hand critical reports is the change in his evaluation of a motet composed by Lucchese, *maestro di capella* at Bonn. The first edition calls the composition charming, but, probably as a result of Ebeling's critique, the second terms the piece admirable.[160]

Ebeling was also responsible for the deletion of a portion of a conversation Burney had with Emanuel Bach. The context of the passage is curious, "Mr. Bach gives you his thanks, but he wishes the passage of blushing in his speech to be left out, notwithstanding you made it as soft as possible." The speech referred to is one in which Bach told Burney "that if he was in a place, where his compositions could be well executed and well heard, he should certainly kill himself by exertions to please." Such was not the case in Hamburg, and Bach concluded that he was "now reconciled to my situation; except indeed, when I meet men of taste and discernment, who deserve better music that we can give them here." Thereafter, in the first edition follows the offensive passage: "Then I blush for myself and my good friends, the Hamburghers."[161]

The majority of the score of additions to the second edition of the *Tour* merely update the work.[162] Several notes record the progress of Burney's own work and inform his readers of his developing personal relationships with the most illustrious German musicians. The note added to page 350, for example, relates the arrival of a "very polite letter" from Hasse, accompanied by "a present of several of his compositions." The arrival of a packet from Emanuel Bach is similarly noted,[163] as is the inception of a correspondence with the German musicologist Martin Gerbert.[164] These, while adding nothing to the value of the book, do serve to enhance the reputation of the author.[165]

There are numerous slight reworkings of prose throughout the two volumes, but most do little to change the substance of the text. One exception is the inclusion of a qualifying phrase on the use of the orchestral crescendo by Stamitz at Mannheim, which the second edition notes was "stimulated by the productions of Jomelli," an important correction.

The revisions in the second editions of the *Tours* (especially in the evaluations of music which he heard) on the suggestions of other critics are disturbing, inasmuch as they seem to evince a degree of insecurity and inconsistency. However, these revisions must be viewed within the context of his travels.[166] As Edward Reilly observed, "Burney's views are of greatest use when approached as they were intended, not as a final verdict, but as a traveler's opinions based on limited knowledge."[167] It was undoubtedly respect for opinions more informed than his, rather than a lack of principle, that accounts for Burney's revisions.

Although he had the opportunity to make whatever alterations seemed necessary between the publication of the first and second editions of the *German Tour*, Burney seems to have felt that to make substantial alterations in the text would undermine his veracity. It was not until the publication of the final volume of the *History* that he unreservedly recanted his statement on German genius. He concludes his chapter on "Music in Germany During the XVIII Century" by "totally disavowing the opinion of another person, which was inconsiderately inserted in the first edition of my *German Tour*, before I was able to examine its truth." In drafting his lengthy apology, he assimilates the most telling point of his critics, noting that the statement was "not only unjust, but inconsistent and absurd; particularly in a book of a man who, during his whole life, has been an enthusiastic admirer of German musicians, from Handel and Hasse to Bach and Haydn." He has, he says, "been as angry with myself as the most patriotic German can be, for ever having given admission to such a reflection."[168] Why the confession was delayed until 1789 is unclear. It may well be that the wrath of the entire German intelligentsia served to impress upon him an awareness of German attainments; but it may also have been due in part to his growing relationship to the Court of George III, and his whetted desire for a higher position in the King's Band.

Burney's daughter Fanny, in July of 1786, was appointed as one of the keepers of the robes to the queen, and Burney believed he was in an advantageous position to benefit from royal favor. His sensitivity to his earlier criticisms of all things German is evident in Fanny's report of the queen's request for Fanny's copy of the *German Tour*. "I had fancied it was to look for some passage herself, and immediately concluded it must be that upon German Genius!—and then thought I, 'tis all over with us for ever!"[169]

There had apparently been some warning of the royal interest in Burney's *Tour*, for two weeks before he had sent to Fanny a copy specially prepared for her to read aloud.

> I have ferreted out a new Copy of my German Tour, which you shall have to prepare to your own mind for the loud lecture, if it should be wanted—I found a copy of the pages reprinted, but am sure they would not go down well. Indeed I was betrayed by the late Mr. Devisme to make a *national* reflection on the dulness of the Germans, which they can never forgive, and indeed it was unjust and inconsistent. I have always praised Handel as a man of great Genius—I have doated on Emanuel Bach, and on Haydn—have greatly admired Hasse, Gluck, Fischer, etc.—and then to say that "if Genius has fixed his residence on Earth, Germany certainly is not the place he has chosen." It was flippant and offensive, and I long to make a public recantation of my Errors rash declaration [sic]. I had been jumbled, and hardly dealt with on the road by individuals, and was certainly tired of my Journey; but what I met with at Vienna, Dresden, Munich, Hamburg, etc. which I heartily praised, make the above uncharitable and unjust conclusion very indefensible. These are my private feelings, but would avail nothing in the perusal in Question, if made public: therefore the book must be guardedly read, and previously prepared.[170]

Possibly, then, Burney's apology was genuinely motivated by his reaction to perpetrating an injustice. If so, he was contrite about only a single reflection out of an entire two-volume work that, as has been related, outraged his German critics practically page by page. Although he was literally tormented by his indiscretion in including Devisme's opinion, his critical position on German music never enters into his regrets.

By undertaking his expensive, exhausting musical tours, and publishing his journals, Burney established his reputation as a writer and critic. He succeeded in capturing the attention of both literary and musical society in England and on the Continent. On his travels he heard a good deal of music, and amassed an immense collection of books and music, neither of which he could have done at home. His correspondence with Ebeling shows that the writings of German critics and scholars were revealed to him only as a result of his travels. Ebeling's and Bode's translations of the *Tours,* censorious though they were, nevertheless placed him before the German public, and generated considerable interest in his forthcoming *History*. He was particularly well established with the *Encyclopédists* in France, and they, too, served to promote his work and reputation on the Continent. In Italy his cordial relationship with Padre Martini was sufficient to gain the respect of many musicians. Taken together, his personal acquaintance and easy familiarity with the greatest musicians of Western Europe gave him a particular prestige which had hitherto eluded truly professional music critics of any nationality.

There is little evidence that the experience of the tours occasioned any significant change in Burney's taste or philosophy in music. He was not a young man of uncertain taste when he began his tours, but a fully prepared, if nascent, critic who seems to confirm the correctness of his judgment and taste at every turn. Quick to judge the numerous compositions and performers he heard on his travels, he appraised them against his mature and well-defined critical precepts, and judged them accordingly. Many new names were assimilated, but very few new ideas.

William Newman has postulated a change in Burney's style of composition at this time, stating that the changes reflect especially the extent to which he became enamoured of Italian as against French music after his tours.[171] There is precious little that can be called French in any of Burney's music. What change is evident is a more modern form of his thoroughly Italianate style. The "fuller texture and careful attention to design" which Newman says "betray the scholar, or perhaps some German influence" was not the result of his travels. The cosmopolitan musical life in London, especially after the establishment of J.C. Bach and Abel in London, was sufficient to give a musician as active as Burney a sense of being abreast of the latest Continental fashions. His belief that he was hearing in London the very best music of every country encouraged him to be unequivocal in his taste.

Before he left on his journey to Germany, he wrote Ebeling:

> ... I think the best of all contrivances in Music, is to please people of discernment and taste without trouble. A long and laboured Fugue, *recte et retro* in forty parts, may be good entertainment for the *Eyes* of a critic, but can never delight the Ears of a Man of Taste.[172]

After returning from his travels he drafted an essay in which he attempted to delineate the respective merits of the music of Germany and Italy.

> Much discrimination is necessary in giving a comparative Judgment /view/ of the different degrees of Merit in the German and Italian Music and Musicians. The former are apt to be laboured long and Elaborate—the latter hasty, careless, incorrect and Trivial. The one studies too much; the other too little. Music seems work to the Germans and play to the Italians. The former regard length in a musical Composition, and even in a Sermon, as a great proof of Merit. I remember a German Gentleman speaking of the superior Talents for preaching in one of his Countrymen: "He was a fine Man. He would preach upon a Text extempore two hours, without ceasing." They love a great deal of everything good—and deny /reject/ the truth of our old proverb, "too much of everything is good for nothing"—and replace it by "one can't have too much of a good Thing." The Italians, however reprehensible in other respects, are never prolix: and with all their faults it must be owned that they are the only Musicians in Europe who can trifle with grace.
>
> The Germans are prone to Excess in every Musical fashion. In the days of Fugues, their compositions of that kind, were the most elaborate, complex and crowded in Europe. And now melody is polished, and rendered piquant by frequent appoggiaturas of semitones foreign to the Original Key or real Modulation, their productions are so overcharged with Embellishments that it is not easy to say whether they are most difficult to execute or disagreeable /disgusting/ to hear. At present the whole music of Germany is rendered hateful to all lovers of simplicity by a laboured and learned Modulation which continually disappoints the Ear and by affected ornaments which offend it.[173]

Little has changed in the philosophy of the critic. His exposure to the wealth of German contrapuntal music did not increase his tolerance for elaborate counterpoint in most styles of music. The tours brought about a revolution in Burney's life, but there was no concurrent revolution, and little evolution, in his musical taste.

5
Music to 1450:
The Reluctant Historian

> The subject itself of ancient music is so dark, and writers concerning it are so discordant in their opinions, that every intelligent reader who finds *how little there is to be known,* has reason to lament that there still remains so much to be said. Indeed, I should have been glad to have waived all discusson about it: for, to say the truth, the study of ancient music is now become the business of an Antiquary more than of a Musician. But in every history of music extant in other languages, the practice had been so constant for the author to make a display of what he knew, and what he did *not* know concerning ancient music, that it seemed absolutely necessary for me to say something about it, if it were only to prove, that if I have not been more successful in my enquiries than my predecessors, I have not been less diligent.[1]

Burney's distaste for the prospect of writing a history of ancient music did not wane as he began his task. As the *Plan* shows, he had no expectation of being able to add anything of significance to the debate about ancient music and its superiority or inferiority to modern music. Although he had little interest in the subject in general, there was one issue in the debate on which he was unequivocal:

> ... As to the superior or inferior degree of excellence in the ancient music, compared with the modern, it is now as impossible to determine, as it is *to hear both sides.*
> Indeed it is so entirely lost, that the study of it becomes as unprofitable as learning a dead language, in which there are no books; and yet this study has given rise to so much pedantry, and to such an ambition in modern musical authors, to be thought well versed in the writings of the ancients upon music, that their treatises are rendered both disgusting and unintelligible by it. *Words* only are come down to us without *things.* We have so few remains of ancient Music by which to illustrate its rules, that we cannot, as in Painting, Poetry, Sculpture, or Architecture, judge of it, or profit by examples; and to several of these terms which are crammed into our books, we are utterly unable to affix any precise or useful meaning. To write, therefore, in favour of ancient music now, is like the emperor Julian's defending paganism, when mankind had given it up as indefensible, and had attached themselves to another religion.[2]

Moreover, he observed that had ancient music survived, it might have had a negative effect by tying later composers to a precedent, in much the same manner as modern Latin writers, who never "dare hazard a single thought or expression without classical authority."[3]

Aside from the wish to record his view on the merits of ancient music, he had little interest in the other issues which were part of the so-called "Quarrel of the Ancients and Moderns."[4] He felt compelled, nonetheless, to treat the subject, rather than appear ignorant or dilettantish to his readers. The topic was so extensive and speculative that Burney decided to set apart the discussion in a "Dissertation on the Music of the Ancients" as a preface to the *History,* and to confine the body of his book to "circumstances merely historical." This device was recommended by Thomas Twining, a clergyman from Essex who was a classical scholar, and who, after reading Burney's *Tours,* offered his assistance. His offer was readily accepted, and it is probably fair to say that he is at least as responsible as Burney for the first volume of the *History;*[5] but even Twining, with his training in the classics, was not enthusiastic about "meddling with the *Old Stuff.*"[6]

Burney was uneasy about presenting to his public a first volume of such complexity; it is hardly a book that "every Miss who plays o'top o' Spinet" could make her manual.[7] He prefaced the work with a harsh critique of other writers on ancient music, asserting that often those "who were most diffuse upon the subject, knew the least of the matter," and that using "technical Jargon," they loaded each page with "unintelligible pedantry" so that "not an eligible thought could be found, in exploring thousands of them."[8] By contrast, Burney assured his readers he did not wish to appear profound, but to write his discussion "in such a manner as was likely to engage the attention of those that are unable, or unwilling, to read treatises written, for the most part, by persons who were more ambitious of appearing learned themselves, than making others so."[9]

Whether the subject or the author be at fault, the book is difficult reading. Since only the first volume of the *History* was published in 1776, Burney sought to impress upon his readers that it was not his intention to write yet another book to sit on the shelf with "all such reading as was never read."[10] His feeling was that obvious and labored learning was antithetic to taste, as a reflection contained in his notebook attests:

> As it is the Business of Art to hide Art, so a truely learned Man should conceal his learning as carefully as his vices or indeed his virtues, for true Science and true piety/goodness/are alike free from ostentation.[11]

Despite the formidable obstacles presented by is subject, Burney succeeds to a remarkable degree in making the "Dissertation" palatable. His subject may be the music of the ancients, but contemporary issues are frequently drawn into the discussion through observations and reflections which, though seemingly extraneous, allow the charm and taste of the author to penetrate his arcane subject. In a thorny discussion of mutation in Greek music, for example, he cites a passage on "modulation" in Plutarch's *Dialogue,* which notes a "modulation" passing from B to G; in a footnote Burney relates that:

> Handel is the only one that I know of who has hazarded a modulation from B to G with a flat third; a passage of this kind occurs in the last act of the Oratorio of *Athalia,* which is so bold and wonderfully happy in expressing the words, that I shall insert it here as a great stroke of the composer as well as of musical imitation.[12]

Similarly, an example from Purcell's *Mad Bess* is given in a footnote to a discussion of Sir Francis Stile's theory of modes in Greek music, and if the example is not all that necessary to illustrate the point, it does provide the reader with a moment's diversion.[13]

In support of his belief in the supremacy of modern music, he constantly encourages his readers—whom he embraces as persons of taste—to exercise their own judgment in determining merit. When Burney notes that the system of modes provided a greater accuracy of intonation in ancient music than can be indicated by modern notation, he immediately counters with a defense of modern music:

> ... Notwithstanding the defects of modern music in some particulars, I may venture to affirm that it has arrived at a very great degree of perfection; and I appeal for the truth of this assertion to the daily experience of persons of good taste and refined ears.[14]

Burney constantly pits taste, judgment, and reason against myth, claims of superiority for earlier music, and classical authority. If the music sounds better to modern ears, it is to him sufficient evidence of its superiority. He invites the reader to compare every aspect of ancient music to the modern, a device which allows the historian to move back and forth between the two eras with ease, introducing subjects of interest to contemporary readers. For example, after commenting that Greek rhythmic structure, based on the poetic feet of the text, fatigued the ear with "uniformity where it requires change; and distracted by change where it requires uniformity," he says of the grace of modern rhythmic structure:

> Modern music, on the contrary, by its division into *equal* bars, and its unequal subdivision of these bars by notes of various lengths, unites to the *pleasure* which the ear is by nature formed to receive from a regular and even measure, all the *variety* and *expression* which the *ancients* seem to have aimed at by sudden and convulsive changes of time, and a continual conflict of jarring and irreconcileable *Rhythms*.[15]

Such observations create opportunities to pillory his favorite target: French serious opera. In response to Isaac Vossius's charge that it had been over a thousand years since music had lost its power over the affections for lack of the proper use of rhythm, and that all modern music is of one style and color, Burney answers:

> We will not defend the age in which Vossius wrote from the charge, nor the music of the present *serious* opera in France; but the compositions of Italy and Germany are certainly free from the

censure, as music is now more divided into phrases and sentences, and time is more marked and more easily felt than it has ever been since the days of Guido. What it was before, is not very well known; but to confess the truth, it is my opinion, that whatever it has comparatively lost in some particulars, it has gained in others, as I shall endeavour to manifest in the course of this work.[16]

Despite his modernist tendency, Burney is careful to proclaim that he is not an enemy of antiquity. To the contrary, he claims to have admired the productions of the ancients as models of writing, sculpture, painting and architecture, and if facts "sufficiently numerous, clear and indisputable" can be found, he is most willing to recognize the superiority of their music as well.[17] In order to determine the matter fairly, Burney collected every known fragment of ancient music, as examples could be "more decisive in proving the truth or falsehoods of the effects that have been attributed to it, and its comparative excellence with the modern, than the strongest arguments that can be drawn from history, or the dark dry musical treatises that are come down to us."[18] He provides a "minute account" of each fragment, carefully comparing different versions and transcriptions of each piece, and even furnishing a rhymed translation of the text. Lest the reader tire of these fragments from antiquity, Burney notes that one example of the Greek melodies, the "Ode of Pindar," is manifestly in the key of E minor," and that by "reducing it to a regular time," and setting a bass to it, it has the "appearance and effect of a religious hymn of the present century" (ex. 5.1).[19] The piece thus represented has only the remotest connection with Pindar's Ode, but it does provide amusement for the reader. But he found that even his keyboard arrangements did not offset the weakness of this music, and though he tried these fragments of melody in every key and measure that the verse would allow, he was "unable to augment their grace and elegance."

If the chapters on rhythm, melody, and mutation allowed references to modern music, the chapter on the dramatic music of the ancients threw wide the door. The chapter abounds with references to opera approached by way of the supposed similarity between Greek dramatic music and modern recitative. In the course of the chapter, Rousseau's *Devin du village,* Metastasio, and even David Garrick, are included in the discussion.[20] Several pages are spent arguing against the proposition that the combined poet-musician, such as Rousseau in the composition of *Devin,* creates a work superior to that of the musician setting another's text. Burney found the opposite to be true because "by being separated, each of these professions receives a greater degree of cultivation," and he concludes with a surprisingly sharp barb that must have rankled a number of his professional friends: "The music of the ancient 'philosophers' and the philosophy of modern musicians, I take to be pretty equal in excellence."[21]

One subject on which Burney seems to have curbed his witty attack was the powerful effect or ethos attributed to the music of the ancients in myth and chronicle. The authority of the ancients was not to be challenged lightly. He had

Ex. 5.1. "Ode of Pindar"

written to Twining that many of the stories of ancient music's magical powers were to be scorned, and one of the surviving notebooks compiled during this period sets aside several pages for "stories to be laughed at."[22] In the end, though, he maintains a fairly respectful attitude toward many of the ancient tales, and seeks, without totally discrediting the stories presented by the classical writers, to account for the effect of music by a reasoned inquiry. Thus, to Pythagorus's account of a young man becoming enraged by a flute being played in the Phyrigian mode, Burney responds:

> ... it certainly would not be difficult to render a company of drunken fellows furious, by a bad hautbois, or tabor and pipe; but, when the first rage had spent itself, if the hautbois were to play a graver strain, and retard the measure by degrees, we should soon see these pot-valiant heroes fall fast asleep, without reflecting any great honour upon the excellence of the music, or performance.[23]

His tack is, "without disputing the truth of the facts," to enquire whether, in those early ages, it was necessary for the art to have been brought to great perfection in order to operate so powerfully. Ancient music could be allowed its superiority in its "simplicity" and strict adherence to metrical feet when applied to poetry," but "as *music* considered abstractedly," it appeared to have been "much inferior to the modern, in the two great and essential parts of the art, melody and harmony."[24] By disallowing the absolute supremacy of ancient music, and by giving reasoned demonstration that external stimuli—such as poetry or merely rhythm—could account for the magical effects attributed to it, Burney was able to discredit most of the arguments of the lovers of musical antiquity without violating classical authority. He was even able to turn back the most influential of all appeals upon its advocates: the precept that art should imitate nature was a strong argument in favor of the Greek arts, for it was believed that the Greeks had achieved a truly imitative art.

> The nearer the people of any country are to a state of nature, the fonder they are of noisy music: like children, who prefer a rattle and a drum to a soft and refined melody, or the artful combinations of learned harmony.
>
> It is not, therefore, difficult to conceive, that the music of the ancients, with all its simplicity, by its strict union with poetry, which rendered it more articulate and intelligible, could operate more powerfully in theatric, and other public exhibitions, than the artificial melody, and complicated harmony of modern times; for though poetry was assisted by ancient music, it is certainly injured by the modern.[25]

The witty vehemence Burney frequently brings to his history of ancient music may be best understood by recognizing the opposing point of view: not that ancient music had value in its own social setting, or some charms that could be appreciated by a modern audience, but that it was completely superior to the modern. Its advocates held that through a rediscovery of the ancient art, music could be diverted from its present degenerate course. But in Burney's view there were "classics in poetry, sculpture, and architecture which every modern strives to imitate; and he is thought most to excel, who comes nearest to those models... As far as we are able to judge, by a comparative view of the most ancient music with the modern, we should gain nothing from imitation."[26] He did not hold that the music of the ancients, in its own time, did not please or could not have pleased contemporary audiences. He believed that "great effects may have been produced by their Music, whatever it was, and however it may essentially have differed from our own." For this reason he did not compare the musicians of antiquity with any but their contemporaries. He wishes the reader to "mount up to each particular period" of which he writes, and "consider Music of antiquity as relative to the knowledge of those who heard it," "since nothing is more certain than that the best Music of the time, in all ages has greatly delighted its hearers."[27]

By demonstrating to his readers his familiarity with the authorities and their arguments, presenting evidence in the form of the music that did survive, and letting reason and taste determine the case, Burney succeeds in writing an appealing and convincing discussion of a complex and abstruse topic. In so doing, he is able to establish his authority as a man of taste and to present his position in such a reasoned manner that little disagreement is possible without declaring oneself to be among the "exclusive and blind" admirers of antiquity.

Once Burney had completed his speculation on the theory and practice of ancient music, there remained the task of establishing a chronology. He disallowed the idea that music was invented by any single person or race, averring "the *art* or *practice* of music cannot be said to have been *invented* by any one man, for it must have had its infancy, childhood and youth before it arrived at maturity." Thus, he begins his history with an account of music in Egypt, the country from which "all human intelligence seems to have sprung." He still had only myth, legend, and the exhausted speculation of other writers upon which to rely. His task consisted of collecting, sifting, and reporting on the most reliable of the earliest reports of music in Egypt. He found, to his regret, that the mythology of Egypt, like that of Greece, contained accounts of early cultivation of music, and that "some slight mention" was unavoidable.

There was substantial evidence about Egyptian musical instruments, and a large portion of his brief chapter is devoted to a discussion of the earliest flute and lyre.[28] He was able to capitalize on the recent return of James Bruce, an "intrepid and intelligent traveller" who had made an extended visit to Africa. Bruce provided Burney with a lengthy account of the musical instruments he had seen, two plates, and an extensive letter, which were printed in the *History*. Burney was thus able to provide readers with some new information from "an excellent judge of the subject of music," and seize upon the popular interest in one of the season's most discussed personalities.[29] Burney expanded Bruce's letter (with his consent), and in one of his additions he follows his practice of alluding to contemporary music at every possible opportunity.

> As the application of the pedals has enabled us to disengage the modern harp from its multiplicity of strings, and brought it nearer to Theban simplicity, I hope our artists, and Merlin in particular, will likewise endeavor to introduce into its form a little of Theban elegance. It is the favourite of the fair sex, and nothing should be spared to make it beautiful; for it should be a principal object of mankind to attach them by every means to music, as it is the only amusement that may be enjoyed to excess, and the heart still remain virtuous and uncorrupted.[30]

The beauty of one of Bruce's instruments, the Theban harp, was sufficient "to encourage a belief, that arts, after having been brought to great perfection, were again lost, and again invented, long after this period."[31] It is the "ignorance and barbarism into which it is possible for an ingenious people to be plunged, by the tyranny and devastation of a powerful and cruel invader" that he holds responsible for the loss of an entire culture.[32] Burney refers to a period of excellence, in music at least, which existed long before the era of Greek achievement, normally regarded as the apogee of the arts. He does not, however, seem to have entertained a similar possibility for music since the fall of ancient Greece.

While evidence regarding the music of the Greeks, Romans, and Egyptians was open to dispute, there was no such problem confronting the historian in his discussion of ancient Hebrew music: the Bible was his source. His task was to "collect the passages" reported in "true and genuine simplicity" in the "sacred writings" and arrange them in chronological order.[33] Burney called this a "trivial" task, and did not look forward to it. When he first surveyed the topic, he wrote to Crisp, "I shall first get over the Drudgery of Jewish Music—Padre Martini—Don Calmet—the Bible—and some Hebrew priests with whom I will converse by Means of my friend Franks, will suffice for that part of my Enterprize."[34]

Though the facts presented in the Bible were indisputable, there were still difficult topics.[35] Burney barely touches on these, preferring instead to stress the relationship of the music to poetry and prophecy.[36] The complexities of the Bible had been thoroughly debated by translators and scholars, and he made no attempt to challenge their authority as he had the commentators on the ancient poets. Rather, when faced with a problem such as the listing of the musical instruments mentioned in the Psalms, he provides six different translations by various commentators to show "that there is no dependence upon any one of them, or hope that these points can be cleared up."[37]

Although Burney ridicules most of the legends about the miraculous powers of music,[38] he does acknowledge music to have some helpful psychological effects.

> If it be possible for music to operate medicinally with success, it may be imagined a palliative, at least, if not a cure, for a troubled spirit. The human mind, under the pressure of affliction, or warped and agitated by the contention of warring passions, seems a fit subject for soft and soothing strains to work upon, as powerful anodynes.[39]

"The whole of David's power" to soothe Saul could be "attributed to his skilful and affecting manner of performing upon the harp."[40] As the affliction of Saul was a mental distraction, music could realistically be credited with "mechanical effects on the nerves and animal spirits."[41] Some authorities, such as Richard Browne, felt that only lively, gay strains were "medicinally appropriate," but Burney disagreed.

> ...on the contrary, in affliction, pain, and sorrow, as well as in hypochondriac and calamitous cases, when gay and lively music is to the last degree offensive, we rather enlist with those who think grave music, if it cannot radically cure, can sooth, alleviate, and afford a temporary relief.[42]

Moreover, there was recent evidence for such belief—Philip V, King of Spain, had (like Saul) suffered from an "evil spirit," or disorder of the mind. The effect of the great singer Farinelli on his ailment was legendary: he had sung the disturbed monarch to sleep every night for ten years with the same four arias, two by Hasse and two by Leonardo Vinci.[43] Burney gave credence to the story, and recommended a similar treatment for George III, who had been seized with a serious mental disturbance which defied the doctors' attempts to cure it.

> Now let me tell you what struck me last night in reading over my acct. of Farinelli, by way of finding faults for the Errata of my Book. His singing in a case nearly similar to that of our dear and good King had such an effect on the King of Spain—on its being heard unexpectedly in another room, as makes me ardently wish an experiment was to be tried on our suffering Monarch; either by some such sweet and touching voice as that I mentioned singing at a sufficient distance merely to be heard, some Air of Handel in which his Majesty used during health to take particular delight—or one of his favourite Choruses, being extremely soft in the neighbouring Room ... In nervous cases I have great faith in the power of soft music on those who like the King were fond of music when well. And the story of Farinelli is so much in point, and has always been thought so authentic, that I am doubly eager to have the experiment tried, if possible. It is not like a Quack medicine, that *may* do harm. Among the greatest and wisest Physicians of Antiquity Music in certain Cases has been thought medicinal. Particularly by Asclepiades who applied it on all occasions, where mental tranquility and calmness were wanting. Perhaps this will all appear too Romantic, and perhaps you will if you see it in another light, want opportunity to mention it where it is most likely to be of any purpose. I cannot however help telling you my thoughts on so important a subject, as I think our most worthy and excellent Sovereign the most likely, from his true and real love for Music, to receive benefit from my Prescription. Without a natural Passion for Harmony and melody, I should never have an idea of its efficacy but laughed at it, as at almost all the Miraculous Powers ascribed to Music by the Ancients and by a few enthusiastic Moderns.[44]

If Burney's experiment was ever carried out he does not mention its outcome.

Although Burney did not question the facts presented by scripture, or even the solutions to textual problems provided by the commentators, he did challenge reports of the great beauty of Hebrew music. The Hebrew language, which "had originally no vowels," the extensive use of percussion instruments, and performers numbering in the thousands, convinced him that Hebrew music must have been very crude. He found no evidence to the contrary in the singing in modern synagogues which he felt, at least in the chorus, was composed of clamor and jargon. "These circumstances," he observes, "must have escaped those who have highly extolled the ancient Hebrew music, or they have been utterly ignorant of the art of singing."[45] Despite his reservations about the merits of Hebrew music, he inserted several examples of ancient Hebrew chant to allay the curiosity of his readers, but "without a hope of their being either edified or delighted by such music."[46]

Placing the discussion of Greek theory and practice of music in the "Dissertation" freed Burney from the necessity of interrupting his *History* with difficult speculations, but when he approached the writing of "Music History in

Ancient Greece," a subject "involved in darkness, which no human light can penetrate," he was faced again with the legends, myths, and reports of dubious accuracy. According to Burney, it was "national vanity" that gave rise to those "practical fictions" which comprised the only evidence antiquity had left the historian. Nonetheless,

> ...as the fables of ancient historians, and the wild imaginations of mythologists, have employed the sagacity of the wisest and most respectable writers of modern times, to digest into system, and to construe into something rational and probable, I shall not wholly neglect them, but, with the assistance of such guides, shall travel through the dark labyrinth of remote antiquity, with all possible expedition.[47]

The most striking feature of the six chapters on the history of Greek music is the extensive quotation of poetry. Most of these poems are translations from Greek and Latin classics, some translated by Burney himself. Twining had objected to the inclusion of so much poetry and strongly criticized some of his translations,[48] but Burney retained a surprising number. As Burney's allusions to contemporary music, these serve, as he confessed to Samuel Crisp, in part, to appeal to the dilettantes among his readership:

> ...I am now got to the Olympic and Pythian Games, whose Musical Contests can perhaps furnish some Biographical amusement, at least, to my readers, who I must endeavor to *divert* when I have not the least chance of Instructing them. My first volume will necessarily consist of more of the History of Poets and musicians than of Music; for till frequent Specimens can be given how is it possible to reason upon the kind of Music that was in use and admired at any distant period of Time.[49]

Doubtless much of the material in Burney's history of Greek music could have been omitted without substantially altering the historical content, but however willing he was to "part with the miraculous powers of their music," he was "unwilling that persons, whose talents have been so long celebrated, should be annihilated, and their actions cancelled from the record of past times."[50] Yet he repeatedly apologizes to his readers for his reliance on legend and myth, and as he approached the "Music of Heroes and Heroic Times," he confessed that the periods could better be called poetic than heroic,

> ...for, though little better than a blank in history and chronology, they have notwithstanding been filled up by poets and fabulists with wonderful events, in the same manner as the vacuity in parts of the Pacific Ocean have been filled up by navigators and geographers with whales, with dolphins, and with sea monsters.[51]

It is surprising that he carried this portion of the work to such length. He must have realized that the inclusion of quantities of poetry and even selected borrowings of material from other writers[52] would make it impossible to conclude his *History* in only one more volume.[53] Yet Burney continued to insert the lengthy descriptions and digressions over Twining's protests. Even Burney, in the midst of the third chapter, felt compelled to explain:

> The following lines are so beautiful, and applicable to the present subject, that I cannot help inserting them, though I have already, perhaps, been too profuse of quotations; not with the design of swelling the volume, or from a scarcity of other materials, but because the passages interested me, and inclined me to hope, that they would be equally striking to the reader.[54]

One cannot help but feel that Burney is striving for recognition for his poetic abilities. Poetry was, after all, an important accomplishment for a man of taste, and was commonly "thought to be the highest of the arts, the most delightful, the most intellectual, and the most useful."[55] Though he must have already realized that his work must expand beyond two volumes, he promises the completion of his work within that space in a passage toward the end of his first volume.[56] He does curb his poetic citations thereafter, but continues to write about poets, because "poetry and music, in the early ages of those arts were so much united, that all the lyric, elegiac, and even epic Bards, were necessarily and professedly musicians."[57]

Surely the most remarkable discussion in this lengthy chapter is that which Burney builds around his treatment of Sacadus, the poet-musician who was "the first upon record who detached Music from Poetry, and who though a good Poet himself, engaged the public attention in favour of *mere instrumental Music;* a *Schism* that has been as severely censured as any one in the church."[58] Here Burney places himself squarely in opposition to the sister-arts theory of the interrelationship of separate art forms.[59] In the consideration of the sisters, music was invariably ranked beneath poetry. "From the beginning of the century to the end the cry was the same: The decay of modern music is due to the separation of poetry and music."[60] Such was the cause which stirred Dr. John Brown to publish his *Dissertation on the Rise, Union and Power, the Progressions, Separations, and Corruptions, of Poetry and Music* in 1763. Brown's view was not reactionary—the debate, among aestheticians at least, continued into the nineteenth century. Indeed, "no matter what any practicing musician may have thought, the English gentleman-critic assumed as a fact that music is an associative art, taking its expressive powers largely from the expressive tones of the human voice."[61] Therefore, the separation of instrumental music from its role of merely heightening the effect of poetry was the first step in music's degeneracy. But Burney, who after all *was* a "practicing musician," boldly asserted the contrary.

> The censurers, however, have forgotten that such *Schisms,* in the *Arts,* are as much to be desired, as those of religion are to be avoided; since it is by such *separations* only, that the different Arts, and different branches of the *same* Art, becoming the objects of *separate* and exclusive cultivation, are brought to their last refinement and perfection.[62]

He was for this cause, moreover, willing to fly directly against classical authority. After quoting Aristotle's objection to the "artificial and difficult trick of instrumental music," Burney retorts,

> These were the sentiments of the learned, long after the separation of Music and Poetry, and these are the objections that still recur, and ever will recur, to those who regard music as a slave to syllables, forgetting that it has a language of its own, with which it is able to speak to the passions, and that there are certain occasions when it may with propriety be allowed to be a free agent.[63]

Burney would not allow that a person of great talent or even taste in one art would necessarily be as discerning about music. The men of letters and poets who were responsible for so much of the polemic about ancient music were usually not musicians; while he would defer to their opinions in their respective fields, he was not unduly influenced by their musical speculations or judgments.

> ... Some of the wisest men, and of the greatest talents, in other particulars, I am sorry to say it, have not had ear enough for music to discover the difference, not only between good and bad music, but between one tune and another. And yet these great and wise men, in other particulars, think themselves qualified to write, talk, and decide, about music, in a more peremptory manner, than those of the greatest feeling and genius, who have long made it their particular study. Poor human nature is never to be perfect: however the musician pities the man without ears; and the man without ears, in revenge, heartily condemns the fiddling fool, who can be delighted with such nonsense.[64]

The several chapters on the history of Greek music show Burney striving to form a cogent discussion from great quantities of information. Whatever effort it required to make the material palatable, and even amusing, to his readers, he at least had a surfeit of material with which to work. The chronicles of the Romans offered no such biographical or anecdotal interest, but it was necessary to write the chapter in the same way that one had "to pass through large tracts of desert country, in order to arrive at places better worth examining."[65] The chapter did permit him to include a pertinent digression about the high cost of musical entertainment to English society. The subject was not only of general interest to his readers, but of great personal concern to the writer.

In the midst of writing his book, Burney became involved in an unsuccessful effort to establish a conservatory in London modeled after those in Italy.[66] The plan to train musicians at the Foundling Hospital was first approved, then abruptly cancelled, greatly embittering Burney, who was to have been one of the directors of the conservatory at a substantial salary. He was, monetary considerations aside, sincere in his enthusiasm for establishing a school in England, where, to his ears, good native singers were rare.

Something of the attitude of the opponents to the conservatory scheme can be gleaned from a satire of Burney's *Tours* produced as a direct result of his involvement in the project. Written under the pseudonym Joel Collier, *The*

Musical Travels Through England (1774) were advertised as "printed on a proper Size to be bound up with the celebrated Musical Tours to France, Italy, Germany, Netherlands, and United Provinces, to which it is intended as a Supplement." The work was dedicated to the governors of the Foundling Hospital, and the sarcastic dedication leaves no doubt about the intended victims of the satire.

> Gentlemen,
> While I was extracting the following observations, anecdotes and adventures from my Journal, as a Specimen of my laborious investigation of the present state of *Music* in this country, I was somewhat at a loss to whom I could with most propriety inscribe my work. Whether to *Doctor Burney*, as the original inventor of this species of composition, and the first musical traveller of our nation, of whom I might so truly say in his own words, "that he has long been my *magnus Apollo:*"—or to the King of *Prussia*, as the greatest *Dilettante* performer of the age; who, like another *Nero*, is playing his new *Solfeggi* to the groans of the miserable *Poles*, and ruined *Dantzickers*. This dilemma, however, was at an end, as soon as I learnt that Dr. *Burney*, and Signor *Giardini*, had, under your authority, and in imitation of the *Italian conservatorios*, just founded a school for music in the *Foundling Hospital*, where deserted orphans, instead of being placed out to trades and services, in which they can have no opportuntiy of making any *noise* in the world, are, in future, to be trained to harmony from their infancy; where they are to be constantly employed in the study of the science of sound; and from whence, in process of time, they are to take their regular degrees in music, till all our public orchestras shall be filled with *Giardinis* and *Bastardinis detta Inglisene*. When I was informed of this important event, I hailed the happy omen, the dawn of an *Augustan* aera; and resolved to dedicate my work to a set of gentlemen, who have shewn so distinguished a zeal for the interests and advancement of music.[67]

The writer, probably John Bicknell, concludes that "when we have rivalled the *Italians* in music it will be time enough to think of our navy and our agriculture."[68] Clearly Burney is responding to Bicknell, and men of his ilk, in his comments on the fall of Greece and Rome.

> It cannot be dissembled, or passed over in silence here, that arts and sciences have been frequently charged with contributing to precipitate both the Roman and Grecian states into ruin, by rendering the minds of the people effeminate, involving the Great in idle and useless expence and luxury, and by calling off their attention from military and political concerns, which alone can acquire and preserve dominion. In the infancy of a state, or in times of danger and calamity, this may be true: but that man was designed for no other purposes than to enslave or destroy his fellow-creatures, or to live a gloomy life of inanity and penance, never composed a part of my creed. A nation become affluent by conquest and commerce, must have amusements in time of peace. The question is, whether these amusements shall be merely corporeal and sensual, or whether elegance, refinement, and mental pleasure, shall bear a part in them?...
> It is difficult to acquire wealth by fair means, but it is much more difficult to use it rationally. And, in our own country, and times, there are at least ten men who have talents of accumulation sufficient to amass great riches, to one who distributes them among his fellow-citizens, with benevolence, taste and judgment...

> The cultivation of Arts and Sciences in a great and flourishing kingdom is expected by its neighbours, and a debt to posterity. It was long the fate of our own country, like that of the ancient Romans, to admire the polite arts more than to cultivate them. We imported the productions of foreign painters, sculptors, and musicians, at an enormous expence, without conceiving it possible to raise a school for the advancement of those arts at home. With respect to the two first, all Europe now allows that genius, diligence, and travel, under the auspices of royal protection and public patronage, have made wonderful strides within the last twenty years towards perfection, and forming a school in our own country; but, as for Music, we have little that we can call our own; and though more money is expended upon this favourite art in England, than in any other kingdom upon the globe; yet, having no school either for the cultivation of Counterpoint or Singing, we acquire by those arts neither honour from our neighbors, nor profit to our natives. Both take wing together! and without a scarcity of genius for contributing to the pleasures of the ear, we purchase them with as little necessity as we should corn at a dear and foreign market, while our own lands lay fallow.[69]

Burney was greatly annoyed and chagrined by the appearance of the Collier parody.[70] He perhaps had himself more in mind than Timotheus when he wrote of this much-maligned musician, "An exalted character is a shooting butt, at which satirists, and wicked wits, constantly point their arrows; ... the abuse, therefore, of this musician, which abounds in ancient authors, is perhaps as great a proof of his superiority, as the praise."[71]

There is no indication that Burney ever warmed to the subject of ancient music, despite his years of dedication to rendering its mysteries palatable, and bringing its dusty darkness to light. His letters to Twining reflect the labor of selecting and digesting the mass of available material. There seems to have been no joy and little satisfaction in writing this portion of the *History*. Years later, in response to a letter from Samuel Wesley, pointing out an error in the notation of the Hyperiastian mode in the *History*, he remarked,

> ... it is so long since my first volume was published, or that I have bestowed a single thought about Greek music that I forgot all about it. The dissertation which cost me more trouble than all the four Volumes of *History* has I am certain been the least read. However, such as it is, I am glad it is there, as it is proof that I did not *shirk* difficulties or leave their solution unattempted from want of diligence.[72]

With his first volume Burney attained an unquestioned triumph over Sir John Hawkins, a triumph which, if not timeless, was secure in its time. Although it is true that Burney manipulated two of the most important reviews of Hawkins's *History*, his efforts, shameful though they were, could not have been enough to cause Hawkins' great work to be stillborn. Only a consensus that Burney's work, despite its incompletion, was superior to Hawkins's work could account for the acceptance of Burney's book over that of Hawkins. It is remarkable that he was able to win his readership while treating only the music of antiquity, a subject which was exhausted by other writers long before he began his task. His sober description of the responsibility of a historian of this period speaks eloquently of the obstacles he overcame:

> History can only consist of quotations, when we write of times anterior to our own, or concerning things of which we have not been eye-witnesses. In treating, therefore, every subject which relates to anitquity, it is necessary to give the sentiments of those who have written upon it before, either in support of our own assertions, or to confute those of others. And indeed all that is left for an historian of ancient music, is to collect the scattered fragments, hints, and allusions, relative to it, which occur in old authors; to arrange them in chronological order, and to connect and explain them by reflection and conjecture.[73]

It was through the process of connecting and reflecting that Burney succeeded in tantalizing and captivating his readers. His undeniable taste, judgment, and the authority he displays as a historian were sufficient to overcome the completed work of the antiquarian Hawkins.

It was not the relative merit of the treatment of their subject that was the determining factor; rather it was their ability to reach an audience. Hawkins, by finishing his *History* first, was temporarily the victor, but his work was devoid of taste and style. He captured some votaries among the intellectuals, but few among the greater audience. Time and a change in fashion and taste were necessary before the intrinsic value of the histories could be assessed. Burney, better than any, knew that taste was evanescent, and deliberately wrote for an immediate audience. Still, as a historian, he was prescient that his work also would be important to later generations. In one of the footnotes designed to tantalize his readers with the content of his following volume, he wrote:

> Here the reader will probably reflect how much curious information, and how many interesting gratifications of curiosity are, and ever have been, lost to posterity, from the unwillingness of authors to inform the present generation of what it is supposed to know already, or to write as if they expected their books would ever become obscure. It is from this cause that we are now in such doubt concerning the Enharmonic Genus, Music in Parts, Modes, etc. which a word or two might have cleared up; and if this *History* should reach a distant period, will not its readers wish to known some particulars concerning Agujari? how high she went? and what were the other peculiarities of her talents? an opportunity will, perhaps, offer itself in the second volume, of gratifying curiosity with respect to the powers of this particular performer: I wish it were as easy to satisfy it in other instances where the scantiness of information may awaken it in vain![74]

Burney knew that he had established only a temporary hold on musical fame with the first volume. He had surveyed innumerable books in compiling his own and knew full well with what critical eyes future historians would survey his work. Yet, he had succeeded brilliantly in the first volume in the task of instructing and pleasing the audience of his day, without putting them to much trouble in the process.

Burney concluded his first volume by expressing his hope that his next would be "more interesting to the reader in proportion as he advances towards Certainty, and the account of things that we are not only sure *have* existed, but of many, though of ancient origin, which *still* exist."[75] He enthusiastically began work on his second volume almost immediately—so soon, in fact, that Twining called him a "hero of a man"—but his optimism was soon curbed. Once underway, the obstacle that Hawkins's completed *History* represented became apparent. Having just begun his second volume, he had to "rewrite part of his opening chapter merely to avoid what might have seemed plagiarism."[76] His reluctance to trod the same path as Hawkins prompted Twining to caution him not to leave anything out of his work that should be there, simply because it had already been treated by the other historian.

By placing a model before the public, Hawkins unwittingly became responsible for much of the content and tone of Burney's second volume. To be sure, Burney anticipated that his style would be more pleasing than Hawkins's, but Hawkins had now set standards of content which had not existed prior to the writing of Burney's first volume. His frustration at following Hawkins was heightened by the realization that the topic of early music, if not as speculative as the subject of ancient music, was as abstruse, presenting few opportunities to amuse or entertain his readers. In September, 1778, he confided to Mrs. Thrale, "The Eel of Science to me becomes more slippery every Day—my hooks are broken and decayed; and from want of success, my former eagerness after this kind of fishing is greatly diminished."[77]

The earliest music which survived in substantial quantity was that of the Roman Catholic Church. Burney doubted that "a new species of music was invented for the purpose of praising God." He believed rather that the Christian hymns were adaptations of pagan hymns.[78] Chant would thus serve to reflect the nature of the earliest music inside as well as outside the church. Music in the church also interested Burney because "in all nations the first *public* use of music has been in the celebration of religious rites and ceremonies." The actual chants, however, he found "simple, artless, and insipid," though the church used "every [other] allurement which could captivate the vulgar, and render its ceremonies pleasing to the senses."[79]

Though Burney appreciated the historical significance of early church music and studied its theory, his lack of sympathy with it led him to some peculiar conclusions. Surely he knew that semitones existed within the tonal structure of every mode. His insensibility to the sound of the modes led him to state that,

> As to the want of variety with respect to modulation, such as are much accustomed to the ecclesiastical tones, pretend that a very different effect is produced to the ear by these *different species of octave,* even though the idea of the key be not changed: and it must be allowed that these tones, which seem all to belong to one key and scale do admit the variety of minor and major...[80]

He does little to enlighten his readers with what he does understand about the modes. To avoid the complicated theoretical discussions that comprised the "Dissertation on the Music of the Ancients," he provides only a very cursory description of the church modes—certainly insufficient to give his readers a thorough understanding of the sound of the modes—dismissing the subject summarily.

> Such are the outlines and general rules of the ecclesiastical modes and Canto Firmo; there are indeed peculiarities and exceptions to most of them; but as the book is designed chiefly for the perusal of my countrymen, who have little curiosity, and *no use* for these modes, it seems unnecessary to enter minutely into a discussion of their anomalies.[81]

He was not so unsure of his knowledge that he avoided making stylistic judgments about the music. Early in the chapter he brings evidence to bear to discount the examples of Ambrosian chant printed by Gafurius in his *Practica musica*. He pronounces Gafurius's examples "very supicious, not only as they have a much more modern appearance than even the ancient Gregorian chants that are come down to us, but on account of the number of modes in which he gives them."[82] Despite the apparent confidence of this statement, Burney was unclear about the difference between Gregorian and Ambrosian chant. He requested assistance from J.C. Bach, former organist at the "Duomo at Milan," Signor Fioroni, then *maestro di capella* at Milan, and Padre Martini, but despite their aid, he was unable to state the difference between the two chants.

Burney viewed the venerability of chant as one of its chief virtues, in that its age and antiquated style were appropriated solely to the church, but he also held that the canons of the church which were responsible for the preservation of chant were also responsible for the "long infancy and childhood of the art of music" which was unnaturally prolonged "until music broke loose from the trammels of the church and mounted the stage as secular amusement."[83] There were those in Burney's time who wished to return music to its former trammels. Dr. John Christopher Pepusch, the German-born theorist, had advocated a return to modes in order (according to Burney) to return music to its "original imperfection." To those who argued for a retrogression of the arts, Burney retorted:

> If perfection in one place be perfection in another, let a mutilated scale be a meritorious characteristic only in the church; for on the stage and in the chamber, where zeal and gravity give no assistance to the composition or performance, every refinement and artifice are requisite to stimulate attention, and captivate the hearer. Let all the sharps, and six of the seven single flats be excommunicated; let them have no admission within the pale of the church; but let them not be cut off from all society elsewhere, or the anathema be extended beyond its limits.[84]

The style of the first three chapters is remarkably stodgy in comparison to the first volume, which, though full of complex material, evinces an apparent good humor. In the second volume, Burney seems intimidated by Hawkins's *History* into a style of history foreign to his nature. His extensive discussion of notation, for example, which he thought "a subject of inquiry not unworthy the curiosity of musical readers," approaches the "vain and useless display of erudition" for which he had so reproached earlier writers.[85] Burney's original plan proposed an investigation of ancient and modern theoretical systems, but the *History's* chapter-by-chapter examination of treatises, of little interest to any but the erudite, is reminiscent of Hawkins. There seems to be a demonstrable shift in the audience Burney is attempting to satisfy: certainly little of the first volume was written merely for "the studious in music antiquities," to whom substantial portions of these chapters are dedicated.[86] Throughout his dull summaries he characteristically inserts apologies to his readers of taste for relating so much about music which is "not indeed of so exquisite a kind as to make us lament the loss."[87] Despite the elaborate discussion he gives of early theory, he candidly informs his readers that "so few will be their opportunities of making use of any knowledge they may acquire . . . that it would be like learning a dead language in which there are no books."[88]

The latter part of the first chapter, a chronicle of the development of church music in England and France, is somewhat more interesting.[89] It provides Burney with an opportunity to relate a quarrel between French and Italian musicians, and to jibe at his favorite target, the French, who "after every great defeat, revive with still greater clamour their pretensions to a *Titular Sovereignity,* without having the least claim to it, either from inheritance, conquest or former possession."[90]

After struggling through the first chapter, his readers must have been dismayed to encounter the first sentence of the second, "The ingredients which I have now to prepare for the reader, are in general such as I can hardly hope to render palatable to those who have more taste than curiosity."[91] His lengthy chapter on "The Invention of Counterpoint, and State of Music, from the time of Guido, to the Formation of the Time-table" is daunting indeed. Even the author, midway in his discussion, is moved to insert an explanation of this and succeeding chapters with which most readers then and today must heartily concur.

> I shall be thought too minute, perhaps; but however dull such disquisitions may appear to miscellaneous readers, they certainly constitute the *Business* of my History. These are facts, the rest but flourishes; for it is unfortunate with respect to the music of the middle ages as well as of the ancient Greeks and Romans, that when so little is known there should still remain so much to be said.
>
> Mere music, however says nothing to eyes that cannot read, or ears unable to hear it. To such, therefore, as are both blind and deaf to musical signs and sounds, and contentedly ignorant of both, I fear this chapter will be far from amusing. But as there are many things belonging to a work of this kind, which though few will read, yet, if omitted, many would miss, I shall endeavour to animate myself with the hopes that the few will at least have curiosity and perseverance sufficient to travel with me to the dusty shelves of Gothic lore, and to the gloomy cells of Monks and Friars, where I am forced with great toil, and small expectation, to seek my materials.[92]

Burney does provide the reader with some amusement with his now familiar methods. He scoffs at early authors and contemporary commentators for their abuse of early writings about music, inserts a personal note about his solfege training at Chester[93] in the midst of a history of solmization systems, and enlivens his narrative further with a report of a conversation between Hasse and the singing master Giambatista Mancini on the merits of a particular solfege system.[94] And, in the tradition of Pindar's ode from the first volume, the reader is given a keyboard transcription of organum in triple meter (ex. 5.2).[95]

Ex. 5.2. Organum

(c) This harmony, if performed in triple time, would not offend modern ears: I write the *organum* an octave lower than Guido, for the convenience of keyed instruments.

Early counterpoint did not please him. He describes it as "such harmony as will not only offend the ear, but set our teeth on edge."[96] Yet he notes that "this kind of harmony, miserable and nauseous as it would be to our palates, did not offend Guido." "The definition of an art at one period of time does not prove what art was at another, of much more remote antiquity."[97] Although asserting this ideal, he continually judges his examples by modern standards. Only a few pages later he prints an example of two-part counterpoint from Marchetto da Padua's *Lucedarium in arte musicae planae* (1283), with the observation that "it contains nothing which the modern rules of Counterpoint will not allow."

In Marchetto's *Lucedarium* Burney discerns great advances in the use and resolutions of discords, enough to convince him that the "laws of Harmony" were at last "tolerably settled," and with the art of music having arrived at this state, he concludes his investigation of the development of harmony. He does not close without firmly fixing upon the "Romanish" church the responsibility for the slow development of music from its beginning to the style of Marchetto. The "laity," he says, was guilty of the "sin of innovation" by deviating from the true and simple path described by Hucbald, Odo, and Guido, and "amidst contempt and persecution" brought "Harmony under regular laws and united science with the pleasure of the ear."[98]

Burney's third chapter, "Of the formation of the Time-table, and State of Music from that discovery till about the middle of the fourteenth century," breathes a new spirit, whether from the nature of the subject or a change in attitude by the author. The contemporary speculation on the origins of counterpoint, and Hawkins's influence, seemed to require the minuteness of the discussion in chapters I and II, but chapter III treats the reader to a sweeping survey of a topic that certainly could have been discussed as minutely as the earlier subjects. When he embarks upon an entertaining panegyric against the learned, who think that the application of measured time injures poetry—or, as Burney expressed it, those who "think the liberty music acquired at this memorable revolution has often been abused by her sons, who are frequently *enfans gâtes*"[99]—the reader is once again struck by Burney's enthusiasm for his subject. He is now locked in combat with the musical Philistines, those men of greater learning than experience or taste, who were responsible for aesthetic speculation and theory up until Burney's time. He avers that poetry, far from being corrupted by music, receives "additional dignity and energy from lengthened tones," and he takes evident delight in throwing up "innumerable scenes of the admirable Metastasio," the "accompanied-recitatives and airs in Handel's Oratorios," and Purcell's "Mad Bess" to refute the critics of music.

There are fewer of the wearisome summaries of treatises, such as those which weigh down his earlier chapters,[100] and he refrains from explaining the rhythmic modes or Franconian rhythmic divisions.[101] Whereas in chapter I he printed the most complex and undecipherable examples of Greek notation, with statements implying that some of his learned readers might profit from them, he now writes of the theory of rhythm of the same music: "These rules, however, are too numerous, complex and useless, to merit the reader's attention, or an attempt at explaining them."[102] In rationalizing this omission, his taste, which earlier had seemed subservient to his learning, is strongly reasserted: "When we are arrived at compositions *worth* deciphering, such of the primitive characters as occur in them shall be explained."[103] He allays any doubts about his own ability to read the notation by including a transcription which he characteristically provides with bar lines and a modern bass.[104]

Although much of the Hawkins-inspired pedantry is absent in this chapter, the content is irrefutable evidence that Hawkins's work remained constantly before Burney. Subtle gamesmanship is often evident in Burney's discussions of material already treated by his rival. In his article on John de Muris for example, he proudly reports on his *personal* examination of four manuscripts in Continental libraries, manuscripts unseen by Hawkins, though not unknown to him.[105] Whenever possible Burney challenges Hawkins directly, but always without mentioning his name or his book. Burney's lengthy and seemingly extraneous discussion of the nationality of de Muris takes on new significance when viewed as a direct rebuttal to Hawkins. Hawkins had proudly advanced "definitive" evidence on the question of de Muris's nationality:

> The general opinion is, that he was a native of Normandy; but bishop Tanner has ranked him among the English writers; in this he has followed Pits, who expressly asserts that he was an Englishman; and though the Oxford antiquary, following the French writers, says that he was a Frenchman of Paris, the evidence of his being a native of England is stronger than even Pits or Tanner themselves were aware of; for in a very ancient manuscript, which it no where appears that either of them had ever seen, and of which a very copious account will hereafter be given, are the following verses:—
> "Ihon de Muris, variis floruitque figuris,
> Anglia cantorum nomen gignit plurimorum."[106]

Burney responds directly to this new evidence. The Latin distich, Burney asserts,

> ...can add but little to its weight, when it is known to come from the most ignorant and monkish of writers, the author of a treatise *De Origine et Effectu Musice,* written 1451; who tells us that "Cyrus lived soon after the deluge; that one king *Enchiridias* was a writer on music," mistaking, I suppose, some *Enchiridion* which he had seen, for the name of a royal author. And that "Thubal kept a blacksmith's shop, at which Pythagoras adjusted the consonances by the sound of his hammers."
> But if, instead of a distich, we take the four last lines of these barbarous verses, with their true punctuation, thus:
> "Pausa, juncturas, facturas, atque *figuras*
> *Mensuratarum formavit* Franco *notarum;*
> *Et* Ihon De Muris, *variis floruitque figuris.*
> *Anglia cantorum omen* [f. nomen] *gignit plurimorum"*
> they will be found no more to prove John de Muris an Englishman, than Franco, as both contributed to the progress of music in this kingdom; and it may as well be insisted upon, that, because Metastasio has enriched this country with many beautiful songs, he must consequently be a native of England. Indeed, it is difficult to assign any meaning to the last verse; or even to divine what it is "to beget an omen."[107]

Burney's care in citing his personal inspection of treatises which Hawkins only knew by references in other books is an indication of the difference in the preparation of the two writers. Hawkins, for instance, could only quote Morley and other writers on the invention of the minim, as expressed in red notes, by Phillipe de Vitry. Burney was able to enter into evidence his personal copy of Vitry's treatise against the second-hand authority of Morley, Ravenscroft, and Butler.[108]

Burney prints a sample of an early motet from Vitry's period that was originally published by Gerbert. Though he finds it "too contemptable [sic] for criticism," and rather pedantically marks all of the parallel fifths and octaves, it is noteworthy that he criticizes the piece because it follows none of the contemporary rules of Franco, Vitry, or de Muris. The survival of such wretched music in the church, after the improvement of the art in secular music, baffled and annoyed him. That the church

> ...ever should have allowed such jargon to disgrace her temples, or pollute the sacred service, and should long prohibit the use of better harmony, when better was found, must make the profane doubt of the infallibility of those councils, by whose decrees the one was received, and the other rejected.[109]

Burney's discussion of the secular vocal music of this period takes a circuitous and often unnecessarily prolix route. He chooses to begin with an essay entitled "Of the Origin of Modern Languages, to which written Melody and Harmony were first applied; and general state of Music till the Invention of Printing about the year 1450." The chapter is far more philological than musicological. Twining, still Burney's collaborator, complained several times that the chapter was too long, and that too much space was "occupied by *language* and *Poets;* and to [o] small a portion by *Music.*"[110] Apparently he was not the only observer who objected to Burney's frequent literary digressions: Twining informed him that "the objection which I have always heard to your first volume, when *any* has been made, has been always that there was too much in it that had nothing to do with music."[111]

Twining recognized the "necessity, or at least, the amusement" of the digressions for the readers "whose *amusement you consult,*" but he was concerned that Burney would be forced to curtail his later discussions "such as will be intelligible and interesting to *all* musical people."[112] Burney, however, was less interested in his "musical people" now than when he began. "Three years as a member of the Streatham Circle, as well as of the most fashionable literary society in London, had done nothing to diminish his desire to appeal to readers who were neither professional musicians nor antiquarians."[113] In many cases verse translations destined for the fourth chapter were actually read at Streatham, and received the approval of Samuel Johnson and Mrs. Thrale. At least two of the illustrious people gathered at Streatham, Johnson and Sir Joshua Reynolds, had no ear for music whatever, and his translations provided one certain way in which Burney could entertain his prestigious friends with what would otherwise seem an unreadable book.[114] Thus, despite Twining's objections, the content of the fourth chapter was dictated by the interests of the polite audience which had played such an important role in shaping the first volume. And since the first three chapters of this second volume are easily as dry and uninteresting to the general reader as the most barren stretches of the first, it is not surprising that Burney determined to develop his fourth chapter sufficiently to compensate his readers, and insure their approbation. His verse adaptations did secure the approval of at least one famous reader: William Mason, the distinguished poet, wrote to him years later that he "was much pleased of your Versions from the Provençal, etc. in your history."[115]

Nonetheless, even Burney seems a bit concerned about the relevance of much of the chapter. After some preparatory remarks on national music—"Of this artless Music, which is best learned in the nursery and street, I shall speak with due reverence hereafter; and at present confine my disquisitions and enquiries to *real Music*"—he begins his chapter by soliciting the understanding of his readers.

> As the origin of Songs and the formation of the language of every country are so nearly coeval, I hope the reader will allow me to bestow a few pages upon a subject, which though it be thought not absolutely necessary for a musical historian to trace, yet it lies so near his path that he can hardly proceed on his way without its being often impressed upon his mind, fortuitously.[116]

Thereafter, many pages pass before music per se finally makes its appearance, with a discussion of the troubadours.[117] Burney believed that, "By singing and writing in a new tongue," that is, Provençal, and by freeing themselves from classical authority in their poetic structure, the troubadours "occasioned a revolution in literature and the human mind." That being the case, as he saw it, he felt free to quote his lengthy verse adaptations in his musical history.[118] Throughout the chapter poetry predominates, and even when music is present, it often seems only a device to introduce his poetic adaptations. His presentation of the "Song from Thibaut, King of Navarre," is an example. The tune is printed in the original notation, then adapted with a bass and an English translation. This seems valid and useful, but it is more difficult to justify the inclusion of six full stanzas of translated text, especially since the last was incomplete in the source. Undaunted, Burney "amplified [it] in English to supply a sufficient number of lines for the melody."[119] Occasionally, his poetic insertions are digressions within digressions, as in his discussion of the lai (or lay), which includes neither musical examples nor even the poetry of the songs. Instead, he quotes six different poetic descriptions of the use of these early secular songs, which tell the reader nothing of their form or style.[120]

Little of the ground Burney was working was new. He was preceded not only by a number of recent studies on early language and poetry, but by Hawkins's work as well. Burney is able to divert his readers with transcriptions of songs found during his own archival research, each "with a base in modern notes to which the translation is adjusted."[121] There is very little similarity between his transcriptions and the originals. His "Fost chausa [*sic*]," for example, regularly barred and accented, bears little resemblance to the original monophonic *Fortz chauza es que tot lo major dan* (ex. 5.3).[122] Even so, his readers must have been pleased by the illusion that they were performing authentic medieval minstrel songs at the spinet or harpsichord. They were probably not disturbed by the modernization of the tunes, a common practice at the time and long thereafter. Most folk tunes of whatever national origin or antiquity were usually published in an adaptation suitable for parlor performance. In settings of this type, presenting first the original and then a more elegant setting, he was able to meet the needs of the scholars among his readers and amuse the dilettantes.[123]

Burney's speculations on the instrumental accompaniment of medieval music reflect the research undertaken on his tours. During his travels he sought to identify precisely the location and time of the origin of counterpoint, as well as the use of the bow for stringed instruments. While he was unable to provide a definitive date for the advent of counterpoint, he did discover archaeological evidence suggesting the first use of the bow in 752 A.D. Surmising the bow to be of much greater antiquity in France than any other country,[124] he provides five illustrations for his discussion drawn from early pottery and sculpture, much as he had anticipated in his *Plan.*

The only polyphonic French music Burney mentions is that of "Guillaume de Machu" (Machaut). He had never seen any of his compositions, and only knew what Abbé Lebeuf had written concerning them.[125] He turned to the newly published history by Jean Benjamin de La Borde, expecting to find an illuminating discussion of polyphony, but was disappointed.[126] He did find a sample of early French polyphony in a British Museum manuscript, which he transcribed. He responded favorably to the result, for "we admire a little Melody in these early productions, as we do of first dawnings of reason in an infant." Although he presented this sample as the only early polyphony in the chapter, he declined to evaluate the "Harmony or Base" because "when the manuscript was unintelligible and conjecture failed me, I supplied deficiencies by modern rules of composition."[127]

Despite the length of his discussion of early French music, its beauties escaped him.[128] Provoked by the disagreeable nature of this music, he compares it with modern French music, discovering similarities which may have been as surprising to contemporary readers as they appear to us.

> Indeed, when they are written in modern characters, accompanied by a base, and the measure is regulated by bars, they remind us of many French airs of the present century, and shew that vocal melody has remained nearly stationary in France, ever since the beginning of the thirteenth century.[129]

The discussion of early French music gave rise to many comments reflecting Burney's prejudice against modern French music, so it is not surprising that his treatment of medieval Italian music inspires many favorable

Ex. 5.3. Burney's Adaptation of "Fortz Chauza"

Ex. 5.3, continued

reflections. The Italian language having "long been universally allowed to be more favourable to singing" than any other—"a language so favourable to *vocal purposes* as to be more musical in itself, when merely *spoken* with purity, than any other in Europe"—the section provides Burney with the opportunity to speak at length about his favorite language, and his three favorite early poets: Dante, Petrarch, and Boccaccio.[130]

Burney's initial discussion concerns the gradual separation of the Italian language from its Latin origins. The French, he notes, began to write in their own language much earlier than the Italians, but French was not brought to perfection until the seventeenth century, while "the writings of the Italians, of the fourteenth century, are still regarded as models of perfection, with respect to diction, and construction."[131] All the nations of Europe had subsequently cultivated their "own language and poetry; but the fruits of none retained their taste and sweetness except the Italian."[132] The bulk of the essay is taken up with descriptions of music, musicians, and "diction" as reflected in his favorite poets. The only actual music introduced is an early example from the *laudi spirituale* repertoire. His example, "Alla Trinita" (i.e., "Alta Trinita"), is fitted with a bass, but, unlike the French examples, is set to the original, untranslated text, perhaps because the Italian was closer to the modern tongue than was Provençal.[133]

Burney uses the poetry of the period chiefly to show "in what rank music was held at this early period, and what use was made of it in polite assemblies."[134] From the writings of Boccaccio, for example, he discerns the existence of two distinct types of music.

> One species of music was a plain, simple and popular melody, generally understood and practised by all persons well educated, on whom nature had bestowed good ears; and the other an elaborate and artificial species of music which professors only or persons of equal genius and application, were able to execute.[135]

The scant mention of instrumental and vocal performers prompted Burney to "deduce" that music was "so simple and inartificial as to require no great abilities or dexterity in the execution."

Burney's discussion of English medieval music was much more circumscribed than that of Continental music. The formation of the English language, and the early poetry, had been amply treated by recent writers of the highest repute who left him with "no excuse for entering upon *that* ground, unless in pursuit of my own game." Yet, he not only had to enter upon their ground, but admits he may occasionally have "accidentally run into them; yet the subjects of our pursuits have been extremely different."[136] He had to work around these writers, as well as Hawkins, who had dealt with the subject extensively; he persevered nevertheless, heeding Twining's advice not to fear covering materials contained in Hawkins's *History* and other works. Yet he remained uncomfortable with the situation.

> In pursuing the history of English Minstrels I am frequently obliged to recount circumstances which have lately been rendered familiar to many of my readers; but these circumstances are such as seem so naturally to belong to my work, that those who peruse it would have cause to complain should they be put to the trouble of seeking them elsewhere. There are certain events which every writer *must* relate, however they may have lost the charms of novelty by frequent repetition; for by omitting them he would be equally absurd with that historian, who in writing the annals of Charles the First, should suppress the circumstance of that unfortunate prince's decapitation, because it has been already so often related.[137]

He was evidently quite constrained by the work of other writers. He gives only three musical examples during the entire discussion of English music, all of which had previously appeared in print. Hawkins printed "Sumer is i Cumen in," and Guido's "Omnes penitus Dissonantias quasi Consonantias includens." The "Song on the Victory at Agincourt 1415" was published by Stafford Smith in his *Collection of ancient English Songs for three and four voices in score.*[138] The appearance of Smith's publication was a particular disappointment to Burney, who had laboriously transcribed the piece at Cambridge.[139] Burney acknowledged Smith but, not being willing to reduce his book "to a mere *Supplement,*" he republished the composition. He promises his readers, moreover, that when he uses the work of other authors, he will "not copy with servility, or without examining the original sources of their acquisitions with my own eyes, which will sometimes perhaps see them in a different light." The different light extended not only to the resolution of difficulties in transcription, but taste as well, and with this in mind Burney altered his editorial technique for this piece: the example is accompanied by footnotes correcting the composition, and suggesting changes.

Only Chaucer's poetry is used to illustrate music and its role in medieval English society. No music from Chaucer's time could be found, but Burney rather bluntly observes that "if we may judge by what has escaped the ravages of time, of a later date, the loss of our musical compositions of this period may be supported without much affliction."[140]

The last portion of this chapter betrays the influence of Hawkins once again. The latter's exhaustive descriptions of manuscripts in the British libraries compelled Burney to review them as well. Burney's discussion is replete with apologies for these dull summations, apologies which pillory Hawkins, though Burney is following his model. It is, he remarks sarcastically, "only in charity to the curious in Music Antiquities" that he reviews these works, in order to deter them from impairing their own eyes and patience "in search of scientific treasures."

Burney attempts to reveal Hawkins's errors whenever possible. Both men, for example, examined the *Quatuor principalia artis musicae* in a manuscript at Oxford. Hawkins, on the authority of Tanner, ascribes it to John Hanboys. Burney, after investigating the manuscript and citing the opinions of other authorities (omitting Hawkins from the list), concludes that there is insufficient evidence to ascribe it to any particular author.[141] Thereafter, Burney delights in mentioning some important manuscripts he discovered at Oxford, which had eluded Hawkins's industrious scavenging in English libraries.[142] But despite his enjoyment at outdoing Hawkins in the location of these manuscripts, Burney expressed a hope that the works "may henceforth remain peaceably on the shelf, without much loss to the art or science of music."[143]

A comparison of the treatment of early English music by Hawkins and Burney reveals distinctly different approaches to the same material. Hawkins, throughout his *History*, is content to cite other authors, hazarding few conjectures. Burney, in contrast, consistently examines the evidence first-hand in an attempt to overturn popular myths and misinterpretations, and to correct errors. This dissimilarity was surely apparent to alert readers of the histories, who no doubt enjoyed Burney's sallies against the accuracy and taste of the antiquarian Hawkins.

Burney knew next to nothing about German medieval music. The four short paragraphs he bestows on it do little more than state the obvious: the Germans must have had some type of music "in their own language, set to melodies formed upon the Guido scale."[144] He was unaware of the meistersinger and minnesinger traditions. Not a single treatise is reviewed nor composition transcribed. He can only close his chapter by promising the Germans "a very considerable share of the honour due to the Cultivators of Harmony, in the subsequent part of this work."[145]

Burney concluded his discussion of music before 1450 with noticeable relief.[146] The last chapter of his second volume—"On the State of Music, from the Invention of Printing till the Middle of the XVth Century"—finally brought him to the "era when the principal materials for musical composition" had all been developed.[147] In contrast to the scant materials with which he had to work in writing of music of earlier periods, he now faced an embarrassment of riches; he no longer had to trod the same path as his predecessors, the difficulty of finding materials was replaced by the much more pleasant task of selecting examples from the many he had collected.

The printed polyphonic music was in part-book form, and as the individual parts meant little, Burney spent many hours scoring compositions, "not only of the same age, but sometimes of the same author." In score, he found, "the eye may compare their several relations at a glance... They must be *scored* before their beauties or defects can be discovered." The obsolete notations presented great difficulties, but he was "determined to speak of no music with which I am unacquainted, or of which I am unable to furnish specimens."[148]

Despite such difficulties, his satisfaction at having at last reached a period of "real music" is evident. Before quitting his second volume, the reader would be shown the riches of the sixteenth century, an era in which church music at least could please discerning readers. Moreover, he was finally able to write the history of "practical musicians" and performers, not just theorists. The former, "however wonderful their powers, are unable, from the transient state of their art, to give permanence to their fame...[but] the reputation of a Theorist is insured by means of books which become obsolete more slowly than musical compositions."[149]

The chapter begins, like so many others, with a delightful collection of reflections ranging from the transient state of music at any period to the need for a well-ordered national library of music, for which he furnishes a plan of classification.[150] The theoretical discussion, which follows, occupies several pages and is more pertinent than the endless analyses of medieval treatises with which earlier chapters had been burdened. At last theory could be applied directly to music of measurable merit. The reader is taken systematically through problems in note values, ligatures, and prolations with sufficient thoroughness to instruct them in the fundamentals of reading early printed music.[151] A discussion of harmony, dissonances and their treatment, and fugues is given before Burney's first analysis of a composition, so that the reader may understand his critical precepts. Each discussion is sufficiently clear to instruct his "Top o' the Spinet" readers, especially that regarding discords and resolutions.[152]

With his reader thus prepared, Burney began the first portion of his *History* for which he displays any genuine enthusiasm. From this point forward his writing reflects the traditional divisions of church, chamber, and theater, and his critical precepts for each are best considered under their individual headings.

6
Sacred Music: The Domain of Counterpoint

Burney's public evaluation of a musical composition was generally directed to its merits rather than its deficiencies, thus an understanding of his stylistic requisites becomes essential to the interpretation of his criticism. He was guided by a set of precepts which specified the qualities he felt were appropriate to the distinct styles of music for the church, theatre, and chamber. These guidelines designate certain qualities as absolute for each style, and also state, or at least imply, an ideal balance of those attributes. In church music the most important attribute was propriety. Sacred music was always to be distinguishable from secular.

> In *Church Music,* whether jubilation, humility, sorrow or contrition are to be expressed, the words will enable the critic to judge; but the degree of dignity, gravity, force and originality of the composition, few but professors can judge in detail, though all of general effect.[1]

The earliest sacred music, chant and early polyphony, had propriety as its chief virtue. Its "venerability" and exclusive association with the church were in Burney's view its only assets; aside from these merits, he hardly considered chant and early sacred polyphony to be music at all.

Renaissance polyphony was more to his taste and was, in his opinion, the very basis of modern music. The study of this music presented some difficulty to a musician trained exclusively in the modern style, as can be gathered from Thomas Twining's lament on his own studies of the sacred music of this period:

> You, from long habit, have your ear in your eye, and can, perhaps, hear all the effect of complicated harmony by reading it. So can I, tolerably, in modern music, and modern notation; but in this old church music, with its clefs, its points, its unobvious contrivances, its equally-distributed melody—that is, everywhere and no where—its keyless modulations and its discretionary supplement of flats and sharps, etc.—in this music I can do nothing but at a keyed instrument; and even so I cannot with much readiness get through the harmony.[2]

The earliest sacred music "in parts" Burney knew from first-hand examination was that of Johannes Ockeghem. It is uncertain how much of Ockeghem's music Burney knew, and his judgment would certainly be affected by the music available to him. Most of his essay on Ockeghem's music concerns the riddle canons. He clearly delights in his ability to solve the difficult canons (although one of the solutions he presents is incorrect), and informs his readers at length of his struggles. It is probably not coincidental that he uses a canon published by Hawkins (who also erred in his solution, and compounded his mistake by misreading the prolation signs).[3]

Burney's evaluation of Ockeghem's music is curiously noncommittal. The only truly critical comment he makes is directed generally at the music of the late fifteenth century:

> These compositions are given rather as specimens of a determined spirit of patient perseverance, than as models of imitation. In music, different from all other arts, learning and labour seem to have preceded taste and invention, from both which the times under consideration are still very remote. But as the chants of the church were the ground-work of all composition at this period, the ears of the congregation seem to have been less consulted than the eye of the performer, who was to solve canonical mysteries, and discover latent beauties of ingenuity and contrivance, about which the hearers were indifferent, provided the general harmony was pleasing. However, the performer's attention was kept on the stretch, and perhaps he gained, in mental amusement, what was wanting in sensual.[4]

The earliest music in which Burney discoverd both mental and sensual amusement was that of Josquin des Prez. With notable enthusiasm he declares that Josquin is the inventor of the "true and genuine style of choral composition" a hundred years before the "great musical illuminaries of the sixteenth century": Palestrina, Orlando di Lasso, Tallis, and William Byrd.[5] It is remarkable that Burney became so enamoured of this music. It had been, in part, Sir John Hawkins's comment about the superiority of early music over that of the eighteenth century which initially provoked Burney into writing a history of music. Yet, in the light of the beauties of Josquin's music, he modifies his position and credits Ockeghem and Josquin with creating the "Augustan Age" at least of the "elaborate and learned" style of composition.[6] Twining relates the process through which Burney passed:

> In your last letter you told me how it stole upon you as you studied it, after a long intermission perhaps, and, from some prejudices against it, brought you to relish its real beauties and be its apologist.[7]

There were many beauties to be found in Josquin's masses, but it was the motets that Burney came to admire most. These were not based on borrowed tunes as were the masses, but were "composed on subjects of his own invention," and displayed a "style more clear and pleasing." In Josquin's motets, especially his *Miserere a 5,* Burney found the "model of choral composition, without instruments."[8] His enumeration of the attributes of this composition echo the precepts for church music from his "Essay on Musical Criticism": "the subjects of the fugue and imitation are simple, and free from secular levity; the style is grave and reverential; the harmony pure; the imitations are ingenious."[9]

His remarks on Josquin's *Misericordias Domini* are curious. In his review he draws attention to two "points" (i.e., contrapuntal subjects) which remind him of subjects from Handel and Corelli. He goes so far as to say that one served as a "Model to Corelli."[10] It is extraordinary that Burney would be struck by such details in music of diverse styles. The passages to which he refers are easily located, but it is doubtful that the relationship would strike the ears of a modern musician (exx. 6.1 and 6.2). Comparisons such as these between styles may seem of dubious value today, but at the time, Twining regarded them as "among the most valuable parts" of Burney's work.[11]

In Josquin's music Burney discerned "little Air or Melody," but he also found that this defect was amply compensated to "Contrapuntists, and lovers of Choral Music, by purity of harmony, and ingenuity of design."[12] The importance of "pure harmony" in this style is apparent in Burney's examples and his accompanying notes. He printed a number of the examples with figured bass numerals inserted at various points to highlight dissonance treatment or unusual progressions.[13] Audacious but acceptable harmonic combinations receive particular notice,[14] and though perhaps questionable from a purely pedantic view, were judged acceptable if they did not offend the ear.[15] Progressions which seemed remarkably modern are also noted. For example, the cadence *"alla moderna"* in e minor from Benedictus Ducis's *In Josquinum a prato* is cited as "beautiful and unexpected." The modernity of the cadence is due to the *ficta,* which Burney carefully justifies. The F♯ in the tenor is needed to prevent a "false fifth with the B in the Base; and a D♯ in the Soprano, as a major third to that same B, previous to its falling a fifth" (ex. 6.3).[16] Technical insights such as these mark the beginning of Burney's presentation of a genuine history of musical style.

Burney's delight in Josquin's ingenuity of design is evident throughout his discussion. He gives a number of examples from Josquin's *ouvere,* all of which contain canons. Captivated by the elaborate contrivance and contrapuntal gamesmanship of this music, he entered into its spirit fully. Citing Josquin's four visual proportions from the *Missa di dadi,* he suggests another proportion which the composer could have used to complete the faces of the die (ex. 6.4).[17] The reader is invited to join in this pleasant, if learned, diversion: after giving several hints to the solution of his two prolation canons, he leaves it "to the sagacity of his readers to work out the solutions."[18] He doubtless anticipated that his "musical readers" would be as "drawn on and amused by the author's ingenious and curious contrivances" as he was.[19]

Ex. 6.1. Josquin: "Misericordias Domini"

Ex. 6.2a. Josquin's Point as Used by Handel

Ex. 6.2b. Josquin's Point as Used by Corelli

130   Sacred Music

Ex. 6.3.   Cadence *"alla moderna"*

Ex. 6.4.   Josquin: *Missa di dadi,* Die Faces

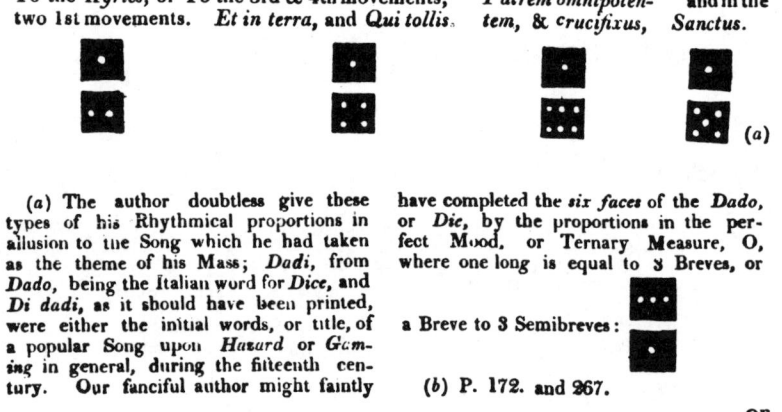

(*a*) The author doubtless give these types of his Rhythmical proportions in allusion to the Song which he had taken as the theme of his Mass; *Dadi,* from *Dado,* being the Italian word for *Dice,* and *Di dadi,* as it should have been printed, were either the initial words, or title, of a popular Song upon *Hazard* or *Gaming* in general, during the fifteenth century. Our fanciful author might faintly have completed the *six faces* of the *Dado,* or *Die,* by the proportions in the perfect Mood, or Ternary Measure, O, where one long is equal to 3 Breves, or a Breve to 3 Semibreves:

(*b*) P. 172. and 267.

or

    A number of the examples of Josquin's music are printed with editorial additions of *musica ficta,* though some are printed without chromatic alterations. When he does indicate *ficta,* the accidentals are printed on the staff without editorial brackets. Under only one of the examples does Burney note that "no accidental Flats or Sharps occur in the ancient Copy," and, suggesting something of the subjective nature of the markings, he remarks that "those which are inserted will not satisfy every Musical Reader."[20] There is room for discussion of some of his choices, but it is easy to justify all of his decisions according to the generally accepted rules governing *ficta* procedures. Although he failed to distinguish his *ficta* from printed accidentals in the *History,* he was not insensitive to their significance. The original manuscript examples of these pieces in his "Extracts" in the British Museum show the *ficta* marked in red, in contrast to the black notation.[21]

In Josquin's work Burney found music he could admire. His enthusiasm was communicated to Twining, who, after reviewing the manuscript of this chapter, responded in part:

> As religious music, I really think we have had nothing comparable to it since. And more than that may be said in its praise; but you have said it all so well, and in such unison with my own ideas of the matter, in your apology for this old music, that I can do no more than refer you to yourself—vide Burneium. As for Master Josquin, I go all length with you; he was an admirable fellow, and I had no conception that such harmony existed near a century before Palestrina. Surely there is nothing of this last composer superior in richness, sweetness, clearness of harmony, and ingenuity of contrivance to Josquin's Misericordias Domini—is there? There is even contrast too, which the moderns think they have all to themselves; for he throws in passages of beautiful simplicity and stable solemnity in the midst of all his art and complication.[22]

Burney's approval of Josquin's music was not unlimited; the parody masses built on secular tunes violated the very propriety which was the chief merit of sacred music. He is adamant that music for sacred purposes should only be constructed on suitable melodies.

> That Chants, and the Canto Fermo, to which the Hymns of the Church had been sung for many ages, should be made the subject, or basis of Counterpoint, in the Church, had something of piety and propriety in it, which would naturally silence censure, and incline the heads and rulers of ecclesiastical rites to excuse, if not encourage the attempt; but when Composers polluted pious ears with the light and contaminated strains of the vulgar and licentious, most profanely adapted to humble supplications, Hymns of praise, or sacred injunctions, the sentiments of which must be perpetually driven from the minds of the congregation, by the frequent repetition of these profane fragments, in all the several parts of a Chorus, they abuse the privilege they had obtained of harmonizing the Chants, and discovered an egregious want of understanding, decorum, and reverence, for the religious rite which they were appointed to direct.[23]

Josquin was, for his time, "the type of all Musical excellence," and his contemporaries, as Burney saw them, "appear to have been but his imitators."[24] He awards to Josquin his most exalted label: that of *original genius*.[25] It is rewarding to have Burney's assurance that "these [Josquin's] productions are not only precious from their age and scarcity, but intrinsic worth."[26]

Burney's reviews of the other composers of Josquin's era are brief. Since he had explained Josquin as the *originator* of a style, he felt "less need be said of his contemporaries, who appear to have been but his imitators." Although he appreciated the beauties of their music, and general characteristics of their style he did not grasp the more subtle stylistic points that distinguish the works of one composer from another. The music of the era seemed in general to be written in a clean, clear, and masterly counterpoint, but he found his examples, "so much resemble each other, that the specimens already given exhibit almost all the variety of melody and pleasure which the productions of a whole century can furnish."[27] Nonetheless, his qualitative evaluations differ. Antoine Brumel, for example, did not display "much invention"; however, his harmony in general, was "pure and melody and notation more clear and simple than was common in the period when he flourished."[28] Philippe Bassiron, in contrast, wrote much which was "dry, awkward, and devoid of invention and contrivance."[29] Jean Mouton similarly failed to impress Burney.[30]

Burney's "apology" for Continental Renaissance sacred music, which so pleased Twining, is worthy of quotation.

> This species of laboured composition has been frequently censured, and stigmatized by name of pedantry, and Gothic barbarism, which, perhaps, it would now deserve, out of the Church; but in the time of Josquin, when there was little melody, and no grace in the arrangement, or measure of single notes; the science of harmony, or ingenuity of contrivance in the combination of simultaneous Sounds, or music in parts, as it was the chief employment of the Student, and ambition of the Composer, so the merit of both, and the degree of regard bestowed upon them by posterity, should be proportioned to their success, in what was their chief object, and not in what had no existence at the time in which these musicians lived. Another apology offers itself for Josquin, as well as for his scholars and followers, who composed for the Church: which is, that pure harmony, and contrivance, are less favorable to that kind of levity which is inseparable from Airs clothed with little harmony, which seem unfit for the gravity of Ecclesiastical purposes.[31]

Burney attempted to organize his discussion of sacred music of this period by national schools, but the international style of the fifteenth century, and the mobility of the composers of this time, prevented him from so doing. He expected to find that the Italians excelled in this style, as they had throughout history, but as inclined as he was "to celebrate the activity, talents, enthusiasm and success" of the Italians, he found instead that the best contrapuntists were foreigners. "Tinctor was at the head of the Neapolitan school, and Josquin of the Roman,"[32] and Isaac was the chief luminary of Florence. Outside of Italy, the situation was no clearer. Burney was unable, for example, to assign Pierre de la Rue and Philippe Bassiron to any school, and he assigns Antoine Brumel, Antoine de Fevin, and Gaspar van Weerbecke to the French school, despite their diverse nationalities.

The nationalities of composers working in England posed no such problems, but Burney's discussion of early English sacred music was circumscribed by the unavailability of the music. He knew the names of Lionel Power, Pasche, and others from Morley's treatise, but was able to find only fragments of their music. The earliest collection he used in this part of his work was a set of part books located at Oxford that contained masses and services to Latin words dating from before the Reformation. From these he studied the music of John Taverner, Dr. Fayrfax, Avery Burton, John Marbeck, William Kasar, Hugh Aston, Thomas Ashwell, John Norman, John Shepherd, and Dr.

Tye.[33] He found "an appearance of national originality, free from all limitations of the choral productions of the Continent."[34] The national originality, however, was due in substantial part to the paucity of features which most redeemed Josquin's music, apparently because the arts of "Canon, Inversion, Augmentation or Diminution" were not yet practiced by these composers. Burney was not pleased by the results of his long hours spent studying the works of the English School.

> I have scored several Movements of such Masses and Services of our old masters, as were composed to Latin words, before the Reformation; but must confess, that the reward I received for my labour was very inconsiderable. Indeed, none of the rules of Harmony are violated, by these venerable Contrapuntists, but there is such a total want of Design, Subject, Melody, and attention to the Accent and Meaning of the Words, that the Notes seem to be thrown upon paper at random; nor could they be more devoid of meaning, if the sounds of such keys as these pieces are written in, had issued from a mill, or been ballotted for in the Laputan manner.[35]

Burney had Sir John Hawkins's work very much on his mind as he wrote about the music of this period. Several times he diverts his attention to Hawkins's writings, especially the note to Walton's *Angler* which so provoked him.[36] Burney took the same list from Morley's *Introduction* which Hawkins quoted so favorably and, using this list as a foil,[37] he severely censures each of the composers admired by Hawkins. Burney's comments could not be directed specifically against Hawkins's critical view, since Hawkins almost never makes a real judgment about individual compositions in his discussion of music. Rather, Hawkins typically writes short biographical notices of each composer accompanied by musical examples. These are often printed without comment, leaving the reader to make of them what he will. Burney, in contrast, prefers to present judgments and opinions along with his musical examples,[38] and often omits biographical data entirely (at least in this chapter).

From this point forward the historical method of the two men clearly diverges. Both had begun chronicling what was known of early history by drawing upon other people's opinions and historical documents. Hawkins continues using this technique, now itemizing composers as, previously, he had the chapters of treatises. Burney, on the other hand, begins a history of musical style, carefully drawing his reader's attention to the merits of composers through his examples, and tracing the advancement of musical history and literature toward excellence.

Although Burney had now freed himself from the necessity of repeating material used in Hawkins's *History,* he continues to build parts of the *History* around his rival's book. He actually mentions Hawkins several times—never favorably—and once directly criticizes his taste and knowledge. He takes special exception to Hawkins's discussion of John Shepherd. Challenging

Hawkins's assessment as well as his knowledge of Shepherd's music, he implicitly attacks his taste:

> If we were to judge of JOHN SHEPARD [sic] by a specimen that has lately been given of his abilities, he would seem the most clumsy Contrapuntist of them all, and not only appear to be less dexterious in expressing his ideas, but to have fewer ideas to express; yet, in scoring a Movement by this author, from a set of MS. books, belonging to Christ-Church College, Oxon, he appears to me superior to any Composer of Henry the Eighth's reign...
> This shews the fallacy and injustice of determining an author's character by a single production; of whom, when more can be found, the best should be chosen.[39]

Of all the composers active before the Reformation in England—that is setting Latin texts (Burney's guide to dating this music)—he found merit only in the works of Robert Johnson and Robert Parsons. The former "disposed his parts with intelligence and design," and displayed "considerable art and ingenuity, in the manner of treating subjects of Fugue and imitation." The latter constructed rich and "curious harmony and modulation."[40] His praise is bestowed upon the two composers who wrote works more strictly contrapuntal than those of their contemporaries: without learned contrivance there was little to commend this style.

With the exception of Josquin's, Burney found music throughout pre-Reformation Europe to be similar in type and merit:

> Before the Reformation, as there was but *one* religion, there was but *one* kind of music in Europe, which was Plain Chant, and the discant built upon that foundation; and as this music was likewise *only* applied to *one* language, the Latin, it accounts for the Compositions of Italy, France, Spain, Germany, Flanders, and England, keeping pace with each other, in style and excellence.[41]

Through the increasing international commerce of the sixteenth century, Burney believed musical style was "communicated to every part of Europe; which not only stimulated the natives to adopt and imitate them, but to improve and render them more difficult by their own inventions and refinements."[42] The style common to all Europe was thus diffused, and began its separate development in each land. This rationale allows Burney to return to his original plan of tracing the history of music in each country separately[43]— an approach he adopts as he commences his third volume.

The Reformation left England with two legal and proper sacred musics: metrical psalmody, modeled after Continental practice, and the full choral service. Burney dutifully chronicles the rise of metrical psalmody as the music of the reformed church, but it is a music he disavows at every turn. He credits the early reformers of church music, among them Luther, Calvin, and John Knox, of "stripping it of all the energy and embellishments of measure and melody."[44] If metrical psalmody had any merit, it was its "venerability" and solemnity of effect, which totally precluded every idea of secular music[45]—very much the same, and very limited, virtue he found in Gregorian chant. He did find evidence of skill in harmony in some of these simple settings,[46] but even this single merit was lost, at least in contemporary services, because of the generally intolerable performances.

> Lovers of mere harmony might receive great pleasure from Metrical Psalmody, in parts, devoid as it is of musical measure, and syllabic quantity, if it were well performed; but that so seldom happens, that the greatest blessing to lovers of Music in a parish-church, is to have an organ in it sufficiently powerful to render the voices of the clerk, and of those who join in his *out-cry,* wholly inaudible. Indeed all reverence of the Psalms seems to be lost by the wretched manner in which they are usually sung; for, instead of promoting piety and edification, they only excite contempt and ridicule in the principal part of the congregation, who disdain to join, though they are obliged to hear, this indecorous jargon.[47]

One of those who supported metrical psalmody was William Mason, the well-known clergyman, composer, poet, and author of *Essays, Historical and Critical, on English Church Music.*[48] Burney's involvement with Mason and his work is an interesting case study, indicative not only of his attitude toward this "dull subject of unisonous and metrical psalmody," but also of Burney's public and private demeanor in professional matters. Burney had known Mason since 1764 and publicly referred to him as "as good as Musician or Painter as Poet" and a man of excellent taste in modern music.[49] Burney read the manuscript of Mason's *Essays* and provided the author with some suggestions for improving the work. Mason expressed his gratitude by sending Burney the only gratis copy given when it was published. Burney, in return, sent him a long and tactful letter with suggested alterations and corrections for the second edition.[50]

Publicly in the *History* Burney referred to the *Essays* as excellent, but he also reviewed the book for the *Monthly Review* in an unsigned article, giving it a rather less favorable assessment. His review is polite, but considerably more critical than his comments in the *History* or in his letter to Mason. The review states in part:

> In Mr. Mason's new way of stringing the harp of David, [i.e. reforming sacred music] not only air but science is to be banished from the church. In our old ecclesiastical music, *learning* and *ingenuity* made us amends for want of air, and even accent; and musicians might well be alarmed, if Mr. M. were supposed to be as good a judge of musical as of poetical composition: but *their craft,* we trust, will not be in much danger, beyond York cathedral, though he attacks the *citadel* of choral music as boldly as if he headed an army of ecclesiastics from the council of Trent... Whether our gifted poet's recipe for composing church music will not be thought too methodistical for any thing but parochial psalmodists, we know not; it will come with weight from so eminent a writer: but it seems likely to put an extinguisher on all genius and ingenuity in our church composers, if adopted wholly and exclusively.[51]

In the guise of anonymity the reviewer notes that "Dr. Burney, it seems is not so partial (in his history of music) to parochial psalmody as Mr. M. wishes; and here an amicable controversy begins."[52] Their controversy, so long as it was carried on openly, was amicable, but as the review demonstrates, Burney could be considerably less agreeable when his identity was protected.

Burney ends his discussion of metrical psalmody in the *History* with the blunt pronouncement that "it is time to speak of a superior species of Church-Music," that species being the cathedral service. His source for most of the music he discusses is William Boyce's *Cathedral Music*,[53] a choice which allowed him to assume that many of his readers would have access to scores of the music under consideration.[54] He gives a prominent place to Robert White, whom Boyce overlooked, a composer who preceded Byrd and Tallis, and who was an "excellent composer in the style of Palestrina."[55] The fact that Hawkins dismissed White in one sentence and could not distinguish Matthew from Robert White, may have influenced Burney's selection.[56] In any case, Burney devotes most of his attention to Thomas Tallis and William Byrd. These two composers, he wrote, could be called the "fathers of our genuine and national Sacred Music," not only because they were the earliest competent composers, but because their works continued to be performed.[57]

The music of Tallis, Byrd, and some of their contemporaries marked an epoch of which Englishmen could be justly proud. It was the single period of which Burney would allow that "no choral compositions in other parts of Europe, of equal antiquity," could be found "superior to those which have been preserved of these authors, the pride of our country, and honour of their profession."[58] Indeed, when Padre Martini asked him in 1770 to name the "English School," Burney began his list with John Tally (i.e., Thomas Tallis), William Byrd, and Thomas Morley. The merits of Tallis's music—"gravity of style, purity of harmony, ingenuity of design, and clear and masterly contexture—exactly matched Burney's concept of perfection in sacred music. He even ventures to suggest that if any music other than Handel's were included in the Annual Congress of Musicians concert, Tallis's "Song of Forty Parts" [Spem in alium], "a stupendous, though perhaps Gothic, specimen of human labour and intellect... and others of Tallis, Bird, Gibbons and Purcell, should have the advantage of such a correct and numerous choral band."[59]

Such an observation may surprise scholars who view Burney as an irresponsible advocate of all that was then new and novel. In sacred music, he was quite conservative. This is not surprising, since English churches continued to present the choral masterpieces of the sixteenth and seventeenth centuries. The Academy of Ancient Music (founded 1710) and the Concerts of Ancient Music (founded 1776) are often cited as early examples of English historicism. These concerts represent only a secular manifestation of the long tradition of performing venerable music during sacred services. Boyce's printed collection and other manuscript collections enshrined this tradition, but it is evident that there was also a living tradition of performing this music as a regular part of the worship service. The tradition was so strong, and the music of Byrd so well known to his readers from Boyce's collection and the "admirable [musical] monuments still remain[ing] in all our cathedrals," that Burney felt it unnecessary to publish examples.[60]

Undoubtedly this same tradition played a dominant role in the formation of Burney's taste. Against this background, his claim that "at all times in my life I honoured an elaborate and learned composition for the Church, whatever its age and country, and at all spare hours I was scoring pieces of Bird, Morley, Luca Marenzio, Stradella; and studying Palestrina" takes on new credence. It is difficult to speculate about when or how Burney came into possession of music by Marenzio, Stradella, or even Palestrina, but music by Byrd and Morley was right at hand.

Burney's discussion of Thomas Morley's compositions is interesting primarily because of two immense footnotes that are actually longer than the entire text to which they are appended. The first note is a review of Morley's *Plaine and Easie Introduction to Practicall Musicke*. Its inclusion was provoked by the recent reprinting of the treatise. It alarmed Burney that, in the absence of any more recent book, students of composition might seriously study Morley's book:

> It has been my wish constantly to do justice to the learning and contrivance of old masters, and to recommend the study and performance of their works to my readers as curious and historical specimens of the best Music of their own times; but not as the sole studies and models of perfection to *young* professors, who wish to please, prosper, and are expected to keep pace with modern improvements. To such I would *first* recommend the study of the best *modern* authors; and then, as matters of curiosity and amusement, to enquire into the productions, and genius of former times, in order to extend their knowledge and views, and prevent embarrassment or surprize, whenever they happen to be called upon to perform or speak of such works.[61]

Burney recommends the examination of music in score as "... of infinitely more service to a student, than the perusal of all the books on the subject of Music that were written during the sixteenth and seventeenth centuries."[62] Even for its time, Morley's *Introduction* did not impress Burney. Morley, Burney found, was often "not very nice or accurate" in his examples given as models of excellence, and Burney devotes considerable space to demonstrating his faults.

The other lengthy footnote[63] is a detailed analysis of Morley's *Burial Service*, a piece Burney had heard in 1760 at the furneral of King George II. This note shows the kind of useful technical analysis Burney could have employed throughout his *History* had he thought it suitable to his audience. He not only analyzes the music, but makes suggestions on improving the piece by rewriting the text. Unfortunately for readers today, Burney felt discussions of this type were useful only to professors of music, not a general audience, and he is seldom so minute in his evaluations.

Burney's treatment of sixteenth-century Continental composers need detain us only briefly. Inevitably he wrote at length about Palestrina, but his account does not credit Palestrina with the invention of a style. Rather, Burney is slightly equivocal, stating only that Palestrina "brought his style to such perfection that, the best compositions for the church since his time are proverbially said to be *alla Palestrina*."[64] He refrained from giving examples of the music by other Italian composers, since they seemed to be so similar in style. He confessed his confusion to Ebeling in a letter:

> The rest of Italy [outside of Rome] has a series of Able Composers for the church, but to characterize their different styles would be no easy Matter, as every Age has its *mode* of composition, which 2 or 3 original geniusses [sic] at most render prevalent. The rest come all under the denomination Imitatores, servum, pecus.[65]

As a consequence, much of the chapter on Italian music is about secular music.

While it is unfair, and not particularly useful, to criticize Burney's *History* for what it does *not* contain, it is equally inappropriate to fail to note consistent omissions. The chapter on German music in the sixteenth century is only eleven pages long—a good deal longer than the single footnote in which he dismissed the German minstrel tradition, but only slightly more informative. Burney attempts to pass some of the responsibility for his failure to write an adequate history of this period on to the German people by claiming that the "Germans seem as fickle in their taste as the Italian," and more willing to neglect their old masters.[66] He has virtually nothing to say, but regards it his "duty [as] an historian to record, at least the names of artists who were once dear to their contemporaries."[67] Thus the chapter is little more than a list of Latin treatises published in Germany. No musical examples are given, nor does he mention the Netherlandish and Italian musicians who supplied much of the music for the courts, despite his acknowledgment that:

> In the Elector of Bavaria's Collection of Music during the sixteenth century, the most complete in Europe, among innumerable Italian composers, there are many works preserved by German masters, of that period.[68]

Burney's discussion of sacred music in France is equally limited, though the chapter on French music of this period in general is quite extensive. Burney's bias against modern French music seems to taint his treatment of sixteenth-century French music. He dismisses the music of France, remarking: "The inhabitants of this kingdom, though ever active in the cultivation of the arts, made small progress in any of them, if we except war, during the sixteenth century."[69] France simply lacked the "internal peace and domestic tranquility" which in Burney's view were necessary to the cultivation of the arts.[70] He seems preoccupied also with demonstrating the superiority of his book over La Borde's *Essai sur la musique*.[71] La Borde—"a very diligent and patriotic enquirer after every species of Music that can do honour to his country"— clearly disappointed Burney as a resource for his investigation of the music of this period. He found that he was sometimes better prepared than the Frenchman. He was able to print a *Noel* by Eusache du Caurroy, which La Borde knew "only by tradition."[72] Besides this *Noel* and one motet, sacred music is mentioned only in lists of titles. Burney was aware of the foreign composers active in France, and had chronicled the development of French psalm settings earlier in the volume, but most of this chapter is given over to secular music.

There was little information available to Burney about the music of sixteenth-century Spain. His deductions about the excellence of the music of Spain are based on the parallel phenomena of the emigrant Italian musicians of his own time:

> ...If we judge by the musicians it furnished to the Papal Chapel, both composers and singers, we may conclude, that the richest and most powerful nation in Europe as Spain then was, would not breed slaves as the Africans do slaves or Circassians women, merely to transport them for the use or pleasure of others; they could doubtless then have afforded to keep a few for their own amusement.[73]

The brevity of his discussion of Cristobal de Morales is not due to the unavailability of his music; Burney transcribed two motets and a magnificat in his "Extracts." Yet the chapter is largely a catalog of musical works, offered apparently, to refute Hawkins's observation that the Spaniards made *"a slow progress"* in music.[74]

Burney's treatment of "Music in the Netherlands in the XVI Century" is both amusing and revealing. He does not subscribe to the Franco-Flemish concept of musical style: instead, he sees the French as avaricious usurpers of Flemish musical excellence. He seems to regard the proponents of the Franco-Flemish school as conspirators, stating that "Flemish and French musicians are so constantly confounded *by the natives of France* in their musical writings, that few readers are able to separate them."[75] Since an effort on his part to overturn the claims of the French "would perhaps appear invidious," he declines to do so, leaving the nations involved to settle the "right to appropriation."[76]

He discusses very little sacred music in the chapter, despite his acknowledgment of the excellence he found in the works of earlier Netherlandish composers. He does, however, compare the styles of Cipriano de Rore and Orlando di Lasso to that of Palestrina, finding their works "much" inferior to those of Palestrina in *a cappella* settings. "Their attempts to be grave and solemn created only dull and heavy music; ... What is unaffected dignity in the Roman, is little better than the strut of dwarfs upon stilts in the Netherlanders."[77] He then ascribes this difference to the Netherlandish composers having spent the "chief part of their time in the courts of princes," and thereby acquiring a "lighter and more secular cast of melody."

Burney admired the *a cappella* style, but gives little of its chronology. Once he notes the establishment of style in the late fifteenth and early sixteenth centuries, his discussion veers off toward secular vocal music. In this style, which is freed from the conservatism of the church, he felt better able to trace the development of style and expression.

His evaluations of sixteenth-century sacred music are consistent with the precepts contained in his "Essay on Musical Criticism." Sacred music from this period did not, however, contain all of music's beauties:

> Taste, rhythm, accent, and grace, must not be sought for in this kind of Music; indeed we might as well censure the ancient Greeks for not writing in English, as the composers of the sixteenth century for their deficiency in these particulars, which having then no existence, even in idea, could not be wanted or expected; and it is necessarily the business of artists to cultivate and refine what is in the greatest esteem among the best judges of their own nation and times. And these, at this period, unanimously thought every species of musical composition below criticism, except canons and fugues. Indeed what is generally understood by taste in Music, must ever be an abomination in the church; for as it consists in new refinements or arrangements of notes, it would be construed into innovation, however meritorious, till consecrated by age; thus the favorite points and passages in the madrigals of the sixteenth century, were in the seventeenth received as orthodox in the church; as those of the opera songs and cantatas of the seventeenth century are used by the gravest and most pious ecclesiastical composers of the eighteenth.[78]

On the other hand, he was considerably less tolerant of this same style when employed in secular music.

> To check Imaginations's wild vagaries and restrain her wanton flights ... when addressed to the Divinity; during the celebration of sacred rites in the temple, is not only required by propriety, but duty. Yet, as the confining Music merely to religious purposes borders on fanaticism, so the treating of secular and light subjects with ecclesiastical gravity; making a fugue of every movement, and regarding grace, elegance, and fertility of invention, as criminal, or, at best, as frivolous, are equally proofs of want of taste, and want of candour.[79]

Burney's chapters on seventeenth century music lack the tolerance he extended to even the most ordinary of sixteenth-century music *alla Palestrina*. When he initially surveyed the materials for the chapter on music in England, for example, he wrote to Twining that except for a few compositions for the church by Pelham Humfrey, Wise, and Blow, all music "from Orlando Gibbons to Purcell [is] unmeaning, dull and despicable."[80] Although in print he is more circumspect, he does not hide his low opinion of most seventeenth-century English music.

Indeed, amidst many dull and worthless secular productions, the *Church* was furnished with some good compositions; but these, it is to be feared, will only prove, that such Music may be produced at all times with less genius than that which requires imagination, as well as science, to support it; as it depends more on mechanical rules and labour than invention.[81]

Nonetheless, Burney writes a very detailed and extensive chapter on English music, in which cathedral music has a substantial place. Apparently his firsthand examination of the music somewhat ameliorated his initial unequivocal condemnation, for he was able to praise William Child for his "remarkably easy and natural" style, and modulation, which, at the distance of time, struck him as solemn, having a "seemingly new effect on our ears."[82]

The civil war and the interregnum, in Burney's view, dealt a "grievous wound to sacred Music, not only checking its cultivation, but annihilating as much as possible the means of restoring it."[83] So thorough was the destruction that "when the heads of the church set about re-establishing the cathedral service, it was equally difficult to find instruments, performers, books and singers able to do the requisite duty."[84] This view has since been substantially discredited,[85] but to Burney the disruption accounted for the dismal state of music until the establishment by Charles II of the Chapel Royal.

In light of Burney's statement to Twining, that Humfrey, Wise, and Blow were three exceptions to the otherwise dismal state of music in the seventeenth century in England, his harsh assessment of John Blow's sacred music is initially surprising. The kindest sentence he wrote was "Though there are strokes of pathetic, and subjects of fugue in Blow's works that are admirable; yet I have examined not one of them that appears to be wholly unexceptional, and free from confusion and crudities in the counterpoint."[86] In support of his severe criticism, he includes one of his most extensive examples: his famous "Specimens of Dr. Blow's Crudities."[87] There have been various modern attempts to explain Burney's criticism of Blow as indicative of an absolute misunderstanding of seventeenth century style.[88] Watkin Shaw's statement that Burney's strictures were "undiscerning," and that "Burney was simply making Blow the scapegoat for typical seventeenth-century [harmonic] procedures which the eighteenth century considered bad manners" is typical.[89] Such generalizations overlook Burney's very clear discernment of merit in Blow's contemporaries. He says of Humfrey, for example,

> ... he seems to have been the first of our ecclesiastical composers who had the least idea of musical pathos in the expression of words, implying supplication or complaint.
>   His anthem for three voices, *Have mercy upon me O God,* has great merit on the side of expression, for the time in which it was composed, as well as harmony, in which there are several combinations that seem new and boldly hazarded for the first time, at least in choral Music.
>   In his verse anthems, many new effects are produced by modulation and notes of taste and expression.[90]

Moreover, in a footnote to this passage Burney acknowledges that a harmonic progression which he finds offensive "appears in all the composers of the last century; and yet I never can let it pass uncensured."[91] His evaluation of Michael Wise's music likewise stands in refutation of Shaw's assertion:

> The first movement of his verse anthem for two voices, "The ways of Zion do mourn," is so beautiful and expressive, that I shall give it here as a specimen of grave and pathetic composition for the church, which no Music of other countries that I have hitherto discovered, of the same kind, and period of time, surpasses. The use the author has made of chromatic intervals at the word mourn, is not only happy and masterly, but new, even now, at more than a hundred years distance from the time when the anthem was produced! The whole composition seems to me admirable; and besides the intelligence and merit of the design, the melody is truly plaintive, and capable of the most touching and elegant expression of the greatest singers of modern times; the harmony too and modulation are such as correspond with the sense of the words, and enforce their expression.[92]

Burney, then, was not as insensitive to the stylistic features of this music as his critics assert. His footnote to this article complains of several harmonic effects, but he concedes that "The sharp third and flat sixth so frequently occur in all the composers of this school, that it is endless to stigmatize this hateful combination any further."[93] He was, moreover, sensitive to the evanescence of taste, and to the prejudices of modern musicians. After criticizing the "passing notes and embellishments" of this period as "uncouth in melody and licentious in harmony," he observes, "Perhaps those of the present times, in less than a century, will be equally unpleasing to the ears of posterity; and yet we fancy that both melody and harmony have received their last polish."[94]

It is clearly incorrect to term Burney's criticism of Blow as "undiscerning," or as an over-enthusiastic attack on the style of the period in general. He distinguished between the harmonic practices of that era and his own, and accepted or rejected elements of the idiom as they struck him. Blow's "crudities" were to Burney's ears exceptional, and beneath the general level of his contemporaries. Burney was aware of and somewhat defensive about the force of his criticism.

> I am as sorry to see, as to say, how confused and inaccurate a harmonist he was; but as it is necessary to speak of an artist so celebrated and honoured by his contemporaries, to dissemble his faults would surpass candour, and incur the censure of ignorance and partiality; for it is as much the duty of an historian to blame as to praise, when justice and integrity require it. Indeed, upon whatever subject a man writes, he should aspire at nothing so much as speaking truth, if he wishes for the approbation of his conscience, which is not only the most comfortable of all praise, but luckily the most within his own power. The abilities of the dead, I can have no interest in depreciating; and if my opinion should be unjust, the mischief will recoil on myself; for the dead have more friends than the living, who are ever ready to vindicate such wrongs.[95]

It was in "justification of so much seemingly severe censure of Dr. Blow's counterpoint" that Burney allotted so many expensive engraved examples. He praised Blow's extraordinary harmony when it produced good effects, but he found much which was indefensible to the ear and the eye.[96] The care which Burney lavished on the preparation, presentation, and defense of his analysis is extraordinary. Many other composers had been dismissed in earlier pages as vulgar or inept without hesitation. Blow, however, was famous even in the eighteenth century, and had inexplicably (to Burney) been praised by Boyce in his *Cathedral Music*. Nonetheless, it is probably to Sir John Hawkins's evaluation that "among church musicians he has few equals and scarce any superior" that Burney's essay is addressed. Burney's methodical presentation of the evidence of Blow's barbarisms may well have been calculated to explode, once and for all, Hawkins's credibility as a critic.[97]

In his dutiful trudging through the music of seventeenth-century England, there seems to have been only one compensation: his discovery of the music of Henry Purcell. His enthusiasm is best displayed, not in the *History*, but in a letter to Twining written at the time of this discovery.

> ... Are you much acquainted with Purcell? If you are not, for heaven's sake! get every note you possibly can of his, *curled* and *uncurled*—why 'tis another Haydn. In the midst of barbarians, in savage times, before an opera, an opera singer, or the works of Corelli had been heard on the Island, to have such resources of force and expression, is more wonderful than that Haydn, who with his own property has incorporated the best of all others during the present century, should be so perfect, so bewitching and Charming!!!—I shall speak of Purcell from an *actual survey*, or *review* of all his works, consisting first of his *Church Music*, or Anthems and Services... —these, with his Printed *Te Deum*, form a large body of Church Music, of a more expressive and varied kind than I have ever seen of any Composer, of any Country. Palestrina was Grave, Sweet, and sublime in his way; but it was all in *one* way. Carissimi and Stradella, more constantly elegant and polished than Purcell; but with less feeling and variety. Handel more grand, masterly, full, and flowing; but by no means so original, so impassioned, so superior to Art and study, yet at times discovering the effects of the deepest labour and Meditation. Purcell's *Expression of English words* must I think frequently make Englishmen feel what Handel with all his Harmonical resources could never arrive at. At least he frequently *shivers* me: makes my hair creep, and gives me sensations beyond those of the utmost elegance and refinement.[98]

Such adulation notwithstanding, Burney is not uncritical of Purcell's music. In general he censures the same type of "errors" he found in the music of Blow, Humfrey, and Wise: footnotes record errors in text setting, cross-relations, unusual harmony and improper resolution of dissonance.[99] This criticism may have been motivated by his concern that Purcell's music might become a model of imitation by young composers:

> Purcell is so classical a composer for the Church, that his harmonical licenses become authority, and may lead young students into error. It is right therefore, to specify the places... which are most likely to offend cultivated ears at present.[100]

Sacred Music

In England the natural development of music in the seventeenth century had been disrupted by violent changes in society; no such upheaval affecting music occurred in Italy, and the learned and elaborate style continued to be cultivated.

> Yet a revolution in favor of melody and expression was preparing, even in Sacred Music, by the success of dramatic composition, consisting of recitation and melodies for a single voice, which now began to be preferred to Music of many parts, in which canons, fugues, and full harmony were the productions which chiefly employed the master's study and hearer's attention.[101]

Burney dutifully chronicles the most eminent of the masters "in the style of the preceding century," but he is obviously anxious to move on to the development of the cantata and oratorio. The difference between the styles is that to the pure harmony and elaborate contrivance of the polyphonic style, "the best moderns have added melody, a more varied modulation, and not only attention to the long and short syllables, but to the expression of words."[102] In addition, the clear establishment of tonality over modality and the overthrow of what we now distinguish as the *stilo antico,* released imagination from the bonds of pedantry. So limiting had been the rules of counterpoint that "an excellent composition might now be produced, merely from ancient disallowances."[103] Upon reaching the point in history when this revolution in style was achieved, Burney's patience with the old style vanished. He held to a new ideal for sacred music. This style, found in the cantata and oratorio, did not merely "flatter the ear," but was one in which "gleeful, pathetic, and pleasing melody was united with pure harmony and ingenious contrivance ... touch[ing] the heart."[104]

Setting aside the history of the oratorio in the seventeenth century for his last volume, Burney summarily examined the progress of church music in Germany and France during that century in two surprisingly brief chapters. Although he notes that in Germany the "Lutheran religion, as well as the Roman Catholic" were favorable to ecclesiastical music, he virtually omits any discussion of sacred music or its composers.[105] He does provide a catalog of "the most celebrated organists" of Germany, which includes Schein, Scheidt, and Schütz, but no mention is made of the sacred concertos, historia, or chorale settings. One is struck once again with how little early German music Burney knew, at least from the first three quarters of the century. His apology—"So few productions of the numerous German composers of the last century are now to be found"—underscores his priorities as collector and scholar of the early history first of Italy, then England, France, and lastly Germany.

The sacred music of France in the seventeenth century occupies Burney for a single paragraph; he records the names of Boisset and Couteaux, apparently on the authority of La Borde. Indeed, French music as a whole would probably have been as sparsely treated as that of Germany in Burney's writings, were it not for the close cultural ties between England and France, and the vast amount of literature on the music of France available to him, especially the comparatively recent *Essai sur la musique* by La Borde.

The final chapter of the third volume, "Progress of Church Music in England after the death of Purcell," carries Burney's discussion of cathedral music to the death of John Stanley, only three years before the volume was published. Burney's anxiety about criticizing musicians who lived during or shortly before his own time is apparent. Hoping to minimize unfavorable reaction to his judgments, he vowed to "assign specific reasons for censure or panegyric." He also promised to examine only "such movements as, upon recent examination, have appeared to me the most excellent."[106] This is in keeping with his basic critical philosophy of praising what is worthy and overlooking the rest.

Burney, like most historians, found it far more difficult to "mount up" to the period under examination when it was so close to his own. The discussion of music of the early part of his own century or slightly before shows his attitude toward a music that was antiquated but which had persisted into his own era. His familiarity with the style increased his confidence in his ability to judge the compositions, yet its very familiarity betrayed him into consistently applying a modern aesthetic in his evaluation without consideration of the changes in style and taste in the decades since its composition. The results of this are evident in his evaluation of the anthems of William Croft, some of which Burney had played in his youth, but had long since set aside. He now saw these pieces with new eyes.[107]

Burney perceived Croft's anthems to have been strongly influenced by Corelli. He cites the third movement of one of these anthems as "so much in the style of Corelli (see his first solo) that it is difficult not to imagine the author had it in mind when he set to work" (ex. 6.5).[108] In Croft's anthem *Out of the Deep,* the movement "Therefore shalt thou be feared" struck Burney as "in the style of Corelli's sarabands; at least I do not recollect such a regular motion of the base to an air in $\frac{3}{2}$ in our English Church Music previous to the publication of his works" (ex. 6.6).[109] Indeed, he sees Corelli as not only having supplied models for emulation, but also having proscribed certain previously acceptable methods, such as the "fall from D♯ to G-natural, which has never been practised by good contrapuntists since Corelli's works have been known"(ex. 6.7).[110] The subject of the influence of Corelli on English musical taste and practice is not expanded upon elsewhere in the *History;* no musical revolution in England is mentioned in the article on Corelli, though Burney's inference is undeniable in these passages.

Beyond citing Corelli's influence, Burney subjects Croft's music to the same criticism as that of Purcell: pointed notice is taken of errors in counterpoint and harmony. Burney anticipates that readers who are interested in this type of detailed analysis will have Croft's *Musica Sacra* at hand, and he

Ex. 6.5. Croft: "In the Style of Corelli"

Ex. 6.6. Croft: "In the Style of Corelli's Sarabands"

Ex. 6.7. Croft: Harmonic Licence

identifies errors by page, line, and measure number in this work. For example, in his "Song unto God" (ex. 6.8), Burney notes the following:

> Line first, bar sixth, the seventh in the treble, not good in itself, is not to be found in the accompaniment as figured by the author. [a] Line fourth, bar second, the base, in two parts, not good. [b] Line fifth, bar first, the base falling a superfluous or redundant fifth is awkward and unnecessary, as B would have led to A much better, without changing the harmony.[111]

Ex. 6.8.   Croft: "Song Unto God"

Ex. 6.8a

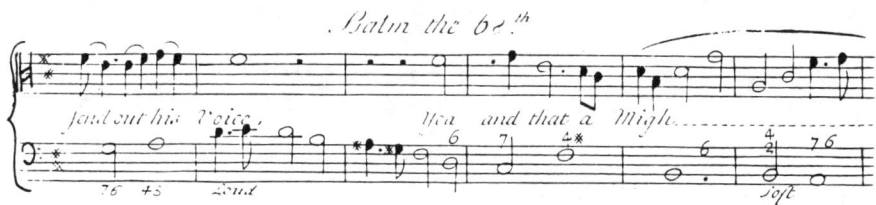

Ex. 6.8b

Ex. 6.8c

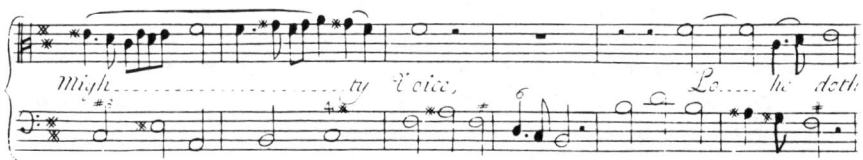

Burney's strictness, which some may be tempted to call pedantry, does not preclude his appreciation of justifiable breaches of technical rules, such as the parallel octaves which occur in the last line of the chorus in Croft's *O Lord Rebuke Me Not,* which Burney calls "one of the most masterly and grand compositions of the kind, which our church, or any other church, can boast." These parallel perfect consonances he ruled may be "easily pardoned, in so many parts, by a good contrapuntist, for the sake of imitations."[112]

148   Sacred Music

Most of Burney's criticisms concern the general value of Croft's music—new, masterly, laboured, etc.—and, in discussions of sacred music, the propriety of music for the church service. Thus, even an anthem such as *Sing Unto the Lord,* in which Burney found little to commend, was "at least entitled to the merit of propriety."[113] Movements containing excessively long divisions or patterns which struck him as too secular are censured as "bordering too much on theatrical levity" (exx. 6.9 and 6.10).

Ex. 6.9.   Croft: Theatrical Levities

Maurice Greene, a contemporary of Croft, was another composer guilty of excessive levity in his sacred music. His most "flagrant" faults were his light divisions, with which "his solo anthems abound, and the repetition of passages a note higher or a note lower in what the Italians call *Rosalia.*"[114] Burney's criticism of the last anthem of Greene's *Forty Select Anthems* in score will serve as a condensed but representative sample of the treatment received by a composer whose eclectic style lacks propriety.

> The last anthem of this volume is made up of common play-house passages; the first movement is heavy and monotonous; the andantes tiresome, by the repetitions of an old harpsichord-lesson passage in the base; the chorus justifies Mr. Mason's censure of this author, by too long and frequent divisions; these are too vulgar and riotous for the church, and, indeed, would have no merit of novelty any where. The vivace, page 151, upon which the last chorus is built, has more of the dancing-minuet, or Vauxhall song, in it, than belong to that species of gravity and dignity which befits devotion. I think I could neither play nor hear this movement in a church, without feeling ashamed of its impropriety.[115]

Ex. 6.10. Croft: Theatrical Levities

Greene's anthem is not very impressive. Taking passages from the score one can, in the spirit of "Blow's crudities," construct a plate showing "Greene's Improprieties," to illustrate Burney's criticism (ex. 6.11). It is in his comments about the propriety of musical settings that Burney seems less than sympathetic to the changes of taste and fashion which affect musical style.

Croft's and Greene's excesses were those of another age, but one very close to Burney's own, too close apparently for him to be forgiving or understanding. He was also, of course, shaping the taste of his readers. The very detailed technical reviews Burney wrote of the music of Croft, Greene, and their contemporaries served to strengthen his position as a critic, and lent credence to his evaluations of composers for whom he did not give detailed criticism.[116]

As Burney reviews the work of composers closer to his own generation he becomes more discreet in his criticism. For example, William Boyce, whose music was easily accessible for detailed criticism, receives only a short biography and brief encomium for his merit as a composer of great originality. Even less is said about the merit of John Stanley, "a natural and agreeable composer," although Burney records in a personal note that he was "a most intelligent and agreeable companion."[117] Burney was clearly unwilling to offend the family or friends of those living or recently deceased by genuinely critical appraisals. From the distance of centuries this is unfortunate, but at the time Burney found it necessary.

The fourth volume of the *History* is almost exclusively devoted to dramatic music, encompassing serious and comic opera, sacred and secular

150   Sacred Music

cantatas, and the oratorio. All of these forms have the use of recitative in common, and it is for this reason that Burney considers them together in the fourth volume. In addition, the oratorio was often very close to opera in other aspects of style as well, and occasionally the only discernible difference between the two forms was the presentation of the oratorios without costume or staging.[118]

Ex. 6.11.   Greene's Improprieties

a.   Heavy and monotonous

b.   Tiresome

c. **Vulgar and riotous**

152 Sacred Music

d. Dancing minuet

Much of the seventeenth-century portion of Burney's chapter, "Rise and Progress of the Sacred Musical Drama, or Oratorio," consists of a catalogue of titles and dates, since very little music was available to him. Libretti were easier to locate than scores, and as a result much of this chapter merely records the dates and the places of performances of works he never examined. He is able to give a scene and chorus Emilio del Cavaliere but apparently the next earliest score he possessed was of a Stradella oratorio. His account of Stradella's untitled oratorio, which was set to music "superior to any similar production of the time," is curious.[119] As he wrote, Burney had before him a rare manuscript score, yet he gives a scene-by-scene criticism which could have had little meaning to his readers who were unable to refer to the music. Burney recognized the logical objections of his readers to his detailed review of inaccessible music, and apologetically noted, "Interested and surprised as I was by the new and unexpected beauties of Stradella's composition, compared with those of his contemporaries, it is to be feared that those who have them not before their eyes, or who compare them with modern productions, will think my account of this oratorio too long."[120] They may have questioned its inclusion altogether.

In Stradella's music Burney found "the germe [sic] of many favourite compositions produced after his death."[121] In "Se nel ben" he discovered that "the natural and clear style of vocal melody appears, which was afterwards much improved by Hasse and Vinci." Burney further credits Stradella with furnishing "the comic motivo, which Pergolesi afterwards perfected in the duet of his *Serva Padrona* in his 'Se Poma Filli.' " He was also "convinced that Purcell made him [Stradella] his model; not in detail, in order to imitate his passages, but general style of composition."[122] When Burney encounters a fugue, his comments reveal the depth of his admiration for Stradella and show that, though he did not consider fugual writing to be truly dramatic, in the church he could still allow it merit.

> This kind of writing is certainly not dramatic, but though it is often Gothic and dull, in the hands of composers of limited abilities, yet when a Carissimi, a Stradella, a Purcell or Handel writes a fugue on any subject, it becomes interesting to every master and judge of good composition.[123]

Stradella is one of Burney's original geniuses, though he does not so label him in this essay. Stradella's works were the first in a new tradition, and these served as models to other composers who adapted his ideas to their own style.

One of Burney's special interests in his survey of early oratorio was the development of the chorus, but he was frustrated by his failure to find examples. Of those that were available, none "anterior to Handel" struck him as worthy. He had great expectations for the choruses of Caldara's oratorios, and was disappointed at being unable to procure a single example from which to judge,[124] particularly since he had seen some of Caldara's masses and motets, and found them very suitable for the church, with their "gravity of style, pure harmony, learning, facility, and correctness in the texture of the parts."[125] This list contains all of the attributes that Burney insisted upon in church music of earlier times, but with the addition in the new style of facility.

Naturally, the works of Handel were the models against which Burney and all other Englishmen measured oratorios. Burney's journal preserves his reflections on the oratorios he heard while in Italy.

> But for this kind of music, that of Handel will, I believe, ever stand superior to all other writers; at least I have heard nothing yet on the continent of equal force and effect. There is often in the composition of others, more melody in the solo parts, more delicacy, more light and shade, but as to harmony and contrivance, no one comes near him by many degrees. I must confess that I had heard some of Handel's music so long, and often so ill performed, that I was somewhat tired and disgusted with it; but my Italian journey, instead of lowering the esteem which I ever had for the best writings of that truly great artist, exalted them in my opinion, and at my return renewed my pleasure in hearing them performed. As yet I had heard little but church music in Italy; however, in that stile, *with instruments,* all other compositions appeared feeble by comparison [with Handel]. The subjects of the fugues were, in general, trivial and common, and the manner of working them dry and artless. Indeed the church stile, without instruments, except the organ, was well known in Italy, and all over Europe, long before Handel's time; and melody is certainly much refined since: it is more graceful, more pathetic, and even more gay; but for counterpoint, fugues, and chorusses of many voices, *with instruments,* I repeat it, I neither have heard, nor do I ever expect to hear him equalled.[126]

Of course, even during his tour Burney was aware of the necessity of favoring Handel in order to avoid alienating a substantial and influential part of his audience,[127] but his late writings show that his admiration for Handel's choruses was genuine.[128]

The concern which Burney always manifested for the sensibilities of the Handelians during the years in which he was establishing his career was sharply increased in 1784 when he was in the midst of writing his last two volumes. In order to illustrate Burney's writings on Handel's sacred music and indeed his criticism of all music contemporary to Handel and even later, it is necessary to digress from the analysis of the *History* to examine the conditions under which Burney wrote at this time.

In 1784 some of England's most influential men of rank and title who concerned themselves with musical matters proposed a magnificent festival to commemorate what they thought was the centenary of Handel's birth (it was later discovered that he was born in 1685, not 1684). The board of directors was to be the same as that directing the Concert of Ancient Music, an important series of subscription concerts dedicated to playing early music (this, by their definition, was music more than twenty years old: in practice the concerts consisted almost exclusively of Handel's music). The king himself was a patron and director of the concerts, and was thus also a director of the Handel festival.[129]

Burney, though not a director of the concerts, was involved in the planning of the event, but by his own admission he was not influential, perhaps because he had great doubts about the efficacy of a performance to be given by more than 500 musicians. He was certainly able to use his masterful skills of accommodation during the five or six dinners at which he had little to do but "to stuff—drink—and be witness to the importance and blunders of the directors."[130] His doubts proved to be ill-founded. The five days of concerts under the direction of Joah Bates were an unqualified success; indeed, the Commemoration of Handel was regarded as the greatest musical event of the century. With belated enthusiasm Burney was struck with the idea of writing a commemorative pamphlet of the event. Not only did the directors approve of the plan, but the king remarked that he was glad such a project was being undertaken, and that he wished to see it in manuscript as it was written. The king was true to his word, and as each section was written it was promptly transcribed on gilt paper and taken by a court page for the king's perusal.[131]

The king's interest was initially welcomed by Burney, who was still anxious to attain some further royal appointment at court. It soon became apparent, though, that the price Burney would pay for this royal notice would be high. The king's musical taste proved to be even more limited than he had imagined—so much so that Burney wrote to his friend Thomas Twining,

Sacred Music 155

> I see that I am in great danger of doing myself more harm than good by this Business—however circumspectly I may Act. But I will not write like an Apostate—I will not deny my liberal principles—I will not abuse the lovers of the best Music of Italy & Germany, and say that they are only admired *though fashion,* and want of good taste and judgment.[132]

Not only was the king to be pleased, Joah Bates, the conductor of the Commemoration, also exerted considerable pressure upon Burney as he worked. Burney was decidedly uncomfortable with his situation:

> I wish there was any other mediator than B.—whom I perceive no praise either of himself or Handel can satisfy—and the K. is full as *intoleratingly* fond of the old Saxon as B.—so that, if I was to act *politically* and *wisely,* I should openly abuse all other Music, Musicians, and lovers of Music in all parts of the world, but Handel and his insatiable and exclusive admirers ... Into what a Scrape am I got?—I may do myself irreparable mischief—and *can* I fear derive no good—considering the hands I am in.[133]

The king did not scruple to make suggestions when he felt Burney's critical judgment missed the mark. Two surviving examples stand in evidence of the extent to which the king suborned Burney's criticism. Fanny Burney, indulging her boundless vanity for whatever increased the prestige of her family, saved and published two notes from George III which contained "suggestions." The significance of the two notes to her father's reputation as a critic presumably escaped her.

The first note is harmless enough, and shows only that Burney was willing to entertain royal preferences when they concurred with his own.[134]

The consequences of the king's second suggestion are much more alarming. The king wrote:

> Dr. Burney seems to forget the great merit of the choral fugue, "He trusteth in God," by asserting that the words would admit of no stroke of passion. Now the real truth is, that the words contain a manifest presumption and impertinence, which Handel has, in the most masterly manner, taken advantage of.[135]

It is hardly likely that Burney "forgot" the merit of the fugue. The king's note suggests that Burney had criticized the chorus for not being sufficiently dramatic: Burney's final version expresses admiration for the very quality he found wanting in his initial criticism:

> The words of the admirable choral fugue: *"He trusted in God that he would deliver him; let him deliver him if he delight in him,"* (Matth. xxvii. 43. and Psal. xxii. 8.), which contain the triumphal insolence, and are prophetic of the contumelious language of the Jews, during the crucifixion of our Saviour, were very difficult to express; however, Handel, availing himself in the most masterly manner of the advantage of fugue and imitation, has given them the effect, not of the taunts and presumption of an individual, but the scoffs and scorn of a confused multitude.

Not only did Burney prudently adopt this suggestion, he also transcribed almost verbatim into the publication an anecdote which the king included in his note.[136]

Burney's capitulation, in this instance, certainly casts doubt upon the reliability of the opinions voiced in the *Account of the Commemoration of Handel,* and his willingness to accept ideas so contrary to his own may have implications for the credibility of his other writings as well.

We must not be too harsh with Burney. Even a man less concerned about the attitudes of the powerful could have done little else in the face of royal influence. The circumstances afforded would hardly have permitted a candid assessment of Handel's music. The book, which was dedicated to the king (and kings were, after all, kings) amounted to an official commemorative program, one destined for the hands of those who were *a priori* ardent admirers of Handel. Yet, rather than acquiesce completely, Burney fell back on his technique of praising "honestly and heartily what he admired and remaining silent about the rest." As the king's note evinces, however, this approach did not always succeed. His capitulation to the Handelians must have caused Burney great concern for his reputation with the substantial portion of the English musical society which was not Handelian in its taste.

One must, then, interpret Burney's criticism of Handel with circumspection. The circumstances under which the *Account* was written were extraordinary and warrant particular care in interpreting Burney's criticism in that source, but he was never free from the practical necessity of carefully considering his audience, particularly when writing about Handel. In writing the history of the oratorio he must have remembered more than once that the oratorio was the king's favorite species of music.

Burney considered oratorios to be essentially dramatic works. His designation of oratorios as *Sacred Dramas* was natural enough for an Englishman, since oratorios were customarily performed in theatrical environments in England.[137] He was not unaware of the hybrid nature of the oratorio; he recognized the dominance of the theatrical style, but nonetheless insisted on the propriety of the music in oratorios on religious subjects. He complained, for example, that in modern Italian oratorios the airs were too often "in a frivolous, light and improper Style for the words to which they were set, as well as for the general Subject of a Sacred Drama."[138] He appreciated many aspects of the airs in the modern style, particularly their great delicacy and contrast. Many of Handel's airs by comparison seemed to him obsolete. By frequent imitation and performance they had become "common," and time had "rendered many of them ungraceful and even uncouth [sic]." These criticisms were written in private; he was never so explicitly critical of Handel in print.

He expected to find the influence of the true church style in the oratorio choruses. Here the emphasis was to be more musical than theatrical. Burney expected to "listen with wonder at the knowledge, contrivance, art of fugue, or richness of harmony" with which they abounded.[139] When he found drama of a type more akin to that of the theatre, such as in the chorus "He comes, he comes to end our woes" from Handel's *Esther,* he was not censorious, though he does note the exception to the common practice.[140]

Burney did not consider the literal musical imitation of motion, natural sounds, or other extra-musical associations to be an appropriate dramatic device. He criticizes Cavalli for doing this, noting, "The trying to express the sense of single words and phrases instead of the general sentiment and spirit of a whole verse of stanza, is a vice of very early date."[141] He leveled the same criticism at Johann Mattheson, who, he says, went to "the infinite trouble" to make the notes on the printed page form a rainbow for that word: "The rainbow story," he says, "may serve as a specimen of Mattheson's taste and judgment with respect to the propriety of musical expression and imitation."[142]

Handel used the same kind of literal depiction, but Burney did not criticize him for doing so. For example, he writes of Handel's "All we like sheep have gone astray; we have turned every one to his own way": "This chorus has a spirit, and beauty of composition of quite a different kind [from "And with his stripes we are healed"]: the base is *costretto,* and moving incessantly in quavers, while the voice parts and violins express a roving, careless kind of pastoral wildness, which is very characteristic of the words."[143] However, it is quite likely that Handel's meandering melodic line on the word "strayed" and the extensive *rosalia* on "turned" struck him as inappropriate or at best naïve.

Burney was particularly concerned with text setting and occasionally found that Handel's music was deficient in this aspect. Since the composer was a foreigner, his pronunciation was inaccurate, and it is to this that Burney attributes his faulty accentuation in setting English words to music. In his "Essay of the Euphony or Sweetness of Languages and their Fitness for Music," Burney states:

> There could be no better guide for a composer of songs, with respect to accentuation, than reading them [the words] first, and afterwards giving only long notes and accents to such words and syllables as require emphasis and energy in the utterance.[144]

By this rule he found that Handel's "He was despised and rejected of men" was very inaccurately accented, and suggested that it be reset (ex. 6.12).

Burney criticizes Handel's accentuation throughout the *Account.* He cites, for example, Handel's setting of the word "delivered" as a disyllable, rather than a trisyllable.[145] His setting of "Sing ye to the Lord" from *Israel in Egypt* is criticised for producing the accentuation "Fŏr hĕ hāth trīumphed gloriously," but the criticism is softened by the observation that in 1738 "our language was not very familiar to him; and he had then but little experience in setting it to Music."[146] The *Messiah,* then as now the best known and loved of Handel's oratorios, is cited for several errors of this type, including the monosyllabic

Ex. 6.12. Burney's Correction of Handel's "He was Despised and Rejected of Men," *Messiah*

(*b*) If we try Handel's admirable and justly celebrated air, as Music, in the Messiah, "*He was despised and rejected of men*," by this rule, it will be found very inaccurately accented. In reading, the accents would certainly be these:- Hĕ wăs dĕspīsĕd ănd rĕjēctĕd ŏf mēn; ă măn ŏf sŏrrŏw, ănd ăcquăintĕd wĭth grĭef; or in musical notes:

Now Handel's accents are: He was despised and rejected, &c.

settings of "cryeth" in the recitative to "Comfort ye my people" and "glory" in "And the glory of the Lord," and the trisyllabic setting of "surely" in "Surely He hath born our grief."

Burney also suggests that Handel's occasional "economies" of self-borrowing might account for some of his errors, for "he often applied words to Music, instead of Music to words; taking from its niche or his port-folio, a movement already composed."[147] This, Burney proposed, is "perhaps" the case with "And the glory of the Lord." However, he does not allow textual considerations to disturb his enjoyment of the music; despite the errors cited in "And the glory of the Lord," he calls it "an excellent composition" which "had a fine effect in the performance."[148] Moreover, after offering a correction, by expanding "blessing and honour, glory and power" from a three to a five-syllable phrase, Burney apologizes for such strictures:

> This little defect would certainly not have been pointed out here, had it not been with the wish of indicating an apology for it, and a cure. In future editions and manuscripts of so classical a production, it seems necessary to recommend the correction of this and a few other similar inaccuracies, lest mere verbal critics, laying too much stress on such trivial defects, should endeavour to diminish the glory of the author and his work. And, indeed, however slight or unimportant such oversights may be to lovers of Music, to mere grammarians and philologers, they appear unpardonable.[149]

One of the great objections of the "*genuine* enemies of counterpoint" was that fugal writing obviated proper text setting because the words were often unintelligible. Burney agreed, suggesting:

> When the verse of a Psalm or Hymn is set in fugue, if the part that leads off the subject were to pronounce the whole verse or sentence, to complete the sense before the answer is introduced, it would perhaps obviate the objection that is made to this ingenious species of composition, on account of the confusion occasioned by the several parts singing different words at the same time.[150]

Burney found merit in Handel's treatment of texts in fugal choruses, many of which follow this pattern: "His yoke is easy," "For unto us a child is born," and many others either present the entire text in a single voice before the fugal answer, or introduce the second line of text in a clear statement midway in the movement, after which the polyphonic texture rebuilds.

Unfortunately, Burney is never so explicit in his remarks on the musical substance of Handel's works. Remarks such as "admirable in fugue, modulation, and counterpoint" do little to inform the modern critic of the precise features which elicited the praise, especially when the same critical vocabulary is applied to movements of widely different character, harmonic structure, and texture.[151] Burney does, however, occasionally identify ingenious or unusual devices which he feels are successful. Twice he mentions cadences which he calls "sublime and truly ecclesiastic." In both instances the cadence is the same: a major chord on the flat seventh of a key (E♭ in F): this, he says, "carries us again to the sixteenth century."[152] He admired the cadence only in sacred compositions, because

> The laws of liason, or relation which have since been established, have banished this modulation from secular Music; but in the Church, when sparingly used, it is not only admirable but productive of fine effects.[153]

The same kind of historical perspective is evident in his remarks on "Sing ye to the Lord" from *Israel in Egypt*.[154] The "sober chanting kind of counter-subject" of the fugue struck Burney in its similarity to William Byrd's *Non nobis Domine*. The rhythmic structure of Handel's theme is entirely different from Byrd's, but the pattern of a conjunct ascending and descending fourth is the same. He does not speculate as to whether the relationship "was taken with design," but admired Handel's setting because "the notes are happily selected, and ingeniously used." Burney's perception is not as naïve as the relation he postulated might suggest: he notes that though tradition, in England at least, attributes the original pattern to Byrd, he has found the same passage in Zarlino and Adrian Willaert, and it is "one of the different species of tetrachord, used by the Greeks, in the highest antiquity."

Burney's criticism of Handel's oratorios emphasizes the need for contrast both within movements and complete compositions. Burney found many of Handel's choruses rich in contrast, particularly "Glory to God," which he said had more *claire obscure* "than perhaps had ever been attempted at the time it was composed." He also admired the contrast produced by alternating small and large groups, such as in "Lift up your heads, o ye Gates,"[155] or the "semi-chorus" "Since by man came death," followed by the full chorus "By man came also the Resurrection of the dead," then the semi-chorus "For as in Adam all die," and the closing full chorus "Even so in Christ."

The effect of contrast in these movements "alternately sung with and without instruments, was so agreeable and striking," that he "wished more frequent use was made of such an easy expedient."[156] Other contrasts were obtained by clearly differentiated subjects, such as those found in the "Hallelujah Chorus." The subject "And he shall reign for ever and ever" Burney calls "the most pleasing and fertile that has ever been invented since the art of fugue was first cultivated." Its principal asset is its contrast with its subordinate themes: "It is marked, and constantly to be distinguished through all the parts, accompaniment, counter-subjects and contrivances, with which it is charged."[157] Contrast could also be achieved through the alternation of polyphonic and homophonic settings within a chorus. "For unto us a child is born," with its powerful homophonic statements "wonderful, counselor, the mighty God, the everlasting Father," Burney called "poetry of the highest class" in music.[158]

Once familiar with Burney's view of Handel, and the circumstances under which the *Account* was written, it is a great temptation to read in criticism where none may exist. His comments about many of the movements performed during the commemoration are succinct, indicating perhaps that the music satisfied him, or perhaps, having nothing good to say, he said little. For example, what is one to make of his comment regarding "But who may abide the day of his coming?": "The Air is in a Sicilian pastoral style, of which Handel was very fond, and in which he was almost always successful."[159]

It is apparently not possible to determine which of the three versions of "But who may abide" was performed at the commemoration. One of the versions is indeed in 3/8 meter throughout; where the modern listener expects the dramatic change of meter and accompaniment that heralds the setting of "for he is like a refiner's fire," this form of the aria is animated only by an elaborate *rosalia* on the word "fire" and divisions in the bass accompaniment.[160] If Burney heard either of the two versions with the strong contrast of the prestissimo written in common time, with its highly animated accompaniment, it seems unlikely that he would have dismissed it as "in the pastoral Sicilian style." Whatever the case, he was certainly not impressed with the drama of the movement. Perhaps his actual opinion was akin to that of the anonymous author of *An Examination of the Oratorios which have been Performed this Season at the Covent Garden Theatre* (1763):

> The next song too, of *But who may abide the day of his coming,* had it been properly expressed by music, might have imprinted on the soul the most awful reverence of that great day it alludes to; but, as it stands at present, has little merit or no effect. The concluding words, *He is like a refiner's fire,* afford little room for musical expression; and though the music is in general good in itself, yet the divisions on *appeareth, a, refiner's,* are puerile, and very much debase the rest.[161]

The enthusiasm for Handel's *Messiah* generated by the 1784 commemoration concerts provided Burney with an opportunity to put Hawkins in a particularly bad light. Hawkins had written of Handel's *Messiah:*

"the airs contained in it were greatly inferior to most of his operas,"[162] an evaluation which Burney counters with "It would not be difficult to point out eight or ten Airs of peculiar merit in this Oratorio; among which, '*Every Valley*—preceded by the accompanied Recitation, *Comfort ye my people*—*He shall feed his flock*—*He was despised*—and *I know that my Redeemer liveth*'—are so excellent, that it would not be easy to find their equals in any one of his Operas or other Oratorios."[163] His opportunistic attack on Hawkins notwithstanding, it is in the criticism of the arias performed at the commemoration that Burney is most vague, perhaps because he was the least pleased with these movements, which, being in the style of Handel's opera songs, were the most dated. Occasionally he let Handel's music pass without comment, choosing instead to praise the performers.[164] Even when one senses that Burney was highly critical of a movement, the criticism is couched in such a way that it is difficult to be certain of his intent. His remarks on "The waves of the sea rage horribly," from the anthem *O Sing Unto the Lord a New Song*, illustrate the difficulty:

> Handel, in the accompaniments of this boisterous air, has tried, not unsuccessfully, to express the turbulence of a tempestuous sea; the style of this kind of Music is not meant to be amiable; but it contrasts well with other movements, and this has a spirit, and even roughness, peculiar to our author.[165]

This passage is devoid of the enthusiasm Burney shows for the most effective descriptive passages in Jommelli's oratorios. We are not told that the music was "picturesque" or "sublime," but merely "turbulent" and "rough," not epithets which Burney uses in sincere praise. The next aria in the same anthem, "O worship the Lord in the beauty of holiness," evoked criticism which, though of a completely different kind, is just as frustratingly vague.

> The solemnity of this movement may, perhaps, seem as much too languid to the admirers of the preceding air, as that may be too turbulent for the nerves of those who are partial to this. The truth is, that both verge a little on the extreme; but a composer, of such extensive powers of invention as Handel, dares every thing, for the sake of variety; and this Duet is much in the admired style of Steffani.[166]

Once again there is an obvious evasion of true criticism of an aria that certainly did not please him.

There is an evident difference in tone between Burney's criticism of Handel's opera arias and his oratorio arias, perhaps in deference to the king's partiality for Handel's oratorios. We are told, for example, that the aria "Sorge infausta una procella," from *Orlando*,

> ...is an Air abounding in that species of ingenious and masterly contrivance, which generally delights the eye and judgment of deep Musicians, much more than the public ear.

> An Opera, however, without such specimens of musical science, is never had in much reverence by professors. But, so changed is the style of Dramatic Music, since Handel's was produced, that almost all his songs seem *scientific*.[167]

Given the close relationship in Burney's mind between oratorio and dramatic composition, there seems little reason not to assume that this criticism reflects on many of Handel's oratorio arias as well, but the *Account* with its biased audience was not the place to express such opinions.

The extent to which Handel's dominance affected other eighteenth-century English musicians has attracted much scholarly interest. Two letters in the Burney papers give first-hand evidence of the constraint the public idolization of Handel had on native composers. In 1784, John Stanley, who was at the peak of his very successful career, holding the position of Master of the King's Band, was approached by Burney with a commission to compose two oratorios. The request was politely refused because of the lack of time, but also because Stanley thought "there is little reason to suppose that any other than Mr. Handel's *Messiah* would succeed. The people in general are so partial to that, that no other Oratorios are very well attended."[168] In a later letter Burney amplifed Stanley's comment to "the public was unwilling to like any other compositions of that kind than those of Handel, though they have heard them so long, that they are heartily tired of them."[169] As has been shown, the same forces that influenced Stanley to reject setting the two new oratorios operated strongly in shaping Burney's treatment of sacred music. As Stanley, Burney had before him the realities of a public which idolized Handel, and a sovereign and dispenser of royal favors who would appreciate no other music. At the time Burney wrote the *Account* he envisaged setting things right in the last volume of the *History*, promising the readers of the *Account* a "critical examination of the entire works of Handel" in that work. However, lack of time and space forced him to forego his promised examination.

Lack of space in the *History* also curtailed Burney's discussion of the oratorio and other sacred music in France, Italy, and Germany. His tours contain some observations of value, as do his reviews for the *Monthly Review* and the article written for the *Cyclopaedia,* but there is nowhere to be found anything approaching a comprehensive history of eighteenth-century Continental sacred music. Of all of the sources, the *Italian Tour* is the most useful in providing insights into Burney's view of modern sacred music. During his tour Burney found two sacred styles: the traditional *a cappella* style, and a modern style, which many thought to be "as light and airy as that of the opera."[170] The modern style differed from opera in only its choruses, which were "long, elaborate, and sometimes well written."[171]

Indeed, Burney says explicitly that all music performed in a church cannot be assumed to be true sacred music:

> I do not call every modern oratorio, mass or motet, *church music;* as the same compositions to different words would do equally well, indeed often better, for the stage. But by *Musica di* [*sic*] *Chiesa,* properly so called, I mean grave and scientific compositions for voices only, of which the excellence consists more in good harmony, learned modulation, and fugues upon ingenious and sober subjects, than in light airs and turbulent accompaniments.[172]

Compositions in this style, such as the one by Antonio Lotti which he had heard at Venice, were in "the true stile for church: it calls to memory nothing vulgar, light or prophane, it disposes the mind to philanthropy, and divests it of its gross and sensual passions."[173] Later recalling the experience, Burney wrote, "We do not remember ever to have received more pleasure from choral music."[174] Music such as Lotti's had, then, the same merit he found in the music of Josquin and Palestrina, although there was some difference: Burney found that one of Lotti's movements "was even capable of expression," and affected him "even to tears," a claim he never made for earlier *musica da chiesa.* Technically most of the music he heard was not *a cappella,* since it was accompanied by the organ, but this did not violate Burney's view of the true church style so long as the organ, or even other instruments, merely doubled the voice parts. Thus, Burney considered Handel's chorus "And with his stripes we are healed" *a cappella,* "as the instruments have no other business assigned to them than that of doubling and enforcing the voice-parts."[175]

Burney's unequivocal definition of the "proper" church style did not preclude his enjoyment of pieces in the modern symphonic style, even in a church. He was favorably impressed by a modern mass by Carlo Monza which he heard at Milan.[176] However, the same day he heard a mass by Giovanni Battista Sammartini and objected to its light style.

> This music would please more if there were fewer notes, and fewer *allegros* in it: but the impetuosity of his genius impels him, in his vocal compositions, to run on in a succession of rapid movements, which in the end fatigue both the performer and the hearers.[177]

He does not specify here that he is objecting to the propriety of this music for use in a church, but years later, when he was not as concerned about offending the partisans of Sammartini, he noted that Sammartini "wrote so fast, that his ecclesiastical compositions were too light and flimsy."[178]

Burney was more pleased with the music in the modern sacred style by Baldassare Galuppi. He met Galuppi at Venice, and heard several of his compositions performed there in the Ospedale dei Incurabile and in St. Mark's Cathedral, at both of which the composer was chapel master. He says that "this ingenious, entertaining, and elegant composer abounds in novelty, spirit, and in delicacy."[179] Galuppi's church music, which was little known in England, he found excellent, though tinctured with operatic style. Just how theatrical Galuppi's music was is evident in Burney's evaluation of the performers: he called the singers "absolute nightingales; they have a facility of executing difficult divisions equal that of birds."[180]

In Galuppi's music Burney found the very best of the Italian style. Nonetheless, his feelings about the propriety of the music in the service of the church is evident. He is, for example, quick to assure his readers that despite the overtly theatrical character of some of Galuppi's music, the composer can also write in the true style; that is, "grave, with good harmony, a good modulation, and fugues well worked out."[181] In addition, Burney goes to the trouble of informing the reader that, though the music was performed in a church (the chapel of the Ospedale), it was not during a sacred service, and the audience sat "as at a concert."

The dichotomy in Burney's view of church music is apparent. On the one hand, Burney as a tourist in a foreign country, listening to a somewhat profane music in a church of a religion quite different from his own, could be quite tolerant. In England, on the other hand, such licentiousness was not acceptable, for there the dispute was still over the propriety of counterpoint in ecclesiastical music. Even in Italian churches there were limits to the admission of secular elements into sacred music, but when the music was as exquisite as that of Galuppi, Hasse, or Jommelli, Burney could be quite liberal. It is not to be forgotten that Burney's experience with sacred Italian music had been limited to study before he left England, and performances in the chamber and concert halls, rather than churches.

Burney averred that there was some excellent modern church music, which he referred to as "*modern* church music *à grand orchestra.*" He found "models worthy of imitation in Hasse, Jommelli, and Perez; these wrote music most worthy of admission, for their gravity and dignity, into the sacred service."[182] It is, unfortunately, very difficult to discern the precise merit of these composers relative to others whom Burney rates highly. Nothing like the detailed analyses of the works of Croft, Greene, and Purcell is to be found in Burney's criticisms of later eighteenth-century musicians (with the exception of Handel). However, one finds lists which expand Burney's triumvirate of "great church composers." The article "Messa" in the *Cyclopaedia* states that "Allessandro Scarlatti, Leo, Pergolesi, Durante, Jomelli, Sacchini, etc. have composed masses, which will be regarded by true judges of composition as masterpieces of the art." Elsewhere, Burney provides a catalogue of worthy composers of sacred music, even suggesting that they could, along with Handel, be played at the Annual Congress of Musicians held in Westminster Abbey:

> There are masses, motets, and psalms, with instrumental accompaniments, by Colonna, Bassani, Steffani, Clari, Lotti, Allessandro Scarlatti, Leo, Duranti, Caldara, Jomelli, Sacchini, Perez, etc. among the Italians; and Fuchs, Sebastian and Emanuel Bach, Graun, Telemann, Hasse, Haydn, Gasman, Rolle, Wolfe, etc. among the Germans; besides our own

> Purcell, Crofts, Greene, Boyce, and many able harmonists of our country, now living, who might contribute toward varying this magnificent exhibition by new productions, and give an opportunity for the best pieces of Handel to be refreshed by rest, which would increase the eagerness of the public to have them revived, and the pleasure with which they would be heard, after being a little forgotten.[183]

Obviously, lists like this one must be viewed with caution. This list is manifestly not exclusively made up of composers Burney regarded as masters, as the study of his reviews of the more secular movements in Croft's and Greene's work has already shown.

The ideal church music in the modern style would balance and blend the grace, elegance, and passion of secular dramatic music with sobriety, the absence of obviously theatrical elements, and contrapuntal writing where appropriate. The master composer who best combined the secular and sacred styles, but whose music still retained propriety was, according to Burney, Niccolo Jommelli. His sacred church music "united elegance with learning and grace with bold design." Most of his sacred works were "learned without pedantry, and grave without dullness," but his *Miserere* transcended the proper balance of these elements. Burney allows the propriety of this long and serious work, but he discerned "a manifest struggle at extraneous modulation and new effects, perhaps too much at the expense of facility and grace." The imbalance was perhaps brought about "in striving at excellence with to[o] great solicitude," and having "recourse to art and study, instead of giving way to his own feelings." Here Burney himself is at the extreme limit of his taste. Jommelli's *Miserere* was too difficult for the "comprehension of common hearers," but those listeners of greater musicianship, "able to read score, or to follow the performers through the labyrinths of art," could derive "great pleasure" from the piece.[184]

Burney praises Jommelli's *Isacco figura del Redentore* for its effective music. The admiration he expresses particularly for the recitative and aria "Chi per pieta mi dice, il mio figlio che fa?" illustrates Burney's preference for a high level of drama in the oratorio.[185] Burney, however, would not have subscribed to a recent evaluation of the dramatic oratorio of his time: "The oratorio, of course, was not normally staged, and had two acts to the opera's three, but otherwise its only fundamental distinguishing feature was its sacred subject."[186] Although an accurate description of many oratorios, it was not Burney's ideal. This, he partially outlines in a letter to Lord Mornington regarding Italian oratorio:

> Your Lordship will often find me a Defender of the *Moderns* against the Prejudices of outragious admirers of antiquity—here I must give them up. The modern oratorios of Italy are in general too light and are too much in the style of Theatrical Music.—a Line should certainly be drawn between the Church and Stage; but, as the French say of the universal finery and Foppery of all ranks of People: "il n'y a Point d'Etat." Jomelli and Bach have

> Composed some admirable Oratorios, in the true Church Style, with Good Choruses, and slow airs that are truly pathetic, with others that are full of Passion, or cheerful, *Cum dignitate.*[187]

Burney wrote very little about the flagrantly dramatic oratorios produced in Germany, but one of his remarks is revealing of his conception of oratorio. He owned the score of Johann Heinrich Rolle's *Thirza und ihre Söhne,* but criticized it only generally, saying that it "is full of good taste, new passages, pleasing effects and true pathos."[188] This is the critical vocabulary he employed in discussing opera, not sacred music. It is used here to emphasize the affective nature of the music, and underline his view of oratorio as a dramatic work. In the *History,* Burney avers that when oratorio libretti adhere to the dramatic unities of time and place, they may "reasonably be called sacred musical tragedies."

> And such, indeed, oratorios ought to be, even when sung in still life: as, when the laws of time and place are observed, the events of the piece interesting, and the characters well supported, the attention of the audience will be more easily excited. Indeed, as these pieces are at present performed without action, the figures of the personages are not presented to the eye, as in other dramas, but the ear.[189]

Burney's ideal of a sacred subject presented with suitable dignity and gravity in the descriptive, picturesque style of the Neapolitans was exemplified in the best works of Jommelli. Jommelli's music, Burney concludes, will always "be regarded with reverence by real judges of composition, as there is no mixture of trivial or fantastical movements or passages in his truly classical, and often sublime works."[190]

In contrast to Jommelli, the other two composers given on Burney's first list of masters of sacred music, Hasse and Perez, seem to have pleased Burney only with their grace and facility, not their profundity. Burney specifically criticizes Perez for his lack of mastery of "fugues or learned contrapuntal music for the church." Hasse he always mentions with respect, but if he ever examined his sacred music, he chose not to evaluate it. He did hear a *Salve Regina* sung when he visited Hasse in Vienna, which he calls "an exquisite composition, full of grace, taste and propriety."[191] Unfortunately, it is not possible to identify this *Salve Regina* from among the eleven settings which survive.[192] In the *Cyclopaedia,* in support of his claim of Hasse's fecundity as a composer, Burney says only that his sacred music and "chamber duets in the style of Steffani" are "innumerable."

Hasse's name occurs at every turn on Burney's lists of excellent composers of vocal music of all kinds. Burney told Hasse in Vienna that "from his works I had received a great part of my most early pleasure... and that he had long been my *magnus Apollo.*"[193] In surveying Burney's criticism of Hasse's works, one is struck with the thought that Hasse's music was Burney's first love, and,

Sacred Music 167

like most first loves, was never quite forgotten, though long since supplanted by greater beauties and attachments.

Throughout his life, Burney preferred a separation of sacred and secular styles. As the Neapolitan style permeated all of Europe, fewer composers maintained the distinction. One who did was Antonio Sacchini.

> Sacchini was one of the few modern masters who kept his sacred and secular style of composition separate and distinct. In his theatrical compositions, to look at the score, there seemed so much simplicity, that a mere contrapuntist would have imagined him to have been a feeble harmonist;... But his ecclesiastical compositions are not only learned, solemn, and abounding with fine effects, but are clothed in the richest and most pure harmony.[194]

The haste with which Burney compiled the last volume of the *History* and the severe limitations of space he suffered make evaluation of Burney's view of the sacred music of his own time difficult. His shortage of space is apparent throughout the last chapters of his work: chapters such as "Opera composers employed at Rome" and "Musical Drama at Venice" are merely catalogues of composers and treatises. Even his article on Galuppi, a composer for whom he had the greatest respect, is perfunctory, as is evidenced by a footnote to the evaluation of Galuppi's compositions: "I find in them his usual fire, grace and originality."

Burney confesses difficulty in properly completing his task, and renders an explanation and apology at the outset of his chapter on eighteenth-century German music:

> The materials for this chapter, which I collected in my German tour, have been so much augmented since, by the acquisition of subsequent publications and a constant intercourse with the natives of that country, that an entire volume would be insufficient to contain them. But to do justice, individually, to *all* the great musical professors that Germany has produced during the period which I have now to describe, would occupy much more space in my works than it is my power to allow. Indeed, the curiosity and wants of the generality of my readers will probably be less pressing about foreigners, whose names and talents have hardly penetrated into our country, than about such as tradition has celebrated or acquaintance endeared. It is therefore hoped, that omissions of minute details, or deep researches, concerning the Music of every other country but our own, will be excused.[195]

Thus, Burney's "history" of sacred music in eighteenth-century Germany is little more than a catalogue; moreover, it is one taken from Ebeling's *Versuch einer auserlesenen musikalischen Bibliothek,* which was then nineteen years out of date.[196] Burney lists Fux, Sebastian Bach, Fasch, Stölzel, Telemann, Hasse, Graun, and Handel. In reality Burney knew next to nothing of the music of Fasch, Stölzel, and Telemann; Fux's he knew only from extracts in *Gradus ad Parnassum* and Martini's *Saggio di Contrappunto*. He did, however, have several manuscripts of Bach's music. Burney has been frequently ridiculed for his failure to appreciate Bach fully, but most of his comments deal with Bach as a keyboard composer and performer. It is generally overlooked that Burney owned a manuscript of a Bach *credo*, which he calls "one of the most clear, correct and masterly I have ever seen," and he calls the remainder of the vocal music known to him "excellent in harmony and expression."[197]

Burney's scant observations on Bach's sacred music are more detailed than his remarks on the music of any other German composer, but, however briefly, something was said of the sacred music of Germany; French sacred music is ignored in the *History*. Despite the possible expedient presented by La Borde's *Essai sur la musique*, Burney chose not to mention anything beyond the names of a few of the most famous cathedral organists.

The Neapolitan School fares better, understandably, since this was Burney's favorite group of composers. Yet even this chapter has obvious oversights. Durante, for example, is scarcely mentioned in the *History*, but in the *Cyclopaedia* Burney writes, "his masses and motets abound with elegant movements ingeniously and richly accompanied; in which there is learning without pedantry, and gravity without dullness."[198] Such criticism, while adding little to our understanding of Burney's critical precepts, does illustrate his acquaintance with a great deal of sacred music which is not mentioned in the *Tours* or *History*.

The *History*, in a very real sense, is an unfinished book. When Burney finally reached music he admired, and about which modern readers are most curious, he was virtually forced to abandon his concept of a history of style, and resort to merely recording the biographies and general merit of his favorite composers. It is easy to imagine a fifth volume to Burney's *History*, filled with plates of "Jommelli's Beauties," "Haydn's Innovations," and "Sacchini's Excellencies." The articles for the Ree's *Cyclopaedia*, though often very illuminating, were also composed in haste. Burney was pressured by the immense size of the project he had undertaken, and fearful that he would not live to complete the task. Thus many of his articles are taken verbatim from the *Tours* and *History*. Composers such as Durante and Colonna, who were passed over in silence in the *History*, receive brief notices, but these are not enough to compensate the modern reader for the history of musical style which Burney never completed.

The most intriguing references to sacred music, made during the last decades of Burney's life, were never published. His papers relate his gradual discovery of the beauty of Mozart's masses and Haydn's oratorios. Burney was the London agent for Haydn's published score of the *Creation*, and an enthusiastic admirer of the work. He first heard the composition performed on 21 April 1800, and his diary entry for that date records the reception of the piece by the London audience.

> Haydn's Oratorio of [the] *Creation*, was performed at the Opera-house Concert Room, under the direction of Salomon, who took great pains to have it well executed. Many parts of this sublime composition had a great effect; and was felt by the audience; other parts were so

new that it could not be understood the first time of hearing it, even by unprejudiced Professors.

See a paper written immediately on my return home, after hearing it; describing its effect on myself.[199]

Burney's descriptive essay records not only his own rapture evoked by the most effective moments of the oratorio, but also relates the strength of the Handel partisans at the beginning of the nineteenth century.

> If I had leisure, I could write a folio dissertation on the beauty of that divine Music, and the intelligence, the mind, and conceptions, of the matchless composer! The Handelians, who are most of them utterly unable to judge Handel's real merit, are all as jealous of that of others, as if they themselves had composed Handel's works, and pert, as well as flippant soi-disant Connoisseurs, have handed it about as a *bon mot,* that the opening of the *Creation* is so confused, that "Chaos is come again." and what *should* be come again (may be asked) but *Chaos,* when Chaos is to be described? Were sounds to be arranged in harmonic and symmetric order before order was born? It struck me as the most sublime idea in Haydn's work, his describing the birth of order by dissonance and broken phrases—a whisper here—an effort there—a groan—an agonising cry—personifying Nature, and supposing her in labour, how admirably has he expressed her throes! not by pure harmony and graceful melody, but by appropriate murmurs which applied to any other purposes would be downright jargon; but here, *in loco,* are sublimely beautiful! Yet if the hearer does not help the composer, musical imitation is so feeble that his designs and conceptions will never be understood. But if this is not picturesque music, it is in vain ever to be attempted. When dissonance is tuned, when order arises, and Chaos is no more, what pleasing, ingenious and graceful melody and harmony ensue! What a new and powerful effect had the encored chorus on the feeling part of the audience! who unable to stay till it was finished, to express their rapture, broke in upon the performers with impassioned applause, both times, before the movement was ended; and what a flash of harmony on the last word of the sublime text of genuine Scripture—"God said let there be light, and there was LIGHT."[200]

In addition to Haydn's *Creation,* Burney owned several of his masses, and, by 1803, several full scores of Mozart's masses as well. In Mozart's sacred music he found many "lovely strains and true devotional music,"[201] and though, like most of the musical world, he came to recognize Mozart's genius only a decade after his death, he then became an enthusiastic admirer.

Burney's writings on sacred music encompass a greater period of musical history than his writings on the other two categories of chamber and dramatic music. He began his writings apparently thinking, like most of his contemporaries, that Palestrina was the inventor of the true church style, but his own investigations carried him back to Josquin, and the revelation of the great beauty which could be wrought in even the most complicated of "artificial" music. His recognition of Josquin and general appreciation of the best music in his style represent some of Burney's finest achievements as a historian. Burney viewed the true church style, once established, as basically static. He perceived degrees of relative merit in different composers, and was aware of changes in technique, but viewed the *a cappella* style from Josquin to his own day as essentially one style, and judged all the music of that style by the same criteria regardless of age.

In contrast, he saw dramatic sacred music, along with opera, at the forefront of advancement in the art. In his criticism of early sacred music he seeks to point out invention and the progression toward refinement which led to the style of music of his own time. His analytical treatment of the music of Wise, Blow, Croft, Purcell, and others demonstrates that, when time and space were available, he was capable of providing solid reasoning to support his judgments of taste. There is every reason to believe that, had his sensibilities permitted, he could have been equally explicit about music from the first half of the eighteenth century. He certainly would have never engaged in the minute analysis of the kind written by Abbé Vogler in his *Betrachtungen der Mannheimer Tonschule* (1778-81), a work far too elaborate for English tastes. Yet had he not been constrained by lack of space and by cabal, the last chapters of the *History* would probably bear a closer resemblance to the third volume, containing lengthy and informative analyses.

Based on their impressions of the fourth volume of the *History*, Burney's critics have asserted as fact that his view of musical history was totally dominated by opera. They are generally unaware of the practical considerations which limited the last chapters of the *History*. Burney's writings on sacred music from the fifteenth to the nineteenth centuries, though less than comprehensive, show him to have been as knowledgeable about and appreciative of sacred music as secular. His taste certainly led him more happily to opera, but as a historian he recognized an *a cappella* sacred tradition spanning four centuries, and a tradition of modern sacred music which paralleled the development of opera.

7

Chamber Music: Burney the Progressive

In the traditional division of style, chamber music encompasses any composition which is neither sacred nor theatrical; it is essentially a catch-all category for instrumental and secular vocal forms. Burney's *Plan* included sections dedicated to church music and sacred and secular drama, but none for secular vocal music or instrumental forms. Section eight mentions "the history of several modern instruments... with their refinements with regard to both their construction and their use," but does not mention the development of the sonata, solo concerto, symphony, or chamber music. The history of instruments, and even their players, does not constitute a history of instrumental style. The lack of systematic organization in Burney's discussion of chamber music is apparent throughout the *History,* often resulting in the omission of music he certainly knew. The collection of his scattered remarks into three sub-categories—secular vocal music, instrumental music, and keyboard music—facilitates analysis, and provides a semblance of order where none exists.

Secular Vocal Music

The little that Burney said of secular vocal chamber music generally appears almost as an afterthought to the discussion of sacred music. He projects an obvious intolerance for early secular compositions, as has been shown by his treatment of the music of the troubadours and trouvères. Thereafter, the earliest pieces he reviews in the *History* are found in the Fayrfax Manuscript. Delighted with the opportunity of presenting specimens of such early English music, he printed four complete songs, but his analysis reveals that he was more interested in the pieces as antiques than music. The rhythmic complexity of the music confounded him, particularly the mixed measures, "a contrivance that occasions nothing but confusion to the Ear; which is utterly unable to form a determined Idea of the Measure in which any one of the parts is moving."[1] Burney is completely tied to the bar line. When confronted with a passage with shifting accents, he finds that "confusion is occasioned by all the parts, continuing to perform in Common Time, passages that are absolutely in Triple Measure,"[2] and suggests two different solutions in triple time (ex. 7.1 a, b, and c). His summary of English sixteenth-century music bespeaks his attitude: "little of our secular music of the beginning of the sixteenth century is preserved; however there must have been plenty of it, such as it was."[3] He knew of the existence of songs and madrigals by Continental composers from the same period, but was able to find "little, either in print or manuscript of higher antiquity than near the middle of the sixteenth century."[4]

The devotees of English Elizabethan music have been among the most severe of Burney's critics, and justly so. Joseph Kerman summarized their position well in his reference to "Burney's notorious neglect."[5] His neglect was not occasioned by the unavailability of this music: his library catalogue shows a large and diverse collection, with many examples, including *Musica transalpina* (1588 and 1597), and the best music of the English madrigalists. Whether from a lack of interest or from hostility toward the lovers of madrigals, who were generally musical conservatives like Sir John Hawkins, Burney certainly did not do justice to this period of secular music. His annoyance with the lack of symmetrical phrasing and strict accentuation is apparent throughout his discussion. Characteristic are his remarks on Thomas Morley's "Cease Myne Eyes": "those who are not accustomed to the music of the sixteenth century, will be much embarrassed with the broken phrases and false accents of the melody, in which there is so total a want of rhythm, as renders the time extremely difficult to keep with accuracy and firmness."[6] Burney's scoring of this music with bar lines obscured one of the most appealing attributes of the rhythmically and accentually free settings of the Elizabethan madrigal; he fails to consider the possibility of a nonmetrical and irregularly accentuated reading once he has barred the music. As Fellowes perceived, "If its original shape is distorted and its beautiful free prose shackled, Elizabethan music will necessarily be misunderstood and will fail to excite admiration."[7] He writes a passage which could well have been penned by Burney.

> ... the particular temptation of the madrigalists lay in the simultaneous introduction of a number of cross-rhythms, overlapping, and combined through the exercise of extraordinary contrapuntal skill, but appearing to the brain through the medium of the eye, rather than to the heart through the ear.[8]

No music more appealing to the eye than the heart would capture Burney's approval. If an informed critic like Fellowes could consider the music overly complex on occasion, it is not surprising that a man of Burney's tastes reacted as he did. His sweeping condemnation of much of this music may have been intended to rebut those of Hawkins's persuasion (including many gentlemen and noblemen) who valued it more highly than did Burney;[9] these admirers of

Ex. 7.1. Mixed Measures: Burney's Solution

a)

All the Compofers in Europe, about the end of the Fifteenth Century, feem to have had a paffion for MIXED MEASURES; and there is not one Song in the Fayrfax M.S. without inftances of one part moving in COMMON TIME while another is in TRIPLE: a contrivance that occafions nothing but confufion to the Ear, which is utterly unable to form a determined Idea of the MEASURE in which any one of the parts is moving. But at the latter end of each Strain of this Song, ftill more confufion is occafioned, by all the parts continuing to perform, in COMMON TIME, paffages that are abfolutely in TRIPLE MEASURE: fee at this mark ‡ where the accent feems to require that the Notes fhould be executed thus.

b)

or thus

c)

the "old stuff" comprised a powerful musical lobby that Burney viewed as detrimental to the progress of music.

Burney failed in his attempt to consider Elizabethan music with the needed historical perspective, and his study did not lead him to an appreciation of the style of the individual composers. In the course of writing the chapter he complained to Twining, "What a mob of them have I been forced to score, in order to be able to say that they are all so *alike* that they might pass for the productions of an Individual."[10] He provides several examples, but confided to Malone that Thomas Weelkes's "My Flock's feed" was "the longest specimen I have inserted of our old Madrigalists; not because the Music is superior to other productions of Weelkes or his cotemporaries, but on account of the words being from Shakspeare [sic]."[11]

Burney's avowed preference for the Italian madrigal over the contemporary native madrigal was motivated as much by the quality of the poetry as the music. Spenser and Shakespeare aside, he judged English lyric poetry to be "in a state of utter barbarism." Indeed, he ranked the madrigals inferior in poetry "to the present Christmas carols of London bell-men."[12] Italian madrigals were set to better poetry, verses which "indicated to the musical composers traits of melody, more airy and marked, perhaps, than we could derive from the prosody or phraseology of our own language." The composer who best exploited these traits was Luca Marenzio.

> There are no madrigals so agreeable to the ear, or amusing to the eye, as those of this ingenious and fertile composer. The subjects of fugue, imitation, and attack, are traits of elegant and pleasing melody; which, though they seem selected with the utmost care for the sake of the words they are to express, yet so artful are the texture and disposition of the parts, that the general harmony and effect of the whole are as complete and unembarrassed as if he had been writing in plain counterpoint, without poetry or contrivance.[13]

It is difficult to judge how Burney came to this conclusion, but it is certain that his taste for Marenzio's music is genuine, as it is documented in his correspondence, as well as in the flattering appraisal in the *History*. His approval is not surprising; Marenzio's eminence was commonly acknowledged. By the latter part of the century he was as highly regarded for his madrigals as Palestrina was for his sacred music.

Marenzio represented the Roman school of madrigal composers, and, as Burney's chapter is arranged around geographical locations, his discussion next turns to composers at Naples.[14] One Neapolitan who could not be overlooked was Don Carlo Gesualdo, the "Prince of Venosa." Like Marenzio's music, Gesualdo's works, difficult and abstruse though they were, were well known and admired in London.[15] Burney, in this case, did not subscribe to traditional assessments. Rather, he heartily disagreed with those who spoke of Gesualdo as "the greatest composer" of the time, and as one who, "quitting the beaten track of other musicians, had discovered new melodies, new measures, new harmonies, and new modulation."[16] Gesualdo's most recent admirer was Hawkins, a member of both the Academy of Ancient Music and the Madrigal Society. Burney's essay, a specific rebuttal to Hawkins, contains his most extensive review of any secular vocal music, but even this does not communicate the seriousness with which he undertook his evaluation. He scored a number of the works[17] in a collection which Glenn Watkins calls "a remarkably varied sampling."[18] and wrote marginalia which is as lively as his published evaluation. Next to the first seven measures of "Belta poi che l'assenti" he noted, "Let the admirers of Venosa's sweetest modulation conceivable' defend the following fragment of a madrigal (the 2nd, op. 6) in G minor."[19] His analysis of the first five measures reveals his approach to the music (ex. 7.2). Using contemporary theory based on figured harmony as a standard, the piece was to him inexplicable. His rejection of Hawkins's evaluation—"fine contrivance, original harmony, and the sweetest modulation conceivable"—is categorical:

> As to *contrivance*, it must be owned that much has been attempted by this Prince; but he is so far from being happy in this particular, that his points of imitation are generally unmanageable, and brought in so indiscriminately on concords and discords, and on accented and unaccented parts of a bar, that, when performed, there is more confusion in the general effect than in the Music of any other composer of madrigals with whose works I am acquainted. His *original harmony*, after scoring a great part of his madrigals, particularly those that have been the most celebrated, is difficult to discover; for had there been any warrantable combinations of sounds that Palestrina, Luca Marenzio, and many of his predecessors, had not used before him, in figuring the bases, they would have appeared. And as to his modulation, it is so far from being the *sweetest* conceivable, that, to me, it seems forced, affected, and disgusting.[20]

The extensive evidence presented to support his criticism is augmented by the inclusion of the complete madrigal "Moro lasso" from Book VI as a "specimen of his style, and harsh, crude, and licentious modulation." The harmonic offenses committed in the first bar are, in his eyes, sufficient to condemn the piece (ex. 7.3). The beginning of the piece on C♯ major instead of the "key note" of A minor is censured, but the progression from C♯ to A minor in first inversion is abominated as "repugnant to every rule of transition at present established," and "extremely shocking and disgusting to the ear." Most offensive is the lack of relation, "real or imaginary," between the two chords, for the second chord is "wholly extraneous and foreign to any key to which the first chord belongs."[21] Gesualdo's licenses were too excessive to be justified by the demands of text-setting, and they did not advance the art of music. "New modulation, when guided by science and a nice ear, is always welcome, and certain in its effect; but when it only consists of such licentiousness and offensive deviations from rule, as have been constantly rejected by the sense

176   Chamber Music

Ex. 7.2. Gesualdo: "Beltà poi che l'assenti"

and intellect of great Professors, it can only be applauded by ignorance, depravity or affectation."[22]

Unlike Gesualdo, Claudio Monteverdi achieved the desired balance between pedantry and innovation; his licenses advanced music, his work forming "a memorable epoch in the history of the art."[23] His unusual harmonic practice pleased the public ear and was soon accepted not only by dilletantes, but professors. Burney says little about Monteverdi's style; the bulk of the essay eulogizes the momentous changes brought about by the rift between the *prima prattica* and the *seconda prattica*. His definition of the *seconda prattica* reflects its importance to his concept of history: "it was in his [Monteverdi's] madrigals and operas that he ventured to violate such established rules of counterpoint as precluded variety, energy, pathos, and every bold expression of words, which have since been so necessary in the picturesque and impassioned scenes of Dramatic Music."[24]

Burney dated Monteverdi's as the period from whence "every fortunate breach of an *old rule* seems to be regarded as the establishment of a *new;* by which means the code is so enlarged that we may now almost pronounce every thing to be allowable in a musical composition, that does not offend cultivated ears."[25] Burney's glowing evaluation of Monteverdi says little about how his music surpasses that of his contemporaries within the madrigal style. His opinion is probably traditional, though confirmed by his own investigations.

Burney, like all historians, relies heavily on tradition to supply him with a starting point for his historical investigations, but he seems always to have

Ex. 7.3. Gesualdo: "Morro lasso"

ratified these opinions by his own investigations.[26] His knowledge of music in the sixteenth century was wide-ranging. As a student of earlier writings, he knew the tradition attached to composers, but his own perception was shaped, at least in part, by the availability of music. Even when he had specimens by a great composer, it was probably not possible for him to determine how representative they were of either the composer's style or the period. It is thus impossible today to evaluate his historical judgement of early music with any degree of certainty or fairness. Nonetheless, Burney's failure to recognize the full range of genius in the Netherlandish and Italian composers seems justly censurable. He found Philippe Verdelot's name in many catalogues, and in the writings of Zarlino and others, for example, but having scored several of his pieces, he found "no characteristic excellence" to recommend them. Other composers *"a dozzina,"* including "Giaches de Wert, Lupus, Lupi, Philip de Monte, Peverinage, Waelront and Verdonk," are similarly passed over.

Burney did admire the madrigals of Cipriano de Rore and Lassus as excellent in the style of the times, but refrained from giving examples, so similar was their music to that of their contemporaries. The style of these madrigals, with their "laboured and equivocal modulations," was often learned and ingenious, but sometimes loaded with so much "caprice and affectation as to fatigue the attention, and disgust the ear." Such music could only suit "depraved ears that are grown callous to everything that is easy and natural." Burney still awaits the arrival of opera to improve style.

> The Italians, when they quitted madrigals, and no longer aspired at the applause of fastidious chamber-critics, whose approbation was bestowed on no compositions that did not smell of the lamp simplified their secular Music... Authors of all kinds, who seek for applause, conform to the taste of their judges; ... In Music, the learned are few, and silent; the ignorant numerous, and noisy: in the chamber it was right to please the former, and in the theatre, where
> "—the fair, the gay, the young
> Govern the numbers of each song,"
> there is no choice. A public and mixed audience is such a many-headed monster, that all its ears cannot be pleased at the same time; and whether good or bad predominate, the greater number must be gratified at the expence of the less.[27]

Burney boldly pronounced that music was manifestly on the decline in England during the seventeenth century.[28] The vocal chamber music in seventeenth-century England consisted of late madrigals, ayres, dialogues, and, in a separate category of social chamber music, rounds, catches and glees. His evaluation of the music found in collections from this period is harsh. Surveying John Playford's first publication, *Select Musicall Ayres and Dialogues* (1653), which contains works by Henry Lawes, Coleman, Lanier, and others, he remarks, "the whole collection does not contain one ayre which now seems worth engraving, either as a specimen of individual genius, or national taste."²⁹ Playford's collection published in 1673 is dismissed as containing "not one air that is either ingenious, graceful, cheerful or solemn. An insipid languor, or vulgar pertness, pervades the whole."³⁰

One would expect a more satisfactory and enlightened treatment of this repertory, judging from the rather substantial collection of music from this period in the catalogue of Burney's library. Modern scholars have been slow to examine the works of the lesser luminaries of the mid-seventeenth century— Nicholas Lanier, John Hilton, and Henry and William Lawes—but have at least accorded due attention to John Dowland and what Fellowes styles as the "English School of Lutenist Songwriters." Burney highly regarded John Dowland as a virtuoso lutenist, but as a composer he was astonished by his scant abilities in counterpoint, "and the great reputation he acquired with his contemporaries...continued to him either by the indolence or ignorance of those who have had occasion to speak of him."³¹ His perception of the rest of the century is equally limited.

Burney recognized the influence of Italian monody on English music, but found that "the beginning of the enterprise was not more fortunate here" than in Italy. Composers surrendered harmony and contrivance, but did not replace it with accent, grace or invention. He finds little reason "for sacrificing music to poetry," for if the "sentiments of the poem are neither enforced nor embellished by the melody," they are better read than sung.

He amusingly related to Twining his disenchantment with seventeenth-century English composers in doggerel written while in the throes of writing the chapter. Annoyed by the "very pompous and minute" discussion of the composers in Hawkins's *History,* he composed his own critical catalogue of the composers represented in Playford's editions of *Select Musicall Ayres and Dialogues.*

> The Base of *Laniere*
> Is too frequently queer,
> And the Treble he gives
> Too like Recitatives.
> Of the dull Doctor *Wilson*
> Our ears get their fill soon;
> His Passages old
> Stuff 'em up like a cold.
>
> The renown'd Harry *Lawes*
> You will find has his flaws,
> For his Treble's Psalmodic
> & Base immethodic.
> While *William's* too rude
> To be patiently chew'd;
> But since knock'd on the head
> There's no more to be said.

> Billy *Webb* is a Bumkin
> Insipid as Pumkin.
> I own I am loth
> To call *Colman* a Goth;
> But you'll see by his paces
> He knew not the Graces.
> And yet master *Ned*
> In his heels has more lead.
>
> With Jeremy *Savill*
> E'er far I w^d travel,
> I'd freely submit
> To have my Nose slit.
>
> Then for *Child*, & for *Rogers*
> Two fumble-fist Codgers,
> They're only prolific
> In Strains soporific,
> Which, Sleep to procure,
> Are than opiates more sure.
>
> As to *Jenkins,* he seems
> But a dreamer of dreams;
> And the Scrapers sh^d fly all
> From Kit *Simpson*'s *Viol*,
> And ev'ry *Division*
> Regard with derision.
>
> *Coperario*'s a fop
> Whose Ears I c^d crop,
> For forging a name
> And bringing to shame
> Two Countries at once,
> Yet *still* be a Dunce.
>
> The bold blade *Captain Cook*,
> Who his King near forsook,
> And when all was despair
> Kept his dread *Nom de Guerre,*
> Only fit seems through Life
> For a Drum or a Fife:
> The *Canons* he fir'd
> 'Twas Mars that inspir'd;
> A God who Apollo
> Could always beat hollow.—
> Yet, when Charles was restor'd,
> Cook as Sovereign Lord
> Was annointed the King
> Of the Pipe and the String. — —[32]

Amidst his wholesale condemnation of seventeenth-century secular music, Burney's regard for canons, catches, and rounds is notable: he consistently maintains a respectful attitude toward these most artificial yet social compositions. Apparently the genial social purpose of these charming tunes obviated criticism of their complete subjugation of poetry to music, or of their distinct lack of melodic grace and harmonic variety. Doubtless for the sheer pleasure of his readers, Burney published nine complete examples from *Pammelia,*[33] of which he remarks, "Great musical science is manifested in the canons, and the harmony and contrivance of the rest are excellent."[34] John Hilton's *Catch as Catch Can* (1652) he praised for containing admirable compositions "which still afford great pleasure to the lovers of this species of humorous and convivial effusions."[35] Burney himself may have been among these as he composed a number of canons, catches, and glees, several of which became quite famous and appear in collections to this day.[36] Four canons from Hilton's collection are published in the *History;* "Non nobis Domine" is printed with six markers, indicating errors in composition. By the standards Burney normally applies, this would condemn the piece outright, though there is no further mention of the composition in the text. Elsewhere, however, he speaks of the defective harmonies which often arise in canonic writing.[37]

Purcell's catches were much in favor among all lovers of such diversions. They were continually performed, and comprised a substantial portion of many of the numerous collections of catches published throughout the century. In Burney's opinion, Purcell's songs were vastly superior to any produced in his era, so superior "that his compositions seemed to speak a new language... His songs seem to contain whatever the ear could then wish or heart could feel." Purcell's most famous collection was *Orpheus Britannicus,* of which Burney says:

> Here were treasured up the songs from which the natives of this island received their first great delight and impression from the vocal Music of a *single voice.* Before that period we had cultivated madrigals and songs in parts, with diligence and success; but in all single songs, till those of Purcell appeared, the chief effects were produced from the words, not the melody. For the airs, till that time, were as unformed and misshapen, as if they had been made of notes scattered about by chance, instead of being cast in an elegant mould. Exclusive admirers of modern symmetry and elegance may call Purcell's taste barbarous; yet in spite of the vicissitudes of fashion, through all his rudeness and barbarism, original genius, feeling, and passion, are, and ever will be, discoverable in his works, by candid and competent judges of the art.[38]

Purcell revived and invigorated music after the decline it suffered in the seventeenth century. Indeed, but for his untimely death, Purcell might have, in Burney's view, changed the course of English musical history. Henry Purcell, Orlando Gibbons, and Pelham Humfrey all died young. Had they "been blest with long life," says Burney, "we might have had a music of our own, at least as good as that of France and Germany... as it is, we have no school for composition, no well-digested method of study, nor indeed models, of our own";[39] even in his imagination he could not conceive of an English school superior to that of his beloved Italian school.

Once Burney arrives at the eve of the birth of opera, he neglects the chronology of the smaller forms of vocal chamber music.[40] Seventeenth-century Italian vocal music consisted principally of sacred and secular cantatas. Burney's discussion of the Italian cantata is extensive, but aside from that he pays vitually no attention to Continental vocal music. No mention of the German cantata appears in the entire chapter on seventeenth-century music. The *cantate françoise* and *air de cour* are similarly slighted in the discussion of the French. It is no exaggeration to say that this repertory did not exist in Burney's mind, or was so insignificant as to require no chronology.[41] After the seventeenth century, the few references to cantatas occur in discussions of the style of composers best known for their dramatic music (cantatas are closely associated with opera in Burney's *History* and will be discussed in the chapter on dramatic music).

There was a large market for individual songs in eighteenth-century England, and, to a lesser extent, cantatas. When Burney began his chapter on the "General State of Music in England during the Present Century," the first thought which came to his mind was of the songs heard at the playhouses.

> Music at all times has been called in to the assitance of the weak plays and unattractive actors of our national theatres; and incidental songs, and singing between the acts, have been found so alluring, that when there was no plan formed for exhibiting musical dramas, singers have been engaged at considerable salaries, expressly for that purpose.[42]

Innumerable songs were produced for the playhouses and the fashionable pleasure gardens of London, especially Ranelagh and Vauxhall Gardens. There was a thriving commercial market for these songs in vocal arrangements, as well as in settings for the transverse flute and guitar. The songs were, above all, written to be popular, and the recurrence of well-known songs by Purcell (especially "Mad Bess"), Arne, and Handel in many anthologies show these publications to be designed for quick profit.

Several collections of popular songs, including Bickham's famous *Musical Entertainer* (1738), were elaborate productions, featuring vignettes at the top of each song and occasionally showing scenes from the gardens. One collection in imitation of Bickham, *Clio and Euterpe,* contains several of the songs Burney composed for *Robin Hood,* each with its own vignette (ex. 7.4).

Burney makes the claim that English vocal music "seems to have remained near stationary for near half a century"; he finds that the change from a vulgar taste to one of some degree of refinement "was begun by the compositions and instructions of Dr. Arne, who endeavoured to refine our melody and singing, more from Italian than English models."[43] This change, he notes, coincided with a change in Arne's style. He states that in 1738 Arne

Ex. 7.4. Burney: "The Man to My Mind"

> ...introduced a light, airy, original, and pleasing melody, wholly different from that of Purcell or Handel, whom all English composers had hitherto either pillaged or imitated. Indeed, the melody of Arne at this time, and of his Vauxhall songs afterwards, form an aera in English Music; it was so easy, natural and agreeable to the whole kingdom, that it had an effect upon our national taste; and till a more modern Italian style was introduced in the pasticcio English operas of Mssrs. Bickerstaff and Cumberland, it was the standard of all perfection at our theatres and public gardens.[44]

Into the national song, with its English and Scottish characteristics, Arne assimilated Italian elements.[45] The new Italian taste caught hold of fashion, from which Cocchi, Vento, Giardini, and other Italian masters profited handsomely. Later in the century Sacchini, Piozzi, and others continued to supply the best instruction, completing the revolution in taste.[46] The revolution in singing, however, did not increase the originality of English song composers. Burney remarks with apparent disdain that Dibdin, Shield, and Dr. Arnold "very judiciously complied with the reigning taste," imitating the latest fashion.[47] Conscious attempts to be popular, even in a composer of Handel's stature, invariably drew Burney's disapproval, because the popular English taste seemed to him conservative and trivial.

Burney's attitude toward popular songs and the public taste (or lack of it) is revealed in a number of letters about his own songs written in the 1790's. Rear Admiral Horatio Nelson's defeat of the French fleet in Abu Qir Bay, near Alexandria, on 1 August 1798, was an occasion for great celebration. Burney, a devout loyalist whose letters reflect his anguish over the French Revolution and possible threat to the English monarchy, was an enthusiastic celebrant of the victory. He composed a commemorative song for the occasion which he described to Fanny as "a song on the Five Naval British heroes of the present War, to an easy and popular tune, which any one with a good ear may sing by memory after second hearing it."[48] The song of 1798 does not appear to have been published, but similar patriotic fervor motivated his setting of Courtenay's *Four Patriotic Songs,* also in the popular vein (ex. 7.5). There can be no mistaking his opinion as to their artistic merit, as he dismissed the songs as trifles and *Hullabaloo.*

It was in part the miserable quality of English verse, and the unsuitability of English compared to Italian as a language for singing, which accounted for Burney's prejudice against English vocal music. He complained bitterly about the dreadful state of English lyric poetry to Mrs. John Hunter.

> My notions of long for good music are very different from those of mere rhymers and ballad-mongers, who being totally ignorant of music, and still more of good singing take no thought of the necessary symmetry .f melody, of its corresponding with different stanzas to the +form turns+ of harsh words, and +mute+ terminations of a thought or a verse, when the voice is either corrupted by a nazal [sic] or guttural sound, such as in n^{r}n [sic], or hissing double ss, snarling up or utterly stopt by a mute consonant, such as d, k, p and t—There

wants[s] attention even in the most Trifl[in]g ballads written for old or new tunes—but for songs intended for good music and good singing, you, dear Madam, and my late old friend Mr. Mason are the only lyric poets who have thought of anything but the wit and the rhymes of their songs. For the last and most refined species of song, I have long seen that Metastasio who wrote for composers or singers, and auditors of the first class, is the best model.[49]

Burney's taste ran to the Italianate. The best of the new Italian opera songs and cantatas could be heard at concerts and private gatherings at the home of Charles Rousseau Burney, and other houses featuring the best modern music. The popular English vocal composers produced hundreds of songs of fleeting popularity, but Burney shunned these popular effusions in favor of a more artful variety; history has ratified his judgment.

Keyboard Music

The earliest keyboard music Burney reviewed was contained in *Queen Elizabeth's Virginal Book,* now known as the *Fitzwilliam Virginal Book.* He was impressed by the great difficulty of the pieces, but not by their quality. In reviewing William Byrd's fantasies he allows that "it was not yet the custom in composing fugues to confine a whole movement to one theme," a statement which reveals his lack of perspective on these pieces. His researches into early, imitative keyboard music were motivated by a wish to locate "the first regular fugue," but, having found it in a piece by Peter Philips, he proceeds to criticize it for not being constructed according to modern practice.

> The harmony is very full, but the modulation being chiefly confined to the key-note, and its fifth, is somewhat monotonous; and the divisions in accompanying the subject, are now become to[o] common and vulgar to afford pleasure, or even to be heard with patience, by fastidious judges of modern melody.[50]

These pieces were simply out of fashion, and Burney pays little attention to their intrinsic merit. Burney concurred with Marpurg's claim that fugues had a greater longevity than any style of composition, but only so long as the subjects of the fugues were "sober, pleasing, and rigorously persued, without extraneous episodes or fashionable divisions, which being the *agrémens,* or *trimmings,* of the times, becomes antiquated, and often ridiculous, in a very few years."[51]

Burney was not at all impressed by the "old tunes with variations" contained in the *Fitzwilliam* collection. These, he discovered, merely proved that the vices of his day were practiced in the sixteenth century as well.

> It has been imagined that the rage for variations, that is, multiplying notes, and disguising the melody of an easy, and, generally, well-known air, by every means possible, was the contagion of the present century; but it appears from the *Virginal Book,* that this species of *influenza,* or *corruption of air,* was more excessive in the sixteenth century, than at any other period of Musical History.[52]

Ex. 7.5. Burney: "Britannia's Triumph"

Ex. 7.5, continued

2
Though France and haughty Spain combine
 For empire o'er the main;
Howe's, Vincent's lightning fires their line,
 And bids Britannia reign.
                Cho: Britannia, then, &c.
3
Batavia's fleet, 'midst shoals and isles,
 In vain the combat tries;
Bold Duncan shakes her trembling piles,
 And wins the glorious prize.
                Cho: Britannia, then, &c.
4
Hibernia tunes her joyful lyre,
 For lo! in wild dismay,
Gaul's banner strikes to Warren's fire,
 And yields the brilliant day.
                Cho: Britannia, then, &c.
5
Let Egypt tell our Nelson's praise,
 Heroically brave;
While Gallia's navy sheds a blaze
O'er old Nile's blood-stain'd wave.
                Cho: Britannia, then, &c.
6
At Britain's call, his dreaded line
 Now shakes yon hostile shore;
See Danish valour only shine
 To add one trophy more.
                Cho: Britannia, then, &c.
7
While victory crowns our sea girt isle,
 And hearts of oak rejoice;
His best reward is beauty's smile,
 And sweet exulting voice.
                Cho: Britannia, then, &c.
8
What noble acts our triumphs grace!
 From patriot zeal they flow;
We own the bleeding sailor's race,
 And sooth the widow's woe.
                Cho: Britannia, then, &c.
9
Danger and death Britannia braves,
 Say can she ever fall?
Her circling trench the foaming waves,
 And fleets her floating wall.
                Cho: Britannia, then, &c.
10
Let wine and joy illume each brow,
 While loyal plaudits ring
To Vincent, Duncan, Nelson, Howe,
 And England's laurell'd King.
                Cho: Britannia, then, &c.

Surveying this collection, he discerned "a manifest superiority" in Byrd's works over the rest in texture and design. Yet his assessment of Byrd's capabilities, though respectful, founders on his failure to consider these pieces on their own terms.

> In a later age his genius would have expanded in works of invention, taste, and elegance; but, at the period in which he flourished, nothing seems to have been thought necessary for keyed-instruments, except variations to old tunes, in which all the harmony was crowded, which the fingers could grasp, and all the rapid divisions of the times, which they could execute. Even nominal *Fancies* were without fancy, and confined to the repetition of a few dry and unmeaning notes in fugue, or imitation. Invention was so young and feeble, as to be unable to go alone; and old chants of the church, or tunes of the street, were its leading-strings and guides.[53]

John Bull's compositions astonished Burney by their technical demands, even more than Byrd's, but their difficulty did not compensate for their lack of interest. Though he acknowledges that he "should greatly admire the hand as well as patience, of anyone capable of playing his compositions," he judged that "as *Music* they would afford me no kind of pleasure."[54] In "mercy to modern performers," he assures them that "the loss to refined ears; would not be very great, if Bull's pieces should for ever remain unplayed and undeciphered."[55]

Nowhere is the influence of Burney's Miss "o 'top o' the Spinet" reader more apparent than in his discussion of Elizabethan keyboard music. Here, for the moment, he forgets all pretense of historical objectivity in order to come to the defense of the taste of his readers. He dismisses out of hand the respected opinion of Dr. John Pepusch that Bull's compositions were preferable to those of Couperin and Scarlatti. Burney felt that this view proved rather "that the Doctor's taste was *bad*, than Bull's music good."[56] Hawkins's taste as well as his historical judgement was also on trial. Burney published "Specimens of Dr. Bull's difficult Passages":

> ...in order to invalidate the vulgar cant of such as are determined to blame whatever is modern, and who, equally devoid of knowledge and feeling, reprobate as *trash* the most elegant, ingenious, and often sublime compositions, that have ever been produced since the laws of harmony were first established.[57]

Having vanquished Hawkins with polemic supported by musical examples, Burney pauses to compare the style of Bull and Byrd to the latter's advantage. The determining factor is Bull's "violation of all present rules and sensations," and bad taste in modulation. Byrd's modulations, by comparison, were natural and pleasing, but only because they more closely conformed to Burney's expectations.[58]

Great gaps mar Burney's history of keyboard music and players. There is virtually no mention of the development of the organ or harpsichord, or their literature outside of England. The names of Andrea Gabrieli and Rocco Rodio pass fleetingly by in other contexts, but the wealth of Continental keyboard music remains uncelebrated. Although Arnolt Schlick is briefly mentioned, even organ music in Germany is passed over quickly. Music for the organ and harpsichord in France is not even mentioned.

Burney's history of seventeenth-century music is similarly circumscribed. Jan Pieterszoon Sweelinck is not referred to in the *History*. The greatest representative of the German school, Michael Praetorius, is passed over without mention,[59] and Samuel Scheidt, Heinrich Scheidemann, and several others are dealt with summarily in a brief list of celebrated organists. Walther's *Lexicon* provided Burney with a list of the titles and dates of publication of German organ music, but if Burney knew of any of the music he refrained from comment. His treatment of seventeenth-century Italy omits any mention of Adriano Banchieri or Giovanni Maria Trabaci. A number of organists are listed, but only one, Girolamo Frescobaldi, receives any critical attention.

Considering Burney's apparent lack of knowledge of early keyboard literature, his essay on Frescobaldi is extraordinary. Frescobaldi, as a composer for organ, is credited with adding "new dignity and attractions" to the organ by composition of "masterly fugues which were soon imitated all over Europe."[60] He is able to evaluate these pieces within their historical context, and judges them to be "of great merit, if we consider the state of instrumental Music at the time they were produced."[61] His criticism of the fugues echoes his standard for church music: "the subjects are well marked and pleasing, harmony pure, and the style chaste and clear." In fact, Burney attributes Frescobaldi's success in organ composition to his reputed excellence as a vocal composer, though Burney apparently had not seen any of his vocal compositions. He is respectful, but less enthusiastic, about Frescobaldi's *Toccate d'intavolature di cimbalo et organo* (1637), which contained full pieces of difficult execution. The presence of "the fashionable divisions and graces of the times" dated these pieces more than those in the church style, but even in this style Frescobaldi's music contained more merit than any other "harpsichord [i.e., keyboard] music of the same age."[62]

The organists of France in the seventeenth century are represented in the *History* by only a brief list probably taken from La Borde's *Essai sur la musique*. Keyboard music in seventeenth-century England is virtually ignored. The greatest English composers—Orlando Gibbons, Thomas Tomkins, John Blow, and Henry Purcell—are discussed at length, but their keyboard works pass unnoticed. Purcell's biography and criticism of his works occupy more pages of the *History* than those of any other composer except Handel. Nonetheless, his keyboard works are not mentioned, despite the presence of his *Choice Collection of Lessons for the Harpsichord or Spinet* (1696) in Burney's library. This gap in the *History* is quite surprising in light of his extensive treatment of Elizabethan virginal music. It is tempting to regard Burney's oversight as intentional.[63]

Reviewing the literature for organ in the sixteenth and seventeenth centuries, he apparently discerned nothing noteworthy after the music of Frescobaldi.

> Our Bird, Dr. Bull, and Giles Farnaby seem to have been the greatest organ players in Europe during the sixteenth century, and the beginning of the next, till Frescobaldi introduced a superior style of treating the organ, divested of rapid and frivolous divisions which disgrace that most noble and comprehensive of all instruments. Indeed the fugues in the ricercari of Frescobaldi are worked with such genius and learning as have never been surpassed, unless by those of Sebastian Bach, and Handel, which seem to include every perfection of which this ingenious and elaborate species of composition is capable. Indeed, if we except these fugues, all instrumental music, particularly that for keyed instruments, seems to have been in a very rude state at this time throughout Europe. It was dry, difficult, unaccented and insipid.[64]

Burney's writings on eighteenth-century keyboard music present at once a plethora and a poverty of material. His visits to Europe's leading virtuosi on his tours, and his interviews with their close associates (for example, Abbé Augier, friend of Domenico Scarlatti), have been invaluable for scholars and collectors of anecdotes. But, as was the case in his discussion of the secular vocal music of this period, there is little true criticism to be found amongst any of his published material. Burney was an organist, harpsichordist, and composer for keyed instruments; nonetheless, his writings sketch only the merest outlines of the development of eighteenth-century keyboard music. He seizes upon the most revolutionary changes, enthusiastically reporting on the genius of Domenico Scarlatti and Emanuel Bach, and the taste of Domenico Alberti, but he gives only the most general idea of their styles, probably because he felt that the music would be well known to his readers.

Burney believed he had been a witness to all of the great changes of style in the keyboard music of his era, but his writings more accurately reflect the history of his own changing taste in keyboard music than the true historical progression.[65] Nonetheless, his view was sufficient for an English history of music. A manuscript in Burney's hand dated 1744 gives us an idea of the repertory he was studying at this time, a time during which he copied a "prodigious" amount of music to advance his knowledge of composition.[66] It is an impressive selection of fairly current music of the best native and foreign musicians active in London. Beside twelve sonatas by Geminiani, the collection consists of three suites of lessons by J.C. Smith, two concertos by Handel, and one solo by Dr. Arne. It can be surmised from this sampling and corroborative biographical data that Burney's taste was quite conventional for an emerging young provincial English musician. He explained to Twining that

Handel, Geminiani and Corelli were the sole Divinities of my youth; but I was drawn off from their exclusive worship before I was twenty, by keeping company with travellers and heterodox gentlemen, who were partial to the Music of more modern composers whom they had heard in Italy.[67]

Domenico Scarlatti, who became Burney's hero in the 1750s, composed sonatas "so wild, fanciful, difficult and eccentric as to be truly inimitable, and this was the only genius who had no Issue, who formed no school, and whose property was out of reach of free looters, pilferers or counterfeiters."[68] Scarlatti may have been inimitable, but Burney has been accused of being one of his would-be imitators. Burney's first set of sonatas for harpsichord (1761) show the influence of Scarlatti's techniques. William Newman's evaluation of Burney's sonatas focuses on these similarities, especially in the fast movements, which "skip about naively from one favorite Scarlatti device to another."[69] Frequent hand-crossing and repeated notes do characterize several of the movements, but there is more to these pieces than mere imitation of Scarlatti. The forms of the sonatas differ totally from Scarlatti's; they are all multimovement works. Five of the six begin with a rhapsodic prelude unknown in Scarlatti's works, but found in Handel's.

No single form is characteristic of English sonatas or lessons from this period. The genre for English composers was quite new, having been established in 1747 by the appearance of James Nares's first sonatas. His were followed in 1756 by those of Burney's master, Thomas Arne. Neither composer adhered to a single form, their works containing variously one to four movements. Each wrote one sonata with a prelude, and if Burney derived his form from any model, it may have been Arne's third sonata, the prelude of which has an obvious kinship to Burney's.

Stylistically, it is easy to identify elements of the modern Italian style, such as the modified Alberti bass figures, in Burney's Sonatas I ii and II iii. This device was not new in England; it had appeared in Giuseppe Jozzi's plagiarisms of Alberti's sonatas in 1745, and in Alberti's sonatas published by Walsh in 1748.[70] The device was popularized also by Italian composers active in England, among them Giovanni Battista Pescetti, whose modified Alberti bass in the second movement of his seventh sonata is echoed in Burney's Sonata II iii. Also evident in Burney's works are moments reminiscent of Emanuel Bach, especially the *affetuoso* of the fourth sonata, with its diverse rhythms and ad-libitum cadenza at the end of the movement.

One feature of these sonatas, the occurrence of long stretches of repeated notes, as in Sonata V ii, gave rise to criticism of Burney's skill as a composer in an anonymous pamphlet published in 1780. The writer was either unaware of Scarlatti's music, or, unlike modern critics, did not deem the occurrence of repeated notes indisputable evidence of Scarlatti's influence.

BURNEY, DOCTOR

Has written a learned and elegant history of Music. We can't say much in his praise as a composer, his lessons having nothing remarkable in them, but the frequent repetition of one note, which *trick* we think rather ill-adapted to the harpsichord. He first wrote lessons for two performers on one instrument, which are very inferior to some since published by Mr. Bach.[71]

There can be no claim for originality or great genius for Burney's sonatas, but they are more than copies of Scarlatti's. They are eclectic, hovering on the verge of imitating the several styles of Scarlatti, Bach, Handel, and Alberti and the other "modern" Italians, yet never becoming blatant copies. Burney, who as a critic was ever vigilant of the plagiaries of musicians, avoids plagiarism, but not imitation. His pieces exemplify how strongly Continental music affected English composers. In Burney's view eighteenth-century English composers were solid craftsmen, but had limited genius; Burney himself falls comfortably into this category.

After Scarlatti, Burney saw the next "revolution in style" as establishing the modern Italian manner best represented in the keyboard works of Domenico Alberti. The "more natural and elegant style of Alberti captivated the public and was an object of easy imitation in composition throughout Europe."[72] Alberti's special merit is explained in a second autobiographical recounting of the development of Burney's taste, which includes his experience up until December, 1781: in a letter to Twining he relates what he calls his *profession de foi*.

As to Harpsichord Music besides the study of Handel's *Lessons*, which in that elaborate style are admirable, I was early a great admirer of the original Fancy, boldness, delicacy, and Fire of Domenico Scarlatti, so different from all lessons before and since! Then the Taste, refinement, and elegant *Chant* of Alberti, struck me as new in instrumental music; and though the easy monotony of his division Bases is so easy to imitate, yet none of those who have used the like expedient for supplying the short-lived tone of the Harpsichord by this kind of bustle, have equalled him in the taste and elegance of his treble part. From the time his pieces were first printed Composers of all kinds seem only to pour water on the *leaves* of others till the German Symphonies appeared by Stamitz, Filtz, Haultzbaur, Canabich, etc. The two Martinis indeed had original merit, the one on the old plan, and the other on the new; but the Sonatas of Zanetti and Campioni seemed models of grace and elegance till those of Schwindl and Abel appeared... you know my opinion of our friend Em. Bach, Schobert, Eichner, and now and then Echard, are *stock* composers for the P.F. with me, and since then I can recollect—nothing like a new *genre* struck out.[73]

The presence of a number of German symphonists on Burney's list reflects the popularity in London of keyboard arrangements of the latest symphonic literature, an interest evidenced by another document, a receipt made out to one Miss Hoare, a student of Burney's.

Miss Hoare's Acct. to Chas. Burney. 1778

Entrance	£ 4. 4.0
From May 6th. 1778 to July 18th 22 Lessons	11.11.0
Augt. 29. Octr. 6.10.24.31 Novr 21.28)	
Decr 5.12.19.23.—11 Lessons)	5.15.5
2 Sets of Schoberts Sonatas	0. 8.0
2 Do. Harpd. Duets, 6d	1. 3.0
Eichner's 1st. Set 3 Sonatas	0. 5.0
2 Overtures, Vanhal	0. 4.0
Blank Bk.	0. 5.0
	£23.15.6

1779

From Jany. 20th. to May 1st. 24 Lessons	12.12.0
Eichener's 2d. Set 3 Sonatas, 3d. Set 6 Do.	0.16.0
1 Set Bach's Sonatas	0.10.6
Schobert Completed	2.11.6
	£16.10.0
Total	£40. 5.6

30th. Septr. 1779
Recd. the full Contents
Chas. Burney.[74]

Emanuel Bach, like Domenico Scarlatti, held a special position in Burney's catalogue of composers. His "delicate, refined and original style" was "universally imitated in Germany," but was, according to Burney, "nowhere sufficiently known or familiar in England to supply food to predatory professors," a curious remark, since Walsh pubished a set of Emanuel Bach's music in the 1760s, and his music was widely available in manuscript copies. So enthusiastic was Burney for Bach's genius that he proffered him as a model to refute Mainwaring's assertion that "great imagination and perfect taste are seldom united." He responds, "The concurrance however happens sometimes. Instance Domenico Scarlatti and C.P.E. Bach."[75] In 1771 Burney wrote to Ebeling that Bach

> stands so high in my opinion, that I should not scruple to pronounce him the greatest writer for the Harpsichord now alive, or that has ever existed as far as I am able to judge, by a comparison of his works with those of others, and by my own feelings when I hear them performed.[76]

The enthusiasm evident in the above passages and the glowing appraisal of Bach in the *German Tour* waned in later years. In November, 1783, Burney sent a package to Twining, including "a new set of Em. Bach Pieces—chiefly Rondeaus—with many new kicks, and detours—But he seems reduced to *recherché* and caprice in order to be new—and to say the truth, his Elève Haydn seems to have given him the *go by* on his own ground."[77] An undated passage in his notebook reports that he was finding Bach becoming "every day more *manière,* hasty and careless in his production."[78] Occasionally the difficulties of Bach's music annoyed him, and when asked by Twining to finger a particularly arduous passage, he responded "what queer toads!—yet they are Bach's—would not one think they were written by a man who had never laid his hand on a keyed instrument?"[79]

By the time the *History* was published in 1789, Emanuel Bach is listed, along with his father Sebastian Bach, as a composer who could have profited from composing for the

> stage and public of the great capitals, such as Naples, Paris or London... the one [J.S. Bach] would have sacrificed all unmeaning art and contrivance; and the other been less fantastical and *recherché,* and both, by writing in a style more popular, and generally intelligible and pleasing, would have extended their fame, and been indisputably the greatest musicians that ever lived.[80]

There has been a good deal of sanctimonious cant about Burney's "failure" to appreciate J.S. Bach. The erroneous impression, now given the status of "truth," is that Burney did not recognize Bach's genius and neither appreciated nor understood Bach's music. The misconception is traceable to Samuel Wesley's correspondence. This was published by Eliza Wesley to ensure the "accord of Honour to whom Honour is due" for her father having introduced Bach's music to England. Eliza states that it was through her father's "discernment and zealous perseverance that Bach's transcendent genius was made known and appreciated (although tardily, and through much opposition) by the English musical world."[81]

The first letter in Eliza's anthology presents Wesley's colorful account of Burney's supposed first real encounter with Bach's music, following which he claims Burney recanted his earlier criticisms of Bach as imprudent, incautious, and ignorant. Wesley in a later letter asserts that he completely converted Burney to Bach's music. Although Burney's own letters to Wesley display considerable interest and enthusiasm, his enthusiasm may well have been augmented by his satisfaction at being consulted on musical matters after he had essentially retired from public life. He was, no doubt, flattered by the attentions of a new generation of musicians. At the same time, he was distressed by the great fuss Wesley was making over his "discovery" of Bach. An annotation on a draft of his letter to Wesley of 17 October 1808 is illuminating: "I can boast of being the first to make my country acquainted with J. Seb. Bach, for when my *German Tour* was first published, there were perhaps not above four professors in the Kingdom who had ever heard his name."

The account of the Bach "conversion" is more likely a reflection of Wesley's and his daughter's enthusiasms than an accurate chronicle of a substantive change in Burney's opinion. Burney was well acquainted with Bach's music years before his meetings with Wesley. As early as 1750 he witnessed a child prodigy who astonished every auditor with his performances of "Sebastian Bach's most difficult harpsichord lessons."[82] He probably had other opportunities to hear Bach's music and certainly to study it, for specimens of Bach's works were scattered throughout many of the most important theoretical works of the last half of the eighteenth century.[83] Burney's friend A.F.C. Kollman published the "Prelude and Fugue in F minor" from Book II of the *Well Tempered Clavier* in his *Essay on Musical Harmony* (1796), and in his *Essay on Practical Musical Composition* in 1799 he printed all of the riddle canons from the *Musical Offering,* the "Prelude and Fugue in C" from the *Well Tempered Clavier,* Book I, and an organ trio. Burney's own canons appeared in this last collection, and he reviewed the publication for the *Monthly Review.* Surely, if he had required any reintroduction to Bach's music, he would have discussed it with Kollman more than five years before Wesley began his efforts.

Another publication reviewed by Burney, William Shield's *Introduction to Harmony* (1800), included the "D minor Prelude" from the *Well Tempered Clavier,* Book I. In addition, a London edition of the "Forty-eight Preludes and Fugues" was published in 1800-1801, which predated Wesley's edition by a decade, and seems to contradict Eliza Wesley's implication that Samuel was the first to publish Bach's *Well Tempered Clavier* in England. One can thus dismiss Wesley's claim that Burney had never heard any of Sebastian Bach's music, an assertion which was absurd in any case.

None of Burney's comments on Bach created a stir in Germany until the German translation of the *Account of the Commemoration of Handel* appeared. Burney evaluated Handel's "full, masterly and excellent *organ-fugues,* upon the most natural and pleasing subjects," and found that "he has surpassed Frescobaldi, and even Sebastian Bach, and others of his countrymen, the most renowned for abilities in this difficult and elaborate species of composition."[84] Many Germans were provoked, including Emanuel Bach, who sent an acrimonious letter to Johann Joachim Eschenburg, translator of the *Account,* in which he took exception to Burney's comparison, finding it absurd that an Englishman should make such a judgment, since most English organs lacked pedals; as a result Burney could have had "no insight into what constitutes the excellence of organ-playing," and other "innumerable things."[85] Moreover, Bach found the styles of his father and Handel so disparate as to make comparisons meaningless. One can certainly concur with him that "Comparisons are difficult and are not even necessary," but the comparison was made, and there is no reason to suspect that Burney's judgment was not sincere. Even had Burney believed Bach to be the superior organist, he probably could not have presented such an idea in a booklet which was a commemorative program prepared for persons predisposed to regard Handel as the greatest of all musicians.

As indefensible as Burney's judgment appears today, he was not alone in his view. Johann Friedrich Reichardt, surely as patriotic a critic as ever lived (and a severe one, if we may judge by his criticism of Burney's *Tours*), wrote in 1782 that "Never did a composer, not even the best and deepest of Italians, exhaust all the possibilities of our harmony as did J.S. Bach... Had Bach the high sense of truth and the deep feeling for expression that animated Handel, he would have been far greater even than Handel himself; but as it happens, he is only much more artful (kunstgelehrter) and laborious (fleissiger)."[86] Thus, even a critic raised with full knowledge of the German organ tradition at one time entertained a judgment similar to Burney's. Reichardt revised this passage in 1796, omitting the passage comparing Bach and Handel. It is probably not coincidental that he did so after the publication of an article very similar to Bach's letter to Eschenburg in the *Allgemeine deutsche Bibliothek*.[87] The similarity of Burney's and Reichardt's assessments challenges contemporary and modern opinions that nothing but ignorance can explain Burney's judgment of 1784.

Burney was certain that he had accorded Bach full honor, so much so that he questioned the necessity of Forkel's new biography. He felt that when he was in Leipzig in 1772 he had "procured from Mr. Hiller, music director there, all the information I could concerning him. From Mr. Marpurg at Berlin, the same, and at Hambro his illustrious and most admirable Son, Carl Phil. Emanuel, and I never met or conversed together, without his father (for whom he had a great veneration) making a part of our discourse. How Dr. Forkel can have procured authentic materials since that time to furnish a Book, I know not."[88] Burney obviously thought that he had done a creditable job of informing the musical world about Sebastian Bach and, indeed, took pride in having done so.

He could be equally confident that his critical evaluation of Bach was correct and sufficient. Taken as a whole his criticism of Bach is very favorable. He is respectfully mentioned in every volume of the *History,* and in the second volume is referred to as one of the "greatest musicians that ever existed."[89] He is referred to in the *German Tour* as the "great Sebastian Bach," a descendant of a "constant succession of great musicians,"[90] and one on whose model "all the present organ-players of Germany are formed."[91] Burney called a credo by Bach which he scored in manuscript "one of the most clear, correct and masterly [works] I have ever seen."[92]

In Burney's estimation, Bach had an abundance of genius and invention, but these were not adequately balanced by taste. With such qualities, he was a great, though not universal, musician. Burney's attitude that canon and fugue were a form of the art of music properly practised only by professors also shaped his judgment of Bach's music, for Burney was writing for a dilettante audience. Marpurg asserted that Bach was "profound in science, fertile in fancy, and in taste *easy* and *natural.*" Burney countered that his examination of Bach's organ music showed him to be "constantly in search of what was new and difficult without the least attention to nature and facility."[93] One can perceive the relationship between Bach's genius and the fashion of the day in Burney's assessment of Charles Frederic Abel:

> Abels' musical science in harmony, modulation, fugue, and canon, which he had acquired under his great master Sebastian Bach, and taste under Hasse and the great singers employed in the performance of his operas at Dresden, had made him so complete a musician, that he soon became the umpire in all musical controversy, and was consulted in difficult and knotty points as an infallible oracle.[94]

Bach was not the greatest of all musicians in Burney's estimation, but he never assigned that honor to anyone because in his view music was in the process of continuous refinement. Bach's music was out of fashion during Burney's day, but fashion and genius are not the same thing and Burney knew it. He could celebrate Bach's wondrous creativity and mastery of technique, and at the same time stigmatize his music.[95]

Burney's tour to Italy in 1770 did not cause him to change his view of the development of keyboard music. Italy was home of the greatest vocal composers, but the genius and taste which gave rise to the finest vocal music seemed to him to be antithetic to that required for keyboard music. Reflecting on this curious circumstance, he asked Twining:

> But who writes perfectly well for an instrument of which he is not an entire master? When Sacchini, Vanhal, Jomelli, Piccini, or any first rate Composer for voices or other instruments writes for the Harpsichord, what flimsy, awkward stuff it is.[96]

A passage from the *History* amplifies Burney's opinion of the defects inherent in the keyboard writing of vocal composers.

> Perhaps the superiority of vocal expression requires fewer notes in a song than a sonata; in which the facility of executing many passages that are unfit for the voice, tempts a composer to hazard every thing that is new. Thus the simplicity and paucity of notes, which constitute grace, elegance, and expression in vocal Music, render instrumental, meagre and insipid.[97]

It is curious that Burney, in drafting these opinions, overlooked the operatic experience of Scarlatti and Alberti: both had composed operas before writing their keyboard works. He also overlooked the approximately 100 sonatas of Galuppi, one of his favorite opera composers, which are thought today to be the best of their kind by an Italian master.[98] Nonetheless, with the exception of Domenico Scarlatti and the dilettante Alberti, Italy, in Burney's opinion, gave birth to no other composer of any merit for keyed instruments.

During Burney's German tour he discovered many great organists, but they astounded him with the elaborate style of performance and full textures, rather than with their genius or taste. He does, however, acknowledge that "the organs of Germany in magnitude, and the organists in abilities, seem unrivalled in any part of Europe particularly in the use of pedals."[99] J.S. Bach's style, as Burney saw it, dominated German organ music. But for the harpsichord and pianoforte, Germany had also Handel, the younger Bachs, Schobert, Wagenseil, and Müthel.

Christoph Wagenseil is the only composer on this list whose name does not appear in Burney's writings prior to the *Tours,* (although Burney was certainly acquainted with his music before he left England.)[100] He was among the first to break away from the old fugal manner of playing in Germany, and his compositions, according to Burney,

> till Emanuel Bach changed the style of playing on keyed instruments throughout Germany, were in favor throughout Europe, and mostly admired for their spirit and originality; as he had quitted the dry, laboured, and crowded style of his predecessors, and given way to fancy, with no unsuccessful attempts at new effects in his compositions.[101]

Wagenseil, in his originality, was one of a few exceptions to the generality of German keyboard composers aping Emanuel Bach's style. Bach was

> ...soon imitated so universally in Germany by writers for keyed-instruments, that there have been few works published for them since, which are not strongly tinctured with his style; those of Wagenseil, Schobert, and Schultz excepted; but Geo. Benda, C. Fasch, Fleischer, Ernst, Benda, Reichardt, etc. etc. are strong Bachists.[102]

Burney's notable enthusiasm for Johann Schobert's music stems from his apparently justifiable claim of having been the first to introduce Schobert's music to England, following his journey to Paris in 1765.[103] Schobert's favor in England was limited by the gradual victory of the pianoforte over the harpsichord as the popular instrument, for "the spirit and fire of his pieces require not only a strong hand but a *harpsichord* to give them all their force and effect. They are too rapid, and have too many notes for clavichords or piano forte."[104] His contribution to the keyboard style was "the use of the pedal of the Harpsichord and Pianoforte" in his "bold and powerful pieces." In particular, Burney notes Schobert's "means of imitating the light and shade of an Orchestra; and the contrast and effects of a numerous band in the execution of the Symphonies."[105]

After the music of Emanuel Bach, Wagenseil, and Schobert, Joseph Haydn's keyboard music next caught Burney's attention. Haydn "candidly confessed" that he made Emanuel Bach his model in writing for keyed instruments,[106] but unlike Bach, he kept his invention within the bounds of taste. The influence of C.P.E. Bach's music was so apparent in Haydn's works that

> Whoever studies the productions of this author will discover him to have been the model of the admirable Haydn, particularly in writing for the P.F. and indeed in Bach's compositions we may sometimes see the germ of many of Haydn's comic strokes and what may be called his musical *bons mots*. Modulation too had been greatly extended by Em. Bach before it was quite unchained by Haydn. I mean not however, by any means, to diminish the just title which Haydn has to originality of which he has more perhaps in Melody and effects.[107]

Unfortunately, Burney does not review any of Haydn's sonatas, but his own sincere interest in promoting Haydn's sonatas is attested to by his arrangements of Haydn's "Op. 13, 14 and 17 for Violin and Piano."[108] In addition to the sonatas, Burney arranged for the use of his own students Haydn's "Symphony in D" (Hob.I, 53), and recommended the pianoforte arrangements of the "Symphony in E♭" (Hob.I, 74, adapted by Giardini) and the "F Major Symphony" (Hob.I, 67) to Twining.[109] His enthusiasm for Haydn's keyboard music is similarly evident in his library catalogue, which contains thirty-eight lots of music by Haydn, most of them for piano.

Two documents shed light on Burney's taste in keyboard music after 1789. The first is a letter written in 1797 in which Burney continues to recommend Haydn's works. He favors piano arrangements of the London symphonies with violin accompaniment, but informs his correspondent that "They are dear, long and difficult; but deserve all the trouble they give the performer."[110] In the same letter the name of a new composer, Daniel Steibelt, is mentioned. Steibelt arrived in London in 1796, after a successful stay in Paris, and he published a number of compositions in quick succession. Burney described him as "a young man with a great hand on his Instrument and possessed of knowledge and *real Genius.*" Though standard reference works do not mention the fact, Burney states that "he was a scholar of our old great favourite *Emanuel Bach.*" He was, however, not a mere imitator of Bach or Haydn; his works always had elegant and natural melodies, and avoided the current fashionable vice of long passages in chromatic scales, which he supplanted with "better resources."

Burney's evaluation of Mozart's piano music rested upon his acquaintance with Mozart's earliest compositions. Mozart's "harpsichord lessons" frequently appeared in London, but according to Burney, they seemed very experimental. "They were full of new passages and new effects; but were wild, capricious and not always pleasing." One feature of Mozart's keyboard music which did not suit him is mentioned in the article "Accelerando" in the *Cyclopaedia.*

> Daring imitators of the bold modulation of Haydn, and of the rapid running up and down the keys in half notes, as Mozart did in his juvenile days, have deformed melody and corrupted harmony. These great masters knew when to stop; but their apes think they can never season their productions too highly.

The same complaint is voiced in William Jackson of Exeter's *Observation on the Present State of Music in London* (1791), and though Burney scorned many of Jackson's judgments, he concurred with his objections to chromatic passage-work.

> He condemns, we think justly, the *staggering octaves*, and the perpetual running up and down the keys on the piano forte in *semi-tones*. Once in a year, perhaps, the rapid *ascent* in half-notes may be borne: but *downward*, the effect is as detestable as if the keys were swept with a broom, or as if the performer had taken an emetic;—and yet every *master*, and every *miss*, who is able to atchieve [sic] this feat, never omits it at a close, be the piece to which it is applied grave, gay, or graceful.[111]

Mozart's "Variations," printed in London in 1800, however, he judged the "most beautiful, amusing, and useful compositions for the piano forte that have ever been produced since the invention of that instrument." In Mozart's variations he found "peculiar difficulties of execution, refinement, and expression to vanquish, at which it is in vain for mediocrity to aspire."[112]

It is difficult to trace the chronology of Burney's acquaintance with Mozart's keyboard music. His library contained the *Oeuvres Complettes* for the pianoforte with accompaniments, printed in Leipzig in 1799, but he also must have owned earlier editions published in London.[113] Though Burney was late in admiring Mozart's keyboard music, there were those who were even later. His diary entry for 21 March 1806 records his hearing "the foremost and most difficult of Mozart's pieces, which were not understood or listened to by three people in the room."[114]

The contemporaneity (by English standards) of Burney's taste in keyboard music almost up until the time of his death is remarkable, as is evident in a list of composers recommended as models to aspiring young composers. The list appears in the *History* (1789) and the *Cyclopaedia*, where it is revised to approximately 1806.

History	Cyclopaedia	
Alberti	Alberti	Mozart
D. Scarlatti	D. Scarlatti	Beethoven
Emanuel Bach	Emanuel Bach	Clementi
Schobert	Schobert	Steibelt
Eichner	Eichner	Dussic [sic]
Kozeluch	Kozeluch	Cramer[115]

Surprisingly, Johann Müthel is absent from both of these lists. Müthel's "Duetto for two clavichords, two harpsichords, or two piano fortes," printed by Hartknoc at Riga in 1771, was a stock piece at the famous musical evenings held at the Burney home, and his daughter Hetty and nephew Charles Rousseau were famous for their rendition of this difficult sonata. Müthel was a pupil of Sebastian Bach, and later a close friend of Emanuel Bach, whose influence is apparent in his sonatas. The sonatas are exceedingly demanding technically; Burney suggests that should a young virtuoso think that he has conquered all the difficulties of his instrument, and nothing remains to be vanquished, he should attempt the "compositions of Müthel."[116] His essay on Müthel in the *Cyclopaedia* is especially revealing about his own knowledge of Continental keyboard music. The approbation contained in the *German Tour* is here tempered by the following admission.

> From having in 1772, seen few of the works of Vanhal or Haydn, and none of Mozart, except his childish productions... we admired the taste, invention, high finishing, complication, and equality of grace and melody which he gave to all parts of his concertos... But after having lost them for many years, on recovering and deliberately examining them, we find the two laws laid down by Rousseau, and generally adopted infringed: the want of *symmetry* and *phraseology* in the number of bars and *unity of melody*.[117]

But Burney allows that Rousseau's laws were probably unknown in Germany at that time. Despite Burney's invocation of Rousseau's theory in judging Müthel's composition, he admits that Rousseau "pushed *simplicity* and *unity of melody* perhaps too far: there are effects produced by harmony and modulation, occasionally quite independent of melody." Compared to Emanuel Bach, Müthel was inferior in grace, but superior to him in the originality of the solo parts of his concertos, in which no vulgar or ordinary passage was to be found. Though captivated by the difficulty and wild fancy of Müthel's pieces in the 1770s, Burney later came to regard them as somewhat undisciplined, in the same way he turned away from C.P.E. Bach's later keyboard music.

It is noteworthy that, despite Burney's reputation as an incorrigible Italianate, his list of the greatest keyboard artists is heavily balanced on the side of the Germans. Among the new names on Burney's revised list in the *Cyclopedia*, the inclusion of Beethoven and Dussek are indeed surprising. According to Burney's memoranda, he first heard Beethoven's piano music performed by one Miss Tate in 1803 during his seventy-seventh year. He found his compositions so full of novelty, taste, grace, and masterly designs, "that we should not hesitate to rank them among the greatest of the last and present age."[118] Burney's tastes were thus still quite open to the best new music.

The appearance of Jan Dussek on Burney's list is somewhat more expected, since he was one of Emanuel Bach's pupils. Dussek was established in London in October, 1789, by which time he had given some instruction to Charles Rousseau Burney. Burney met him at his nephew's home and became one of his many English admirers, noting that he composed and played in the style of his old favorite Emanuel Bach more than any other.[119]

202   Chamber Music

Burney was to come to know another of the important pre-romantic pianists, Johann Nepomuk Hummel. A young prodigy, Hummel studied with Mozart for two years, after which he left on a concert tour, arriving in London in 1790. Like many of the foreign virtuosi before him, Hummel's father sought to enlist Burney's support for the youthful musician in London. Hummel was introduced to Burney by none other than William Mason,[120] who in a very condescending letter urged Burney to hear the prodigy. Burney's letter to Fanny following the young man's audition is one of the most remarkable documents in the Burney papers, and in a sense brings Burney's career as one of London's leading musicians full circle.

> I had just stuck the little boy down to my large Piano forte which in the morning I had tuned very nicely; when behold the Pac. came. I made him begin the Piece again, which was one of his master Mozart's, as I found—a French Air with very difficult and ingenious variations, which were executed with the utmost precision. The little boy seeming to think the touch of my large piano forte somewhat hard, I carried him into the study, where I had a small one of Broadwood's, which had luckily been tuned two or three days ago, and this suiting his hand better, I had it carried instantly into the parlour. He then played another lesson—equally neat—and on being asked if he played extempore at sight, accompanied or composed, he was modest in his answer; but said he would play us some variations of his making (to an English tune: the plough-boy, I believe, by my old scholar Mr. Hook) These Pac. said he liked better than Dussec's variations to the same tune—they were ingenious and full of difficulties. I then brought him some Music I have just received from Germany—ill printed, but good composition. He first played a song by Mozart, which he entered into the Spirit of very well. (It is in a periodical work to which I have subscribed, printed at Speier, called *Bibliothek der Grazien,* Library of the Graces. The title is affected, but the music often excellent.) I next set the little man to work at a very fine Symphony of Haydn's, but extremely *recherchée* and difficult—He first of all had the prudence to cast his Eye over each page to see what he was to expect; and afterwards played the whole in masterly manner. If it was at sight, as I really believe it was, I can venture to say that there are very few Masters who could have played it so well.
>
> Upon the whole, I think him a very extraordinary performer, for his age; and that with his natural fire and love of Music, he who has begun so well, must end in a great Musician. I think his hand (of which however I am not quite satisfied with the carriage) is capable of anything that is worth doing or fit to be heard in the way of difficulty. His taste and expression will of course be improved by hearing other great performers, more especially *singers.* I like the character of the boy; it is natural, docile, and civil. And I shall be very glad to be of use to him in whatever is in my power. Pac. is very kind to him on Mr. Mason's account as well as his own and mine. He has invited him on Saturday Evening when I shall be there, and perhaps he will hear some singing. I shall propose him to Mr. Burney and Hetty the next time they have Music. I advise him not to make himself common till the town is full, and he has a benefit, or plays at some great Concert. He should be heard at the Professional Concert, which Cramer might manage for him for a word from Royalty.
>
> It is odd that 30 years after his Master Mozart had been recommended to me, and played on my knee, on subjects I gave him, that this little Man should also claim and merit my kindness.[121]

Burney's activities on behalf of other musicians have drawn little attention, yet a great deal of evidence suggests that in almost all circles of London musical life (the notable exception being the playhouse community) Burney exercised considerable influence. One of London's most fashionable teachers after his return to the city in 1760, he was welcomed in the best homes, and could surely influence the scheduling of concerts and even capture the king's ear on musical matters. It is small wonder that his support was so eagerly sought. Mozart was in London before Burney carried sufficient influence to help or hinder his success. He was able to sponsor a number of later musicians, and his papers record his auditions of a number of prodigies, both English and foreign, who sought his patronage. Most notable among the English musicians were William Parsons and the young William Crotch. The latter received strong support from Burney until he was well established. Hummel was similarly favored, as were other greater and lesser composers and performers whose names are now forgotten. Fanny's editorial work has deprived us of the full record of his service to other musicians.

According to his own assessment, Burney was more in touch with keyboard music than with any other genre. His taste for Italian opera has drawn great attention, but keyboard music was the heart of his professional life, not as performer or composer, but as teacher. Doubtless his teaching, which he continued until 1804,[122] kept him abreast of the latest fashion, as did the musical evenings he attended after he discontinued teaching. He had an opportunity of reviewing his *Cyclopaedia* articles until at least 1808, if not later, allowing him to chronicle, however sketchily, the change in style from Bach and Handel to Hummel and Beethoven.

Instrumental, Chamber, and Orchestral Music

Like the other categories of chamber music, instrumental chamber music receives very unsystematic treatment in the *History*. The status of chamber music as "house music" may account in part for this sparse treatment. The smaller instrumental forms (chamber music in the modern sense) were immensely popular in England, especially the trio sonata and the accompanied sonata. Practically every minor fiddler, flautist, and harpsichordist, including Burney, published compositions, often just to peddle them to students, a practice which may also account for the historian's casual attitude toward most of these productions. Burney's history of instrumental music may lack the order convenient to the modern reader, but his chronicle, irregular and incomplete though it is, provides a vital, first-hand account of an era.

Early instrumental music, which to Burney was even more passé than early secular vocal or keyboard music, receives little notice, and that little is none too objective. Burney was aware of the use of viols to support voices in madrigal performance, or to fill in for missing voice parts in sixteenth-century compositions, but he was searching for purely instrumental music. Examining the records of Elizabethan times, he concluded that there must have been a strong preference for military music, and mockingly remarked that music for viol and lute was "too feeble for the obtuse organs of our Gothic ancestors." The sources available to Burney seemed to show that madrigals, "which were almost the only compositions, in parts, for the Chamber, then cultivated," were suddenly supplanted "by a passion for Fantasias of three, four, five, and six parts, wholly composed for viols and other instruments, without vocal assistance."[123] Burney's belief in progressive history, with its increasing refinements, is reflected in his explanation of the change in practice: purely instrumental music was encouraged because the words of the madrigals were unintelligible and the singing "often coarse and out of tune."

His ability to chronicle the development of the Elizabethan fantasy was not hampered by a lack of music. He possessed "several considerable manuscript collections of fancies," but he regarded them as "very dry," and enjoyed a bit of pun by labeling them "fanciless." It was to him curious "how ingenious and well disposed the lovers of Music, during the former part of the last century must have been, to extract pleasure from such productions."[124] In short, these pieces were a product of the "infancy" of instrumental composition.

Early pieces were adopted from vocal models but performed instrumentally; they thus had neither poetry nor the virtues of first-rate instrumental music to recommend them. Even a composer of the stature of Orlando Gibbons fell miserably short in writing for instruments, his compositions lacking a number of the attributes which Burney's eighteenth-century orientation required. No knowledge of the expressive power of the bow was evident, and it was apparent that air, accent, grace, and expression were "equally unknown to the composer, performer, and hearer." Indeed, Burney judged that up until 1625 "all instrumental music but that of the organ, seems to have been in a very rude state at this time throughout Europe; and if we except the fugues of Frescobaldi, all the Music, even for keyed-instruments, is dry, difficult, unaccented, and insipid."[125]

Though he was merciless in his evaluation of the music of seventeenth-century English composers, Burney recognized the fame that these musicians had acquired in their own time, even if the cause of their celebrity escaped him. He drew heavily from the *Memoires* of Roger North, printing for instance, a lengthy appreciation of John Jenkins without challenging North's favorable assessment of Jenkins's skill as a composer of fancies. Though Burney seems largely to have forgotten his duty as historian in favor of that of critic, an occasional indication of historical perspective is apparent in comments such as his note that the encomiastic verses prefixed to Christopher Simpson's *Division Violist* only show "with what perishable materials musical fame is built."[126]

Burney, always at his most entertaining when writing about music or musicians he disdains, treats the reader to the following reflection on the period of transition from viol to violin.

> It was at this time an instance of great condescension for a musician of *character* to write expressly for so ribald and vulgar an instrument, as the violin was accounted by the lovers of lutes, guitars, and all the *fretful* tribe.[127]

The advantage of the violin over the viol was its "superior power of expressing almost all that a human voice can produce, except the articulation of words," and because of that expressive capability, the violin ranked highest among all instruments. But Burney's displeasure was not rooted solely in his dissatisfaction with the instruments. Although he had managed to remain mildly respectful in his attitude toward some of the vocal music of seventeenth-century English composers, he spared nothing in his condemnation of their instrumental pieces. William Lawes's *Royal Consort,* for example, is classed as "one of the most dry, awkward, and unmeaning compositions I ever remember to have had the trouble of scoring."[128]

Burney found few works written during the reigns of James I and Charles I, the interregnum, and the reign of Charles II that he could heartily praise. The exception was the music written by Purcell, the composer "who is as much the pride of an Englishman in Music as Shakespeare in productions for the stage, Milton in poetry, Lock [sic] in metaphysics, or Sir Isaac Newton in philosophy and mathematics."[129] Yet, Burney's view that a "truly English" composer never existed is maintained when he says that Purcell, "with great personal humility," acknowledged the modeling of his trio sonatas [1683] on the "most famed Italian masters."[130] He praises the sonatas as "infinitely superior in fancy, modulation, design, contrivance, to all the Music of that kind, anterior to the works of Corelli,"[131] but the praise bestowed in this historical judgement is considerably diminished by his critical assessment several pages later that Purcell was

> so little acquainted with the unlimited powers of the violin, that I have scarcely ever seen a becoming passage for that instrument in any one of his works; the symphonies and ritornels to his anthems and songs being equally deficient in force, invention, and effect. And though his sonatas contain many ingenious, and, at the time they were composed, new traits of melody and modulation, if they are compared with the productions of his contemporary Corelli, they will be called barbarous.[132]

Burney's explanation for the inferiority of Purcell's instrumental music harkens back to the reason he advanced to explain the flimsy keyboard music of the Italian vocal composers: Purcell was not a violinist, while Corelli was; to a critic raised in an era when most concertos were played only by their composers, this was a logical and satisfactory explanation.

With the restoration and coronation of Charles II, music in England came under the strong influence of Continental models. The imitation of Louis XIV's *Vingt-quatre violons du roi* by Charles II firmly established the violin as a popular instrument in England. The end of Charles's reign saw the decline in the influence of French music in favor of the Italian. Nicola Matteis was one of the immigrant Italians responsible for the shift in taste, and Burney had a special interest in his activities as a result of his studies on the violin with Matteis's son.[133] The chief distinction of the elder Matteis was "his *arcata,* or manner of bowing, his shakes, divisions, and, indeed, his whole style of performance." In these particulars he excelled all the violinists heard in England in his day.[134] But instrumental technique had developed so much since the time of Matteis that now "no one can have the least idea of these pieces having ever been difficult."[135] Burney displays unusual tolerance for Matteis's music, probably for sentimental reasons, finding that his pieces "still retain such a degree of facility and elegance, and so many traits of the beautiful melody that was floating about Italy during the youth of Corelli, as render them far from contemptible."[136]

Burney's concept of the history of instrumental style is revealingly displayed in his chapter "The Progress of the Violin in Italy from the Sixteenth Century to the Present Time." His work is a history of personalities first, and of style in the broadest sense of the word only insofar as it helped define the personality and contribution of the artist. He does not mention the inherently diverse natures of a concerto by Torelli or Corelli, and a quintet by Boccherini. The music serves one purpose: to exemplify the ability of the virtuoso composer and performer. Burney uses the technical and expressive demands of the compositions as indicators of the virtuosity of the performer-composer whom he has never heard. In tracing the history of performance techniques he gives special attention to bowing. He says of Giovanni Legrenzi's sonatas of 1677, for instance, that "there is considerable merit in the texture and contrivance of the parts, yet, for want of knowledge of the bow, or the particular energies and expressions of the violin, these compositions have been long since justly superseded and effaced, by superior productions of the same kind."[137]

Writing the history of the violin and its performers of Corelli's generation presented Burney with a delicate task. Corelli's music was favored by many dilettante performers and could not be flippantly dismissed as antiquated. Giuseppe Torelli, Corelli's contemporary, was not held in as high esteem, and Burney spurned his music as "now so superannuated, as almost to cease to be music." Corelli was the superior composer, but he, too, needed to be set aside in the interest of protecting the public taste and promoting the superiority of the modern style of instrumental music. While Burney was willing to acknowledge Corelli's merit, he was aware that most of Europe had long since given up the old-style concerto grosso. In England, however, Corelli's music continued not only to be performed, but to be reissued in new publications for "music societies and academies of ancient music," this at the same time that "J.C. Bach was delighting audiences with his galant concertos."[138] Archangelo Corelli's works, we are told, were in 1781 "thrown aside as antiquated lumber by some, and regarded as models of perfection by others"; Burney was compelled to take a stand.[139]

Burney's objection to the old style in comparison with the new is worthy of quotation because of its succinctness, and because it is characteristic of Burney's style at its best and most informative. Oddly, it does not appear in the discussion of Corelli, or indeed any instrumental composer, but in the middle of the chapter on Italian opera in England.

> What was now called writing upon a theme, or adhering to a subject, was very convenient to a sterile fancy; this subject was to be heard as often in a simple melody of one part, as in a fugue of many parts, which occasioned such incessant repetitions of the same passage, in scale, in the fifth, the fourth, with a major and a minor third, as to our ears at present are very dull and tiresome... Corelli hardly ever fails to repeat the same passages in three different keys, generally rising a note higher each time. Such repetitions, however, in all the relative keys, discover much less ingenuity in the composer, and afford less pleasure to the hearer, than such passages as naturally arise out of the subject and are connected with it in melody, measure, and style. In no other art, except architecture, is identity, or exact repetition, a beauty; and in that, symmetry requires the same pillars, windows, and ornaments to be multiplied; but in the sister arts of poetry and painting, the same figures, lines, or ideas, are never presented to the eye or the mind. There are, indeed, happy effects sometimes produced in Music by a precise repetition of the same passage in passionate movements, by which the sentiment is enforced and impressed deeper in the mind, as a nail is driven farther by repeated strokes of the hammer; but this energy is not given to passages by the cold, dull, and barren iteration of the same series of sounds through all possible keys, at which the ear recoils, as a nail does by strokes too frequently repeated. The excess of every style in Music, as well as of every moral virtue, borders on vice; and the adhering too closely to a subject in music seems to have been the vice of the last age, which by repressing invention, and manacling imagination, frequently occasioned dulness and monotony.[140]

Though willing to allow the "grace and elegance" of Corelli's works, Burney faults them for lacking "true pathetic and impassioned melody and modulation."[141] Corelli could not be considered an original genius either because his special quality was not creativity "but a nice ear and most delicate taste."[142] Models for his concertos could be found in Torelli's works, and for his sonatas in those of Bassani and other contemporary composers. Moreover, the redundancy of "certain favorite passages" betrayed "a want of resource," and, Burney concludes, "the musical index to his works would not be long."[143] Burney tempers his strictures by acknowledging Corelli was the first composer of instrumental music whose works will be "respectable, and fixed in their use and reputation, in all probability, as long as the present system of Music shall continue to delight the ears of mankind."[144] He weakens this praise though, by suggesting that the classic appeal of Corelli's music could "only be accounted for on the principle of ease and simplicity."[145] And though Burney concludes his lengthy consideration of Corelli with the observation that his music has "only given way to the more fanciful compositions of the Martini's, Zanetti, Campioni, Giardini, Abel, Schwindl, Boccherini, Stamitz, Haydn, and Pleyel," he was keenly aware that, for many of his readers, Corelli's works had lost ground to *no* later compositions.[146]

Perhaps the greatest disappointment Burney suffered during his Italian tour came from having arrived in Padua just months after the death of Giuseppe Tartini. Tartini was legendary as a violinist, composer, teacher, and founder of the "School of Nations" for violinists. His music was well known in London and occupied a prominent place in music catalogues of this period.[147] Englishmen were so well acquainted with Tartini's merit that Burney declined to produce any panegyric on them in the *Tour*. The special attraction of Tartini and his students derived from their composition of "divine" and expressive adagios, as well as their mastery of bowing in the performance of these works. Tartini is credited as the "first who knew and taught the power of the bow." Almost immediately upon his return from the Italian tour Burney published a translation of the *Lettera del defonto signor Giuseppe Tartini alla signora Maddalena Lombardini*, a particularly timely translation, as the original appeared in Venice in the same year. The *Lettera*, "an important lesson to performers on the violin," is primarily concerned with developing complete expressive control of the bow.

Mastery of the bow was requisite to produce the expressive cantabiles for which Tartini's melodies were noted. Indeed, Burney found that "many of his adagios want nothing but words to be excellent pathetic opera songs."[148] Tartini consciously imitated operatic style in his instrumental music, but Burney credits him nonetheless as being "one of the few original geniusses [sic] of this age, who constantly drew from his own source."[149] In spite of this appraisal, the sole example of Tartini's music printed in the *History* is an "adagio quasi recitativo" entitled "Aria del Tasso."[150]

When Burney wrote the article on Tartini for the *History*, he was perhaps as many as eighteen years removed from the assessment printed in the *Tour*. On reviewing Tartini's works, Burney found him "to have had a larger portion of merit as a mere instrumental composer than any other author who flourished during the first fifty or sixty years of the present century." Yet years had elapsed, and even in England, a backwater of conservative violin music, Tartini's style had become dated. Not only did Tartini's music appear to be dated, but the violinists formed by his School of Nations were old-fashioned, for though their adagios were "exquisitely polished and expressive, yet it seems as if that energy, fire, and freedom of bow, which modern symphonies require, were wanting." The opinion he gave in the *Tour* was his honest evaluation at that time, but since then "Boccherini, Haydn, Pleyel, Vanhal; and others, have occasioned such a revolution in violin music, and playing by the fertility and boldness of their invention, that compositions which were then generally thought full of spirit and fire appear now totally tame and insipid."[151]

Aside from his comments on the Italian virtuosi, Burney says little about Continental instrumental music before the middle of the eighteenth century. His short discussion of German seventeenth-century violinists records the great number mentioned by Walther, but there is little commentary on the music, though the works of several of the German composers were known in England.[152] Heinrich Biber, whose solos were "the most difficult and the most fanciful of any violin music" of the period, was the only German master active in the seventeenth century who aroused his interest.[153] Burney was much more impressed with the peculiarities of Biber's tunings and scoring than with the quality of his compositions, and his assessment is essentially a summary description of some of Biber's eccentric techniques.

Burney's discussion of seventeenth-century French violin music in the *History* is disjointed and inadequate. He recognized the value of French dance music, and he realized that Lulli's overtures were imitated all over the Continent, as well as in England, but he allowed Voltaire to speak for him in a long quotation. Voltaire remarked in part, "Our instrumental Music, though less offensive to strangers, is somewhat affected by the monotony and languor of the vocal."[154] Burney's quotation of the remark extends his prejudice against French vocal music to encompass the instrumental as well. This is a result of carelessness or oversight, for elsewhere he comments favorably on the quality of French instrumental music and especially French instrumentalists. Nonetheless, he refrains from any substantial criticism of French instrumental composition in the *History*.

Burney's history of violin music on the Continent is really only a chronicle of the Continental influences that reached England. Thus, his history of instrumental music outside of England in the eighteenth century is severely limited. Only Stamitz receives any critical attention among the masters active in Germany during the first sixty years of the century; for the latter part of the century he merely gives a list of the names of more than fifty composers. His list includes some of the most important composers of the period, but only a few of the composers receive even slight consideration, and the "matchless Haydn" alone receives anything approximating a satisfactory treatment. Considering the brevity of the chapter on German instrumentalists, it is not surprising to find an even less thorough treatment of French composers. Burney was aware of the activities of the *Concert Spirituel,* and remarked favorably on the instrumental music he heard at performances there while on his tour. The works of several French writers for the violin, especially Mondonville and Le Clair, were well known in England, but Burney excuses himself from discussing their works by referring the reader to the accounts "displayed with patriotic zeal by M. de la Borde, in his *Essai sur la musique."*[155] Thus French musicians do not find an appropriate place in Burney's criticism even when their music merits attention, for Le Clair's pieces were performed at the Burney concerts of a Sunday evening, and were well regarded.

Like his history of Italian opera in England, Burney's history of violin music in England is largely a record of the comings and goings of the virtuosi. One of the first to arrive in England was Geminiani, a student of Corelli. Burney says that the violin at this time was in such favor that "the English were said to have stripped Italy" of all of its violins, and that neither the ignorant nor the learned would hear anyone's music except Corelli's, until Geminiani arrived and demonstrated that higher cultivation and improvement was possible.[156]

Burney's remarks on Geminiani provide the rationale for his idea that the history of violin music was the history of performers rather than the development of a repertory. According to Burney, around 1739 "it became more than ever the fashion for public solo players to perform only their own compositions, and others were unable to execute them."[157] Indeed, after a short summary of the miscellaneous performances and general state of practical music to about 1720, the reader is advised that Burney intends thereafter to mention "a short record of such new performers as afterwards became eminent, and of such new exhibitions as were remarkable for their singularity."[158] The most telling of Burney's comments states that upon his arrival in London in 1744 "Handel, Corelli and Geminiani, with some introductory *Musicks* of Purcell, furnished both the bands [Drury-Lane and Covent Garden] with all the pieces they ever attempted."[159] This limited repertory seems to have persisted until the arrival of another virtuoso, Felice Giardini in 1750, brought the taste of the newer Italian style of Tartini and Sammartini.

Burney's account of this period may well provide glimpses into his own changing taste. He marks this time as the beginning of the fashion for private concerts, "as are now frequently given by the nobility and gentry at their own houses."[160] He records that the first occurred at Lady Brown's home, under the direction of Count St. Germain. Her Ladyship, he states, "distinguished herself as a persevering enemy to Handel, and a protectress of foreign musicians in general of the new Italian style."[161] The mid-century was indeed a period of great change for some music lovers:

> Content with our former possessions and habits, we went on in the tranquil enjoyment of the productions of Corelli, Geminiani, and Handel, at our national theatres, concerts and public gardens, till the arrival of Giardini, Bach, and Abel; who soon created schisms, and at length, with the assistance of Fischer, brought about a total revolution in our musical taste.[162]

This "total revolution" in taste which Burney celebrates was not universally welcomed. Charles Avison, in his *Essay on Musical Expression* (1752), blamed the modern symphonic style for the corruption of music. The charge prompted

Burney to sketch a rebuttal in his pocket book which eloquently asserts the merits of the new style.

MODERN OVERTURES

> Mr. Avison attributes the decay and corruption of Music to the Torrent of modern Sinfonies with which we are overwhelmed from foreign Countries and Composers. But I must beg +here+ to differ totally from him in this matter. For I on the Contrary think it is the Spirit, the Taste, Effects and the endless variety of passages in these Compositions that Instrumental Music owes its greatest Improvement and refinement. Effects have been produced by Contrast, by +   + and Judicious use of the *Crescendo* and *Diminuendo*, by the almost unlimited power of the Bow, in varying the Expression of the same Notes, as well as by the invention of new phrases of melody, as can no where be found in the Music of past ages. In their slow movements every Species of Cantabile and Delicacy has been used in the Melody which has pleased in vocal music, and every kind of accompaniment, of harmony and modulation which could give relief to their Melody has been tried and often with great Success, in order to vary our musical pleasure, by heightening the Colouring of the whole, and rendering the Light and shade as conspicuous and pleasing as possible.[163]

Burney's advocacy of the new style is striking, but it is difficult to follow the process of change from old to new in the *History*. His reflection, linking Giardini with the Bach-Abel concerts, puts into juxtaposition events actually separated by fifteen years. The chronology in the *History* slips almost imperceptibly from 1750 to 1762, a gap explained by Burney's absence from London from September, 1751, until 1760.

Burney's own compositions reflect the dramatic changes in musical style. His works fall into three general, though not exclusive, periods. As a young, developing musician in London, he composed primarily dramatic songs between 1748 and 1751. After leaving London, he began a period of instrumental composition, publishing trios and concertos in the old style, and the six "Scarlatti" sonatas for the harpsichord. Upon returning to London in 1760, he abandoned composition, perhaps because of his awareness of the new style. Only around 1770 did he resume composing, publishing his accompanied sonatas, piano duets, and a "sonate à trois mains," all in the new *galant* idiom. It is possible, then, that Burney was either not knowledgeable of or was not won over to the new style until after his return to London in 1760. When he began publishing again, he was firmly pointed in a new direction and was disdainful of the old.

During his absence from London, the music of the Mannheim symphonists became well known. Walsh, for example, one of the London publishers least likely to risk publishing speculative works, released Johann Stamitz's *VI Sinfonies or Overtures in Eight Parts* in 1765, indicating something of the fashion for the symphonies by this time.[164] Of course, more modern German and Italian music was available from other publishers, including foreign ones, and more importantly, in manuscript copies brought to

England by immigrant Germans. The importance of the earl of Kelly in bringing the Mannheim style to England has been stressed by Percy Young. Kelly began studying with the elder Stamitz in 1750. When he returned to England he brought with him and promoted the music of the Mannheim symphonists, as well as his own works in a similar style.[165]

> When he quitted Great Britain to make the tour of Germany, according to Pinto, he could scarcely tune his violin; but stopping at Manheim [sic], he heard the best instrumental music in Europe, and shut himself up with the elder Stamitz, whose originality and fire set his young pupil in a blaze, and so congenial were the taste and disposition of the scholar and the master, that they seemed the growth of the same soil. The same energy and enthusiasm which had lifted Stamitz above his fellows of the Manheim school, stimulated the young earl to study compositions, and practise the violin with such serious application, that, on his return to England, there was no part of theoretical or practical music in which he was not equally versed with the greatest professors of his time.[166]

Lord Kelly, then, through advocacy and imitation, did much to advance the new style, preparing the way for the Viennese symphonists, including Vanhal and Haydn.

Burney's history of music in Germany sheds little light on his perception of the revolution in instrumental styles which took place mid-century. He does recognize the importance of Jommelli's overtures to the emerging Mannheim symphonic style. The new symphonists seemed at first "little more than an improvement" on Jommelli's style by the Mannheimers, until "by the fire and genius of Stamitz, they were exalted into a new species of composition, at which there was an outcry, as usual, against innovation by those who wish to keep music stationary."[167] To Burney, "the variety, taste, spirit, and new effects produced by *crescendo* and *diminuendo* in these symphonies, had been of more service to instrumental music in a few years, than all the dull and servile imitations of Corelli, Geminiani, and Handel, had been in half a century."[168] Contrast was also an important feature of modern symphonies. Johann Christian Bach, who along with Abel composed much of the music heard at their subscription concerts, was, according to Burney, the first who "observed the law of *contrast,* as a principle... Bach in his symphonies and other instrumental pieces, as well as his songs, seldom failed, after a rapid and noisy passage to introduce one that was slow and soothing."[169]

The staple names which appear on Burney's lists of composers in the new instrumental style are Boccherini, Haydn, Pleyel, and Vanhall. Because there is much less information about instrumental music than about vocal or keyboard music in the Burney papers, changes in Burney's taste are difficult to trace with surety. Perhaps his reflection that the Bach-Abel concerts, which began in 1764 (not 1763, as he records), revolutionized taste in England implies that his own taste changed then. It is certain that he was among the enthusiastic admirers of Vanhall. The earliest symphonies he knew were written in 1767 and "soon circulated in manuscript all over Europe;" however, they were not known in England until the duke of Dorset imported them about 1771. Vanhall's compositions subsequently became prominent in London music catalogues around 1774 to 1776. Vanhall's music, at least to those listeners of Burney's taste, attracted more attention than any other until the introduction of Haydn's symphonies in London. Though Vanhall's name is constantly linked with Haydn's in Burney's writings, Burney recognized a vast difference in their creativity. Haydn's invention seemed inexhaustible, while Vanhall "composed too much perhaps... but his symphonies, quartets, and other productions for violins certainly deserve a place among the first productions, in which melody, pleasing harmony—and a free and manly style are preserved."[170]

Of Burney's three great writers of string music—Haydn, Vanhall, and Boccherini—the first and last are praised for their exquisite adagios. The relative abilities of Haydn and Boccherini was the subject of an interesting exchange of letters with Twining. Twining, an amateur violinist—he possessed a Stradivarius violin—claimed some knowledge of string compositions, and he believed that Boccherini's adagio movements were superior to Haydn's. Burney's final word on the subject leaves no doubt as to his own judgment.

> I'll allow that Boccherini is more constantly serious than Haydn—nay that he is always serious and Charming—but in Haydn's works, more serious Compositions in the true gran Gusto, may be selected, then Boccherini has ever produced—and then you have all his fun, fancy, extravagant if you will and Capricious, for Gigantic players, *di plus*—God bless 'em both, I say; but if I were forced to part with one of them—I should not hesitate a moment in locking Haydn fast in my Arms, and only sending a sigh after the other.[171]

Twining was unlikely to make headway in Boccherini's favor against sentiments as strong as these, but Burney did recognize Boccherini as a first-rate composer who had "perhaps supplied the performers on bowed-instruments and lovers of music with more excellent compositions than any master of the present age (1782), except Haydn."[172]

Burney knew something of Haydn's music in 1771, for his name appears on a list of musicians "whose musical productions and performances have given me great delight." What he knew of Haydn's instrumental music probably was in manuscript or in Continental editions, as the first quartets, opus I, were not published in England until 1772 by Bremner. It is evident in the *German Tour* that Burney became more aware of and delighted with Haydn's music throughout his stay in Vienna. He first records hearing some Haydn quartets "performed with the utmost precision,"[173] and then, a few days later, refers to "some exquisite quartets by Haydn."[174] He found that the symphonies and quartets of "Hofman, Haydn, Ditters, Vanhal, and Huber" were "perhaps among the first [i.e., highest rank] full pieces and compositions, for violins, that have ever been produced."[175]

Burney's enthusiasm augmented interest in Haydn's works in England, at least among his friends. William Bewley, who received much advice from Burney, wrote in 1777 that Haydn and Vanhall were his favorite composers, a view which by 1783 was widely shared. Haydn's popularity was sufficient for the directors of the Professional Concert to attempt, from 1782 through 1788, to attract him to London as an instrumental composer.[176] In 1783, Haydn's works figured in all but two of the twelve concerts sponsored by Willoughby Bertie, fourth earl of Abingdon. These works were selected from the already large number of his compositions available in England.[177] By January, 1785, the *Gazetteer and New Daily Advertiser* called Haydn "the Shakespeare of music, and the triumph of the age in which we live." His domination of musical life in England among the modernists was challenged by only one figure: Ignatz Pleyel.

Burney first heard Pleyel's string quartets in 1785. While working through the material for the last volume of the *History,* he recorded his opinion in a notebook, which amplifies the cautious appraisal of Pleyel that was eventually published:

> He's called a scholar of Haydn, and is not an unworthy disciple of such a master; having imitated his style without stealing his passages. He is now settled at Thasburg (1787). His Quartets are truly republican. The melody and brilliant passages being equally divided and *requiring* equal abilities in all the several performers. Whereas those of Haydn are more monarchial: the first violin being soverign invested with riches and splendor, while the other parts are subordinate, and humble attendants. This is the specific difference between the writing of the master and scholar in this species of composition. I think however that though Pleyel's +treasures+ and resources in these pieces are considerable, it is but a single vein: — but Haydn +'s veins+ lie in all directions, and flow to every style and part of the musical system, as the arteries and great blood vessels from the heart.[178]

The details of Haydn's triumph over Pleyel during their concurrent London visits in 1791 are too well known to require retelling here. The relationship of the two men was so cordial than when Pleyel conducted his first performance for the Professional Concert in 1792, he performed not only one of his symphonies, but also one by Haydn and one by Mozart.[179] But it was Haydn who returned to London in 1794, and eventually his victory over Pleyel was complete.

Burney's admiration for Haydn and his tireless advocacy on behalf of his music are well known.[180] Indeed, he is exuberant in the introduction to Haydn's biography in the *History*—"I am now happily arrived at that part of my narrative where it is necessary to speak of HAYDN! the admirable and matchless HAYDN!"—and continued to be so to the end of his public life.[181] Haydn's allegro movements "exhilarate every hearer," but it is in his adagios that Burney finds his genius best displayed. He especially admires the adagio theme and variations because about the middle of the last century, the musical world was overwhelmed with dull unmeaning variations to old and new tunes, which consisted of nothing more than regular multiplication of notes, without fancy, taste, or harmonical resources; till Haydn, in the slow and graceful middle movements of his quartets and symphonies, by richness of imagination, by double counterpoint, and inexhaustible resources of melody and harmony, rendered variations the most ingenious, pleasing, and heart felt of his admirable productions *a grand orchestra.*[182]

Burney's appraisal of Haydn's instrumental "Passione, The Seven Last Words," attests to the power Haydn's lyric movements held over him. "Though all the strains are slow and affecting, they are so varied, that the same passage is not to be found in any two movements;" It is "the most sublime composition without words to point out its meaning that has ever been composed."[183]

It must strike many readers of the *History* as curious that Burney's unbounded enthusiasm for Haydn did not extend to Mozart. Mozart figures in the *History* only in a brief passage which notes that, having astounded all of Europe as a prodigy, he "is now no less the wonder of the musical world for his fertility and knowledge as a composer."[184] Only in the almost unknown article in the *Cyclopaedia* does Burney record his discovery of Mozart's worth. Like most of the rest of the musical world, he failed to recognize Mozart's genius until a decade after his death. The credit for the promotion of Mozart, as well as Beethoven, in England lies largely with the impressario Salomon, which may help to explain why the two composers are so closely linked in Burney's discussion of instrumental music. Landon's recent research on Haydn's London years reveals that Mozart's instrumental music was somewhat more frequently heard than has formerly been realized. According to Landon, Salomon's series of concerts in 1786 included symphonies of Mozart and Haydn *"inter alia."*[185] Some of Mozart's symphonies were introduced by Pleyel and Haydn in 1791, and Salomon continued to perform them occasionally after Haydn's departure.[186] In addition, two of Mozart's piano concertos were performed in 1792 by Haessler and Hummel. Nevertheless, it was Burney's impression that "we knew nothing of his [Mozart's] studies or productions, but from his harpsichord lessons" until after his death.[187] It seems likely that Haydn's deep affection and respect for Mozart, and his acquaintance with the young Beethoven, showed Burney the error of his ways, and led him into a fuller appreciation of both Mozart's and Beethoven's genius.

The first linking of Mozart's name with Haydn's as an instrumental composer occurs in Burney's 1791 review of the *Observations on the Present State of Music in London* by William Jackson of Exeter. Jackson, like Avison forty years earlier, complained about the degeneracy of the modern symphony, and the obsolescence of the old concerto form. He remarked that "composers, to be grand and original, have poured in such floods of nonsense, under the sublime idea of *being inspired,* that the present Symphony bears the same relation to good music, as the ravings of a bedlamite do to sober sense."

Burney's retort adds Mozart to the group of superior composers he had supported for many years: "Now, might not the ingenious writer as well have said, at once, that the authors of these *floods of nonsense* are *Haydn, Vanhall, Pleyel,* and *Mozart,* and the admirers of them tasteless idiots, as leave us to guess who he means." Burney's new appreciation of Mozart is also reflected in the article "Symphony," which carries the chronology of Burney's taste to 1804.

> [The] symphony had been highly cultivated in Germany, particularly at the Manheim [*sic*] school, by Stamitz, Holtzbauer, Canabich, Toeschi, and Filtz; by Vanhal, Ditters, and Kozeluch, at Vienna; and since that period, the symphonies of the immortal Haydn have exceeded in number and excellence all that modern times can boast, and seem to include every perfection that can render instrumental music interesting and sublime; invention, science, knowledge of instruments, majesty, fire, grace, and pathos by turns, with new modulation and new harmonies, without crudity or affection. All these excellencies the admirable Mozart had nearly attained; and perhaps he is only inferior to Haydn in the number of his symphonies from the shortness of his vital course! Beethoven (pronounced Baythoven) a disciple of Mozart, is now [1804] so rapidly advancing into fame, that there would be little risk in predicting that, if he lives, he will be a great man among musicians of the present century, as Haydn and Mozart were of the latter end of the last. He is said to be a young man; but writes with the freedom and boldness of long experience, and a fertility of invention that promises inexhaustible resources.

Once Burney became committed to Mozart's cause in England, he was a fervent apostle. William Jackson was only one opponent: more influential was William Crotch. Crotch, in a series of public lectures at the Royal Institution of London, denigrated Mozart's work and joined with those who venerated Handel above all other composers. The exchange of the wise old critic with the younger, but more conservative, lecturer is representative of the state of English national taste, still strongly divided half a century after Handel's death.[188] Burney's defense of Mozart confesses his own initial reservations about

> the inexhaustible Mozart, whose compositions I did not like at first; they seemed to [o] capricious and as if he were trying experiments, till he began to compose vocal music of which we knew nothing till after his decease; but which, both in his serious and comic operas, seems to me, and innumerable others, the most delightful music that has ever been composed.[189]

Crotch's defense of his partiality to Handel written in response to Burney refers mostly to remarks made against Haydn. He mentions Mozart only in passing, but clearly pronounces that he favors Handel. "Handel united grandeur, elegance, and embellishment with the utmost propriety, and on this account I ventured to pronounce him, upon the whole, the greatest of all composers."[190] Burney wrote to Christian Latrobe about the controversy in detail, making it evident that Crotch was not alone in his views:

But here (in a whisper) I must entreat you not to quote me, concerning my differing opinion with the lecturer about Mozart. He offended Salomon, and lovers of the German school, last year, by his arrogant manner of censuring Haydn, to the great delight of the exclusive admirers of Handel, and the English School; and this year, he only speaks of Mozart as an innovator and capricious composer; in which he is hallooed on by the Catch and Glee singers and those who regard Dr. C-1--tt [Calcott] as a great conjurer... And as C[rotch] is going (as they say) to print his lectures, should you wish that posterity should regard such men as Haydn and Mozart in no higher light than the lecturer has done, or should think that we did not understand their works?... C[rotch] has foolishly excited a rage in all those who most admire and best understand the great musical Phenomenon, Mozart... [191]

In the last decades of his life, Burney recognized that the best instrumental music emanated from Germany and found that "no praise is too strong for the instrumental music of Germany." In Mozart, "and his scholar Beethoven, it seems as if instrumental music, at least, was arrived at its acme of perfection."[192]

Just how much of Beethoven's instrumental music Burney knew is impossible to ascertain, but it is certain that prior to his death he already recognized the absolute dominance of what has come to be known as the Viennese classical school of composition. His early recognition of the greatness of Beethoven is fascinating, particularly since he could not have heard one of Beethoven's symphonies (at least at a concert) until his seventy-seventh year. Salomon first programmed a composition by Beethoven, his *Septet*, in 1801. Burney either did not attend or forgot the event, as he dates his first acquaintance with Beethoven's music as 1803.[193] He does not specify what composition he heard, but lists only "some instrumental works which are such as incline me to rank him amongst the first musical authors of the present century."[194] The year 1803 was indeed important for the introduction of Beethoven's music to England: the first performance of a symphony occurred in May of that year. By 1804, when the article "Symphony," with its encomium on Beethoven, was drafted, Burney would have had an opportunity to hear both the first and second symphonies. Before 1810, the year in which he effectively withdrew from public life, it is possible that he had heard all of the first six symphonies, with the exception of the fourth, which was not performed in England until after 1820.[195]

Charles Rosen has speculated that Burney was the first to recognize what has become famous as the triumvirate of the Viennese classical school by his linking of the names Haydn, Mozart, and Beethoven in 1807.[196] Burney may well be the first; if so, he is entitled to credit for an even greater prophecy, for as we have seen, the linking of the three names in the article "Symphony" dates from 1804. His association of these names should occasion no surprise: it was a judgment probably more easily made by an octogenarian music lover removed from Continental musical life, than by a more youthful critic in, for example, Vienna. Doubtless the music appealed to him, but the influence of Haydn and certainly Salomon must also be considered as having brought these composers to Burney's attention. Nevertheless, his joint reference to the three composers was not merely fortuitous. The three are also linked in Burney's commentary to his translation of Rousseau's article "Music" in the *Cyclopaedia,* where he remarks on the expressive power of instrumental music, asserting that "instrumental music brought to its present degree of perfection in the trios, quartets, quintets, and symphonies, such as those of Haydn, Mozart, and Beethoven, can amuse, interest, and delight cultivated ears even to rapture." In an undated letter to Samuel Wesley, Burney writes that German composers certainly studied melody from the Italian vocal composers, and adds that composers "such as Haydn, Mozart, and Beethoven" in their slow movements "surpass the Italians themselves."[197]

The modernism which marked Burney's awareness of keyboard music is apparent throughout his appreciation of instrumental music as well. In the now-familiar lists from his article on Morley,[198] Burney extends his recommendations to include composers of instrumental music whose works he must have first heard in his seventy-eighth year or even later:

Symphonies, Quartets, Trios,
Duets and Other Music for Violins

HISTORY	CYCLOPAEDIA
Haydn	Haydn
Vanhal	Mozart
Boccherini	Boccherini
J.C. Bach	J.C. Bach
Abel	Abel
Giardini	Giardini
etc.	Beethoven
	Pleyel
	etc.
FUGUES [same in both sources]	SOLO VIOLIN [*Cyclopaedia* only]
Corelli	Tartini
Handel	Giardini
Geminiani	

Another classification of composers in the article "Stilo" arranges into separate categories composers who gave an "original stamp" of excellence to a style:

SYMPHONIES	QUARTETS, QUINTETS
Stamitz (the elder)	Haydn
The Mannheim School	Mozart
Haydn ⎫	Boccherini
Mozart ⎬ Vienna	
Vanhal ⎭	

Perhaps the most intriguing aspect of Burney's list is the inclusion of music which he knew throughout his life. At the end of his career there is none of the disdain for music of older styles which is evident in his earlier critical writings, especially in the 1770s, when his taste could encompass only instrumental music composed in the prior quarter century. At the end of his life he allows the value of music which had pleased him at any point in his life. It is easy to ascribe this broadening of taste to a critical vanity which would not allow that music which had once pleased could ever be in bad taste, but perhaps the idea of a standard repertory of instrumental music of all periods, one not subject to evanescent fashion, was only then becoming acceptable to Burney and his modish contemporaries. Perhaps also the persistent tradition of historicism in England, which maintained the greatest music of three centuries in an active repertory, albeit on a limited scale, finally began to lessen the power of fashion. What is certain from Burney's own musical autobiography in doggerel is that he recognized that Haydn and Mozart had established a mark of excellence which would not be wiped away by time or fashion. The poem summarizes this view of the passing from fashion of his own compositions:[199]

> Dramatic Pieces long since old,
> Concertos, trios, many fold;
> Lessons, Sonatas; Organ-pieces,
> Fugues on dry and barren theses...

the superiority of Viennese classical music over any other:

> For who can hope with utmost pains
> To equal such enchanting strains,
> As Haydn and Mozart have found
> Which lift each hearer off the ground,
> Where taste and genius ever flame,
> Whence all their inspirations came?
> And still the road to fame is stopt
> And ev'ry verdant laurel cropt,
> By that gigantic youth, Beethoven,
> Whose feet, beyond a doubt, are cloven...

and points to the future, prophesying his own place in musical history.

> My days in labour, study, toil
> Have long been spent, and nightly oil...
> Not to acquire for self a name,
> But loud to sound the trump of fame,
> And with an honest zeal to sing
> Each brother of the pipe and string.

8

Dramatic Music:
Burney the Covert Conservative

> The annals of modern Music have hitherto furnished no event so important to the progress of the art, as the recovery or invention of *Recitative,* or dramatic melody. Musicians till this period having been chiefly employed in gratifying the ear with "the concord of sweet sounds," without respect to poetry, or aspiring at energy, passion, intellectual pleasure, or much variety of effect.[1]

Thus Burney heralds a new epoch in music history with the first sentences of his chapter on dramatic music. Opera dominates Burney's affections as overwhelmingly as it does his critical writings. He probably felt it was only a slight exaggeration when, at the end of his lengthy chapter on Italian opera in England, he wrote "as the OPERA includes every species of Music, vocal and instrumental, its annals, if faithfully and amply recorded, seem clearly to comprise the whole history of the art."[2] And though he never so states, it is evident that in Burney's view the writings of Jean-Jacques Rousseau, the *Dictionnaire de musique* (1768) and the *Lettre sur la musique français (1753),* comprise virtually the entire aesthetic of the opera. He worked on English translations of both works shortly after their publication, and as late as the final years of his life he relied on the *Dictionnaire* as the basis for his articles on dramatic music in the *Cyclopaedia.* The *Dictionnaire* was more than thirty years old at the time, and the experience with Italian opera upon which Rousseau based his work came principally from his one year visit to Venice in the 1740s (and the performances of the Italian comic troupe in Paris), but Burney saw little need to revise most of the articles he translated. In his steadfast adherence to Rousseau's ideals, Burney clung to an aesthetic formed more than sixty years in the past.

In interpreting Burney's remarks on opera, the reader must take care to determine the critical posture Burney is displaying at any given moment. Burney's views addressed to his fashionable English readership are quite different from those intended for an international audience. Nowhere is this more apparent than in his discussion of opera as drama. On the one hand he advocates the observance of conventions by which dramatic integrity is preserved. He adheres to the Metastasian ideal, recognizing the significance of the libretto reforms of Apostolo Zeno, especially the elimination of "tragi-comedy and buffoonery" in opera seria. He calls the period previous to the reforms of Zeno and Metastasio, who "purified and sublimed the libretto," the "nonage" of opera.[3] He condemns the substitution of arias from opera to opera, and the *pasticcio* form of opera, with its flimsy plot and string of arias pulled from unrelated sources, a practice which, Burney says, inclines "the good people of England to imagine the words of an opera to be *all nonsense.*"[4] He criticizes the addition of arias to the London performance of Gluck's *Orfeo* because "the unity, simplicity, and dramatic excellence of this opera, which had gained the composer so much credit on the Continent, were greatly diminished here by the heterogeneous mixture of Music, of other composers, in a quite different style."[5] Gluck's style was exceptional, but Burney lodges a similar protest against interpolated arias in more traditional forms as well.[6]

On the other hand, he defends the practice of encoring songs in the middle of an opera because the "Business of the drama is chiefly transacted in the recitative, and as few people interest themselves in England about an Italian drama, the evil would not be insupportable."[7] Burney specifies that this position is appropriate only for England, where the poetry of an opera had little to do with its success, and where "it is generally upon *singing* that its favour entirely depends."[8]

> Frequent airs are of infinitely more use and importance in an Italian opera performed in England, than Italy; for the public in general being ignorant of the language can receive but small amusement from the *recitative* or narrative part, compared with that which the *airs* afford them; where the richness of the harmony, ingenious complication and design of the several parts, and elegance of the principal melody, all conspire to captivate and charm without the assistance of poetry, fable, or intelligence of the words; as an air well sung, is of all languages, and must ever afford a delight much superior to that which the same air played on an instrument could produce.[9]

"In France and Italy, on the contrary, where operas are performed in the language of each country, the poetry and conduct of the drama are of infinite consequences to its success."[10] He does not dispute that understanding the words would render opera "more rational and more complete," but even without that advantage opera was still the *"completest concert,"* combining the "most perfect singing, and effects of a powerful and well-disciplined band" with "excellent acting, spendid scenes and decorations," and dancing.[11]

Notwithstanding the critical attention he gives the libretto, he regards suitable libretti as mere vehicles for the support of music. Early in the chapter he challenges the assertion made by Angelo Ingegnesi in his *Della poesia rappresentativa* (1598) that music is the "*third* and *last* part of dramatic representations." Without qualification Burney retorts, "Music is the *first* consideration in operas and oratorios."[12]

Since the lyric poetry of an opera is to be sung, it must of a necessity differ from other poetical forms.

> Verses full of philosophy and ethics, strong reasoning and bold metaphors, or epigramatic wit, must be enfeebled by music which conveys them slowly to the mind; though passion, sentiment, graceful and pleasing images and descriptions are embellished by it.[13]

Good poetry is only harmed by music; "sublime poetry leaves the musician nothing to do." Indeed, he avers that a good opera will always be a bad tragedy unless substantial changes are made to the text, and the converse is equally true. Tragedy requires expansive dialogue for the development of the characters, while in

> ... an opera, the narrative must be short, the incidents numerous and rapid in succession, the diction rather sweet and flowing, than strong and nervous: as the words of an air should merely serve as an outline for melody to colour.[14]

Burney's definition of lyric poetry not only clarifies his idea of a good libretto, but also explains his criticism of the more dramatic opera style which emerges in the second half of the century.

> The charactertistic of lyric poetry, which distinguishes it from all others, is *dignity* and *sweetness*. As *gravity* rules in heroic verse; *simplicity*, in pastoral; *tenderness* and *softness*, in elegy; *sharpness* and *poignancy*, in satire; *mirth*, in comedy; the *pathetic*, in tragedy; and the *point*, in epigram; so in the lyric, the poet applies himself wholly to soothe the minds of men, by the sweetness and variety of the verse, and the delicacy and elevation of the words and thoughts; the agreeableness of the numbers, and the description of things most pleasing in their own nature.[15]

Good lyric poetry, then, provides the composer with images which move the passions of the listener without becoming overly passionate or violent.

The poet most gifted in achieving the desired balance of expression and taste was Metastasio, the favorite lyric poet of the eighteenth century. Burney's admiration for him is apparent throughout the *Tours* and *History*, and especially in his *Memoirs of the Life of Metastasio*, which he regarded as a "kind of supplement to my *General History of Music*."[16] Describing him as a man of exquisite taste, Burney proclaimed Metastasio "the best lyric poet and writer of operas, or dramas for music in Italy, during the last century, or perhaps during any age, or in any country."[17] His works breathed the "purest principles of virtue and morality," a feature sufficiently important to prompt Burney to describe the moral object of each drama in an appendix to his biography of Metastasio.[18] Burney's glowing description of Metastasio's character seems to reflect the personality which Burney himself strove to project:

> In all his productions, religion, government, sound policy, morals, manners, and even innocent prejudices, are so highly respected that the most extreme delicacy never finds the least sentiment that can offend or alarm. His doctrines and practice in the particulars so perfectly agreed, that he constantly discountenanced in conversation all tendency to licence, disrespect, and disputation on moral and sacred subjects, though naturally cheerful, and pleasantly metaphorical, in his conversation.[19]

Metastasio was the first to achieve in his librettos "the difficult task of rendering so wild and incongruous a compound of seemingly heterogeneous ingredients and absurdities, as an *opera,* a rational entertainment."[20] But rationality was not the most important feature of opera: music was to dominate.

The balance between poetry and music was delicate, and there was often great friction between composer and librettist. Burney frequently speaks of the jealousy of the sister arts toward one another, notably poetry and music.[21] Invariably he sides with music against poetry, asserting that "there never was perhaps a lyric poet who did not *listen* with an *evil ear* to the rapturous applause givien to a singer in performing an air, of which 'nobody would think of reading the words, but the author.'"[22] His chief rebuttal to those who challenged the propriety of musical settings which injured the poetry was that

> Music is more the object of sense than intellect; its use is to please the ear, not to improve the understanding. It has been said, that music can awaken and excite sensations, but cannot reason.[23]

He concurred with most critics that the union of poetry and music was best, but remained diffident about ever achieving a balance satisfactory to all parties. Though opera was perhaps "nonsense well tuned," it was nonetheless highly pleasurable to the senses, and efforts to subjugate music to poetry were to him insupportable. The French critic, François-Jean de Chastellux, shared his views on the place of music and poetry in opera. In reviewing the *Essai sur l'union de la poésie et de la musique* (1765), Burney calls the author a deep and original thinker. The *Essai,* he acknowledges, "is certainly humiliating to Lyric poets; but will only seem *unreasonable,* perhaps to them and to those who prefer declamation to singing. To others, the author will appear possessed of good taste, and sound reasoning."[24] The conflict over which art was to dominate opera was long-lived, especially in France, and even the "divine Metastasio" entered into the fray, claiming that his own dramas were well received "in Italy when declaimed *without* MUSIC; but that the most exquisite music which has been set to them would not be equally favoured *without the poetry.*"[25] Burney strongly disagrees, arguing that instrumental music "well composed and exquisitely performed" delighted audiences. Moreover, "when there *is* singing in a concert who attends to the poetry?... If bad music spoils a good drama, good composition and performance, have saved many a one that is ill written."[26]

Notwithstanding his insistence on the supremacy of music in the conflux of the arts that was opera, Burney recognized that the "revolution in music" occasioned by the invention of recitative was not inspired by musicians; these "learned contrapuntists had abused their art," and confined it to such narrow limits that even instrumental music "made no advance in their hands." Rather, the poets, by insisting on restoring the balance of music with poetry, had rescued music, freeing it from the "musical pedants, who, with a true Gothic spirit, had loaded her with cumbrous ornaments, in order as was pretended, to render her more fine, beautiful, and pleasing, after having fettered, maimed, and mangled her."[27] The early lyric poets restored music to the bounds of taste by writing "short effusions of passion or sentiment" which best exercised the powers of musical expression, thus setting music on its proper affective path. Burney's conclusion as to how this meliorating influence came about is revealing: it was through "appealing to the public ear, by bringing music on the stage," that the pedantry of musicians was vanquished.[28] This view helps explain Burney's idea of history, which occasionally seems dominated by mere fashion. Opera, the music he valued most highly, was above all a popular art, legislated by the audience, not the professors, performers, nor even the composers.

The taste of the audience did dictate the state of music in England, and fashion did shape musical history to some extent. Existing without patronage from the court or city, opera in England survived largely on the subscriptions of the relatively small portion of the English audience which attended the Italian opera. Tickets could be obtained without subscriptions, but a sufficient number of subscribers were necessary to guarantee the season. The Italian opera was supported by a "coterie of society people and intellectuals; the middle and lower class theatre goer inevitably preferred the playhouse where he could understand the words."[29] The same select group supplied the pupils upon whose fees Burney was dependent and made up the majority of the subscribers to his *History*. His readers may have thought it flattery when he pronounced them the supreme legislators of the art, but such was the case in England.[30]

Burney began his history of dramatic music with the earliest experiments in opera by the Florentine *camerata*. His narrative consists largely of lengthy extracts from the writings of Giovanni Battista Doni, and though he prints extracts from Peri's and Caccini's *Euridice* in the chapter, they elicit little commentary. In contrast, Burney reviews Monteverdi's *Orfeo* extensively. His analysis reveals his difficulty in treating early opera with any objectivity. Burney was not impressed with much of the music. He found no support, for example, for the claim that Monteverdi was the greatest writer of recitative among the early composers, because "more forms of phrases of musical recitation *still in use* may be found in Peri and Caccini, than Monteverde [*sic*]."[31] As has been noted, he was surprised to find a composer with Monteverdi's reputation to be defective in counterpoint, and gave several examples of parallel fifths and octaves, anticipations which he could not reconcile by the rules of composition, and other instances of "improper" dissonance treatment. In accord with his progressive attitude toward musical licenses, he examines the dramatic intent of Monteverdi's dissonances, but concludes that some, though expressively motivated, were not accepted into common musical language because they were too offensive to the ear. He is less tolerant of the parallel perfect consonances he found, which, he says, "must strike [the ear of] the youngest student in composition."[32]

Monteverdi's rhythmic diversity completely befuddled him. He cited the ritornello to "Vi ricorda, a boshi ombrosi," for example, for its breaks in measure (in modern peformance it is marked $^6_8/^3_4$) a practice he also greatly objected to in French opera. In French opera the rationale for broken meter was that the poetry demanded metric change, but there was no justification for the practice in the ritornelli of Monteverdi because they were "merely instrumental."[33] Despite his objections to Monteverdi's style (which occasionally border on pedantry), Burney appreciated his dramatic flair and praised his expressive recitative,[34] especially "Tu se' morta, se morta mia vita."[35]

Burney's investigation of seventeenth-century opera was hindered by a lack of music. He provides information about a great many operas, extracted from catalogues and theatre histories, but is unable to comment on most of the music.[36] His only substantial discussion of music besides Monteverdi's *Orfeo* focuses on seventeenth-century opera in Venice. His resources for this part of the history were also quite limited. He possessed one scene from Pietro Antonio Cesti's *Orontea* (1649) which he published in the *History* to give his readers some idea of the style of the period. He was also fortunate to have access to a manuscript of Cavalli's *Erismena,* and published an aria not for its intrinsic worth but because it was an early example of *da capo*. His remarks on the aria stand in painful evidence of his inability to treat opera in a historical context, as he had successfully done with sacred music: "It is amusing to see how contented, and even charmed, the public is at one period with what appears contemptible at another." He compares *Erismena* directly to modern opera, and judges it "so deficient in poetical and musical merit, compared with those in present favor, that no perfection of performance could render it palatable."[37] The arias were "psalmodic, monotonous, and dull" in comparison to modern airs. He is more just to the recitatives. He finds the recitatives less "passionate and expressive,"[38] than those of Luigi, Carissimi, and Cesti, but at least he compares them against contemporary rather than modern models.

Burney takes exception to the elaborate staging of seventeenth-century Venetian opera, observing that "much greater care seems to have been taken to amuse the eye than the ear or intellect."[39] He cites this as yet another example of the imbalance of the sister arts in opera, which he says is

> a species of exhibition, which as it originally consisted of poetry, Music, dancing, machinery, and decorations, it is the business of the historian to watch and point out the encroachments which any one of these constituent parts, at different periods, has made upon the rest.[40]

The standard he applies in defining these encroachments is not that of the period under consideration, but that of the second half of the eighteenth century. All of the excesses in decoration and dance he saw as ineffective attempts to compensate for the lack of truly dramatic music. Nevertheless, in the midst of all the spectacle and mythological nonsense of these operas, there was occasionally a moment where "the audience was disposed to give way to their feelings." It was in these moments that the true power of music was discovered.

> Music thus becoming a third art of imitation, had soon a language, expression, and images, of its own, wholly independent of poetry. Harmony even began to speak in the symphonies, without the assistance of words, and frequently sentiments were produced by the orchestra equally forcible with those of the vocal performers. Thus relinquishing by degrees the wonders of Fairy tales, the childishness of machinery, and the fantastical representation of things that humanity had never seen, pictures, more interesting and true, were sought in the imitations of nature.[41]

All of the marvels of spectacle which supported the Italian stage in the seventeenth century, and the French stage throughout the seventeenth and eighteenth centuries, were unnecessary once the power of affective music was discovered. Indeed, he saw the persistence of spectacle and mythological representations on the French stage as indicative of its degenerate state, for without affective music and beautiful singing there remained only dance and spectacle, the most pronounced characteristics of French serious opera.

In tracing the early history of opera Burney attempts to identify the evolution of a style of aria completely distinct from recitative. One stylistic feature which was particularly important was the cadential formula found at the end of each movement or section. The perfect, or formal cadence, in which voice and accompaniment cadence simultaneously is the approved form in arias. In the "true form" of the cadence of recitation, the accompanimental cadence follows directly after the vocal close (ex. 8.1)."[42] Burney expresses particular satisfaction at finding it in the works of the best composers of the period. His preference for the modern cadential formula did not completely blind him to the beauties of early models, however, and he cited several examples with favorable comments.[43]

228   Dramatic Music

Ex. 8.1. Cadence of Recitation

Frustrated by the lack of printed opera scores, Burney relegates most of his discussion of musical style in the seventeenth century to his chapter on "Cantatas or Narrative Chamber Music." Burney's discussion warrants inclusion here, as it elucidates his opinion of the style of the prominent seventeenth-century opera composers: Carissimi, Cesti, and Cavalli. The cantatas of the best composers were readily available in England, and no composer was better represented in music collections than Giacomo Carissimi, whom Burney, in a statement reflecting his values in his examination of seventeenth-century music, credits with "greatly improving recitative in general, rendering it a more expressive, articulate, and intelligible language, by its approximation to speech and declamation."[44] His progressive view of the history of style emerges in practical guise as he tries to distinguish invention and improvements in style at their source, a discrimination which to him seemed at once the most necessary and difficult part of a music historian's business.[45] In Carissimi's melodic style he found the fount of much of the common eighteenth-century idiom, including "more traits of fine melody than those of any composer of the seventeenth century,"[46] and "sweet and graceful passages, which more than a hundred years have not impaired."

Despite their lasting beauties, certain features of the melodies betrayed their age. Burney avers that it is in the patterns of the divisions in opera melodies that the changes of taste are chiefly discoverable. These are the fashionable forms and trimmings, which soon give way to others; "but the principal ground-work, or materials, if good at one time, would not lose their value at another."[47] The fine "principal ground-work" which he saw in Carissimi's cantatas prompted him to print fifteen excerpts with commentary in a plate called "Beauties of Melody and Modulation." His comments attest to the influence he felt Carissimi exerted on later composers: phrases such as "could never be old or common," "plaintive and can never be vulgar," "furnished melody, harmony, and modulation, to the beauties of which the greatest masters have added but little," and this "is a musical phrase that still retains its bloom" are characteristic.[48] In the twenty-two cantatas he studied, Burney discovered "many refinements and subtleties of composition, that are thought new and *recherchées* at present, when used by the first professors in Europe."[49]

Burney is even more explicit about the influence of Cesti on musical style. Cesti's music was sufficiently progressive to incline Burney to believe that his works would fill a "considerable number" of the pages in a collection "of the most elegant and striking passages of the best composers of the last century, which are still, and ever must remain, pleasing."[50] Such a collection, taken from the works of Stradella, Carissimi, Cesti, and others, "would leave but little to subsequent composers who have been the most celebrated for originality and invention." Burney's plates of Cesti's work boldly cite passages and give the names of composers who adopted characteristics of style which in Burney's view were original with Cesti. Handel, Steffani, and Corelli are each listed as having adopted basses, divisions, and even melodic formulae.

Burney's study of the cantatas of Cesti and Carissimi was conducted largely in the British Museum, and at Christ Church, Oxford. He was also able to draw upon one of his own treasures: the music book of Salvatore Rosa. According to Burney, it contained "eight entire cantatas written, set, and transcribed by this celebrated painter himself."[51] Unfortunately, Burney erred when he wrote this section of the *History*. His notes in the manuscript state that the third cantata is in Rosa's own handwriting, but when Burney utilized this source years later he apparently assumed from his note that everything in the manuscript beyond the note was composed by Rosa. Not all of these compositions have yet been identified, but two fragments are, respectively, from cantatas by Cesti and Giovanni Bononcini. Another, in which Burney says that there are several airs "on pleasing subjects, and treated in a manner above mediocrity," is actually by Alessandro Scarlatti. Thus Burney's evaluation of Salvatore Rosa as a composer—"not only admirable for a *Dilettante,* but in point of melody, superior to that of most of the masters of his time"—though misdirected, is indisputable: Bononcini, Cesti, and Scarlatti were certainly superior to most of their contemporaries.[52]

Burney's commentary on other works in the Rosa manuscript demonstrates his willingness to point out stylistic borrowings even in the work of composers he most esteems. For example, he credits Leonardo Vinci with establishing a new era in music, but notes that Alessandro Scarlatti's "Lasciami sola a piangere" from *Gli equivoci nel sembiante* (1679) contained "many beautiful, and then new, traits of melody, of which Vinci afterwards availed himself when he set 'deh respirar lasciatemi' in Metastasio's opera *Artaserse* (1730)."[53]

His essay on Alessandro Scarlatti shows the contradiction between Burney the historian and Burney the critic. Scarlatti, he proclaims, is the "most voluminous and most original"[54] of the composers of the "golden age of cantatas in Italy,"[55] a statement representing his historical judgment. His musical judgment finds the cantatas "not always free from affectation and pedantry." Scarlatti's modulations in particular come in under attack, for "in struggling at novelty, [he] is sometimes crude and unnatural." In addition, he is often guilty of expressing the meaning of a single word, rather than "the general sense and spirit of the whole poem."[56] He is aware of the expressive intent of Scarlatti's harmony, but feels that it often exceeds the bounds of beauty and taste, and gives examples such as setting the words *cangio in dolare* with a "sudden, violent, and extraneous modulation," and "*dura, cruda, Dolente, Strano,* etc., [which] were irresistible temptations to wring the ear with crudities."[57]

These complaints aside, Burney was impressed with the fertility of Scarlatti's invention, and found some peculiar beauty of modulation and melody in every one of his movements. Scarlatti's recitatives particularly pleased him, for in recitative the bold modulations, too pungent for his taste in the arias, seemed appropriate. Tracing the history of musical style through the cantata, Burney found Scarlatti's "property among the stolen goods of all the best composers of the first forty or fifty years of the present century."[58]

Not all of the innovations he found in the works of seventeenth-century masters contributed to the advancement of the art. One innovation upon which Burney did not look favorably was the excessive use of divisions. In his survey of the development of melodic style, he found Luigi Rossi culpable for having "started several flimsy divisions, which afterwards became common."[59] The expression of individual words by literal representation is similarly censured. Burney eventually had to curtail his use of musical examples for many other composers of varying merit, because, though he preferred to let the composers speak for themselves through their music, he feared his book would "have more the appearance of a music book than a history of the art."[60]

Burney's discussion of seventeenth-century opera outside Italy is very limited. The chapter on German opera is as insignificant as that on German sacred music. Only a few titles and names of composers appear in the *History*, and these are taken from Marpurg's *Historisch-kritische Beyträge*. Burney owned scores to five of Reinhard Keiser's operas, and referred to the composer as "the admirable Keiser," but he did not review the operas, nor even list their titles. His summary of Keiser's style is indicative of his attitude toward German vocal music, and serves to explain the insufficiency of the discussion. "For grace and facility I do not recommend him; indeed, they were little sought or known during his time; but for modulation, ingenuity, and new ideas, he scarcely had his equal."[61] Grace and facility were, of course, what Burney valued most in dramatic music. He was willing to grant the Germans of the seventeenth century superiority so "far as harmony, contrivance, complication and diligence could carry them," but this to a man of taste was not very far.

The dramatic music of France fared considerably better, though only in the allotment of space. In tone the chapter is tainted by the unfavorable cast which Burney brings to his writings about French music of all periods. The initial sentence of his discussion of opera captures the spirit of the chapter.

> Though the French have long wished to have a dramatic Music of their own, their most patriotic writers on the subject have been obliged to confess, that they owe the establishment of operas in France to the Italians.[62]

His animosity toward French writers causes him to discredit too much of what they claim for France. He sneers at Blainville's discussion of opera before Lulli, yet his own account is badly muddled, confusing Cavalli's *Ercole amante* with the production of *Xerse,* and overlooking Luigi Rossi's *Orfeo* (1647) altogether.

The greatest part of the essay on French opera is devoted to a biography of Jean Baptiste Lully. Burney shows a surprising moment of objectivity, confessing that "on a recent examination of the operas of Lulli, I am much less surprised at the high favour they obtained in France, than I used to be.[63] He continued to find Lulli's recitative disagreeable, but the arias, choruses, and dances he found "easy and natural." Nonetheless, he challenged La Borde's assertion that music since Lulli's time, "instead of advancing towards perfection, as is imagined, has perhaps lost more than it has gained,"[64] reminding LaBorde of his own "warm encomiums" on Piccinni, Sacchini, Paisiello, and Rameau.

In general, Burney's caustic tone in his discussion of French opera seems to be motivated by the resistance of the French to change, and by the bitter literary exchanges which accompanied the changes that were attempted in France. He saw the *"querelle des bouffons,"* the Piccinni-Gluck disputes, and the Lulli-Rameau upheaval as symptomatic of the reactionary spirit of French music lovers. He had little sympathy with such debates; they were certainly not consonant with his view of music as an innocent luxury. He nevertheless joined in the dispute, pitting the authority of Voltaire, "who had long lived out of France," against the partisans of French music.[65]

Burney's history of native dramatic music in seventeenth-century England consists largely of extracts from dramatic poetry which allude to the use of music in drama. Faced with music which could provide little of interest or amusement to his readers, he spends much of the chapter in a discussion of the references to music in Shakespeare's works.[66] Though entertaining, this has little to do with the history of music. He occasionally mentions recent musical settings of Shakespeare's dramas, including those by Thomas Linley and Arne of the *Tempest* (he neglects, however, to mention his own unsuccessful music for

Garrick's production of *A Midsummer Night's Dream*), but nothing resembling a history of dramatic music emerges in the discussion. Midway in his essay, Shakespeare's lines attacking music:

> Tis good; though Music oft hath such a charm
> To make bad good; and good provoke to harm

provokes this retort from Burney:

> This is a heavy charge, which it would not have been easy for Shakspeare [sic] to substantiate, and does not very well agree with what he says in the Tempest of the *innoxious* efficacy of Music: "Sounds and sweet airs, that give delight and *hurt not.*" Music may be applied to licentious poetry; but the poetry then corrupts the Music, not the Music the poetry. It has often regulated the movements of lascivious dances; but such airs heard could convey no impure ideas to an innocent imagination; so that Montesquieu's assertion is still in force: that "Music is the only one of all the arts, which does not corrupt the mind."[67]

The innocence of music is a theme evident throughout Burney's writings.[68] He acknowledges that music is occasionally present in art that tends to corrupt, but his article "Opera" in the *Cyclopaedia* underscores the culpability of poetry in corrupting the morals, for mere music, without words, cannot suborn. It is not clear to whom these defenses are directed among contemporary writers, but contention in England over the corrupting influence of music certainly had not subsided since Shakespeare's time. Burney's work is the precursor of a number of essays on Shakespeare and music. He was also the first successful annotator of Shakespeare's musical allusions.[69] In his concentration on the poetry to the exclusion of music, he underscores his distaste for seventeenth-century English music in general, once again displaying his interest in poetry in the absence of music which suits him.

Burney's attitude toward the seventeenth-century English composers of dramatic music is most amusingly revealed in the doggerel he sent to Twining which was reproduced in the chapter on chamber music. Burney's essays on these composers in the *History* are brief, but considerably more respectful than his poetic characterizations, with the exception of his commentary on Henry Lawes. Burney calls Lawes's music to the opera *Comus* (1634) "a series of unmeaning sounds," and even offers a critical opinion of his text-setting contrary to that of Milton and other poets, who had praised his accentuation of text. In accordance with his promise to justify his strictures, he prints "Sweet Echo Sweetest Nymphe," citing specific errors in accentuation and overlooked opportunities for expression, and concludes with a challenge to Lawes's partisans: "I should be glad, indeed to be informed by the most exclusive admirer of old ditties, what is the *musical merit* of this song, except insipid simplicity, and its having been set for a single voice."[70]

Only one composer, Henry Purcell, is spared Burney's sweeping condemnation of English seventeenth-century composers. The enthusiasm he shows for Purcell's sacred music permeates his discussion of the dramatic music as well. There is even an undercurrent of challenge to Handel's preeminence.

Burney says, for example, that the first movement of the overture to Purcell's *Indian Queen* (1695) is "equal to any of Handel's," and that the fugue in the overture to *Dioclesian* (1691) is in the style of Handel "with better fugues."[71] Moreover, his comparison of Purcell's music to that of unnamed foreign composers is clearly more applicable to Handel's style than to that of any other composer:

> There is more elegant melody, more elaborate harmony, more ingenious contrivance, in the motion and contexture of several parts in the works of many great composers, but to the natives of England, who know the full power of our language, and feel the force, spirit, and shades of meaning, which every word bears according to its place in a sentence, and the situation of the speaker, or singer, I must again repeat it, this composition will have charms and effects, which, perhaps, Purcell's Music only can produce.[72]

Purcell possessed remarkable abilities for an English composer. Burney especially notes that his secular vocal music was the best composed in that era, a remarkable achievement because that genre had always been dominated by foreigners.

> And, indeed, since his time, nothing can secure success to an English composer, but dexterity at imitation. Handel, Geminiani, and the Italians in general, were long imitated; nor, of late years would the strains of our countrymen have been borne, much less listened to with pleasure, but for the Italian taste and tincture in their composition.[73]

Burney does not consider Purcell an original genius. He perceives Purcell's models to be "Carissimi in the best of his recitatives," and "Lulli in the worst"; it "manifestly appears, that he was fond of Stradella's *manner* of writing, though he never seems to have pillaged his passages."[74] All in all, though, he found Purcell in advance of his time because the passing of a century had not injured many of his movements.[75]

The chapter "Attempts at Dramatic Music In England, previous to the Establishment of the Italian Opera," has much the same tone as the discussion of French opera. Opera was not a welcomed guest in England when it first made its appearance. The propriety of singing in drama was constantly being questioned by critics of the time, whom Burney viewed as "men without taste or ears for Music," and who, neither feeling nor understanding music, thought every music lover a fool.[76] The detractors of opera, he discerned, had interests in the playhouses which competed with the opera for patrons, and were therefore strongly prejudiced. Colley Cibber characterized the establishment of

234   Dramatic Music

opera as "the victory of sound and shew over *sense* and *reason*", to which Burney responded,

> *Opera* is an alien that is obliged silently to bear the insults of the natives, or else she might courteously retort, that nonsense *without* Music is as frequently heard on the English stage, as with it on the Italian;...[77]

Indeed, in Burney's view no true English opera was ever established. The several attempts at English recitative were set aside, and the tradition of stage plays with incidental music and songs continued. Only for Arne's *Artaxerxes* was an English audience found.

Burney's preoccupation with defending opera as an institution clouds his discussion of the musical development of English opera. He singles out one of opera's best known critics, Joseph Addison, and his opera *Rosamond* (1707) for a particularly strong attack, censuring him for "total want of sensibility and knowledge of the art." Burney proceeds with a vigorous cirticism of Addison's work, taking delight in extracting from *Rosamond* "opera absurdities" of the kind which Addison himself pilloried in the *Spectator*. In addition to criticizing him for selecting the incompetent Thomas Clayton to set the music, and for failing to appreciate Handel over Clayton, he attacks Addison on his home ground, accusing him of having an "ear for rhyme [which] was no more nice than for Music."[78] Burney is merciless in his criticism of the literary men who attacked the opera of this and every period.[79]

Burney ends his history of opera in England before the arrival of Handel with a critique of the prominent singers of the period. As these were singers whom he had never heard in performance, his biographical information comes from newspaper advertisements and Cibber's *Apology*. Musically, he judges the performers, with respect to their execution, by the divisions which composers wrote for them. The principal singers receive extensive notice, but the subaltern singers are only listed, with the explanation that "many parts of a building are necessary to its construction, which are never regarded as ornamental."[80]

The most extraordinary features of the chapter "Italian Opera in Eighteenth-Century England" are its immense size, and the exhaustive and exhausting reviews of Handel's operas.[81] The reviews occupy an inordinate portion of Burney's *History,* a surprising amount, considering that they supplement the lengthy discussion of Handel's music in the *Account of the Commemoration of Handel*. The expansive survey of Handel's music in the *History* is curious; Burney's work had more than doubled in size from his original plan, and he was facing a severe shortage of space. The lack of space necessitated the abbreviation of subsequent chapters, forcing him to limit the treatment of the Neapolitan School, the group of composers for whom Burney had the highest critical regard. In his discussion of Pergolesi he laments:

as the works of this master form an era in modern Music... it was my intention to have inserted here, some critical remarks resulting from a late, careful examination of his principal productions for the church; but upon calculating the business I have still to do, and the pages left for its reception, I find that critical discussion must give way to matters of fact, or my volume will be rendered too cumbrous and unwieldy.[82]

Burney's problem grew so acute that he was finally forced to eliminate at least two complete sections of his *History*. In view of circumstances, Burney's appropriation of space for the reviews of Handel's operas seems inexplicable, but there were practical considerations that account for both the length and design of the chapter. Burney found great difficulty in collecting materials for the history of opera, a music which appeared fleetingly on the stage and then disappeared with perhaps only a collection of a few "Favorite Airs from the Opera of ___" to mark its existence. He could rely on newspapers and program collections to construct a calendar of the operatic stage, but little music was available for review even in Burney's extensive library, and he could not expect that most of his readers would have enough music in their collections to justify any lengthy discussion of the majority of operas. The situation was quite different, however, with respect to Handel, for not only were the autograph manuscripts available for his use, but the publication of Handel's music by Samuel Arnold would allow Burney's readers to follow his commentary on the operas literally aria by aria. The sheer bulk of the discussion of Handel's opera must not be mistaken as an indication of the importance which Burney ascribes to Handel as a composer of opera. Though Handel was the dominant figure of the operatic stage for some years, was the favorite composer of a segment of Burney's readers, and was one of the few composers whose works were published, he was not the composer Burney ranked as the greatest of his day. Burney's aesthetic, as has been shown, was rooted in the style against which he judged all others, thus a review of the Neapolitan composers and their aesthetic need precede evaluation of his work on Handel. Burney struggled to review music of his own time objectively. Several times he assures his readers that he is not criticizing a work "in consequence of the extreme difference between this music and that of modern times; but by mounting up to the period of its production, and comparing it with contemporary compositions, lately perused."[83] This adjustment of historical perpsective was necessary, not only in the evaluation of different composers, but individual operas as well, in order to judge fairly the composer's originality,[84] especially in works written and performed in Burney's lifetime.

Despite his best efforts, Burney's attempts at objectivity are frequently overshadowed by his belief in Rousseau's unity of melody theory, particularly the precept that the accompaniment is completely subordinate to the melody. This obsession is not as antihistorical as it may seem, for Burney believed that the style of music in opera had come nearly full circle. He approved of the "very thin" accompaniments of the earliest operas, and noted that "as dramatic music advanced towards perfection," it was found that the orchestra could produce effects which "were picturesque, coloured sentiments and augmented auricular pleasure."[85] When accompaniments became fuller and the semi-polyphonic style (to use Downes's term) developed, however, the balance of voice and orchestra was lost as the orchestra sought too prominent a role:

> ...though much ingenuity and science appear in a rich and full accompaniment *on paper,* yet in performance, the composer and the orchestra frequently abuse their power, and tyrannize over the voice, which they should cherish, and disguise the poetry by complication and noise, which they should help to explain and enforce.[86]

In Burney's own time, though, the operas of Leonardo Vinci and subsequent Neapolitans had returned to a style which in spirit at least was analogous in its accompaniment to the style of the early monodists. In England, however, the taste for Handel's music offset the "reforms." Most Handelians viewed the music of the Neapolitans as insipid in its simplicity.

Semi-polyphonic works, in Burney's view, violated the unity of melody, and made truly dramatic treatment impossible. A passage from his notebook, compiled while he was working on the *History,* speaks of the Augustan age of "the *free, graceful, pathetic, picturesque,* and truly *Dramatic style,*" the style "invented by Vinci, Hasse, Porpora, and Pergolesi [which] has been pushed perhaps as far as it will go, by Jomelli, Galuppi, Piccini, Sacchini, Paesiello, and Sarti." Handel is conspicuously absent from the catalogue of truly dramatic composers, an omission explained in a later passage.

> Vinci and Pergolesi have been imitated near 50 years; and in Dramatic music it must be owned that the symmetry, Grace, accent and beauty of the melodies, and clearness and tranquility of the accompaniments were so near perfection that much deviation from them could not be admitted but at the expense of poetry, nature and simplicity. Melodies loaded with ornaments, and turbulent accompaniments may enrich a score that's made for a fastidious and critical *Eye,* but will always injure the Effect to the *Ear* in performance, unless poetry and passion are wholly sacrificed.[87]

The style of Vinci, which Burney holds as the model of the Neapolitan style, was praised lavishly by Rousseau. The *Dictionnaire* article "Génie" urges the student who questions if he possesses real genius to "Be quick, hasten to Naples, and listen to the masterpieces of Leo, Durante, Jomelli, and Pergolesi." Algarotti, in his *Saggio sopra l'opera in musica* (1755), also turned to Naples for models of excellence, citing Vinci. Burney, in designating Naples as the seat of the new vocal music, is following a well-established tradition. Of all the Neapolitans, he credits Vinci with remembering "that the true characteristic of dramatic Music is clearness." Vinci "seems to have been the first" to call attention "chiefly to the voice-part, by disintangling it from fugue, complication, and laboured contrivance."[88] The Neapolitan School thereafter in Burney's opinion remained the model of good dramatic music for much of Europe.

Looking back on the eighteenth century, Burney reflected on the influence of Naples, and pronounced it the most eminent of cities for vocal music. His list of masters connected with the city (in which he takes a broad view of the term Neapolitan) includes a startling galaxy of stars: the two Scarlatti's, Leo, Pergolesi, Durante, Porpora, Vinci, Jommelli, Perez, Piccinni, Sacchini, Anfossi, Traetta, Rinaldo di Capua, Guglielmi, Gennaro Manna, Ciccio di Majo, Gaetano Latilla, Sala, Cimarosa, and Paisiello.[89] Indeed, he did not scruple to say that "no good composer except Gluck" had abandoned Vinci's style. The "disciples" of Durante, among them Piccinni, Sacchini, Traetta and Anfossi, embellished and rendered the style more elegant, but all were "guided by the outline of Vinci."[90]

Johann Adolphe Hasse, despite his German origins, was a Neapolitan by training, and the principal torchbearer of Vinci's style during the middle third of the eighteenth century. Like Vinci, he excelled in expression; "equally a friend to poetry and the voice, he discovered as much judgment as genius in expressing words, as well as in accompanying his sweet and tender melodies."[91] Burney's evaluation of Hasse in the *German Tour* is radiant with praise for his unencumbered style.

> If the affected French expression of *le grand simple* can ever mean any thing, it must be when applied to the productions of such a composer as Hasse, who succeeds better perhaps in expressing, with clearness and propriety, whatever is graceful, elegant, and tender, than what is boisterous and violent...[92]

Hasse's most famous operas were on Metastasian libretti. To Burney this collaboration seemed the realization of the perfect union of poetry and music. A passage from the notebook reflects on their perfectly complementary roles:

> Dr. Brown pretended to prove the separation of Music and poetry—if he was right, it must however be allowed that this poet and musician are the two *halves* of what...once constituted a whole.[93]

Hasse's slightly younger contemporary, Niccolo Jommelli, whom Burney ranked very highly, intensified the expressiveness of the Neapolitan idiom. After his visit to the composer in Naples in October, 1770, Burney recorded, "were I to name the living composers of Italy for the stage according to my idea of their merit, they would be in the following order: Hasse—Jomelli—Galuppi—Piccini—Sacchini etc."[94] When preparing the list for publication, he expanded his assessment: "Jomelli's works are full of great and noble ideas, treated with taste and learning."[95] Burney detected three periods in Jomelli's development: during his early life he adhered to "the easy graceful flow of Vinci and Pergolesi"; the German sound then influenced him, and he "changed his stile in compliance with the taste and expectations of his audience" for learning and complication; his final years were spent in Naples, and were characterized by a thinning and simplifying of his style, which, however, remained too elaborate for popular Italian taste. This opinion must have been based in part on the discussions of Jomelli's style which he heard in Naples during his tour, and on Mattei's writings, since Burney knew little of Jommelli's music firsthand.[96] Only *Attilio Regolo* (in 1753) and *Andromaca* (in 1755)[97] were performed in England, though other music by him was incorporated into pasticcios and used in concert performances. Burney heard a scene from his *Olimpiade* during the Italian tour, which he found extremely difficult, but he says it was "justly admired for the boldness and learning in the modulation, which is *recherchée* but expressive and pleasing." Mestastasio urged Jommelli to adhere to his simpler style, which "instantly seizes on the heart, without giving the mind the trouble of reflection," but Burney countered the poet's complaint with the charge that "Poets are always ready to join in censuring the composer's science."

> ... it was the opinion of the Neapolitans, that the songs of *Jomelli,* which masters respected for their art, and contrivance, were too elaborate, and gave the hearers too much trouble, to afford them careless delight... but, as the Public is a many-headed animal, with ears of all sorts and sizes, it is to be feared, that some of them will expect learning and science to be displayed by the composer, and powers of execution by the singer, as well as others [of] such artless simplicity, as would reduce an opera to a level with a ballad farce.[98]

Jommelli's particular distinction, as Burney perceived it, was the enrichment of a style that had been vitiated by composers who, lacking genius, captured only the simplicity of the Neapolitan style in their feeble imitations. In Naples in 1770 Burney found that "the general run of Neapolitan music is noisy and monotonous, but while such composers as Jomelli, Piccini, Merula, Mann[a], Paesiello, etc. are in it one would think no complaint need be made of a scarcity of good music."[99] Though as an eclectic composer Jommelli is not credited with original genius, he nevertheless ranks as among the best in Burney's category of truly dramatic composers. It is difficult to explicate the musical features that account for Burney's admiration of the Neapolitan school because there is insufficient evidence; the *History* contains only very brief remarks on *La Caduta dé giganti* by Gluck, *Attilio Regolo* and *Andromaca* by Jommelli, and *Demofoonte* and *Siroe* by Hasse. Otherwise, Burney's remaining thirty-nine discussions of eighteenth-century operas are exclusively devoted to the works of Handel.

Handel's place in Burney's categories is among the "ingenious and artful" composers. Considering Burney's predilection for the Neapolitan style over the semi-polyphonic, his criticism is surprisingly well balanced. Burney seldom criticizes Handel's elaborate accompaniments, although he mentions that the style has changed, and "been long banished from the opera, as undramatic: for the voice-part is so overpowered and rendered so insignificant that she loses her sovereignity."[100] Operose accompaniments, though lacking true drama, created a kind of energy merely by the noise and thematic interplay of the instruments. For example, the second act of Handel's *Amadigi* (1715) is burdened with a particularly heavy accompaniment. One aria, "Ti pentirai, crudel," which Burney credits with having "all the spirited effect of a crowded score," is scored only for violins in unison and bass,[101] and seems rather thinly accompanied to modern ears. However, it is not the number of discrete parts in the orchestral accompaniment that he censures, but their melodic character, especially when they feature polyphonic imitation. This he viewed as an encroachment on the domain of the voice. Some arias which are more fully orchestrated, such as "Crudel, tu non farai, ch'il tuo rigor giami," are not criticized because even though the accompaniments have great spirit they do not interfere with the voice.[102] He did not disapprove of echoes and imitations of a voice part by an instrumental part. The aria "S'estinto è l'idol mio"[103] has prominent imitations of the vocal melody in the violins which echo and even overlap the voice. Nonetheless, he praises it as "one of the finest Handel ever produced," crediting it with a pathetic subject, natural and pleasing imitations, rich harmony, and affecting modulation." The imitation in the aria is restricted to one part and never shared by the other instruments in fugato, except for a short point of imitation in the closing instrumental tutti. Nor does his definition of confused accompaniments include instrumental doubling of the voice part: in the first section the voice is accompanied by unison first violin, and at the lower third by the second violin. He can allow that colorful instrumentation and occasional imitation may be effective, but fugato passages between voice and instruments are rejected.

Not all arias Burney describes as "ingenious" or containing "masterly contrivance" are fugal or even imitative. "Sorge infausta una procella" from *Orlando* (1732) is described as "abounding in that species of ingenious and masterly contrivance, which generally delights the eye and judgment of deep Musicians, much more than the public ear."[104] The accompaniment, though not imitative, is hardly a model of unity of melody. The viola contains a continuous passage of sixteenth notes against the voice during much of the aria, and the second violin has a pattern similarly distracting from the voice part. Such loaded accompaniments may not charm the polite audience, however, Burney notes, "without such specimens of musical science [an opera] is never had in much reverence by professors. But so changed is the style of Dramatic Music, since Handel's was produced, that almost all his songs seem *scientific*."[105]

The richness of Handel's accompaniments seemed appropriate when the aria was written for a singer of no special abilities, as they could compensate for the poverty of the voice.[106] In *Siroe* (1728), for example, Burney says that

Baldi's aria "Frà l'orror" is "set to an admirable instrumental movement in five parts strictly *fugato*." As Baldi was a second-rate singer, the lively accompaniment served to render the piece interesting and was "better worth having than the voice."[107] Burney asserts elsewhere, not altogether convincingly, that "Handel, had frequently been accused of crowding his score with too many parts... but I can perceive no such redundance of parts in his opera songs, when he had a good singer to write for."[108] The articles on arias, composition and opera in the *Cyclopaedia* do not mention this expedient, which seems a mere rationalization.

One manner of accompaniment in Handel's arias which Burney never fails to compliment is "the modern style of iterated notes." He first detects this style in Handel's "Ah! speitato! e non ti muove" from *Amadigi* (1715). The iterated-note technique is described as modern when it applies either to the inner voices or the bass. Some arias combined both styles, such as "Anima infida" from *Xerxes* (1738), which according to Burney, has "a Corelli base, and a modern accompaniment."[109] His genuine opinion of Handel's ability in each operatic style and in mixture is revealed in his review of *Alcina* (1735). An unnamed authority had written that in *Alcina* Handel adopted the new taste of Vinci, Porpora, and Hasse. Burney counters by asserting that "the best and most favourite airs of the opera were composed [by Handel] in his own manner, without leaning to that of others, either by accident or design."[110] He divides the arias in *Alcina* into three categories: "*aria all' antica,* or Handel's own style, twenty-one; *alla moderna,* eight; *antica e moderna,* or of a mixed style, three." Despite an admirable defense of Handel's own style, Burney betrays himself by citing six capital arias from the opera: four of the six are *alla moderna,* one mixed, and only one in Handel's own manner.[111]

A passage from the *Account* best characterizes Burney's perception of Handel's modernism.

> These [arias from *Siroe*] were composed in 1728, about the time that Vinci and Hasse had begun to thin and simplify accompaniment, as well as to polish melody. In the first of these Airs the voice-part is beautiful and a *canevas* for a great singer; in the second, the effects by modulation and broken sentences of melody are truly pathetic and theatrical: the first violin admirably filling up the chasms in the principal melody, while the second violin, tenor, and base, are murmuring in the subdued accompaniment of iterated notes in modern songs. By these two Airs it appears that HANDEL, who had always more solidity and contrivance than his cotemporaries, penetrated very far into those regions of taste and refinement at which his successors only arrived, by a slow progress, half a century after.[112]

The idea that Handel "penetrated" into the modern style was far-fetched, and Burney knew it. The Neapolitan style was already firmly established in Italy. Vinci, with whom Burney most frequently associates this style, died in 1730, at which time the new style was common language. Moreover, Burney cites examples of similar attributes of style in Alessandro Scarlatti's works. Yet this theme of Handel's modern style recurs several times in the *History*. "Scoglio d'immota fronte" from *Scipione* (1726), for example, is described as in a style "as bold, fanciful, and elegant as in any of the best dramatic songs of Vinci and Pergolesi."[113] Weighed against his explicit preferences, these claims seem to have something of an air of accomodation about them.

Notwithstanding his objections to some aspects of Handel's style, Burney genuinely admired the composer's tremendous genius. As he undertook the minute examination of Handel's works, he uncovered even "more reason" for the "long duration of national partiality. Indeed, I have lately discovered beauties of composition which perhaps I formerly did not see."[114] He was most impressed with Handel's variety of design (form) in aria compositions, which surpassed in "variety of style and ingenuity of accompaniments those of all preceding and cotemporary Composers throughout Europe."[115]

Throughout Burney's writings on opera the aria has the most prominent place. Yet only the most general idea of Burney's taste is discernable from his criticism. The arias he cites as being particularly affecting are so diverse in their style and expression as to defy attempts to synthesize a cogent idea of his expectations. His preferences in accompaniments are apparent, but melodic style, as he realized, is peculiarly resistant to analysis and verbal description. It is a great pity that the musical form that most pleased and interested Burney is the least accessible through his writings.[116]

Though the air was the most significant element of an opera, other aspects are frequently mentioned. In his discussion of Handelian opera Burney cited virtually every example of accompanied recitative he encountered, several of which he praised because of the effective expression of the text. Burney was a professional musician, fluent in Italian and knowledgeable of Italian poetry; one might be tempted to infer that he was unusually well equipped to appreciate recitative. But it is evident from his writings that English audiences were perhaps not as oblivious to the expressive significance of recitative as has been commonly supposed. The directors of the Handel Commemoration of 1784, for example, in scheduling Handel's operatic music for the second day of the ceremonies, selected eleven arias and an accompanied recitative from *Julius Caesar,* a recitative legendary for its pathos.[117] To persons "equally well skilled in Music and the Italian tongue," Burney reports, this recitative, when "recited on the stage by Senesino," had an effect "which no Recitative, or even Air, had before, in this country."[118] Clearly there must have been a sizeable portion of the audience at the commemoration capable of appreciating the recitative in order to warrant its inclusion.

In *recitativo accompagnato* it was always the effective expression of the text that elicited praise from Burney.[119] The *History* would have been liberally sprinkled with examples of expressive accompanied recitative, but as Arnold's edition of Handel's works was in the process of publication, Burney, troubled by the expense of engraving and by the burgeoning size of his *History,* was satisfied with only citing their appearance, noting that such dramatic painting in 1742 was "somewhat new, at least in England."[120] This last statement serves to re-emphasize that Burney's "history of Italian opera" is its history in England. He acknowledges that England was not at the forefront of the modern style when, in tracing the influence of Galuppi on Italian music, he records that "many of the refinements of modern melody, and effects in dramatic Music, seem to originate from the genius of Galuppi, at this period, *at least in England.*"[121]

Though Burney cites particularly expressive accompanied recitative, and chronicles changes in aria styles, *recitativo semplice* is seldom mentioned. Burney saw little to mention, for

> ...the Italian recitative, which received its last forms and polish chiefly from the elder SCARLATTI (Alessandro) and PORPORA; seems as fixed and permanent as a dead language; and, while melody is as fluctuating as the waves of the sea, recitative seems, in stability to resemble *terra firma.*[122]

The opera overture was subject to greater fluctuations in style. Burney had no expectations that Handel's operatic overtures would have any dramatic import, and on the whole he was satisfied with them, despite Handel's employment of the old-fashioned French form. However, Handel's frequent use of a third movement in dance form in his London operas displeased him. His criticisms range from tacit acceptance to well-articulated disgust.[123] Not everyone was inclined to disapprove of Handel's third movements: Burney remarks that the lack of a minuet or popular air in the overture to *Radamisto* had "prevented it from being as frequently played as many others,"[124] but he views the inclusion of the jig as a concession to the lovers of banal simplicity, "who, unable to follow a composer through the mazes of learned modulation and complicated parts, listen only to the tune of the principal melody."[125]

In contrast to his general praise of Handel's overtures, Burney is critical of his interstitial symphonies, which he finds frequently undramatic. In the midst of act one of Handel's *Amadigi,* for example, Burney found an overture in the standard slow adagio—fast allegro structure, "good enough for the opening of any serious opera," where the libretto says "an enchanted palace falls to pieces, *al suono di strepitosa sinfonia.*" The thunder, lightning, and ruin pronounced by the poet do not evoke anything "picturesque or imitative" from the composer, a lapse which Burney lamely excuses as perhaps the consequence of orchestras which were "not so powerful or able to execute new and dramatic ideas, as at present."[126] Handel overlooked another opportunity for an expressive instrumental movement in *Admeto,* where another regular overture takes the place of the expected "horrid symphony to express the cries and shrieks of tortured souls in the infernal regions." The text suggested "wild jargon and hellish dissonance" to Burney, but Handel provides only a fugue with a chromatic subject.[127] Burney was not always so disappointed: in *Orlando* he found that the entire last act,

> ...which paints the madness of Orlando in accompanied recitatives and airs in various measures, is admirable. Handel has endeavoured to describe the hero's perturbation of intellect by fragments of a symphony in 5/8, a division of time which can only be borne in such a situation.[128]

Although a full evaluation of the influence of the Handelians on Burney's criticism must be delayed until the conclusion of this study, it is impossible to quit the discussion of Burney's treatment of Handel's operas without reference to the consequences of that influence upon it. It was in the discussion of the operas that Burney was compelled to temper his critical pen. His remarks on Handel's works are by no means consistently favorable, but he does avoid giving a concise assessment based upon his convictions. His notebooks stand in evidence of the frustration he experienced in writing about Handel. They contain a variety of drafts, some aborted after only a paragraph, others after several pages. One speaks eloquently of his difficulties and also contains the definitive assessment of Handel's style which he never gave in print.

> Handel's Merit is so various, and those *virtues* which are ever on the Margin of vices when carried to excess, require such discriminatory Criticism as would fill a larger portion of this work than can be allowed it; even to the transcendant merit of this great Composer. I am not ignorant of the great Number of his enthusiastic admirers who have so long been accustomed to speak of all his Productions with equal rapture that I can expect no quarter from them for daring to say that he had the Concomitant Defects of voluminous and popular writers, whose Genius is often allowed to expand uncircumscribed to the narrow limits of the singers Talents for whom he writes. In a word, Handel's chief defect was want of Delicacy in accompanying his Melodies, as well as in the Melodies themselves. The age for fugues, for imitation, and contrivance as well as for crowding a score were vices of his age into which he plunged deeper than his contemporaries. The ritornels and violin accompaniments of his songs too are frequently very unnatural and awkward for that instrument, and +such+ as when executed with great pains and Labour had no good Effect, either in shewing the instrument in pleasing the +music lover+, or in assisting the vocal performers.[129]

Burney's circumspection in writing about Handel is, in part, motivated by his perception that most of the readers did not share his own wide knowledge of music. When he attempted to determine who was the greatest opera composer, Burney narrowed the contest to Hasse and Handel. His manuscript reflections show the difficulty he faced in presenting what he considered to be a truly objective judgment to his English readers.

> Which was the best of the two I shall not pretend to determine. Both had great merit in different ways. Such as admire manliness of style, richness of Harmony, and ingenuity of Contrivance will vote in favour of Handel; while others who admire Elegant Simplicity, refined Taste, clearness, and a judicious and happy Expression of the Words, will give their

Suffrage to Hasse. But nothing can be more illiberal and unjust than to exalt the one at the expense of the other, especially when it is done, as is frequently the case, *sans Connaissance de Cause* as the best works of Hasse are but in few Hands in England, so that where nine out of ten think it blasphemy to name him in competition with Handel; yet on the Continent little more than the name of Handel carried thither by the English has been heard. How is it then possible either for the generality of English or + + to form a Comparative Judgment concerning the merit of these great composers?[130]

Nevertheless, Burney's choice is apparent everywhere in his writings except when he discusses Handel.

One curious feature of this critical debate is its retrospection. Handel had been dead for thirty years in 1789, and Hasse had neither written an opera since 1771 nor changed his style since 1730. A possible explanation is suggested in a conversation which Burney had with Rinaldo di Capua at Rome. Rinaldo, who is quoted at length about the stagnant state of operatic composition, averred that composers "had nothing left within the reach of their invention to entitle them to the reputation for novelty, but the refuse of thousands, which had been often tried and rejected, either as impracticable or displeasing."[131] Burney published these sentiments without comment, but in the *Cyclopaedia* he states that he "subscribed to these opinions at the time." Looking over the history of musical style, Burney determines that the last acceptable style had emanated from Naples, and reached its apogee in the works of Hasse. Indeed, he seized on the years between 1725 and 1740 as the period in which

> the musical drama in Italy seems to have attained a degree of perfection and public favour, which perhaps has never been since surpassed. The opera stage from that period being in possession of the *poetry* of Apostolo Zeno and Metastasio; the *compositions* of Leo, Vinci, Hasse, Porpora and Pergolesi; the *performance* of Farinelli, Carestini, Caffarelli, Bernacchi, Babi, la Tesi, la Romanina, Faustina, and Cuzzoni; and the elegant *scenes* and *decorations* of the two Bibienas, which has superseded the expensive and childish machinery of the last century.[132]

Thus, in focusing on Hasse and Handel as the proponents of the different styles, he is pitting the golden age of opera in England against the concurrent golden age of the international style emerging from Naples in the first third of the century.

One must not overstate the case, however. Burney did not view the opera of the second half of the eighteenth century as being in a state of decay. The temporary loss of originality among composers was the natural result of the excellence of the previous age.

> When any *style* of poetry or music is brought to perfection, little is left to be done for a long while, but to imitate and vary the thoughts and passages of that style. Milton's epic, Pope's satirical and epistolary style, in poetry, and Pergolesi's in music, must be worn out and nearly forgotten, perhaps, before new styles can be formed or favoured. Handel left nothing new to be done in *his* style of composition. Imitations are ever timid and feeble.[133]

His period lacked the numerous international stars of the golden age, but had its admirable composers nonetheless. Among them was Paisiello, who, along with Haydn and Mozart, eventually dissuaded Burney from his accord with Rinaldo's judgment.

The exhaustion of style resulted in composers "constantly plagiarizing," not only from their own works, but from the works of others. Burney's awareness of the self-borrowings and plagiarisms of composers is impressive evidence of his knowledge of this music. He identified dozens of Handel's self-borrowings, many of which are not whole movements, but individual passages, often in a different genre. Of "Ah, crudel" from *Rinaldo,* he notes that "the whole opening and conduct of this admirable adagio may be found in the author's hautbois concertos."[134] Similarly, he identifies a passage in the second part of "Sovengati o bella" from Handel's *Teseo* (1713) as appearing in the first movement of the overture to *Saul,* and one from "Per salvarti" in *Lotario* (1729) as appearing in the minuet of the *Second Organ Concerto.*[135] Burney frequently is able to identify the transfer of entire movements from one composition to another by relying on Handel's notations in his scores, but his detection of the similarity of many of the movements between Handel's serenata *Parnasso in festa* and those in the oratorio *Athalia* derives solely from his own knowledge of the scores.[136]

His disclosures of the plagiarisms by other composers likewise range from single passages to entire movements. Here again the amount of music he has in his ear is impressive. He faults the overture to Bononcini's *Astarto* as being "but an extract from the last movement of Corelli's first solo,"[137] and in the same composer's overture to *Muzio Scevola* he discerns that the best passages belong also to Corelli.[138] He detects passages from Handel's *Flavius* in a favorite movement of a sonata by Dr. Boyce, "one of the most honest of our composers."[139] Johann Friedrich Lampe "burlesqued a fine passage from Handel's *Atalanta* (1736) for his air 'Oh! Oh! master Moor,' in his *Dragon of Wantley.*"[140] Arne was guilty of plagiarizing several passages in his operas as well,[141] and even Handel is caught using "precisely the same notes" from Lulli's overture to *Persée* (1682) for the slow movement of his overture to *Admeto.*[142]

Handel was the richest source for plagiarists, especially among English composers, whose own genius and invention in vocal music failed to impress Burney. Handel's passages

> ... became the musical language of the nation, and in a manner proverbial, like the *bon mots* of a man of wit in society. So that long after this period all the musicians in the kingdom, whenever they attempted to compose what they called Music of their own, seem to have had no other stock of ideas, than these passages.[143]

As infuriating as this charge must have been to native composers, it is repeated on five separate occasions in the discussion of opera until 1746,[144] and Burney cites several specific examples.[145] The English composers in competition with Handel were dead by 1789, but it is nonetheless surprising that Burney should publish a passage attacking both the composers and their audience.

> There were in England at this time [1732] several candidates for fame in theatrical and choral Music: Arne, Lampe, Smith, Defesch, and Greene, tried their strength against Handel; but it was the contention of infants with a giant. Indeed, they composed for inferior performers as well as inferior hearers; but they appear to have been so sensible of their own want of resources, that the utmost they attempted seems to have been a humble and timid imitation of Handel's style of composition.[146]

As this passage suggests, Burney regarded playhouse musicians and audiences as inferior to those of the opera. He said of his mentor, Thomas Arne, "the doctor had kept bad company: that is, had written for vulgar singers and hearers too long to be able to comport himself at the Opera-house, in the first circle of taste and fashion."[147] He also censured those who came to the opera house because it was fashionable. These auditors flocked to hear new compositions and singers, until, tiring of "the dainties" of Italian opera, they returned to the "plain food of the playhouse." He specifically referred to "the neglect of musical merits and talents" by the fashionable audience whose tastes he called "depraved appetites." The playhouse and public gardens furnished entertainment for the masses; only the most select audience was in constant attendance at the opera.

The same discrimination by class of audience and quality of music is apparent in Burney's discussion of Italian opera in England as well. Comic operas, he states, "are not estimable works, being on the old burletta model, full of buffoonery, and a broad kind of Italian humour, tasted in no other country, though suffered for the sake of the music, which is often ingenious, imitative, and sometimes graceful but more frequently grotesque."[148] The grotesque music which offended Burney was not written by the best comic opera composers. He greatly admired the music of Niccolò Piccinni's *La buona figliuola* (1760), and even *La buona figliuola maritata* (1761), which he said failed in London because it was too difficult, especially for the orchestra, and for the audience, both of whom were glad "to return to the *Buona Figliuola* for their own ease and relief from a too serious attention."[149] Piccinni's fertility astounded him.

> What still more astonishes in such innumerable works, is the prodigious variety which reigns in them all; and the science which never degenerates into pedantry or affectation; an harmony pure, clear, and profound; a melody perfectly suited to the subject and situation of the performers; and a force, an originality, and resources of all kinds, unknown till his time, and of which perhaps the secret will long remain undiscovered.[150]

Baldassare Galuppi is also at the top of Burney's list of great comic composers, as is Giovanni Paisiello, who he says in 1804 is "justly regarded as at the head of vocal composition at the present time."[151] His evaluation of Paisiello's music as "never grotesque" emphasizes the excesses he heard in some Italian comic operas. Moreover, Paisiello is included among the masters of the special feature of comic opera, the ensemble finale.

> The finales of the Italian comic operas are the most ingenious, varied, pleasing, and masterly compositions which dramatic music can boast; particularly those of Piccini, Paesiello, Cimarosa, and Mozart. Such a variety of measure, such fire, grace, passion and pathos, by turns, that the hearer, at the end, is unable to say what movement or passage he likes best. They are extremely difficult to perform, yet the Italians, by dint of study and rehearsal, are no more embarrassed than if, instead of singing, they were only talking and squabbling the whole time.[152]

Paisiello held Burney's affection as the leading vocal composer of the last decade of the eighteenth century.[153] In Paisiello's *Gli schiavi per amore* (1771) he found that,

> ...besides a great number of gay and agreeable airs, there are fragments of excellent composition, in which new passages and effects abound, as usual in the works of that admirable master.[154]

Burney's reviews of comic operas remark on the ingenuity, simplicity, elegance, and genius of the music, but say little about its ability to move the passions. The performers of the comic opera, at least in London, were first-rate actors. They so fully engaged the attention that critics had little leisure left for a severe examination of the music.[155] But he felt they were second-rate vocally, and since Burney considered opera "the completest concert," he was not willing to sacrifice good singing for natural acting and music which was merely charming. His summation of the music of Galuppi's *Il Filosofo di campagna* (1754) is typical. After citing several airs for particular beauties, he remarks, "Other parts of the Music were sufficiently good to support bad singing."[156]

The best known comic opera composer in London was Gioacchino Cocchi, a Neapolitan of little originality. Cocchi's invention, says Burney, was so exhausted before his arrival in England "that he hardly produced a new passage after his arrival." In the comic style, "he was quite contemptible,"[sic] especially in "attempting to clothe comic ideas in melody, or to paint ridiculous situations by the effects of an orchestra." These effects appear to be the grotesqueries which to Burney largely characterized the Italian comic style.[157]

To the modern critic, the most curious aspect of Burney's review of operatic history is the attention given the musical demands made upon the singers. Indeed, it is because of his conviction that Handel and most composers of the first rank were always "remarkably judicious in writing to the taste and talents of [their] performers; in displaying excellence and covering imperfections,"[158] that Burney was able to form judgments regarding the merits of singers whom he had never heard. It is not an over-simplification to state that Burney's chapter on "Italian Opera in England" is as much a history of the virtuoso singer as it is of the development of musical style.

Burney's view of opera as a vocal concert rather than a dramatic entity did not bring him into conflict with contemporary English aesthetics, but the extent to which this outlook pervades the *History* is, nonetheless, extraordinary. The plates generally do not exhibit samples of interesting modulations, new melodic figures, or cadence formulae, but rather show the divisions written for singers in the various decades of the eighteenth century. He viewed these vocal divisions as key elements of style, and perhaps the most telling of all stylistic elements, since "The divisions and embellishments, which, when a song is new, are its most striking and refined parts, soonest lose their favour and fashion."[159] Evanescent fashion not only limited the written embellishments, but those which were improvised as well; the singers themselves were susceptible to changing fashion, and competition between the virtuosi required increasingly elaborate embellishments. No sooner was the audience amazed and enchanted by the powers of one singer than it was ready to hear new and more adventuresome displays.

> It seems to be with musical effects as with medicinal, which are enfeebled and diminished by frequent use. Indeed, such execution as many of Farinelli's songs contain, and which excited such astonishment in 1734, would be hardly thought sufficiently brilliant in 1788 for a third-rate singer at the opera... The singer must not then submit to the limits of nature and facility, but must torment himself day and night in attempting impossibilities, or he will be heard with as much indifference as a ballad-singer in the streets.[160]

Thus, the numerous examples of divisions in the *History* constitute a panorama of operatic style and fashion in singing.

The divisions given in Burney's plates delineate definite changes in style.[161] The earliest examples are taken from several different operas dating from the first decade of the eighteenth century. Throughout the variety of configurations one clear principle is evident: they are all conjunct, and many represent only a written-out trill figure which ascends by step (ex. 8.2). The second plate gives the divisions of a variety of singers of Nicolini's generation, including Valenti, Margarita, and Senesino. The divisions are longer and more varied melodically, but they continue to demonstrate predominately conjunct treatment, although more vocal leaps and distinctive configurations are encountered (ex. 8.3). The third set of plates contain vocal divisions exclusively of Farinelli in various operas from 1734-1736.

Burney considered Farinelli to be the greatest virtuoso singer of the century; his divisions are lengthier than those of Nicolini, much more varied rhythmically, and have a wider tessitura. Several of them contain repeated articulations of the same pitch, rare in the earlier examples (ex. 8.4). Farinelli's divisions characteristically occur on the vowel "a." Burney distinguishes a change in style at "about the middle of the last century," prior to which "many Italian composers gave divisions to a, e, and o indiscriminately";[162] thereafter "a" is preferred.

Ex. 8.2. Divisions

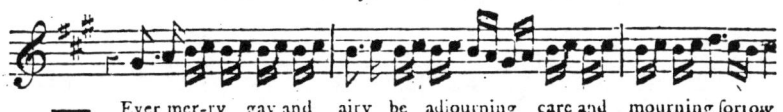

Ex. 8.2, continued

This battered passage occurs in a song of Mrs. Lindsey in the same opera; and in Comus, thirty years after.

Ex. 8.3. Divisions

Ex. 8.3, continued

Ex. 8.4. Farinelli's Divisions

Ex. 8.4, continued

The final plate is entitled "Vocal Divisions and Refinements in Dramatic Music from 1740 to 1755." Here at last the reader is given a few examples of operatic music other than divisions. The examples contain some sample passages from Galuppi and cadences from Lampugnani.[163] However, Burney neglects to explain the reason for the inclusion of several of these examples, and one can only guess at their significance. The bulk of the plate is again devoted to examples of vocal divisions as performed by Carestini, Moscovita, Monticelli, Visconti, Ricciarelli, and Mingotti. The styles are much less varied than that of Farinelli in the previous plate. Repeated notes are prominent, and repetition is a pronounced feature of the samples. Considered as a body, little progress seems to have been made in the art of embellished singing during this period; in fact, one might say that there was a decline, though Burney does not present this opinion (ex. 8.5). Despite his assertion that there was a stylistic break "mid-century," after which the vowel "a" was used for divisions, the first example, from Pescetti's "Diana and Endymion" dates from 1740, later than Farinelli's operas, but the roulades occur on the "o" vowel. Pescetti was, however, according to Burney, a feeble imitator of the Neapolitan style. In the remaining examples the reader is unfortunately deprived of the text. Regrettably, Burney did not carry his specimens into the latter half of the century; his enthusiasm for Pacchierotti's abilities could well have been illuminated by examples of his art.

From the specimens given in the plates one might conclude that Burney favors the bravura aria over all other types. Yet in the text he most often cites arias that are unusually pathetic, or contain a particularly beautiful cantabile. For him these are of a higher form of art, as he explains in the *Cyclopaedia*.

> To be able to play or sing an aria di cantabile, is the highest praise that can be bestowed on a musician. Execution surprises, and for a certain time amuses; but goes no further than the ear; but to sing a cantabile with tenderness and expression, is conveying sounds to the heart.[164]

Burney frequently associates the term *"canevas"* with pathetic arias. He defines the term as a song "left by the composer, as a mere sketch for the singer to grace and embellish."[165] Arias of this type appear in Handel's operas, including "Non vi piacque ingiusti Dei" from *Siroe*,[166] and "Si tornerò" from *Faramondo* (1738).[167] Surprisingly, these *"canevas* arias" appear full and complete to the modern observer, but Burney is quite specific about the character of these arias, "which a great singer only can colour, and souls susceptible of pleasure from the most select and sentimental sounds can truly enjoy."[168]

Burney's criticism of opera makes it clear that a satisfactory evaluation of an eighteenth-century opera can never be made from the printed score itself. To gain an understanding of the music, one must imagine the composition as it would have been embellished in performance; from contemporary accounts, the magnificence and virtuosity of the Italian singers seems beyond

Ex. 8.5. Divisions and Refinements

Ex. 8.5, continued

imagination.[169] Burney is explicit that a composer's style reflects the character of the embellishments which derive from the abilities and limitations of specific singers. Considering Handel's trip of 1729 to the Continent to recruit new singers for his opera company, Burney discerns that "These new performers gave birth to a new style, particularly in divisions, which by writing for nearly the same singer during six or eight years, Handel had often repeated."[170] Another revolution in Handel's style was occasioned by the arrival of Giovachino Conti; Handel "modeled his melody to the school of his new singer." The abilities of a singer so influenced the composer that revivals of operas, even after a period of only a few years, seemed impossible to Burney.

> Songs have... been so much composed to display the peculiar talents and abilities of singers, that operas can never be successfully revived but where the same performers, who sung in them originally, happen to survive..."[171]

Handel even altered his style to suit the "education and talents of his new singers," not only in his operas of various periods, but even for different singers within the same opera,[172] a process which Burney says was commonplace. He notes, for example, that in Handel's *Armino* the songs of modern cast, in "conformity to a different style from his own," were written for Conti and Annibali. At the same time in his opera he returned to his own style for Strada, "a singer formed by himself, and modeled on his own melodies."[173] The singers, then, to a great extent dictated the style to the composer, and most kept to their own style of aria and embellishments.

When Burney says that Guadagni's embellishments are "seemingly extemporaneous," perhaps he is hinting that Guadagni rehearsed his renditions, or wrote out his embellishments, in order to insure their correctness, and then memorized them. Another possible explanation is contained in Burney's article on "Passage" in the *Cyclopaedia*.

> ... in Italy singers are obliged to know how to invent passages extemporaneously upon any given notes; whereas in France, and, we fear, in England, young singers dare not hazard a single passage that has not previously been written down and practised.[174]

The few surviving manuscripts which contain Handel's arias with embellishments, are convincing examples of the singer's role in the creation of the eighteenth-century opera, in which the singers give "adventurous beauties" to arias "which cold notes cannot paint." Care must be taken not to overestimate the value of these manuscript treasures, as models of eighteenth-century virtuostic vocal art, for, as Burney noted of the abilities of Farinelli,

> ... his execution the musical reader will be enabled to judge by a view of the most difficult divisions of his bravura songs. Of his taste and embellishments we shall now be able to form but an imperfect idea, even if they had been preserved in writing, as mere notes would only

show his invention and science, without enabling us to discover that expression and neatness which rendered his execution so perfect and surprising.[175]

It is, then, not inappropriate that Burney's chapter on "Opera in England" is a history of the operatic art as a performer's vehicle, rather than as a true history of musical style, for he viewed Italian opera as it was presented in England: a concert of the most elevated sort, in which the quality of the production was far from solely dependent on the art of the composer. Indeed, a singer of the ability of a Farinelli delighted an audience despite the quality of the music, as Burney assures us in a critique of Handel's "Polypheme."

> The fourth air is languid, common, and uninteresting, on paper; how it was embellished and meliorated by the voice and pathetic powers of Farinelli, those can best imagine, who have been delighted with the performance of a great singer, in spite of bad music.[176]

The importance of exceptional singers to opera in England is stressed throughout his discussion, but nowhere more forcibly than in his explanation for the failure of Handel's *Il Pastor fido* in 1712:

> ...Handel had at this period no real *great* singer to write for...Nothing but *miraculous powers* in the performers can long support an opera, be the composition ever so excellent. Plain sense and good poetry are equally injured by singing, unless it is so exquisite as to make us forget everything else. If the performer is of the first class, and very miraculous and enchanting, an audience seems to care little about the Music or the poetry.[177]

Burney did not scruple to say that "no Music can support an opera, without great and favourite singers."[178]

Burney's preoccupation with vocal art as the stylistic basis of opera of the period is evident in the very structure of his chapter on opera in England. The arrival and departure of composers and singers are noted with equal attention, but much more information is given about secondary singers than secondary composers. The chapter, then, is a series of discussions of several operas, followed by a short critical sketch of the various singers employed at the opera during each season throughout the first three-quarters of the century. The reader is left with the unmistakable impression that if all the composers had perished, opera in England would have continued unabated so long as Italy continued to produce first-rate singers.

The survey of operas performed after 1773 is interrupted so frequently by lengthy descriptions of the singers, that it is easy to lose sight of the chronology altogether. None of the operas produced after 1773 are subjected to an aria-by-aria analysis; only general remarks are given, which, though interesting, tell very little about Burney's view of opera during the years when he was writing the *History*.

Of the Italian composers who arrived in England after 1771, Antonio Sacchini was his favorite. Sacchini had left London in 1781, and was thus a safe subject for criticism. Burney's commendation of Sacchini's abilities contains praise for the same elements of style he cherished in opera from Vinci's time. He lauds both the transparency of Sacchini's accompaniments, which, "though always rich and ingenious, never call all attention from the voice," and the principal melody, which "is rendered distinguishable through all the contrivance of imitative and picturesque design in the instruments."[179] Sacchini interested "the audience more by a happy, graceful, and touching melody, than by a laboured and extraneous modulation."[180] This praise is for Sacchini's Italian operas, not those written during his residency in France. In these Burney detected changes in his style in which he found that "it is manifest... that he worked for singers of mean abilities."[181] This, in addition to French texts, he noted incorrectly, "prevented their circulation in the rest of Europe": even in his favorite composers, Burney was unforgiving of French characteristics.[182]

The opera seasons in London between the time of the publication of the *History* and release of the articles in the *Cyclopaedia* were dominated by the works of Domenico Cimarosa, Luigi Cherubini, Giovanni Paisiello, and Francesco Bianchi. Cimarosa's music suited Burney's conservative taste: it was "always graceful, never grotesque or capricious." Burney admired his accompaniments, which were ingenious, embellishing the melody of the voice part without "too much occupying the attention of the audience."[183] The review of Cimarosa's *Il Matrimonio segreto* (1792) in the *Morning Post* (13 January 1794) is revealing in its mildly enthusiastic reception and its praise for one particular merit.

> Of the Opera, it is unnecessary to say more, than that it is well calculated as a vehicle to introduce some very charming music from Cimarosa to the Town, who certainly is an able master. It has besides the praise of not distressing the Audience by too much Recitative.[184]

Judging from this account, the opera clearly remained the "completest concert" for most of the English audience throughout the century. It is perhaps this view of opera as a mere concert which accounts not only for Burney's conservatism but that of the generality of English opera fanciers.

Predictably, Burney's article on French serious opera harps on the inferior qualities of French singers. He seems often unable to distinguish the intrinsic merit of the composition from the quality of the performance of French vocal music. Burney explained his objections to French performers during his tour of France in 1770. He found that the basic musicianship of the singers at the *Concert Spirituel* as quite good, but grieved "at the abuse of nature's bounty; the voices are in themselves really good and well toned; and this is easily to be discovered, in despight [sic], of false direction and a vitiated expression."[185] It is very difficult to imagine, and probably impossible to recreate, the style of singing which so displeased him, but some clue of its negative attributes can be gleaned from the writings of both Burney and Rousseau.

There was, it seems, a very clear difference between the voice production of French singers and the Italian virtuosi who were charming the rest of Europe. The French voice, complains Burney, "never comes further than from the throat; there is no true *voce di petto*."[186] He defines the *voce di petto* as a "voice which comes from the breast, in opposition to one which is nasal or guttural."[187] The singers further offended Burney's cultivated ears by forcing the voice, which, if truly produced in the throat, would indeed yield an unpleasant result.[188] Burney notes, for example, that at the *Concert Spirituel* Mademoiselle Delcambre had "screamed out Exaudi Deus with all the power of lungs she could muster."[189] A bit later, in the same program, "the principal counter tenor had a solo verse... which he bellowed out with as much violence as if he had done it for life, while a knife was at his throat."[190] Chorus singers, too, were defective in their vocal production, and performed with more force than feeling.[191] The last chorus of this particular evening was "a finisher with a vengeance! and it surpassed all clamour, all the noises [he] had ever heard in his life."[192]

The lack of a "true *portamento,* or direction of the voice" is also cited as a serious fault in French singers. Burney states that the term signifies the conduct of the voice, which is said to be good when it is neither nasal nor guttural. Another definition, given by Thomas Busby, although equally vague, seems to fall within the usage given by Burney:

> A term applied by the Italians to the manner of habit of sustaining and conducting the voice. A singer who is easy, yet firm and steady, in the execution of his passages, is said to have a good Portamento.[193]

Johann Quantz refers to the same sense when he describes the *portamento* as "*Das Tragen der Stimme.*"[194] Although none of the definitions is explicit, the concept seems to suggest a legato style of singing, with careful dynamic control, and the imperceptible passing from one register of the voice to the next.[195] It was considered by critics of the Italian school to be a requisite of good vocal production, and one which Burney says was absent among French singers. He was not alone in his opinion; Quantz provides a succinct comparison of the French and Italian styles:

> The *French manner of singing* is more simple than artful, more spoken than sung, more forced than natural in the expression of the passions and in the use of the voice; in style and expression it is poor, and always uniform; it is better suited to drinking songs than to serious arias, diverting the senses, but leaving the musical intellect completely idle.[196]

Burney did not object to the natural qualities of the French singers, but to their training. Upon witnessing a performance of *Les Contes Moraux,* on a libretto by Favart, with ariettes by Grétry, Burney declares that there was not "one bad voice among the performers," and that one particular actress had a "sweetly toned" voice, "and one of great compass." However, her songs were too difficult for her to perform satisfactorily, and "she joined the national false direction of voice, to forcing, screaming, and bad taste, that incurable and insufferable expression, which is eqally disgusting to the learned and the ignorant of other countries."[197]

Although Burney finds the singing throughout France to be disgusting, it was "at the serious French opera, and by the performance of *slow Music,* and *airs tendres* that those accustomed to good singing are most offended."[198] None of Burney's criticism is sufficiently descriptive to allow the reader to form a clear idea of just what was so offensive about the nature of French taste and expression which Burney feels is so "vitiated."[199] It is therefore enlightening to consider the detailed and harshly critical account of French vocal expression contained in Rousseau's *Lettre sur la musique,* the work which was so influential to Burney's thought. In addition to censuring the defects in vocal production also cited by Burney, Rousseau strikes out at the failure of French singers to keep exact time, claiming that "the time is always vague and undetermined, expecially in slow airs."[200] He asserts that the vocal style prevents composers from writing "drum" basses or subdivided accompaniments, because "if the actor were compelled to keep time, he would immediately be prevented from displaying his voice and his action, from dwelling on his notes, from swelling and prolonging them, and from screaming at the top of his lungs, and in consequence he would no longer be applauded."[201] He also states that in French recitative the "trills and *ports-de-voix* have been multiplied," producing so languid an effect that "hardly anything [is] left to distinguish it from what we call 'air.' "[202] In contrast to Italian practice, French recitatives were apparently heavily ornamented. Rousseau enjoins the listener to try to endure the "extravagant shriekings," the interruptions of "the recital in the wrong place to string some beautiful notes on open syllables without meaning," and the "*Fredons,* cadenzas, and *ports-de-voix* which recur at every moment," and then explain to him "what analogy there can be between speech and this pretended recitative."[203]

There was one point on which Burney was considerably more vehement than Rousseau. Rousseau remarked that "It takes a Fel or a Jelyotte to sing French music," for the beauties of French music, "if there are any, are all in the art of the singers."[204] Burney does not seem to have found even the French singers of greatest fame sufficient to please him. A comparison of Burney's and Rousseau's descriptions of French singing with Burney's definition of good singing demonstrates just how unlikely it was that Burney would find pleasure in the opera house or theatre in France.

> Singing is a faculty that requires the union of so many gifts of *nature,* and so much assistance from *art,* that the complete concurrence and union of both rarely happen. The requisites

from nature are a voice full, flexible and extensive in compass, well-toned, sweet, clear, and interesting; with an ear perfectly correct in time and tune. The acquisitions from art are a good *portamento,* or delivery of the voice from the chest, free from nasal or guttural defects, a good shake, good taste and expression, with a rapid, distinct, neat and articulate execution of divisions, and the power of sustaining a long note with steadiness, and of augmenting and diminishing its force by the most minute degrees.[205]

Just how decisive an effect the French manner of performance had on Burney's opinion of French music is evidenced by his opinion that it was in vain for the French to attempt to imitate the Italian style, for "let this detestable and unnatural expression be given to any music in the world, and it becomes immediately French."[206]

Sound, pass'd thro' them, no longer is the same,
For Food digested takes another name.

Although it was the performance which drew most of Burney's criticism, it is evident that he had little sympathy for French music itself. He claimed in 1770 that the style of composition, though totally changed throughout the rest of Europe, had in France stood still "for thirty or forty years," and had undergone "few changes at the great opera since Lulli's time."[207] He found the style to be "exhausted," yet the French people were unwilling to "relish any new attempts at pleasing them in a different way."[208] In Burney's progressive view, the growth of opera in France had been arrested at an early phase of its development, and the art of operatic composition, "with respect to the two great essentials of melody and expression," was still in its infancy.[209]

Burney's discussion of French opera in the *History* is quite closely related to his early views expressed in the *Tour*. At the heart of the chapter is his analysis of Rameau's *Castor et Pollux,* a work he heard during his visit of 1764-65. The date can be established with certainty because Burney complains about the "vocal outrages of Mademoiselle Arnould."[210]

Burney praises the overture to *Castor et Pollux* as "the best of this author upon Lulli's plan," but in a footnote quotes the authority of d'Alembert that the overtures of Lulli, although "all cast in the same mold," have been the "invariable models of all other overtures for sixty years; during which time, there has been but one overture heard in our operas, if even that can be called one."[211] Without qualification, Burney remarks that the opening symphony [ritornello] to the first aria is beautiful, but then, like Rousseau, queries "why the same melody was not applied, in the same measure, to the poetry" (ex. 8.6). If, in fact, the versification required a different measure, then the symphony should have been constructed to suit the measure, according to Burney. He is applying the principle of the "motto aria" of the Italian style, in which the aria begins with a preliminary statement of the initial motif, to French aria composition, and finding the latter wanting.[212] It was, to Burney, the "eternal

Ex. 8.6. Rameau: Opening Symphony to the First Aria, *Castor et Pollux*

changes in the measure, which teaze and disappoint the ear of all that are used to other Music," which was one of the chief defects of French music.

He also faults the "overcharged tenderness of Rameau's Music" which appears in "all of his slow movements." Part of this overcharged tenderness was created by the too frequent use of "appoggiaturas or leaning notes being incorporated in the harmony," which "renders it crude, and the hanging on every note, as if unwilling to relinquish it, checks and impedes the motion of the air and gives it a slow and languid effect."[213] In this passage Burney seems to be once again confusing the material of Rameau's music with the manner in which it was performed. It has been noted that Rousseau complained several times in the *Lettre* about the breach of time, especially in slow airs. Although Burney is more ambiguous in his criticism, his view is illuminated somewhat by his observations on "Rallentando." He thought that this refinement was "often abused." It has been, he writes, "chiefly practised in France, and favours of [sic] affectation, and that *overcharged tenderness* which renders the national *airs tendres* so disagreeable, or so ridiculous, to the natives of other Countries."[214]

In addition to being marred by breaks in tempo in performance, the accent in French music was disrupted by changes in meter. In the second act of *Castor et Pollux* Burney found Telaïre's "Tristes apprêts, pales flambeaux," though "cast in an admirable mold," was spoiled by frequent and unnecessary changes of measure" (ex. 8.7). The admirable mold, not surprisingly, is the da capo form, the staple of the Italian stage (dal segno in this case, as the orchestral introduction is not included in the repeat). Burney does candidly allow that, in spite of its "defects and the vocal outrages of Mademoiselle Arnould, I was more pleased and affected by this scene, than any other I ever heard at the French serious opera."[215] Mademoiselle Arnould's vocal outrages doubtless included the excessive ornamentation that so annoyed Rousseau. Jean Baptiste Berard's *L'Art du chant* (1755) contains an embellished version of "Tristes apprêts, pales flambeaux." It is quite possible that Mademoiselle Arnould's performance may have resembled the very elaborate realization construed by Berard (ex. 8.8).[216] While Burney was no enemy of embellished singing, the style of the Italian embellishments was very different from the subtle inflections used by French performers. The breaks of strict tempo, apparently necessary for proper performance of the ornaments, were aggravated by poor vocal production, and produced a style which was too languid and affected for Burney's taste.

Sarcastically remarking that Rameau "perpetually discovers himself to be a great harmonist," Burney particularly criticised the *prélude tendre* at the beginning of act 3 (ex. 8.9). He was especially censorious of the "chord of the superfluous fifth [i.e. augmented fifth] which makes all nature shudder except our Gallic neighbours" (m. 11).[217] He also objected to the many "drags [appoggiaturas] which being equally harsh to the ear and injurious to the pulsation, seem to prevent the performer from ever falling on his feet." Rameau

Ex. 8.7. Rameau: "Tristes apprêts, pales flambeaux," *Castor et Pollux*

Ex. 8.7, continued

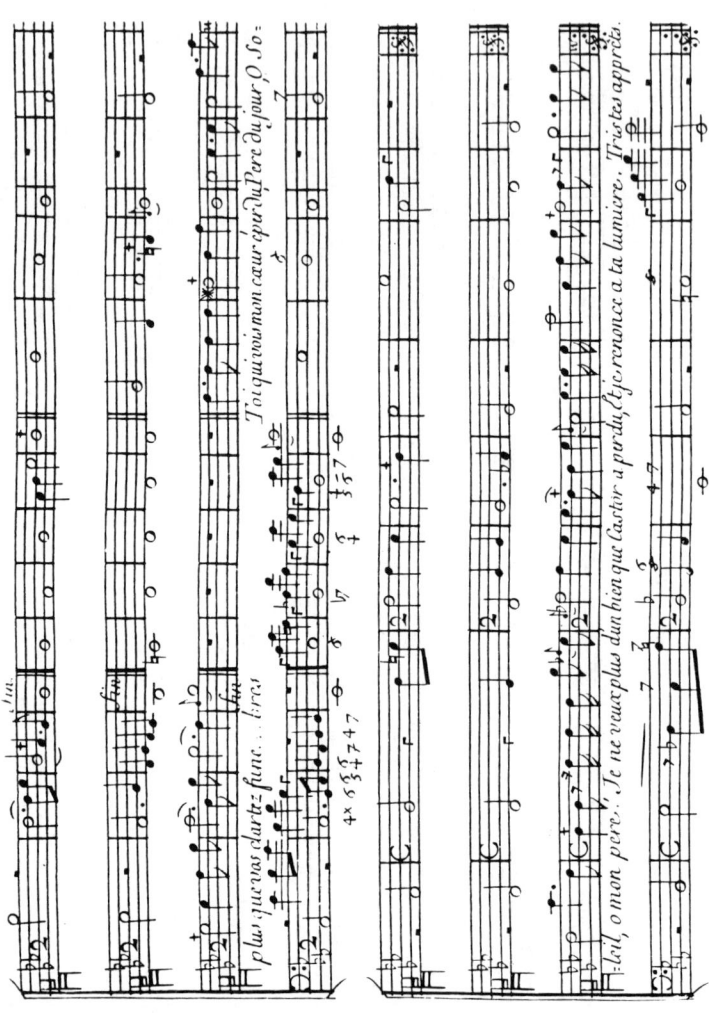

Ex. 8.7, continued

Ex. 8.8. Rameau: "Tristes apprêts pales flambeaux," *Castor et Pollux*. Berard's embellishments

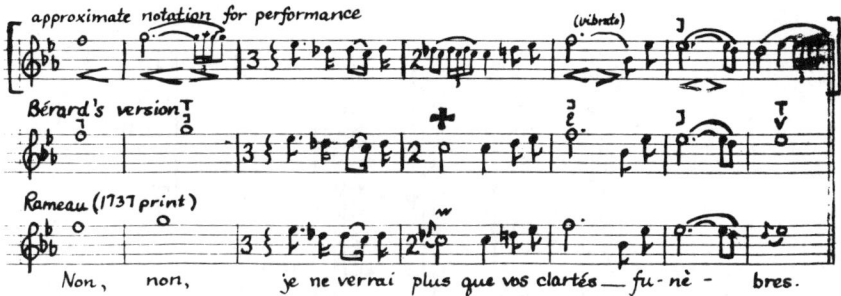

had succeeded only in augmenting the "defects of all predecessors, and rendered what was rude and clumsy in Lulli, still more offensive." Once again Burney has laid the responsibility for the vitiated style of French music at Lulli's feet. Despite his frequent repetition of this charge, Burney did not furnish his readers with a detailed critique of Lulli's style in the *Tour, History,* or *Cyclopaedia*. He was by no means ignorant of Lulli's works, for he possessed seven printed scores.[218] Nonetheless, Burney left his readers in doubt as to his specific objections to Lulli's art.

Although Burney was relentless in his attack on Rameau's vocal compositions, in which he felt "the voice is worse used by the composer than the most insignificant instrument," he found much to admire in Rameau's dance music. The A major minuet of act 4, scene 6, receives praise for its rich harmony and graceful melody (ex. 8.10). It is in his criticism of the dance music that a previously unstated principle of utmost importance finally emerges: in the dances, he writes, "there is a necessity for motion, measure, and symmetry of phrase."[219] The concept of phrase does not appear in the discussion of vocal music, but elsewhere he wrote, "it is in the invention of musical phrases, in their proportion and texture, that the true beauties of music consist."[220] He provided a particularly succinct definition of good music for a German friend, which stressed the importance of meter and phrasing.

> At present it [music] has in good compositions, its accents, its phrases, and its periods; all capable of being as strongly marked by the performer as those of Rhetoric or Poetry by an Orator, or declaimer.[221]

Small wonder that he could not embrace French music.

Rousseau remarked in the *Lettre* that Italian singers, while they sang the French pathetic airs with "the greatest exactness, could never recognize in them either the phrasing or the time; for it was not a kind of music which made sense."[222] For Burney, a singer who feels, marks, and accents passages [here

Ex. 8.9. Rameau: "Prélude tendre," *Castor et Pollux*

Ex. 8.10. Rameau: Minuet, *Castor et Pollux*

meaning phrases] well is a person of taste; such a view, defining phrasing narrowly, in accordance with the symmetrical, regularly accented model of Italian composers, in itself makes impossible an appreciation of French vocal composition and performance. "Nothing," writes Burney, "is given to the voice part but broken accents and dislocated measures."[223] It seems to Burney a truism that, of all the operatic music written by France's most prominent composers, "nothing in Lulli's operas was imitated or adopted by the rest of Europe, but the style of his overtures, or in Rameau's but the dances."[224]

By the last quarter of the eighteenth century the situation in Paris had changed. The Parisian opera houses became the main center for numerous Italian or Italian-trained composers. Gluck, Sacchini, Salieri, Piccinni, and Cherubini did their finest work for Paris. Luigi Cherubini, during his directorship of the *Théâtre de Monsieur in the Tuileries* (1789-92), produced operas by Anfossi, Paisiello, Cimarosa and other Italians. All of this activity Burney saw as advancing the taste of France, though not rapidly, for even the best of the Italian composers, according to Burney's limited and, it must be admitted, prejudiced view, compromised their style in order to appeal to French audiences, and to accommodate the inferior abilities of French singers.

> The French, since the time of Rameau, have often had fine compositions performed in their theatres, and a well disciplined band to execute them *instrumentally;* yet, for want of good singers, the vocal part, which is the best and most interesting in an Italian opera, is the worst in the musical dramas of France. And for this there are two causes which affect the composition as well as the performance of French opera songs: the composer, be he a Gluck, a Piccini, or a Sacchini, having no great vocal talents to display, dares not give way to fancy, or aim at new passages, but, of necessity, *underwrites* the vocal part so much, that the productions of these great masters for the French stage are never in favour elsewhere with their greatest admirers.[225]

In the French *opéra comique* Burney saw a revolution in musical style. He was correct as far as he went, but he restricted the upheaval to France, and failed to perceive the epochal changes which the *opéra comique* inspired. To Burney, the efforts of Duni, Philidor, and Monsigny "had the address to betray the French into a love for Italian melody, or at least a melody resembling that of the burletta operas of Italy then in circulation."[226] Of course, the more Italian the style the better, according to Burney's standards. He particularly approved of the omission of recitative in *opéras comiques,* indeed in all opera outside of Italy, but especially in France, which he believed had the least musical of all languages. He heard six *opéras comiques* during his 1764 and 1765 visits and, though he found the style of singing offensive, he found the operas very pleasurable and extremely well acted.[227] He was especially pleased with Monsigny's operas, averring that "Nothing could be more pleasing and amusing than these dramas to the natives of all Europe, not critics of great singing; for it must be owned, that they are all well written, well set, and well acted."[228]

Returning to France in 1770, he found the *opéra comique* still at the forefront of musical style, while the *Opéra* continued to languish as it had five years earlier.[229] The style of *opéra comique* had been greatly advanced by Grétry who, upon arriving from Italy in 1768 [actually 1767], brought with him the newest Italian taste "in order to please his protectors and judges."[230] Despite this compromise, Grétry "improved the French taste as much as they have corrupted his," bringing them closer to a "tolerable dramatic music."[231] Two of Grétry's operas, *Richard Coeur-de-Lion* and *Zémire et Azor*, were translated and "successfully brought on the English stage" (to stages all over Europe, he might have added), but Burney does not review either production. His admiration for Grétry is apparent, however, in the *Cyclopaedia*, where he states, "Duni, Philidor, and Monsigni were the patriarchs of the comic musical dramas, and Grétry the King David."[232]

Burney was essentially conservative in his operatic tastes. His conservatism is evident in the list of composers he recommends as exemplars to young students in composition, a list which first appears in the *History*, volume III (1789),[233] and then reappears, with alterations, in the *Cyclopaedia* years later. His recommendations for models of vocal composition are:

GHM	Cyclopaedia
Pergolesi	Pergolesi
Hasse	Hasse
Jommelli	Jommelli
Galuppi	Galuppi
Piccinni	Piccinni
Sacchini	Sacchini
Paisiello	Paesiello
Sarti	Sarti
	Vinci
	Perez
	Nasolini

The only changes are the addition of names merely omitted by oversight from the first list—Vinci and Perez, who receive flattering reviews in the *History*—and the addition of a new figure, Sebastiano Nasolini. He is not mentioned in the *History*, and receives no article in the *Cyclopaedia*, but is mentioned in a review in *The Times* (24 February 1802) of his *La Morte di Mitridate*. The article describes a composer fully fitting Burney's operatic taste.

> In the music, composed by Nasolini, there are few movements that can be called truly grand; but those which possess undoubted claims to fine taste and delicacy of expression are very numerous. The melodies in particular are rich and impressive. The Overture is one of the neatest that has been performed for many seasons. It is destitute of all the thunder and crash of our modern compositions of this kind; yet it proved as successful and was received with general applause.[234]

Nasolini's preference for delicacy of expression over intensely dramatic music perfectly accords with Burney's preference in opera from 1750 until his death.[235]

Several other important composers' works were performed during the period between the drafting of the two lists, including Gluck's *Alceste,* which was first given at London in April 1795, and *Iphigénie en Tauride* in April, 1796. Even at this late date Burney had not accepted a new style in opera. His view of opera was so fixed upon Rousseau's aesthetic and his idea that the abilities of the singer could dictate style to the composer, that he failed to perceive even epochal changes in operatic composition. Nowhere is this more apparent than in his criticism of Gluck's operas.

He first wrote about Gluck in the *German Tour,* where he is compared to Hasse, Burney's favorite opera composer. His evaluation fastens upon Gluck's genius and originality in representing the more intense passions, calling him "the Michael Angelo of music"; indeed, "his expression of passion may sometimes be too strong for common hearers."[236] He credits him with being a great friend to the poet through his insistence on the meaningful and rapid unfolding of the drama with a minimum of extraneous repetitions, symphonies, and dances. In contrast to Gluck, Hasse is the Raphael of music. "Whereas Gluck's genius seems more calculated for exciting terror in painting difficult situations, occasioned by complicated misery, and the tempetuous fury of unbrideld passions,"[237] Hasse excels in graceful and pleasing music.

The appearance of objectivity in this comparison disguises Burney's strong preference for the traditional style of *opera seria* over the new reformed style. It also presents a false image of Burney; as his later writings demonstrate, his taste is not nearly as pliable as the discussion implies. Faced with the emergence of a new style and tradition, Burney remains a firm advocate of the old, though always in its newest dress.

In the years between Burney's visit to Vienna in 1772 and the publication of volume IV of the *History,* Gluck produced his very successful French operas, then returned to Vienna, where he died in 1787. But far from seeing fulfillment of the reforms begun in *Orfeo* (1762), Burney views Gluck's French operas as unprincipled capitulations to French prejudices and inadequacies. He says, for example, that *Iphigénie en Tauride* had "all the success that may be imagined from the force of his genius applied to a favourite drama, set in the style of their favourite composers, Lulli and Rameau."[238] He admires the drama of Gluck's works, and declares him unrivaled in "force and effect in his expression of grief, fear, remorse, vengeance, and all the violent passions," but his ideal of passionate expression is more restrained.

Burney's passion is "the augmentation and refinement of the cries of nature, harmonized, and divested of the harsher and more violent effects; adopting such only as penetrate the heart without shocking the ears of the audience."[239] Gluck, genius though he was, did not subject himself to the bounds of taste and propriety.

The violent passions which Gluck so masterfully exploited were not considered the most suitable for opera. Burney admired the pleasing grace evident in the music of Vinci, Hasse, Piccinni and Sacchini, and the expression of lofty sentiments. Gluck was deficient in these qualities. Indeed, Burney attributes the failure of *La Cythère assiegée* to Gluck's inability to express "more delicacy and tenderness than force."[240] Similarly, *Armide* (1777) failed in Burney's opinion because Gluck "did not quite fulfill the ideas of grace, tenderness, and pathos, which some of the scenes required, and auditors accustomed to Italian Music expected."[241]

The intense drama of Gluck's operas was injurious to music, and Burney saw it as but another example of poetry threatening to dominate music. Burney's view of Gluckian opera is best expressed in his biographical footnote on Ranieri di Calzabigi found in Burney's biography of Metastasio.

> The editor, panegyrist, and afterwards dramatic rival, and censurer, of Metastasio's style. He is author of the three operas of *Orfeo, Alceste* and *Paride*, which were set by Gluck, in a new dramatic style, that has been adopted by the French, and violently praised by all those who love poetry better than music. The French who have frequently fine voices, but no great singers, do well to deprecate the vocal abilities of the Italians, which can enchant all other foreign nations, without their having the least knowledge of the language in which they sing. Indeed it is not merely the simplicity of Gluck's style that pleases the French, but the having formed it upon *Lully* and *Rameau*, to whose strains Gallic ears will long continue partial.[242]

Gluck's French operas did serve as "excellent preparations for a better style than the French had been used to," energizing the vitiated performance customary in Rameau's operas through more rapid recitative, and "airs more marked than those of Lully and Rameau."

Burney's prejudice against French opera did not completely deafen him to Gluck's merits. His adverse criticism tends to overshadow his praise, but his review of Gluck's London operas (1746) asserts that "his contemporaries in Italy, at this time seemed to[o] much filed down [i.e., too simple and artless]; and he wanted the file, which when used afterwards in that country, made him one of the greatest composers of his time."[243] Here Burney is tantalizingly close to the truth. But the "filing" which Gluck underwent was not undergone in Italy. Most of the period after his London visit Gluck spent in Vienna, although he occasionally took trips to Italy to produce his operas. Had Burney been more alert to changes around him, he might have fixed the responsibility for the changes in Gluck's style upon French comic opera, from whence they developed. In his biography of Metastasio Burney compared his response to the music of Gluck and the Neapolitan composers[244]:

> I will frankly confess, that I have received great pleasure, though of different kinds, from the operas of Metastasio, on the old model, by Jomelli, Piccini, Sacchini, Sarti, and Paesiello,

and from those of Gluck on the new. The brilliant and beautiful parts of the music and singing in the one, have rendered me as charitable and inattentive to the rest; while the general and continued interest of the other made me forget the beauties of introductory symphonies, the dexterity of difficult divisions, and the genius, art, and extempore powers of long closes.

And yet, perhaps, an interesting drama well set by a composer, who respects the poetry, without sacrificing his own art and the performers, if singers of the first class, with whom the French are but little acquainted, would be a more perfect exhibition, than it is possible ever to render an opera, by adhering strictly either to the *Piccinists* or *Gluckists*.[245]

Burney never did achieve an appreciation of the style created in one of the major reforms in operatic history.

Burney's criticism of opera in Germany also reflects his unyielding Italianate taste. Even the passages most radiant with praise for the Germans betray him. He wrote of the "German School of Composition":

This extensive empire has likewise produced masters who have even equalled the most eminent Italian dramatic composers of the last century; such as Handel, Hasse, Graun, J.C. Bach, Misteweece [sic], Gluck, Naumann, etc., without mentioning the operas, oratorios, and Masses of Haydn, and the dramatic music of Mozart, perhaps the best of its kind.[246]

Under "Naumann, Johann Amadeus" in the *Cyclopaedia* however he states, "this composer had no originality; he had formed himself on the flimsy style of Italy in the middle of the last century." His article on Josef Myslivecek is similarly tepid. He states that Karl Heinrich Graun formed his style on "that of the inventor of the new style, Vinci." J.C. Bach is praised for the richness of his accompaniments, but not for the originality of his melodies, "which however are always natural, elegant, and in the best taste of Italy at the time he came over."[247] Handel, Hasse, and Gluck all appear in the *Cyclopaedia* article "Italy" because "they formed [their] styles on the best models of that country." The more Italianate the style of a German composer, the more highly Burney praised him. Composers who maintained a more distinctively German tradition are passed over in silence, or mentioned only respectfully on the authority of Marpurg, Mattheson, Ebeling or other German critics.

Burney's access to German culture was limited by his inadequate knowledge of the language. Much of the material he wished to ferret out of German criticism was sent to translators, although he attempted short translations himself. His early letters to Brig Fountaine, and later his correspondence with Latrobe, speak of his frustration at the hours it took to read German literature with a dictionary. Moreover, he was incapable of deciphering German handwriting. These hindrances are partially responsible for the imbalance in the *History*, which is not representative of his regard for German musicians, as is evident in his discussions of instrumental music. The imbalance is of little consequence to modern scholars. His allegiance to Italian vocal music, and pro-Italian French criticism, precluded his unprejudiced consideration of the music of France and Germany, and his limitations in the use of materials only aggravated the imbalance.

As it stands, the two most lengthy discussions in the chapter on German opera are of Gluck and Jommelli (who resided at Stuttgart from 1753 to 1769), and these are very brief. For the rest, there is only a list "of the great opera composers" of the century. This list ranges from the famous to the obscure, at least for dramatic music: Hasse, Handel, Mozart, Abbé (Johann) Sterkel, Joseph Schuster, and Ignaz Pleyel. Burney's *German Tour* contains a wealth of information stated with the authority of a firsthand observer, but his historical judgment is of little value except in the cases of those musicians who eventually reached London, or whose music was so widely accepted throughout Europe as to come inescapably to his attention.

One such composer was Wolfgang Amadeus Mozart. His instrumental music reached England rapidly, but his vocal music was almost unknown until after his death. Only one public performance of a Mozart aria prior to 1791 was recorded; "Crudel perche finora," from *Le nozze di Figaro,* was performed in a pasticcio opera in 1789,[248] although much more of his music must have been known. Thomas Attwood, Michael Kelly, and Stephen and Nancy Storace certainly brought Mozart's vocal music to London when they returned from Vienna in 1787, if it was not known earlier. Nancy Storace, after the custom of the day, performed two of his arias, "Deh vieni" from *Figaro* and "Batti, Batti" from *Don Giovanni,* in a performance of Bianchi's *La villanella rapita* in February, 1790.[249] Roger Fiske speculates that the Storaces must have brought a manuscript full score of *Figaro* with them from Vienna. Nancy was Mozart's original Susanna, and must surely have performed other songs in public and private concerts. She may also have performed the scena and aria "Ch'io mi scordi di te" (K.505) composed expressly for her by Mozart in 1786. Kelly, too, sang in *Figaro,* and as one of the most popular singers of his day, he must have also added to a growing awareness of Mozart's gifts as a vocal composer.

Thomas Attwood played a major role in advancing the popularity of Mozart's music in England. He included several arias by Mozart in his own productions, the first recorded example being "Non piu andrai," sung as "Where the Banners of Glory are Streaming" in 1792. This and other selections performed in pasticcios popularized Mozart's vocal works after his death, as Burney noted. Many of the advertisements for Attwood's operas mention that several airs are selected from the works of the late Mozart: The *Morning Chronicle* in May 1795, for example, says of *The Adopted Child,* "The music is by Attwood, with a few airs by Mozart; the original airs prove Mr. Attwood's skill and the selections evince his taste."[250] However popular Attwood and his adaptations of Mozart may have been, they were not sufficient to inspire a full production of any of Mozart's own operas during the 1790s.

The first full-length production of a Mozart opera appeared in 1805, when *La Clemenza di Tito* was performed (King's Theatre, Haymarket, 27 March 1805). Despite the apparent success of this production, no opera of Mozart appeared again until the 1811 production of *Così fan tutte* (King's Theatre, Haymarket, 9 May 1811). A letter to the editor of *The Examiner* proclaimed,

> The lovers of good music have at last been relieved from the dull repetition of the productions of Pucitta, Trento, Guglielmi and others, who have so long strove [sic], with too much success, to suppress those operas of sterling merit, which would have exposed the poverty of their invention, and consigned them to merited oblivion. These pretenders to science have hitherto succeeded to[o] well in their endeavors, from want of a Manager of taste... [251]

Die Zauberflöte was performed the same year (King's Theatre, Haymarket, 6 June 1811) with great success, and thereafter Mozart conquered England.

There is no indication of when Burney began to recognize Mozart's greatness as an opera composer. It may have been later than his recognition of his creativity in instrumental music. His rebuttal of William Jackson's claim that the quality of vocal music had decayed in the early 1790s brings "the beauties of Sarti, Cimarosa, and Paesiello" to the defense of modern music, but Mozart is not mentioned. Yet the defense of instrumental music in the same essay does link Mozart with Haydn as among the best instrumental composers. This suggests that an awareness of Mozart's vocal music came late, and only after the Storaces, Kelly and Attwood had been championing it in London for several years.

Despite Burney's assertion that "we" (i.e. those who had not traveled outside England) knew nothing of Mozart's music until after his death, someone did. On 26 October 1790, a letter was sent by Robert May O'Reilly to Mozart, offering him an opportunity to compose "at least two Operas, serious or comic." O'Reilly's letter was written after he learned "through a person attached to H.R.H. the Prince of Wales" of Mozart's plan to travel to England later that year.[252] Burney himself knew of one vocal piece of Mozart's, his "Scena for Tenducci" ([Anh. 3] 315b). He probably saw the scene around 1780, and wrote his evaluation of the piece in a letter to Daines Barrington, who published it in 1781 in his *Miscellanies*.

> It is a very elaborate and masterly composition, discovering a great practice and facility of writing in many parts. The modulation is likewise learned and recherchée; however, though it is a composition which none but a great master of harmony and possessed of a consummate knowledge of the genius of different instruments, could produce; yet neither the melody of the voice part nor of any of the instruments discovers much invention, though the effects of the whole, if well executed, would doubtless be masterly.[253]

Unfortunately, the scena is lost, making it impossible to evaluate the sagacity of Burney's judgment. His writings on Mozart's later dramatic works, however, could not be more full of praise. Late in his life he proclaimed of Mozart's comic operas: they "must be enrolled among the first for genius, originality, and good composition that modern times have produced."[254] He also stated that the dramatic music of Mozart as a whole was perhaps the best of its kind.[255] His library contained the score of *Don Giovanni,* and one scene from *La Clemenza di Tito,* but it is clear from his article "Mozart" that he also knew scenes from several of his other operas. Possibly he was in attendance at chamber performances of some of the operas; whatever the case, his enthusiasm for Mozart's operas is evident in his late letters and throughout the *Cyclopaedia.*[256] In the "Mozart" article Burney specifically mentions *Idomeneo,* which was not performed in England during his lifetime.

> "Idomeneo" which is full of fine things, the air in E♯ [it is in E♭] at the beginning of the second act, the chorus Alla Siciliana, in the same key [or rather in E maj.], and the quartet in the last act, etc. are exquisitely beautiful, in different styles. But a commentary on the work of this gifted musician would fill one of our volumes.

Apparently then, he had access to one of the piano-vocal arrangements published at the end of the century, though the item does not appear in his library catalogue.[257] The article "Design" from the *Cyclopaedia* gives a summary of Mozart's development which depicts his growth as Burney saw it in retrospect.

> It is, therefore, in the intelligent distribution and arrangement of the several parts, that a perfect design consists. In the latter productions of Mozart it is, that perfection of design appears. The early cultivation of his talents rendered him a profound critic, at an age when others are usually beginning their studies. In his first composition[s] he was trying experiments and vanquishing difficulties; but in his maturer years he gave way to his feeling, particularly in his vocal music, which was little known, except at Vienna, till after his death. But in his operas, both serious and comic, his designs are supported with so much simplicity, grace, and elegance, and fed with such a constant flow of ideas, as if he had trusted to chance for arrangement.

A passage from the biography in the *Cyclopaedia* best summarizes Burney's idea of Mozart's creative life.

> In England we know nothing of his studies or productions, but from his harpsichord lessons, which frequently came over from Vienna; and in these he seems to have been trying experiments. They were full of new passages, and new effects; but were wild, capricious, and not always pleasing. We were wholly unacquainted with his vocal music till after his decease, though it is manifest that by composing for the voice he first refined his taste, and gave way to his feelings, as in his later compositions for the piano forte and other instruments his melody is exquisite, and cherished and enforced by the most judicious accompaniments, equally free from pedantry and caprice.

The only record of Burney's attendance at a Mozart opera is a diary entry for Thursday, 27 March 1806: "Mrs. Billington's benefit[,] the charming Opera of

La Clemenza di Tito by Mozart in which Mrs. Billington looked, acted and sang better than ever I heard her, more pathetic than bravura."[258] Thus, although Burney may have been unreceptive to the high drama of Gluck's operas, he was able to accept an opera like *La Clemenza di Tito,* which evolved from the main line *opera seria.*

Burney began to write of the decline in opera because of poor singing in the early 1780s in England, though many of the composers were first rate. One consequence was a rise in the popularity of the dance, and a concommitant increase in the use of dance in drama. By 1782 this increase threatened the domain of singing, and Burney complained to Twining that the opera was "dwindling again into a mere Dancing Entertainment. The Ballets historiques fill the house more than the singing...dancing at the opera is at best a secondary thing, and should never strike the flag to Music."[259] The situation did not improve during the following year, when, if not for Pacchierotti, "this affected and silly stuff" might have been able to "triumph over Music."[260] In the *History* he remarks that within the last ten years (1779-89) "dancing seems to have encroached upon Music, and instead of being a dependent or auxiliary, is aiming not only at independency, but tyranny."[261]

The degeneracy of the Italian opera in England sparked Burney to make efforts to bring Haydn to London. The negotiations for a time went well, but his goal was never realized. Burney's correspondence indicates that there was contention among the directors of the opera.

> I have stimulated a wish to get Haydn over as an opera composer—but mum mum—yet—a correspondence is opened, and there is a great likelihood of it, if these Cabals, and litigations ruin not the opera entirely.[262]

Haydn did not come, and the opera continued to decline. In December 1784, he had not yet been to the opera because "there is nothing new in the comic line; and Cherubini, the second composer, with Crescentini, the first serious man, and the Ferrarese, the first woman, being all principiants [*sic*], I have no more desire to dress and go into the cold theatre to hear them than to go to a puppet show, or see the giants at Guildhall."[263] Burney's evaluation is supported by Edgcumbe, who reports that "the accounts I received during this time of the Opera in England were extremely unfavourable."[264] By 1785 neither the serious nor comic troupe had one performer "with a marked talent for voice, knowledge, taste, and execution or action...In short the whole band consists but of different degrees of Mediocrity."[265]

The decline, especially in the quality of the subaltern singers, prompted Burney to become one of the twenty-five proprietors of a new opera in the Pantheon, which was remodeled as a theater. His investment was £700, not an unreasonable sum, since he was delegated Foreign Secretary to procure singers and composers at a salary of £360. He did his job well: the season of 1791 featured Sacchini's *Armide,* Pietro Guglielmi's *La Bella pescatrice,* Sarti's *Idalide,* and Paisiello's *La Molinara* and *La Locanda.*[266] Edgcumbe describes both the serious and comic companies as very good, with both Pacchierotti and Mara joining the serious troupe. The season was remarkably successful, but the theatre burned down after only one performance of the 1791-92 season, terminating the company, and costing Burney both his investment and his salary as secretary.[267]

After the destruction of the Pantheon, the opera continued at the Haymarket with an inferior company of singers, and a season filled "with no particular brilliance."[268] Thereafter a sharp decline set in, according to Edgcumbe, until the arrival of Banti in 1794. The decline continued in the 1790s; "Novelty is wanting at present, both to Poetry and Music," Burney wrote, and the "eternal imitation and repetition of what we have heard a thousand and a thousand times" disgusted him. Singers eager to attain reputations as virtuosi degraded the vocal art by imitating the difficulties of instrumental music. Burney believed that instruments had to resort to pyrotechnics because they lacked the expressive capabilities of the voice, but that it "degrades a singer to run races with hautbois, flutes and fiddles."[269] To vocal music belonged the "sentiments and expressions of humanity, and the passions that belong to its nature."[270]

The decline in singing, in Burney's estimation, continued to the end of the century. Mrs. Billington was greatly admired, but she sang in poor company. In 1801 he heard her sing in *Artaxerxes.* "Catch me in France!" he afterward wrote his son; "I would not hear the people who sing with Mrs. Billington at C.[ovent] G.[arden] again for a Guinea a Night."[271] Though Burney had long been a supporter of the opera in all its lavishness, the increasingly high salaries of the principal singers vexed him. At the exorbitant rates only one decent principal singer could be afforded, harming the rest of the company. By 1807 the salary commanded by Mrs. Billington "was more than the pay of the two principal singers in the time of Mingotti and Manzoli." As things stood, he saw no future for the opera, and feared that "We shall never have a good first man and first woman together."[272] Most of Burney's late letters do not mention opera composers at all; rather they contain his opinions regarding the great singers and their activities, especially Mrs. Billington, the Banti, Pacchierotti, and, later, Catalani. His papers substantiate the view projected by his criticism that opera was a vehicle for singers above all else.

Burney steadfastly defended Metastasian opera to the end of his life, trapped into intransigence by an aesthetic derived from Rousseau's *Lettre sur la musique* and *Dictionnaire.* It is ironic that, though he considered himself to be at the forefront of the avant garde, he never relinquished an aesthetic formed on the writings of a Swiss dilettante turned self-proclaimed musician, more gifted in rhetoric than music. Burney possessed more impressive credentials as a musician and an enlarged taste as a critic, but he lacked the enormous assuredness and intensity of feeling which marked Rousseau's character as an author. Burney's criticism of dramatic music suffers from his preference for one style over all others. In writing the history of opera he attempts to shape and improve his reader's taste: advocacy does not create good history, though it does make lively criticism. With the singular exception of the sections on Handel, Burney's writings on dramatic music seek to form taste at the expense of history.

From his first sentence, Burney attempts to mold his reader's opinion, laying the groundwork that must lead him to accept the only true taste. In fastening so firmly on his aesthetic, epochal changes in dramatic music pass unnoticed. It is difficult for any critic to write the history of his own age, and it is easy to understand Burney's caution as a critic in evaluating current changes in operatic style. It is more difficult to understand how, as a historian looking back at the eighteenth century from the early nineteenth, he could fail to discern the immense changes in dramatic style. His lively literary style, and the acceptance of the most modern and innovative instrumental music, camouflage his conservatism in dramatic music, and it is indeed surprising to find him still looking to Naples at the beginning of the nineteenth century.

9

Burney's Achievement as Critic and Historian of Music

There has always been controversy about Burney's achievement as a critic and historian. His *Tours,* though received with critical acclaim in England, inflamed Germans throughout the eighteenth century, and damaged his reputation in that part of Europe. Patriotic Frenchmen also must have been rankled by his irrepressible and often brutal contempt for their greatest national musical institution, the *Opéra.* In England the publication of Burney's *History* in 1776, in competition with Hawkins's work, split English musical and literary circles into two factions, and the relative merits of the works still provoke lively debate. If Burney's accomplishment could be measured by the amount of controversy his work has aroused, it would be great indeed.

The most prolonged and acrimonious debate continues to focus on the relative merits of the two histories of music. This dispute cannot be resolved, for the two books are so divergent in character as to defy meaningful comparison. Their dissimilarity—and the attendant controversy—is attributable to fundamentally different ideas of what constitutes a history of an art. Those who view a work of history as a storehouse of data will inevitably side with Hawkins, while those who believe a history must evaluate and interpret the events chronicled will prefer Burney's work.

During his life, Hawkins was considered by many to be a mere antiquarian and that reputation has remained with him and his work to this day. Much of his *General History of the Science and Practice of Music,* as Burney prompted Bewley to point out, is little more than a repository of information.[1] Pages pass with no intimation of the author's opinion or personality. When Hawkins presents a musical example, it is as if it were an exhibit in a museum; the reader is free to view the work without hindrance, and value it according to his own standard. Though something of Hawkins's thought is conveyed through his selection of materials, his work is largely an impersonal, if meticulously wrought, account.

In contrast, Burney's *History* is an intensely personal record of the history of his art. His personality is as evident in the discussion of Greek theory as it is in the discussion of the music and musicians in England in his own time, and his character is so boldly stamped on his work as to be noticeable when absent for even a few pages. The opening chapters of his second volume, as has been noted, show him consciously struggling to be more scientific and learned, endeavoring to match Hawkins on his own ground; they are the least successful pages in all of his writings. Hawkins's style of history is foreign to Burney's nature, just as these pages seem foreign to the *History*. Once freed of Hawkins's oppressive influence, he is able to resume the predominant tone of the *History*, that of a lively and personal tour through the history of music. In the role of a charming and urbane tour guide he was able to entertain his readers in a way few historians of music have managed since.

Burney takes his topic seriously, yet, consonant with his definition of music as a luxury of society and a daughter of peace and tranquility, he remains light-hearted and generally good-natured about even the most contentious of subjects. He shuns speculative debate on abstruse subjects over which men more knowledgeable than he had already produced book after book and endless debate. Instead, he remains aloof, and tells his readers with pleasant irony that where these illustrious men have failed, he can hardly hope to succeed. He then moves on to more agreeable and fitting subjects, leaving the question unresolved. After all, he reasons, none of the debates over Greek modes, ratios of sound, or even theoretical systems of harmony such as Rameau's, have produced one note of good music. There is thus little reason for a person of taste to become involved in these matters. Let Hawkins explain to his readers notation systems for music which can no longer be revived; Burney defers such instruction until, in the music of Josquin and his contemporaries, he finds music worthy of examination by the tasteful reader.

Burney moves with ease between the roles of historian and critic. Selecting materials from the vast quantity of music available to him, he fulfills his duty as a historian by pointing out the value of a composition in relationship to the music of the era in which it was produced. Having completed his task as historian, he then often obscures what historical perspective he has brought to the subject with his witty sallies against music which has long since lost currency. While "taste" was rejected by Hawkins as an unsuitable legislator of the arts, Burney embraces it. Asserting his authority over his readers as a professional musician and critic, he invites them to acquire musical taste through the knowledge presented in his *History*.

The contemporary critical reception of the two histories has been thoroughly explored by Roger Lonsdale, who revealed Burney's ignoble manipulation of the most important reviews of both his own and Hawkins's books. His sordid but successful machinations to suborn the reviews of Hawkins's book were probably as unnecessary as they were unprincipled. Many of the contemporary references to Hawkins's work that Burney did not instigate are as bilious as those he controlled. Even in death Hawkins was not spared; the obituary in the *Universal Magazine* in August, 1790, is highly unflattering, stating in part:

> The labours of Sir John Hawkins, as an author, will undoubtedly entitle him to the praise of great patience and industry, but not to that of taste and judgment... In 1776, appeared his *General History of the Science and Practice of Music* in five volumes quarto. It is a vast heap of materials, in which the most unimportant narrations and trivial digressions are predominant...[2]

The virulent critical debate provoked by comparisons of the two histories has continued almost unabated for 200 years. Biographers, historiographers, musicologists, dilettantes, and students of literature endlessly compare the two works. But of all the evaluations of the two books written since Burney's death, the best, in reasoning and in perception of the distinctive features of the works, is that published in the *Harmonicon* in 1832. The assessment, part of a biography of Burney, may have been by William Ayrton, a friend of Burney's, and student of both histories:

> Between the two rival histories the public decision was loud and immediate in favour of Dr. Burney. Time has modified this opinion, and brought the merits of each work to their fair and proper level—adjudging to Burney the palm of style, arrangement, and amusing narrative, and to Hawkins the credit of minuter accuracy and deeper research, more particularly in parts interesting to the antiquary and to the literary world in general. Hawkins wrote in the temper, and with all the attachments and even prejudices of an age which, at the moment he gave his labours to the world, had already passed away; so that his musical readers had little or no sympathy with his opinions or his feelings. Burney, on the contrary, felt it impossible to expect that music, which, above all other arts, so much depends on imagination and feeling, should ever be permanent; and that although there are, no doubt, particular periods at which one might wish it to stop if it were possible, yet as that wish cannot perhaps, fortunately, be gratified, it is best to comply with necessity, in good humour, and with a good grace: in fact, that to "stop the world in its motion is no easy task; on we *must* go, and he that lags behind is but losing time, which it will cost him much labour to recover." In conformity with this feeling Dr. Burney marched with the age, and produced a book which carried its own welcome with it.[3]

Ayrton, if it was he, recognized the essential characteristics of Burney's criticism. Burney wrote for the age in which he lived, and with the tastes of his audience always in mind.

Relying on the community of taste for his readership had its drawbacks. Burney's courting of the approval of the great in music, literature, and society, especially those in political positions, required constant catering to wide-ranging taste. He was ever mindful of the sensibilities of men of position, and aware that few such men were likely to admit that they had no taste, or a superannuated taste, in music. Though Burney had very specific and limited musical taste, his careful control of his prose lent an illusion of universality to his opinions. His idealism led him to a critical style which, without giving cause for the majority of his readers to take offense, led them in the formation of taste. As Lipking put it, "Burney tried to be all things to all readers, and momentarily his ambition seemed to be fulfilled."[4] His success was not achieved without sacrifice, nor was his hard won eminence sufficient to ensure a prosperous future.

Despite the wide acknowledgment Burney received from the literary world, substantive recognition of his abilities as a musician was elusive. He made numerous attempts to obtain positions at court, especially the coveted post "Master of the King's Band." Each effort to secure this post met with failure, failure keenly felt. However widely regarded he may have been, he lacked the political or musical power to advance in the court of George III. Perhaps, despite Burney's best efforts to hide the fact, the king was aware that Burney's taste did not fully embrace Handel.

Burney's attempts to gain increased patronage at court have been used to account for several aspects of his work, particularly his circumspection in writing about Handel and the amount of space he assigned to the review of Handel's operas. On this latter point Roger Lonsdale remarked:

> ...his gratitude for the King's generosity in permitting him to use the Handel Manuscripts in the Royal Collection obliged him to deal with that composer's theatrical works at enormous length. Earlier threats about uncensored criticism of Handel which would appear in the *History* were now forgotten and his lengthy and detailed discussion of the operas was obviously written primarily for the delectation of the King: for once Burney hardly cared about his general readers.[5]

This opinion is amplified in Lawrence Lipking's analysis of this portion of the *History*.

> For the sake of Royal approval, Burney was willing to allow the appearance of a flaw in construction [the enormous size of the opera chapter]. We do not need to resort to theory in order to understand this particular unsightly bulge in the *History of Music*.[6]

There doubtless is some merit in these conclusions, but they fail to consider fully the circumstances surrounding the creation of the chapter. Burney's treatment of Handelian opera can even conceivably be explained as a recognition of the interest of his general audience. Little of the music discussed in the first three volumes of the *History* was known first-hand by the majority of his readers. In contrast, the works of Handel were constantly before the public. Many of his readers would have seen the operas, and they were soon to be available in Arnold's edition of Handel's works. The public, whose interest in Handel's music was by this period being stimulated by the annual Commemoration Concerts, would be very interested in the works of the great master. The availability of the music was even more decisive in shaping this chapter than were the preferences of the king. Had Burney been so solicitous of the king's pleasure at this time, he most certainly would not have curtailed his discussion of the king's favorite Handelian music, the oratorios, for which he provides only a brief list of dates and a reference to the *Account*.[7]

Lipking's comparison of this chapter and chapter IX, "Opera Composers Employed at Rome"—"It is almost one hundred times as long"—might have more suitably been drawn between Burney's treatment of English music and that of the music of other countries as a whole. Beginning with volume III, the sixteenth century, the following allocations of pages are given to each nation:

Spain	6
Germany	37
France	52
Italy	244
England	572

Clearly Burney's *History* is above all an English history of music for Englishmen. Omitting entirely the 253-page chapter on "Opera in England," the portion of the *History* dedicated to England still exceeds the total coverage given Italy by 75 pages. Considered in the broad scope, the construction of the *History* is not as absurd as it may initially appear. These observations do not obviate objections to the peculiar proportions of the last volume of the *History*, but they do challenge Lipking's assertion that "By any discernable rule of relevance Chapter VI is absurdly outsized."[8] With more available space Burney might well have expanded the chapters on Germany and Italy to achieve greater balance with chapter VI, but there is no indication that he would have altered one line of the chapter on Italian opera in England. Confronted with severe restrictions of space, he resorted to the not-illogical expedient of referring his readers to the tours of France, Italy, and Germany for the history of music in those countries.

It has been evident in the discussion of opera and oratorio that Burney's concern over the necessity of courting the favor of the king and other powerful Handelians caused him to misrepresent his critical opinion of Handel by omission, obfuscation, and improbity. The extent of Burney's accommodation to the Handelians is evident in the review of a key essay in the *Account of the Commemoration of Handel*. The earliest version of Burney's essay "Character of Handel as a composer" is found in one of the manuscript notebooks; in it he cautiously expresses his opinion of Handel's virtues and defects, prefixed by a short history of his own changing taste.

> After being many years myself a blind admirer of Handel, and studying his works almost exclusively: I became captivated by the Grace and elegance of Italian Music and prejudiced against him by the unreasonableness of his partizans, who were to hear, or at least to be pleased, with the Compositions of no other master. I undertook with the utmost candour into which I could reason myself, to examine all his works in order to do Justice to him and to

my own integrity in drawing up his Character. That Handel was superior in the strength and boldness of his style, the richness of his Harmony, and complication of parts, to every Composer who has been most admired for such excellencies cannot be disputed and while Fugue, contrivance, and full score were thought the first and almost only requisite of good Music he remained wholly unrivalled. + + though the hand of a great Master of Harmony appears in all his works, but particularly those of his younger years; it is not for the interest of his Fame that it should rest on the originality or superior merit of all his productions to those of his predecessors: *Cantatas* we had by Carissimi, Old Scarlatti and Gasparini; *Duets* by Stefano; Vocal Choruses without Instruments by Palestrina and our own Tallis, Bird and Purcell; and with instruments by Paola Colonna; with Violin *Sonatas* and *Concertos* by Corelli and Geminiani equal if not superior to his best productions upon these models.[9]

When this passage appeared in print in the *Account*, it was substantially altered. Burney's private history of his own turning away from Handel was suppressed, and he set aside his critical integrity. The concessions he made to the Handelians are painfully evident, as he retained the same catalogue of composers quoted above, but all are surpassed in merit by Handel.

And though we had CANTATAS by Carissimi, Alessandro Scarlatti, Gasparini, and Marcello; DUETS by Steffani and Clari; VOCAL CHORUSES, without instrumental accompaniments, by Palestrina, and our own Tallis, Bird, and Purcell; and, with accompaniments, by Carissimi, as well as Paolo Colonna; with VIOLIN SONATAS and CONCERTOS by Corelli and Geminiani; yet it may with the utmost truth be asserted, that HANDEL added considerable beauties to whatever style or species of composition he adopted, which, in a larger work, it would not be difficult to demonstrate, by examples. At present, I shall only venture to give it as part of my musical *profession de foi*, that his *air* or *melody* is greatly superior to any that can be found in the otherwise charming Cantatas which Carissimi seems to have invented; that he is more natural in his voice-parts, and has given more *movement to his bases* than Ales [sandro] Scarlatti; that he has more *force* and *originality* than Gasparini or Marcello; that his chamber duets are, at least, equal to those of Steffani and Clari, who were remarkable for no other species of composition; and though the late Dr. Boyce used to say that HANDEL had great obligations to Colonna for his CHORUSES *with instrumental accompaniments*, it seems indisputable that such choruses were infinitely more obliged to HANDEL than to Colonna, or, indeed, than they were to all the Composers that have ever existed. It is my belief, likewise, that the best of his *Italian Opera Songs* surpass, in variety of style and ingenuity of accompaniment, those of all preceding and contemporary Composers throughout Europe; that he has more *fire*, in his compositions for violins, than Corelli, and more *rhythm* than Geminiani; that in his full, masterly, and excellent *organ-fugues*, upon the most natural and pleasing subjects, he has surpassed Frescobaldi, and even Sebastian Bach, and others of his countrymen, the most renowned for abilities in this difficult and elaborate species of composition; and, lastly, that all the judicious and unprejudiced Musicians of every country, upon hearing or perusing his noble, majestic, and frequently sublime FULL ANTHEMS, and ORATORIO CHORUSES, must allow, with readiness and rapture, that they are utterly unacquainted with any thing equal to them, among the works of the greatest masters that have existed since the invention of counterpoint.[10]

It is certain that this version of Burney's essay does not represent a genuine change of heart. Perhaps the king, or Bates, ordered changes in the original, or perhaps Burney stopped short of showing such a critical passage to them; we will never know. The constancy of his true critical opinion is evinced by yet another version of this passage, taken from the article "Handel" in the *Cyclopaedia*. This passage, though written earlier, was published in 1811. The quotation below begins at precisely the same point in the essay. The elaborate catalogue of Handel's ranking against other composers in every style has been deleted: there remains only a brief and fully honest assessment.

> We will not assert that his vocal melodies were more polished and graceful than those of his countryman and contemporary Hasse; or his recitatives, or musical declaration, superior to that of his rivals, Bononcini and Porpora. But in his instrumental compositions there is a vigour, a spirit, a variety, a learning, and invention, superior to every other composer that can be named; and, in his organ fugues, and organ playing, there is learning always free from pedantry; and, in his choruses, a grandeur and sublimity which we believe has never been equalled since the invention of counterpoint.[11]

Thus Burney finally set the record straight in print, and belatedly reasserted his integrity, though many of his original readers were no longer alive to witness the rectification.

The Handelians exerted an overpowering influence on Burney's criticism. Yet even the above record does not fully reveal the stifling force the devotees of Handel wielded over musical life in England. To Burney, it was a pernicious influence, affecting far more than his writings; at the bottom of a page in one of his notebooks there is a passage written for no eyes but his own.

> I dare not say what I have long thought. That it is our reverence for old authors and bigotry to Handel, that has prevented us from keeping pace with the rest of Europe in the cultivation of Music.[12]

As strongly as Burney felt these sentiments, it was not possible for him to express them publicly without the danger of undoing a lifetime of effort. When he finally did publish the mildly censorious but more balanced appraisal of Handel in the *Cyclopaedia,* he was essentially retired, and had long since given up hope of further advancement in the king's service.

Evaluating the effort Burney made to accommodate a variety of tastes, Lipking concludes that one of the defects of his work is that in striving "to incorporate and satisfy every audience, it inevitably hearkens to common denominators, intelligible to every taste and every nation. Burney's writings are popular in two senses: they appeal to, and they are based upon, common opinion."[13] This conclusion is manifestly erroneous. There was a denominator, but it was neither common nor low; Burney's world of taste included the best and most recent music to reach England from the Continent. The constant difficulty he was in with the Handelians bespeaks the less-than-universal opinions contained in his works. Though Burney did capitulate to the Handelians, at least in part—his remarks on Handel's operas are not uncritical—he found fault with Corelli and other composers dear to those of conservative taste. It is easy to forget the realities of his world, and to consider the compromises he made in his criticism as evidence of a want of principles. But the agonized intensity of his letters to Twining, and the numerous drafts of essays on the subject of Handel, stand in evidence of the struggle he underwent before surrendering his critical integrity. What today may be construed as needless improbity in pandering to the tastes of the gentry and nobility may have been to Burney a necessary compromise to ensure the continuation of his prosperity.

Burney's principles have been challenged on other grounds. He has been criticized for accepting an exorbitant stipend, £ 1,000, for his *Cyclopaedia* articles, a charge which appears as early as 1832 in the *Harmonicon* biography. The author sarcastically remarks that "as most of the matter was extracted without alteration, from his *History of Music,* the price was perhaps not inadequate to the service rendered."[14] The statement that many of the articles were extracted from the *History* is accurate. However, there was little reason for Burney to rewrite the articles on Purcell, Morley, Croft, Greene, or other composers long since dead, for he had written all that was needed about these men in his *History.* Criticism would be better directed at Burney's extensive use of Rousseau's writings rather than his own. How much more interesting it would be to have his own thoughts on opera, expression, performance, taste, and numerous other topics, instead of warmed-over Rousseau; with an occasional criticism or addition.[15] Without Rousseau as a crutch for his work, Burney might have been forced to re-evaluate the history of music more thoroughly than he did. The fact that Burney revised Rousseau's work in this way says a good deal about Burney's thought, but not as much as his own original essays could have.

Burney did write a substantial number of new articles. He also felt free to revise in the *Cyclopaedia* his remarks about musicians who had died since the writing of the *History* and, in so doing, he extended the history of music in England up to the turn of the nineteenth century. In light of the remuneration Burney received, these articles may have seemed a poor value to the author of the *Harmonicon* article, but at the distance of almost two centuries, they appear as treasures.

The most serious challenge to Burney's integrity is the charge that he plagiarized from Hawkins's work. Hawkins, though he apparently made no public charges, is reputed to have complained bitterly about Burney's borrowing from his material. Christopher Welch, "intimately acquainted with Sir John Hawkins's grandson," claimed to have

...had more than one conversation with him on the subject of the relations of Dr. Burney with his grandfather Sir John. I have thus been favoured with a glimpse behind the scenes; but what was then revealed it is neither necessary nor desireable that I should disclose.[16]

The original public charge of plagiarism seems to have been lodged by William Chappell, who stated that Burney "took his authorities at second hand, when the originals were accessible; and copied especially from Hawkins, without acknowledgement, and disguised the material by altering the language."[17] Unfortunately, Chappell, a fierce critic of Burney, does not substantiate his allegations.

It is impossible to divine what plagiarisms troubled Chappell, but apparent plagiarisms are evident, and are readily identifiable. The most blatant of these occur in Burney's chapter "Progress of Church Music in England after the death of Purcell." Two examples will suffice to illustrate the nature of Burney's pilferings, which, it must be acknowledged, exceed the bounds of petty theft.

HAWKINS

JOHN GOLDWIN was a disciple of Dr. William Child, and on the 12th day of April, 1697, succeeded him as organist of the free chapel of St. George at Windsor. In the year 1703 he was appointed master of the choristers there; in both which stations he continued till the day of his death, which was the 7th of November, 1719. Of the many anthems of his composition, Dr. Boyce has selected one for four voices, "I have set God always before me," which, in respect of the modulation, answers precisely to the character which the doctor has given of the music of Goldwin, viz., that it is singular and agreeable.[18]

BURNEY

JOHN GOLDWIN, or GOLDING, was a disciple of Dr. Child, and his successor in the free chapel of St. George at Windsor, 1697. In 1703, he was appointed master of the choristers in the same chapel, and continued to occupy both those stations till his decease in the year 1719. Nothing can be more just than the short character given of the productions of this master, by the late honest and candid judge, Dr. Boyce, who, in his short account prefixed to the second volume of his collection, says that "there is in them a singularity of modulation, which is uncommon and agreeeable."[19]

Except for Burney's curious error in naming Weldon's teacher as John Porter instead of John Walton (not Walter, as Hawkins has it), the following passage seems to be either taken from a similar source, or cribbed from Hawkins.

HAWKINS

JOHN WELDON, a native of Chichester, had his instruction in music under John Walter, organist of Eton college, and afterwards under Henry Purcell. From Eton he went to Oxford, and was made organist of New College. On the sixth day of January, 1701, he was appointed a gentleman extra-ordinary of the royal chapel; and in 1708 succeeded Dr. Blow as organist thereof. In 1715, upon the establishment of a second composer's place, Weldon was admitted to it: He had been but a short time in this station before he gave a specimen of his abilities in the composition of the Communion-office, that is to say, the Prefaces, Sanctus, and Gloria in excelsis; and also sundry anthems, agreeably to the condition of his appointment.[20]

BURNEY

JOHN WELDON, born at Chichester, learned the rudiments of Music of Mr. John Porter (John Walton), organist of Eton college, and afterwards received instructions from Henry Purcell. He was for some time organist of new College, Oxon (1694). But in 1701, he was appointed a gentlemen of the Chapel Royal; and in 1708 succeeded Dr. Blow, as one of His Majesty's organists. In 1715, upon the establishment of a second composer's place in the King's chapel, Weldon was the first who filled that station, of which he seemed conscientiously determined to fulfill all the duties; for before he had long been in possession of this office, he gave proofs of his abilities and diligence in the composition of the Communion service, as well as the several anthems required by the conditions of his appointment.[21]

Other examples, including some more discreetly paraphrased, are evident throughout this chapter, and one catches occasional glimpses of Hawkins elsewhere as well.[22] There were, of course, no copyright laws to protect published works; but Burney is "guilty" by the application of the standards he sets for other writers.

Burney was quite annoyed by plagiarism from his own work, as his reviews in the *Monthly Review* evince. At every turn he points out passages taken from his work without acknowledgment, severely censuring the authors for their lapses. He was also plagued by the writers of reference works, especially the author of the article "Music" for the *Encyclopaedia Britannica*. According to Burney, the writer abridged "the *General History of Music* volume by volume and article [by article] without even mentioning the name of the original author" until the very end of the lengthy article. He found his writings in the *Encyclopédie méthodique,* a new edition of the famous *Encyclopédie,* the first volume of which appeared in 1791. The authors of the *Encyclopaedia Perthensis,* who also drew extensively from his work, at least acknowledged "the aid we have derived from Dr. Burney's *History of Music,* the best work on the subject yet published."[23]

German writers borrowed extensively from Burney's writings. Reichardt and Forkel, two of his harshest German critics, used his works frequently in their almanacs and periodicals. Forkel, in the eyes of Burney and his friends, went beyond such petty larceny into grand theft in his *Allgemeine Geschichte der Musik* (1788 and 1801), the appearance of which caused something of a furor in England. The anonymous reviewer of Burney's *History* in the *European Magazine,* probably Thomas Busby, wrote:

...we are told that A Dr. Torkel [sic], in writing a History of Music in that language lately, has so closely adopted his plan, opinions, and manner, in the first volume, chapter by chapter, that people are tempted, notwithstanding the author's science, to call it a translation: even the ornamental pieces have been copied in this work. M. de la Borde and other French writers on ancient and modern music have translated, quoted, and made free use of his materials, frequently without acknowledgment.[24]

So great was the concern over Forkel's plagiarism that a copy was prepared by Latrobe laying out those passages resembling Burney's own. There was a plan to unmask Forkel, in which Burney was invited to join; he refrained, preferring to remain silent, but he later cleverly exposed Forkel in a footnote in the *History*.

> I am sorry that the third volume of this author's *General History of Music* which is confined chiefly to the Music of Germany, was not published before this chapter was written; as it would probably have saved me as much trouble in seeking, selecting, and arranging the materials, as my first volume seems to have saved him, as far as he has hitherto advanced in his work; which from the great resemblance of its plan to that of my own, I can hardly praise with decency.[25]

Other German writers also made ample use of Burney's work. There are more than a score of references to his work in Johann Sulzer's *Allgemeine Theorie der schönen Künste*. Moreover, Heinrich Bossler cites his work frequently in his *Musikalische Realzeitung,* which contains a retrospective *Ephemeriden* (daily chronicle) recording Burney's daily progress on his tour of 1772. The *Musikalisches Wochenblatt,* edited by Friederich Kunzen, published two of Eschenburg's translations of Burney's writings, the "Essay on Musical Criticism" and an essay on Pergolesi.

Annoying as this pilferage was to Burney, it only served to bolster his international renown. Though designed for a national audience, his writings were read on the Continent. His travels, and the publications arising from them, thrust him into international prominence within the space of only three years. Even before he completed the *History* in 1789, his fame was assured. Stefano Arteaga, in his *Le Revoluzioni del teatro musicale italiano* (1783-1788), after giving his own account of ancient music, states that Burney, "the most accurate musical historian existing, confirms our assertions with such a series of facts, and ancient testimonies as is wonderful."[26] In Germany, the *Tours,* translated by Ebeling and Bode, and "The Dissertation on the Music of the Ancients" and *The Account of the Commemoration of Handel,* both translated by Eschenburg, repeatedly placed Burney's name before the German public. His reputation as a historian was built on the foundation of his critical writings, and in Germany his achievements as a historian even overcame much of the ill-will raised by the remark on German genius. Even Forkel, who prefixed his review of volume one of the *History* in his *Musikalisch-kritische Bibliothek* (1778) with a scathing denunciation of the *German Tour,* and Burney's qualifications to undertake the writing of a history of music, was sufficiently impressed by his achievement as a historian to conclude hs lengthy review with a laudatory assessment:

> One cannot deny that Herr Burney has treated most portions of ancient music very well and with order. One also finds a wealth of remarks, often supported with very sound judgments, that show at all events Herr Burney as a man who possesses very broad learning, who has read everything one could possibly read in support of such a task as the writing of a general history of our art.[27]

Years later, in his *Allgemeine Litteratur der Musik* (1792), Forkel specifically linked the resurgence of respect for Burney's work as a historian to his efforts to rectify the damage wrought by the remark on German genius.

> ...the author at the end of chapter X. vol. IV, has formally retracted his earlier verdicts concerning the lack of genius in the Germans in a noble manner, calling them undeserved and absurd; he even made a full apology for it to that nation. This act not only shows his love for justice and truth, but it will cause his readers to have greater trust in him as art critic and historian, than he could previously expect due to his biased and unfounded opinions.[28]

Burney's fame in Germany appears to have been secure by the end of the century. In 1802 a writer in the *Allgemeine Musikalische Zeitung,* in a reference to Charles Rousseau Burney, identifies him (incorrectly) as "son of the famous critic and historiographer."[29] The *Tours,* however, were not forgotten. Though he knew Burney's *History,* Christoph Daniel Schubart's evaluation of Burney (writtin in 1784-85, but not published until 1806) is dominated by his response to the *Tours,* an assessment obviously obliged to Reichardt's criticism. For all of his assured proclamation, Schubart is obviously speaking from ignorance: Eschenburg translated only the "Dissertation on Music of the Ancients" and several isolated portions of the *History,* not the entire work.

> Burney, doctor of music, has become known in all of Europe by his *Musical Travels* and especially by his *History of Music.* Although his *Travels* contain many correct and profound observations and show an extraordinary knowledge of music, his own opinions are too British, i.e. too bold, and are often absolutely wrong. Ebeling, translator of these *Travels,* and Reichardt have emphatically demonstrated this to him, and have also rejected with German courage his defamations of great men. Burney travelled much too fast and too carelessly, to be able to observe with philosophical composure. He treats us Germans with far too little justice, where it is due. He only lets us have virtuosity and diligence, but he denies our musical genius—a defamation which is being refuted throughout the whole history of music, to the honor of our nation. His Musical *History,* which he collected and wrote during twenty years, contains a prodigious amount of erudition, easily available to those with enough money; but the work is full of errors; his opinion is not his own, but mostly French, and his "aesthetic feeling" does not mean much.
> Eschenburg's translation of his work has by now erased many of these obvious errors.[30]

Schubart touches on several interesting points in his evaluation. His is but one of several references in German literature to Burney's wealth (Gerber mentions that he has his own carriage as a sign of wealth). Burney was not a wealthy man, but there seemed to be a certain suspicion among Germans about a musician who had sufficient resources to travel all over Europe to collect materials for his work. Schubart also mentions Burney's French aesthetic, a feature passed over by most of his contemporaries (though he should have attributed the influence to Rousseau, rather than to French writers), accurately distinguishing Burney's disdain for French music from his admiration for the writings of the *Encyclopédists*.

A particularly interesting statement of the German view of Burney's work is found in Ernst Ludwig Gerber's *Historisch-Biographisches Lexicon der Tonkünstler*, published in 1790-92 and revised in 1812-14. The 1790 edition notes the appearance of the *History*, but the editor refrains from criticism, although he does remark on the *Tours*, nothing that Burney traveled "with a haste which was bound to be harmful to his research and his experiences as a writer of history and which made him see many things dimly or from the wrong angle."[31] The 1812 edition contains a supplement to the earlier biography, and it should be noted that the writer praises the lengthy discussion of opera, which has so troubled modern critics:

> He is not content with dressing up carefully all he says, or in other words: he knows how to write about the dullest matters in the most pleasant way, and he also shows his cheerful and witty disposition always at the right place in order to prevent the reader from going to sleep over the long, tedious passages empty of artistic activities. For his compatriots, however, who miss none of his insinuations or sneers, the work must be more attractive, and especially his detailed and complete history of the London opera theatres must interest them a lot. Generally, however, he has added a lot to the history of dramatic music, which was missing in Hawkins and totally unkown to Printz, since before Mattheson's *Patriot* and his *Ehrenpfordte* [sic] no German publications have mentioned the opera by as much as one word. It is lucky for us that a Forkel lives in our century and is now in Göttingen, who is up to such an immense task and who lets us dispense with any foreigners' help in this field; otherwise we would have reason to reach out with both hands for a translation of Burney's works.[32]

The article testifies to the international importance of his *History*, for Forkel was never to finish his projected history.

The dramatic German response to the *German Tour*, or the "trouble with Germans" that Scholes and Lonsdale chronicled, has overshadowed the less dramatic but more significant and durable respect evident in later German musical literature. To most Germans his achievement as a historian eclipsed his indiscretion in printing Devisme's opinion of their creativity. However incensed they may have been by a few of Burney's judgments, they acknowledged his contribution to the historiography of music. It is safe to say that his writings were before the musical public of Germany, either in their original form or in German adaptations, almost as much as before English music lovers.

The French also paid homage to Burney's lifetime of work. The *Journal des beaux arts* in 1780 referred to him as the "famous Dr. Burney, so celebrated in Europe for his *History of Music* and for his voyages."[33] Many other respectful comments in periodicals could be cited—a writer in the *Correspondance des amateurs musiciens* called Burney one of the most celebrated of Oxford's musical graduates,[34] for example—but the most impressive evidence of his French recognition as a critic and historian is his election to the French Institute. He first learned of the proposal to make him a *correspondant* of its *Classe des Beaux Arts* from Fanny in July, 1806, a curious circumstance, since no official record of such a proposal exists in the records of the institute until 1810, when Burney was nominated to fill a vacancy in the class.[35] The minutes of the meeting of 21 April 1810 reveal that there were two places to fill, and eleven names were adopted for consideration, including those of various architects, artists, and musicians. Among those mentioned in the last class were Peter Winter, Alexandre Choron, and Burney. The latter two were listed as authors, and Winter as a *compositeur à Munich*. In the election held a week later, the first ballot was decisive, with Burney capturing fourteen of the twenty-two ballots cast. In contrast, it required five additional rounds of balloting to elect the second new member. Thus it seems that Burney was held in high regard indeed by the members of the Institute, who included Grétry and Gossec.

There are several references to Burney in the official publication of the Institute, the *Notice des travaux de la classe des beaux arts*. One of the earliest (1803) occurs in an article by Joachim le Breton, who makes the curious observation that Burney's *History* was marred by his partiality in favor of the English, a remark which surely would have astounded Burney's countrymen. In 1811, the year after his election, the *Notice des travaux* notes Charles Brack's translation of the *Tours*, and refers to Burney's *History* as a genuinely classic book.[36]

Brack had also planned a translation of the *History*, but the work was never published, if it was completed. His was not the first proposed translation: the library of the *Opéra* contains a manuscript translation of some of Burney's work.[37] This volume, apparently one of an original two volumes, contains extensive translations from the third and fourth volumes of the *History*, and also parts of the *Account of the Commemoration of Handel*. The manuscript is probably not Brack's, as it bears numbers indicating that in 1793 it was in the Bibliothèque du Roi. Though many portions of the work are translated, it is noteworthy that chapter 11 of the fourth volume, "Progress of Music in France," has not been transcribed. Only two blank leaves, and the chapter heading, mark its place in the manuscript; apparently the translator perceived little of value in Burney's discussion of contemporary French music. Whatever the provenance of this manuscript, it is yet another indication of the international readership of the *History*, and the fame of its author.

It was an extraordinary honor to be elected a *correspondant,* and no one was more surprised than Burney; he found it a very "liberal" gesture, "as I have been abusing French Music of the old School, all my life, particulary vocal."[38] Old and infirm at the time he was elected, he sent only one report to the Institute, his inaugural address.[39] Revealingly, his subjects were Metastasio and Haydn, the aged historian's great heroes in opera and instrumental music. In 1814, the *Notice des travaux* announced the passing of the "learned and witty Dr. Burney," and expressed regrets.[40] The French, it seems, like the Germans, distinguished between Burney's shortcomings as a critic and his accomplishments as a historian.

No one familiar with English letters need be told of Burney's fame in his own country. His reputation in literary circles was extraordinary. The critic for the *Annual Review and History of Literature,* in a not completely favorable review of the new *Cyclopaedia,* wrote, "The *musical* articles are by Dr. Burney, or, in other words, are peculiarly excellent; they display practical skill, scientific information, and are written in a style of such lively simplicity as is rarely found in unison with profound knowledge."[41] If we are to judge his accomplishment by the eminence he achieved on an international scale in his own time, it is paralleled only by that of his heroes: Rousseau and the other Encyclopédists. Burney himself would have asked for no more.

Another just measure of Burney's success is how well he met his own expectations. The *Plan* set out an ambitious proposal which he did not fully realize. There are substantial differences in form between the prospectus and the completed *History,* the most notable being the omission of chapter seven, which was to have treated the "national music" of no less than thirteen different countries. It is not found in any form in the *History.* Indeed, America, Russia, and Portugal, which figure in the *Plan,* are not so much as mentioned, and the national music of the other countries listed is mentioned only incidentally. The absence of any substantial discussion of folk music in the *History* led Percy Scholes to the unfortunate conclusion that

> The books of Burney and Hawkins share one narrowness. What happened musically in Ancient Greece or Rome (or even Egypt) they regard as possessing some importance, but they show little interest in what we now regard as the very foundation of the history of music—research into the musical practices by the untutored peasantry and of uncivilized races. Burney had spent his childhood amongst the "folk" and heard the songs of his good Dame Ball, but on becoming an historian apparently forgot all about them.[42]

The contrary is true. Burney's plan to include the essay on national music in the second volume of the *History* was not abandoned, even after the first volume went to press. Amidst a comparison of Chinese and Scottish scales, Burney promises his readers that "all the specimens that I have been able to collect of Chinese melody, several... will be given among the examples of national music in the second book."⁴³ Yet with the exception of a few scattered comments on Scottish, Welsh, and Abyssinian music, no further discussion of national music appears in the *History*.

His decision to delete the section on national music must have been difficult; though he was only slightly interested in the sound of the music, he felt that the examination of it was an important part of his prospectus. In his report of his meeting with Rousseau, he noted that when Rousseau came to the article on national music, he remarked, "ah, that's good, 'tis what I waited for..."⁴⁴ Burney's failure to complete the full report on the folk music of thirteen countries as promised in the *Plan* represents little loss to ethnomusicology. His attitude towards national music, even after engaging in fifty years of collecting material and doing field research, reveals his lack of success in studying the music of another culture. The articles for the *Cyclopaedia* provided him with an opportunity to use some of the material he had collected; he wrote lengthy articles on Welsh and Chinese music, as well as shorter articles on the music of several other countries. But unmoved by the exotic sounds of this music, he concluded of national music in general:

> ...we are inclined to imagine that music in Europe has been cultivated with so much more success than in any other quarter of the globe; our instruments, our harmony, and our melody, are arrived at such a superior state of perfection, that to abandon or neglect them for any refinements or properties which the music of Asia, Africa, or America could furnish, would indeed be letting our cornfields lie fallow, and feeding on acorns; or throwing aside the poetry of Milton, Dryden, and Pope to read and imitate only Chaucer, Gower and Lidgate.⁴⁵

His research upon and experiments with national music foundered on the same shoals of cultural prejudice that impeded most eighteenth-century investigations of ethnic music. Guided by the idea of progress in music, the basic critical precept of his age, he could only consider the music of another culture vastly different from his own as being at some lower level of the progression that must ultimately lead to the apex: a music similar to that of Western Europe.

Another proposal of the *Plan* that was not completely realized is chapter eight, "the history of some modern instruments; that is to say, the clavicembalo, the organ, the violin, etc."⁴⁶ To be sure, copious references to all three instruments exist, but the planned chapters devoted exclusively to the history of the instruments did not materialize. The most extensive discussion of a single instrument in the *History* is chapter IX of book III, "Progress of the Violin in Italy, from the Sixteenth Century to the Present Time," and even this discussion does not fall within Burney's original conception. It is more a history of violinists in Italy than of the violin itself. There are no discussions of violin makers, improvements in the instrument, or the relative value of the various makes, ancient or modern. His discussion of the organ is even less systematic.

The organ in England receives some attention, but the discussion is chiefly concerned with the influx of foreign organ builders; the remainder of the sparse chronology accorded to keyboard instruments is dispersed throughout the four volumes by country and time period.

Another aspect of Burney's *Plan* which remained unfulfilled was his proposal for a dissertation on the "Harp of David" in the chapter on Hebrew music. He was aware of the potential difficulty in writing this essay: he reports Rousseau's reaction upon his reading of the proposed essay, "Ma fois, vous aller [*sic*] bien loin—says he—and I felt a little ashamed of the promise to examine it."[47] Although David as musician is discussed at length, no essay on the harp of David is included in the *History*. His disappointment at his inability to produce this essay was probably tempered by the opportunity to report on James Bruce's Theban harp.

Instrumental music received sparse treatment in the *History*. In the *Plan* instrumental music is mentioned only incidentally. Using his plan as a guide, Burney collected materials for the *History*, and thus, in the later reorganization of his notes, he was faced with a collection of material heavily weighted toward the vocal forms. The emphasis on opera is a natural outcome of Burney's musical taste, but it also reflects the dominance of opera throughout most of the eighteenth century. His bias, of course, reflected the common view of the time which ranked vocal music as superior to instrumental. To a person of Italianate taste such as Burney, the best music in England was Italian, and the best of that was Italian opera. Few of his English contemporaries disagreed, and those who did were probably exponents of German instrumental music, not native English music.

Though Burney ultimately omitted several topics advanced in the *Plan*, he also made several additions. The most substantial of these is the "Dissertation on the Music of the Ancients," which represents a reorganization rather than a true addition. Chapter six of the *Plan*, dealing with musical systems and theorists, was eventually incorporated into annotated catalogues of writers about music found at the end of each chapter. Perhaps the difficulty of treating the music of antiquity without discussing the theory and theorists of the period dissuaded Burney from his original organization, and led him to a chronological scheme. Nothing more need be added to the record of his reluctance to enter into a discussion of ancient music. But once committed to the task, he vanquished it by all contemporary standards, as Forkel's admiration proves.

Another addition to the *Plan* was the chapter on Egyptian music. The impetus for its inclusion did not come from Bruce's willingness to share his discovery of the Theban harp with Burney, as the chapter on Egyptian music had already been printed, and Burney was forced to cancel a number of pages to make room for its inclusion. Perhaps he felt that since he had already engaged in so much speculation in his "Dissertation," he would be remiss in not advancing his conjectures on music in the cradle of civilization.

Two other sections of the *History* are not found in the prospectus: the "Essay on Musical Criticism" prefixed to book III, and the "Essay on the Euphony or Sweetness of Languages and Their Fitness for Music" prefixed to book IV. Burney as a musical historian in the eighteenth century probably found it impossible to resist engaging in a favorite subject for polemic in this period: the nature and suitability of languages to be set to music. One of his first studies in Continental music had been his translation of Rousseau's *Lettre sur la musique française* (1753), and, if only in emulation of his hero, he must have felt obliged to make his contribution in his "Essay on the Euphony or Sweetness of Languages and their Fitness for Music."

The "Essay on Musical Criticism" was undoubtedly prompted by his anxiety about the possible response of his contemporaries to his critical judgments. Well aware of the hazards of setting himself up as a critic, he sought to forestall antagonism with an explanation of his critical viewpoint:

> ... the analysis of this pleasure is, therefore, the subject of the present short Essay; which, it is hoped, will explain and apologize for the critical remarks of this *History*, on the works of great masters and prevent their being construed into pedantry and arrogance.[48]

This essay speaks directly to the issue of prejudice. "A critic," he says, "should have none of the contradictions and narrow partialities of such as can see but a small angle of the art." But Burney himself failed to meet his standard. His first reviewer mentioned Burney's prejudice against French music, a bias apparent throughout his criticism. In writing about Rameau in his last volume, he acknowledged his lifelong intolerance for French music:

> Minutely to discuss the merits of this musician in the practice and theory of this art would occupy more pages in my book than I have now to spare. I shall however, confess the effect his compositions and writings have had on myself, in spite of early prejudices against the vocal Music of France in general, and still more against its execution at the serious opera.[49]

Despite this admission, the more impartial discussion of French opera seemingly promised in the quote does not materialize.

The duality of Burney's aims in writing his *History* resulted in certain contradictions. He wished both to fill a "chasm in English literature" by writing a history of music, and to instruct in the formation of taste. As Burney saw it, a good and true taste was developed by instruction from those possessed of the ability to notice, judge, and appreciate what is beautiful, appropriate, harmonious, and excellent in art.[50] He felt, therefore, that it was his obligation to clearly present those models worthy of approbation and to exclude the rest. This critical system, based as it was on such an indeterminate concept as taste, was susceptible to the prejudices inherent in modernism and progressivism. As such, it did not serve well the objective ordering of an art. However, it did contribute to the creation of an audience in England receptive to the confluence of ideas that crystallized in the Classical style.

Burney's embracing of Rousseau as a model for music criticism induced him to accept a prejudice against French music he need not have entertained. Rousseau's criticism addressed an immediate controversy, one in which two musical styles competed for the favor of one audience in his country. Burney, in an almost quixotic gesture, joined the skirmish only to find that there was no opponent on the field of battle; French serious opera enjoyed no significant following in England. His awareness of his *History* as a work primarily for Englishmen belies the explanation that he was hoping to influence Continental taste. There is, in short, little justification for his having engaged in this controversy at all, and less for having taken such a definite and obstinate stand about music of little interest to an English audience.

One explanation for the intensity of his support of the Italian style over the French may be his frustration at being largely unable to address directly similar issues in his own country. He saw the pamphlet wars waged over opera in France as being not so much an exhibition of two current tastes in opposition, but an example of antiquated and vitiated taste challenged by a modern and purifying taste. It was a classic battle of conservative versus progressive. When Burney linked Handel's name with those of Lully and Rameau, he seemed to be considering the developments of musical style in England and in France to be parallel. He could take an unequivocal position on French musical quarrels, but in writing of his own country all such discussions required circumspection.

The "Essay on Musical Criticism" was a necessary inclusion for Burney, who, ever conscious of his audience, wished to persuade but not to alienate them. With a critical aesthetic based on taste, supported (as he presented it) by the laws of science and nature, he was able to establish himself as sole judge of the music of several centuries and of innumerable composers with conviction and remarkable success.

Perhaps the greatest difference between the *Plan* and the *History* is the organization; the *Plan* is systematic, the *History* is largely chronological. Traces of the systematic organization remain in the *History,* as in the separation of the chapters on sacred music in England, the cantata, the oratorio, and the violin in Italy, but the bulk of the work is arranged chronologically.

Given the breadth of Burney's *Plan,* it is remarkable to what extent he was able to fulfill his all-encompassing prospectus. Only a few omissions, none of them total, have been mentioned, and their places have been more than filled by material not in evidence in the *Plan.* If one should be tempted to regard the omissions of the chapter on national music and of the dissertation on the harp of David as signs of failure on Burney's part, one should recall his meeting with the Abbé Rousseau and a Mr. Lumisden. Upon reading the *Plan* "... the Abbé Rousseau cried out every moment 'ma foi, c'est vaste!' [Burney] told them... it was only what I promised to *myself*."[51]

Rational assessments of Burney's lifetime of achievement are difficult to formulate. As Lipking states, Burney has "a charm and intimacy" which makes "every reader desire to be his friend."[52] This same familiarity has created his harshest critics as well. Even in the eighteenth century, critics took notice of the separation between instruction and entertainment which distinguishes solid scholarship from popular history. The critic of the *European Magazine* pronounced Burney's *History* the best ever written, and "superior in the essential articles of historical information, scientific discussion, general accuracy, and above all taste and candour." It must also be owned, says the critic, "that the author, perhaps to enliven the dry parts of his narrative, has sometimes been so indiscreet as to hazard puns and pleasantries; but in a work of such length readers want relaxation."[53] The critic develops this line of reasoning at some length. He allows that in "poetry, painting and music in which the biography of wild, capricious, and enthusiastic votaries of those arts, is as necessary as knowledge and taste in describing their progress, a smile, it should seem, may be admitted now and then, without derogating much from the dignity of the subject."[54] He also cites Burney's own remark in the preface that he would rather be thought trivial than tiresome. It is doubtful that anyone has pronounced him trivial; the sheer magnitude of his accomplishment requires greater respect.

If we are content to judge Burney's achievement as a critic and historian by contemporary international critical opinion, or by the fulfillment of his own ambitions, his is an impressive and commendable record. It is a record which stands, despite our fairly recent discovery that Burney was not the angelic, faultless character created by Fanny Burney. Nor should changing fashions in historiography, or our expanding perception of the course of musical history, be permitted to detract from his accomplishment. Since Burney's death his preeminence as a historian and critic has gradually been reduced, until his *History* is no longer regarded as a timeless monument of scholarship. His work, which dominated English musical historiography for a century, has assumed a more modest reputation, and is seen today rather as a personal record than as a universal history of music.

Many of Burney's critics, in the process of cutting away the aura of unsurpassable erudition which accompanied his works for so long, have lost sight of the decades of scholastic accomplishment that were necessary to give rise to a far more thorough picture of music than Burney was able to produce. These critics have censured and ridiculed his judgments with as much severity as if they were the product of a modern scholar who had the array of complete editions, bibliographies, indices, reference works, and biographies readily available.[55] As J.A. Westrup has aptly pointed out:

> It has become the fashion nowadays to poke fun at Burney. Writers who have not a tithe of his musicianship or literary skill amuse themselves by ridiculing his opinions because they are supposed to be out of date. This is a tedious pastime.[56]

Critics nevertheless continue to point out Burney's shortcomings with evident pride in their own sagacity. It should occasion no surprise that 200 years of scholarship have done much to rectify misconceptions about the Greek modes, and to elucidate more accurately the dissemination of music in the sixteenth century. Burney was not surprised to find books twenty years old to be out of date, inaccurate, and occasionally ridiculous, but nonetheless of value in understanding the thought of their day. Today's critics, disturbed by and critical of Burney's censure of John Blow's harmony, his distaste for Gesualdo's music, his imagined dismissal of Sebastian Bach, or other such "errors in judgment," are themselves censurable for their naïveté. The *History* is worthy of great respect despite its obvious failings, for, judged in the context of the conditions under which it was written, it is an astonishing achievement.

While it is but just to allow Burney his place of honor, it is also necessary to evaluate rigorously his writings for their reliability as records of history. The scholar turning to the *Tours* or *History,* as so many have, to find the opinion of the "unfailing Dr. Burney,"[57] will be distressed to learn that his writings are often misleading. Joseph Kerman calls Burney "the first and one of the shrewdest of music historians"; indeed, Burney was shrewd enough to mislead Kerman into labeling him "the good Handelian."[58] The point is not Kerman's perception, but Burney's deception. In responding to the forces around him, and in shaping his work to meet the narrow taste of some of his patrons, he produced a work which has, to a greater or lesser extent, misled scholars for 200 years.

As the present study has shown, Burney the critic and historian is as complex and as contradictory as the character so vividly recreated by Lonsdale. The generalities which have been used for years to describe Burney's tastes must be re-evaluated, and many, if not most, abandoned. To cite a few of the most popular generalizations and their controversions: Burney the alleged counterpoint-hater wrote fugues for the organ, and even a capriccio on a four-note ground bass (surely among the most gothic of productions), and in the hours when he was least comfortable and wished to divert himself, he turned to writing canons for amusement. The supposed superficial and modish opera lover held the sacred music of the sixteenth century, and later *a cappella* contrapuntal music, in high esteem. The fashionable critic, moving mindlessly with whatever was new, shunned, both in Gluck's reform operas and in the *opéra comique,* the newest and most epochal movements in opera. Burney the insatiable modernist remained tied to an operatic aesthetic half a century out-of-date, and the model of the "good Handelian" held Handel largely responsible for the stagnation of English music. The agreeable Dr. Burney, under the cloak of anonymity, wrote sharp and often biting reviews in the *Monthly Review,* contrived reviews of Hawkins's work, and composed malicious poetry. Some of these contradictions were created by Burney himself in tailoring his criticism to the widest possible audience, but others have arisen through the misuse of his writings as historical records. Historical documents clarify the past only when viewed in the context of their period and circumstance of creation.

We may cite Burney's own writings in admonishing scholars to remember the milieu of the era in which he worked. He quotes a conversation with Emanuel Bach, who remarked:

> When the critics... are disposed to judge impartially,... they are frequently too severe on works that come under their lash, from not knowing the circumstances that gave them birth, or remembering the author's original intention.[59]

Burney's quotation may be taken as a caveat; with proper attention to this warning much of the misapplication and abuse of his work could be avoided. The user who turns to an index and then extracts judgments without considering the aesthetic of the critic, the meaning of his critical vocabulary, or milieu in which he worked, is in danger of doing both himself and his readers a great disservice. "Knowing the circumstances" means more than an awareness of the biography and tastes of a writer: it also entails an understanding of his cultural environment. A North German critic, for example, though of impeccable musical credentials, would be a poor source for a contemporary appraisal of Haydn's music, because the mixture of serious and comic styles found in Austro-Bohemian instrumental music was in general spurned in North Germany.

In England the boundaries of musical taste were not defined by geography but by the opposition of progressive and conservative taste, and by the contradictory views of professional musicians and men of letters, who fancied themselves superior to musicians and more capable of aesthetic speculation.

For the modern reader, there are prejudices which must be overcome in order to "mount up" to Burney's and other eighteenth-century critical writings: for example, the perception that a vast gulf separates Vanhall and Dittersdorf from Mozart. For much of his life Mozart was considered to be no more than a fine young composer writing in the best taste of the times. Edward Dent was correct in stating that Burney's comments about Mozart published in the *Tours* and *History* should occasion no surprise; in all the vituperative reviews of Burney's works, contemporary with their publication, not a single critic finds fault with his assessment of Mozart.[60] The modern critic who smiles at Burney's failure to prefer Mozart to Sacchini can only congratulate himself for the assurance that he has excellent hindsight. Lipking would have it both ways: praising Burney for his recognition of Beethoven's genius, he remarks that "a critic whose instincts are so fine may be forgiven for liking Sacchini and Schobert."[61] To an uninformed modern viewer, Sacchini and Schobert may not seem to be in the swiftly moving center of the mainstream, but this view attests less to their merits or demerits as composers than to our selective and exclusive view of history, which, if only for pedagogical ease, fastens on one or a few great composers, to the exclusion of many ranked by their contemporaries as equal geniuses.[62]

The well-known existence, and often long duration, of spurious works in the catalogues of Mozart, Haydn, Beethoven, and other masters, should suffice to remind us of the intrinsic value of a great deal of music written by now less-famous composers. So long as we look back to records contemporary to the eighteenth century for confirmation of present perceptions, we will only be confirmed in narrow and exclusive views of musical style. Were this not generally the present practice in musicology, we would not be recording as new the discovery that opera dominated musical development throughout the eighteenth century; virtually every eighteenth-century critic points to opera as the dominant force in musical life. Today, Burney's preoccupation with opera over instrumental music no longer seems curious and eccentric; he recorded the pulse of his time. His dates may sometimes be inaccurate, and his taste narrow, but his very narrowness puts us intimately in touch with one of the epochal movements of his time, the Italian opera.

The study of Burney's papers has placed in relief his limitations as an objective observer of the music of his time. His most important failings derive from a single factor: his sometimes practical, or perhaps merely egotistical, need to accommodate himself to an audience of diverse tastes. This same consideration, more narrowly applied, gave rise to the most extensive prevarication in his work: his evaluation of Handel as a composer. Similarly motivated were his benevolent, cautious, and occasionally deceptive evaluations of living English musicians, or those recently deceased, who were popular or well respected. Judging him in the harshest light, it may be said that his impulse to be agreeable led him to sacrifice objective criticism for praise. If this is so, as it demonstrably is in some instances, the reader who wishes to gain the greatest insight into Burney's criticism would do well to keep in mind his requisites for excellence in each of the styles of music: sacred, dramatic, and chamber. It is also necessary to remember his intention to write a general history of music for British readers, not a universal history for an international audience.

Scholars have failed to recognize the limitations of Burney's critical writings. The result of their deception by his improbity is a legacy of confusion which only makes more apparent the importance of becoming thoroughly familiar with critical sources before relying upon them. Scholars accustomed to relying on the veracity of the "perspicacious Dr. Burney"[63] will find his lack of critical integrity, for whatever reason, vexing. But to dismiss his writings as the work of an unprincipled and unreliable critic would mean overlooking the lesson that Burney's criticism offers, and losing a genuinely important, though neither comprehensive nor infallible, guide to eighteenth-century musical life. Our disappointment and frustration with Burney are founded on expectations based on standards of scholarship and criticism not applicable to much of the music criticism on library shelves. Critics of every era are dependent to some extent on the approval of their readers and everything a critic writes may not represent his candid opinion. The precariousness of the positions of many eighteenth-century critics, because of their dependency on patrons, the gentry and the nobility, or at the very least the support of their professional colleagues, had a telling influence on their work. Burney was told by Marpurg in Berlin that Marpurg himself "had injured his work by partiality to friends, whose productions he had frequently cited against his judgment." Surely other writers found themselves in similar situations, either political or social. Not all may have capitulated to the extent of Marpurg or Burney, but these examples are probably more typical than exceptional.

The unusual resource of the Burney papers sheds light where darkness should never have intruded. It should not require the clues contained in the Burney papers to alert scholars to the contradictions inherent in his works, or to the need to consider his milieu before citing his authority. But the widespread misuse of his writings attests to the need to reassert these ideas. Only when considered in light of the circumstances of their creation will Burney's or any other critic's works yield their fullest reward: a view of an era as men then saw it, not as we imagine it.

Notes

Chapter 1

1. See Joyce Hemlow, *The History of Fanny Burney* (Oxford, 1958), p. 446. See also CB to Latrobe, 14 Nov. 1796 (Osborn).
2. Now in the Berg Collection.
3. CB to CB Jr., 19 Apr. 1806 (Comyn), quoted in Lonsdale, p. 436.
4. *Memoirs*, i, pp. viii-ix.
5. MM, iii, pp. 294-95.
6. *Memoirs*, i, pp. 82-83.
7. GDB, i, pp. 63-99.
8. *Memoirs*, i, p. 213.
9. Berg, 198788B. The year is 1794. Brigitta Banti, Italian soprano, her role in *Semiramide* was her debut performance during her 1794 visit. The music of *Semiramide* was by Francesco Bianchi.
10. *Memoirs*, ii, p. 265.
11. Lonsdale, p. 451.
12. Lonsdale, p. 454.
13. Hemlow, *Fanny Burney*, p. 452; for an exhaustive study of the "Memoirs" and *Memoirs*, see Lonsdale, pp. 432-55; and Hemlow, pp. 446-66.
14. Osborn.
15. Arthur Simmons Collins, *Authorship in the Days of Johnson* (New York, 1929), p. 195.
16. *Memoirs*, i, p. 26.
17. CB to Lady Crewe, Oct. 1807, (Osborn).
18. Fragments of "Memoirs" (Berg).
19. See Paul Henry Lang, *George Frederic Handel* (New York, 1966), pp. 243-257.
20. For a full account of Burney's attempts to gain positions in the court musical establishment, see GDB, ii, pp. 321-27.
21. Quoted in GDB, ii, p. 322.

22. CB to CB Jr., 25 Feb. 1781 (Comyn). quoted in Lonsdale, p. 295.
23. GDB, ii, p. 324.
24. Frances Burney, *Diary and Letters of Madame d'Arblay,* 6 vols. (London, 1904-1905), ii, p. 358.
25. GHM, ii, p. 950.
26. Ibid., p. 973.
27. Burney copied Addison's definition in his notebook with the note "see alternative."
28. CB to Crotch, 17 Feb. 1805 (Coke).
29. C. "Piozzi."
30. CB to Barthélémon, [1789] (Osborn).
31. Ibid.
32. Ibid.
33. GHM, ii, p. 1009.
34. CB to TT, 24 Feb. 1782 (Osborn).
35. C. "Worgan."
36. MM, ii, p. 243.
37. CB to Dr. Harrington, [17] May 1806 (Berg).
38. CB to Mrs. Waddington, Feb. 1807.

Chapter 2

1. GHM, ii, p. 7.
2. C. "Webb."
3. Lawrence Lipking, *The Ordering of the Arts in Eighteenth-Century England* (Princeton, 1970), p. 219.
4. Charles Avison, *An Essay on Musical Expression* 2d ed, (London, 1752), p. 81.
5. Lipking, *The Ordering of the Arts,* p. 225.
6. GHM, ii, pp. 7-8.
7. Ibid., p. 7.
8. Ibid.
9. Ibid.
10. Ibid., p. 8.
11. Jacques Barzun, "Music into Words," *Lectures on the History and Art of Music: The Louis Charles Elson Memorial Lectures at the Library of Congress 1946-1963.* (New York, 1968), p. 88.
12. Ibid., p. 89.
13. GHM, ii, p. 8.

14. GHM, i, p. 378.
15. Ibid., p. 5.
16. "Barbarism." Samuel Johnson, *A Dictionary of the English Language,* (London, 1756).
17. GHM, ii, p. 562.
18. See chap. 6 for a discussion of these plates and the controversy surrounding them.
19. C. "Licence."
20. GHM, ii, p. 357.
21. Ibid., p. 517.
22. Ibid., p. 351.
23. B.M. Add. MS. 48345 f. 5v.
24. Burney later referred to these pieces as among his early "sins" in composition. See notebook in Osborn.
25. GDB, ii, p. 266.
26. Berg, folder 5.
27. CB to Latrobe, 14 Nov. 1796 (Osborn). See also CB to CB, Jr., 15 Jan. 1811 (Osborn), and memoranda for 1794 in Berg.
28. August F.C. Kollmann, *An Essay on Practical Musical Composition,* (London, 1799), p. 69.
29. Ibid.
30. See chap. 7, below.
31. C. "Eximeno."
32. GHM, ii, p. 414.
33. Ibid., p. 172.
34. GHM, ii, p. 124.
35. Ibid., p. 394.
36. C. "Gothic."
37. Lipking, *The Ordering of the Arts,* p. 149.
38. GHM, ii, p. 955.
39. Ibid., p. 745.
40. GHM, i, 766.
41. Ibid., p. 785.
42. C. "Pammelia."
43. GHM, i, p. 770.
44. Ibid., p. 794.
45. Johnson, *Dictionary,* "Artificial."
46. GHM, ii, 414.

310   Notes for Chapter 2

47. CB to Ebeling, Nov. 1771 (Staats-und Universitätsbibliothek, Hamburg, hereafter referred to as "Hamburg").
48. C. "Invention."
49. C. "Character."
50. Ibid.
51. C. "Merula."
52. C. "Voluntary"; see also "Prelude."
53. C. "Extemporaneous."
54. C. "Machine in Music."
55. Johnson, *Dictionary*, "Genius."
56. C. "Genius."
57. C. "Composer of Music."
58. C. "Subject."
59. C. "Gossec."
60. C. "Grazioso."
61. C. "Pergolesi." According to Burney, such composers included Giovanni Lampugnani, Giovanni Pescetti, and Geminiano Giacomelli, among "many others." His evaluation of Giacomelli illustrates the relationship of these lesser composers with those having true grace: "He was the scholar of Capelli but adopted a more high and flighty style, with which the Venetians were much captivated, before they heard the more graceful and expressive airs of Vinci and Hasse." C. "Giacomelli."
62. C. "Marmontel."
63. C. "Jomelli."
64. Johnson, *Dictionary*, "Ease."
65. C. "Counterpoint."
66. C. "Natural."
67. Notebook (Osborn). A similar idea is expressed in Burney's review of *A Treatise on the Art of Music* by William Jones, *Monthly Review* LXXV (1786), p. 107: "... it has been observed, and never contradicted, that we have little in nature to imitate. When we cry, laugh, exult, or repine, it is not in musical tones. The whole is nearly a work of art and imagination; and under the guidance of the fundamental rules of Harmony, that imagination which affords us the highest pleasure and amusement is certainly the best. That men do not agree in this as in the excellence of a Poet's, Painter's, or Sculptor's imagination, is from the variety of imagery in the mind of man, where there is no type in view, to keep it from rambling."
68. C. "Mortellari."
69. C. "Stillingfleet."
70. Ibid.
71. C. "Simplicity."
72. C. "Hiller."

73. PSMFI, p. 316. When Burney amplified his criticism of Paisiello's music years later, he retained the passage as quoted, but added the revealing continuation: "But since that time he has continued *improving* in his style, both in serious and comic operas..." [C. "Paesiello."] Part of this improvement, says Burney, consists of more invention creating less common passages in the vocal melody.
74. C. "Propriety."
75. Review of "Melody the Soul of Music," by Alexander Malleson, *Monthly Review.* XXVII (1798), p. 192.
76. GHM, ii, p. 272.
77. C. "Opera."
78. C. "Pathetic."
79. C. "Morellet." This enthusiasm for the pathetic was not limited to Burney; John Brown called the pathetic style "the highest species of song." When hearing such a song, he remarked, "the noblest faculties of the mind are gratified at once; we judge, we admire, we feel." John Brown, *Letters on the Italian Opera.* (London, 1791), pp. 43, 48.
80. C. "Appoggiatura."
81. C. "Expression." The method of achieving this expressive unity is delineated in Rousseau's article "Expression," which Burney translated for the *Cyclopaedia.*
82. C. "Expression."
83. *The Oxford English Dictionary* (Oxford, 1933).
84. C. "Expression."
85. C. "Effect."
86. C. "Chiarezza."
87. C. "Transparency."
88. Notebook (Osborn). See also C. "Contrast."
89. Review of "Melody the Soul of Music," p. 192.
90. GHM, i, p. 718.
91. Ibid., p. 722.
92. CB to Ebeling 30 Mar. 1772 (Hamburg).
93. C. "Counterpoint."
94. Burney was particularly opposed to the breaks of measure as practiced in French opera arias: "... most of the musicians in Europe, except those of France, ... will affirm, that the frequent change of time in the music of the serious French opera, relaxes the measure, and destroys all idea of the accent and energy by which every phrase in good melody is constantly marked. By two or three bars being in common time, and two or three in triple, as is generally the case in the operas of Lulli and Rameau, the hearer can retain no fixed or precise idea of either; the passges in one mutually destroying the effects of the other; for the traces are either lost, or so slightly impressed in the memory, that the work is always to begin anew. The chief superiority of modern melody over that of former times, is certainly due to the graceful arrangement of sounds, and the exact and continued manner with which they are enforced by the measure,

and the accentuation of the bars. The difficulty of distinguishing the airs from the recitatives in the old music, particularly the French, is owing to the frequent change of measure, and the want of accent in the bars and musical phrases." GHM, i, p. 98.

95. Thomas Busby, *Dictionary* (London, 1811), "Phrases Manquées."
96. GHM, ii, p. 618.
97. Busby, *Dictionary*, "Extraneous Modulation."
98. William Shield, *Introduction to Harmony* (London, 1790).
99. William S. Newman, *The Sonata in the Classic Era: The Second Volume of A History of the Sonata Idea* (Chapel Hill, 1963), p. 698.
100. GHM, ii, p. 384.
101. Ibid., p. 930.
102. C. "Expression."
103. Ibid.
104. C. "Melodia."
105. See C., *Plates for the Cyclopaedia,* plate V.
106. C. "Basse Fundamental."
107. GHM, ii, p. 955.
108. Ibid., p. 11.
109. Ibid.
110. Shield, *Introduction to Harmony,* p. 108. Shield's rules for free *capriccios* state that they must begin and end in the same key.
111. Ibid., p. 109.
112. C. "Modulation."
113. C. "Prelude."
114. C. "Taste."
115. Notebook (Osborn).
116. C. "Taste."
117. Ibid.
118. See Berg 198788B folder 5.
119. PSMFI, p. viii.
120. GHM, ii, pp. 902-3.
121. Alexander Gerard, *An Essay on Genius,* 3d ed. (London, 1780), pp. 421-22.
122. C. "Expression."
123. GHM, ii, p. 261.
124. CB to Mrs. Waddington, 12 July 1805 (Berg).
125. Notebook (Osborn).

126. GHM, i. p. 707.
127. Ibid., p. 378.
128. GHM, ii, p. 124
129. Ibid, p. 380
130. C. "Senaillée."
131. GHM, ii, p. 482.

Chapter 3

1. CB to Mason, GDB, i, pp. 148-49.
2. CB to H. Repton, Nov. 1788 (Osborn).
3. CB to J. Huttner, 15 Aug. 1807 (Osborn).
4. *Memoirs,* i, p. 219.
5. CB to Mason, GDB, i, pp. 148-49.
6. Arriving in France with his copy of the *Plan* in English, it became obvious to him that it would be expeditious to show his acquaintances his plan in their own language. Thus in Paris he had the *Plan* translated into French [MMM, p. 19] and later, for his associates in Italy, into Italian. He had a similar document rendered into German for his second excursion to the Continent in 1772. It is surprising that Burney relied on translators for both the French and Italian translations, considering his own skills in these languages were quite good.
7. MS. I, f. 62. At the point marked by an asterisk the text has been adapted from the preface to the *Italian Tour.*
8. The Italian copy represents only one version of Burney's prospectus. Burney wrote to Twining in April, 1773, that he was sending him "a rough sketch of my *Plan* such as I carried with me into Germany." This probably differed somewhat from that copied by Martini in Bologna, for the revelation that Burney "determined to allay his thirst for the science of music at the true source by undertaking a voyage to Italy, from whence the rest of Europe has obtained not only all of the most celebrated composers and performers, but also all of the ideas concerning what is elegant and of the finest taste in the art of music" would not bring out the most cordial of receptions from Burney's German hosts; a new version of the *Plan* would have been necessary.
9. CB to TT, 28 April 1773 (B.M.).
10. GHM, i, p. 16.
11. GHM, i, p. 18.
12. Burney's views of Tartini's theoretical work illuminates his feelings: "If, instead of wandering in the mazes of conjecture, and calculating, unscientifically, which every dry mathematician can discover, he had given us a well-digested practical treatise on composition, what a treasure it would have been to the musical world!" C. "Tartini."
13. Of Thomas Morley's *Plaine and Easie Introduction to Practicall Musicke,* Burney complained: "Few of the examples are elegant or worthy of imitation, now; and it appears as if the attentive examination of good modern compositions in score, would be of infinitely more service to a student than the perusal of all of the books on the subject of Music, that were written during the sixteenth and seventeenth centuries." GHM, i, p. 87.

14. TT to CB, 28 May 1773 (B.M.).
15. Frank Harrison, *Time, Place and Music. Source Materials and Studies in Ethnomusicology*, (Amsterdam, 1976), p. 161.
16. La Borde's *Essai sur la musique*. 4 vols. (Paris, 1780).
17. PSMFI, p. 34.
18. See, for example, John Brown, *A Dissertation on the Rise, Union and Power, the Progress, Separations and Corruptions of Poetry and Music. To which is Prefixed, the Cure of Saul* (London, 1763).
19. CB to TT, 28 April 1773 (B.M.).
20. GHM, i, p. 19.
21. Dwight Warren Allen, *Philosophies of Music History* (New York, 1962).
22. The catalogue of Burney's library must be reconstructed from several sources: the sale catalogue of his general collection; his collection of music and books on music; and the list of books on music acquired by the British Museum. *A Catalogue of the Miscellaneous Library of the Late Charles Burney*..., (London, 1814). *Catalogue of the Music Library of Charles Burney, Sold in London, 8 August 1814*, introduction by A. Hyatt King, Auction Catalogues of Music, No. 2 (Amsterdam, 1973), with addenda supplied in the review by the present author in *Notes* XXXI (1974), p. 45. The British Museum acquisitions are catalogued in Add. MS. 18191.
23. GHM, i, p. 13.
24. Ibid.
25. Though Burney calls Calvisius a "very learned theorist, and a good practical musician," he was apparently unaware of that author's historical work. (GHM, ii, p. 206).
26. C. "Cerone."
27. GHM, i, p. 475.
28. C. "Praetorius." He was familiar with several of Praetorius's compositions, but he was not favorably impressed.
29. GHM, ii, p. 465.
30. Ibid., p. 459.
31. C. "Kircher."
32. GHM, ii, p. 459. It is curious that Burney lists this work in the 1770 catalogue of his library; perhaps it was one of the many works he loaned to friends which was never returned.
33. C. "Bontempi."
34. GHM, i, p. 17.
35. C. "Bontempi."
36. C. "Bonnet."
37. See *Catalogue* of the auction sale.
38. C. "North."
39. C. "Walther."

40. GHM, ii, p. 948.
41. C. "Mattheson." It is significant that Burney criticized Mattheson's essays for their poor literary style. While he had made reference to the obscure language of earlier writers, this criticism of Mattheson strikes out at the lack of elegance of the author's productions.
42. C. "Marpurg." Burney describes this as the best work extant on the subject, with the possible exception of Padre Martini's *Saggio di contrappunto*. He also describes Marpurg's *Des critischen Musicus an der Spree* (1750) as that writer's "coup d' essai."
43. Ibid. Burney wrote to Callcott, "...Marpurg, though not a man of original genius, as a composer, was a good theorist, and wrote in an elegant and good style in his own language. I found much information in his works concerning the history and practice of music at Berlin during the best period of Frederic's [*sic*] reign, when he had assembled about him all the great men of every country whom he could tempt to enter into his service." Mar. 1797-8 (Osborn). See also CB to d'Holbach, 2 June 1772 (Osborn).
44. CB to Ebeling, Nov. 1771 (Hamburg).
45. C. "Martini."
46. CB to Ebeling, Nov. 1771 (Hamburg).
47. Brown's work is not discussed in any detail, but the four principal references to Brown in the *History* ridicule his theories and his qualifications as a musician. GHM, i, pp. 68, 144, 446, 462.
48. GHM, i, p. 444.
49. C. "Brown."
50. C. "Blainville."
51. C. "Rousseau."
52. GHM, i. p. 13.
53. GHM, ii, p. 99.
54. Ibid. See also CB to FB, 12 Oct. [1806] (Osborn).
55. See chap. 8, below.
56. GHM, i, p. 423.
57. C. "Eximeno."
58. PSMG, ii, p. 319.
59. C. "Gerbert."
60. La Borde's *Essai sur la musique* was also completed before 1789, and Burney made extensive use of it in his work (See below, chap. 5). His manuscript reflections on this work are brief and damning. "The same may be said of Laborde's Essai sur la Musique which is a confused compilation of the best inconsistent and contradictory thoughts of writers on Music, spoiled often by National prejudice, and the Abbé Rousseau's council..." (Osborn). See also Andrew Lumisden to CB, 10 July 1780 (Osborn).

Three works have not been discussed which Allen included in his bibliography. James Grassineau's *Musical Dictionary* (1740) is not mentioned in the *History,* nor does he himself receive an article in the *Cyclopaedia.* The article on Sebastian Brossard contains a brief reference to this work, in which Burney asserts that "Mr. Grassineau might without excessive humility have called his musical dictionary a translation (of Brossard's work)." The *Musical Dictionary* is included in the bibliography of works printed in England, and a copy was in Burney's library. *Essai d'une histoire de la musique* (1757) written by Dom. Phil. Jos. Cassaux (Allen #17) has never been published. The manuscript is presently located in the Bibliothèque National de Paris, but its location during Burney's several visits to Paris is unknown; he does not seem to have seen it nor to have been aware of its existence.

It is odd that M. Dard's *Nouveaux principes de musique* (1769) escaped Burney's notice, since it appeared only one year before his famous tour of France. Yet no mention of it appears in any of his critical writings, and no copy was contained in his library at the time of his death. It seems then that Burney may well have been unaware of it.

61. See the catalogue of Burney's library attached to Martini's copy of the *Plan*.

Chapter 4

1. The first surviving reference of a plan to publish a report of this trip is in a letter to David Garrick, 17 October 1770 from Naples.
2. Ernest Walker, *A History of Music in England*, 3rd. ed., revised and enlarged by J.A. Westrup (Oxford, 1952), p. 273. Walker describes Burney as possessing no "very exceptional qualities."
3. William S. Newman, *The Sonata in the Classic Era: The Second Volume of A History of the Sonata Idea* (Chapel Hill, 1963), p. 697.
4. CB to Mrs. Crewe, 8 Aug. 1773 (Berg).
5. The *Tour* was available on 3 May 1771, and all the copies were sold by 1773.
6. For a full explanation of the machinations behind the reviews of the *Tour*, see Lonsdale, pp. 105-10.
7. *Monthly Review*, XLV (1771), pp. 161-70, 337-44.
8. *Memoirs*, p. 105.
9. His only serious objection was to Burney's attack on the profession of reviewers. PSMFI, pp. 61-62.
10. *Memoirs*, i, p. 51.
11. Ibid., p. 53.
12. *Critical Review*, XXXI, pp. 421-32; XXXII, pp. 1-15.
13. Ibid.
14. Ibid., p. 15.
15. GHM, ii, p. 658.
16. CB to TT, 30 Aug. 1773 (B.M.). See also GHM, ii, pp. 993-94. This is an interesting but far from unique sample of the manner in which Burney extracted material from his correspondence for inclusion in his published work.
17. CB to Samuel Crisp, [31] May [1771] (Osborn).
18. Lonsdale, p. 61.
19. GHM, ii, p. 972, and Lonsdale, p. 61 and 71 n^2.

20. Only one reference to Burney's musical activities during his early Paris visits is extant. In it he writes to Fanny that he has "just come from the Comick Opera, which is here called the Comédie Italienne, where I have been extremely well Entertained." He was, however, exhausted from standing "the whole Time, which every Body in the Pit does..." Burney also saw Rousseau during his 1764 visit (Berg). See PSMFI, p. 39.
21. PSMFI, p. 13.
22. Oliver Strunk, *Source Readings in Music History: From Classical Antiquity through the Romantic Era,* (New York, 1950), p. 640. See also Denise Launay, ed., *La Querelle des Bouffons,* 3 vols., (Geneva, 1973).
23. CB to Gui [1 May 1774] (Leigh).
24. PSMFI, p. 36.
25. MMM, p. 222.
26. CB to Crisp, [31] May [1771] (Osborn).
27. CB to Diderot, Mar, 1771 (Osborn).
28. CB to d'Holbach, 23 May 1771 (Berg).
29. CB to Suard, 24 May 1771 (Berg).
30. CB to Rousseau, late May 1771 (Osborn).
31. CB to Diderot, Mar. 1771 (Osborn).
32. CB to Diderot, Mar. 1771 (Berg).
33. CB to Diderot, 27 May 1771 (Berg).
34. Diderot to CB, 18 Aug. 1771 (Leigh).
35. d'Holbach to CB, 15 Dec. 1771 (Osborn).
36. CB to Suard, 24 May 1771 (Berg).
37. *Journal encylopédie... Bouillon Imprimé du Journal* (1770), pp. 95-100; not available for this study.
38. The extracts are direct translations from the original, without additional notes or critical remarks. *Journal de musique,* IV (1777), pp. 19-53, and V (1777), pp. 19-54.
39. *Early Diary of Frances Burney, 1768-1778,* ed. Annie Raine Ellis, revised ed., 2 vols., 1907, pp. 226-27. See also CB to Ebeling, 15 July 1773 (Osborn). Unfortunately, neither Framery's letter nor Burney's response is extant. The French writers may have been only Framery, in which case Burney may only have received the single critique and not a number of criticisms, as the evidence from Fanny's diary suggests.
40. *Early Diary of Frances Burney.*
41. Book reviews were not a prominent feature of Italian periodicals in the eighteenth century, and as there was no exclusively musical periodical in Italy until the second decade of the nineteenth century, it is not surprising that there seem to have been no contemporary Italian reviews.

    Burney must surely have sent Padre Martini a copy of his *Tour,* but no mention is made of this book in Martini's extant correspondence. There are, however, indications of at least one gap in the surviving letters, and there may well be others. In addition, since most of the letters were hand-delivered by various travelers, some may never have reached the addressee.

See, for example, Martini to CB, 6 Oct. 1781 (Osborn); 24 June 1780 (Osborn); CB to Martini, 20 Oct. 1779 (Osborn). Fanny's early diaries and the dozens of letters from Italian singers and instrumentalists in the Burney Papers attest to the constant flow of the most illustrious Italian musicians in London to the Burney home.

42. Osborn.

43. MMM, pp. 86, 104, and 205. The comments in the *Errata* also lend credence to Scholes's observation that portions of Burney's description of the ancient paintings at Portici seem to have been lifted directly from J.J. de Lalande's *Voyage en Italie*. Several passages in Burney's original manuscript journal reveal that he was carrying a copy of Lalande's work with him on his trip, and may well have turned to it while traveling to supply details to his notes.

One of Burney's responses in the *Errata* is particularly interesting given our amusement at the behavior of eighteenth-century Italian operatic audiences. Baretti challenged his criticism of the lack of attention given to the performance by the audience, who often talked, ate, and even gambled during the performance. Burney responded,

> You asked why you should be attentive: let me in my turn ask you why you should go to a theatre to talk when you would be less disturbed at home...

44. CB to Thomas James Mathias, [1810?] (Osborn).

45. See, for example, *Italian Tour,* i, p. 63.

46. Ibid., p. 70.

47. Ibid., p. 150.

48. Lonsdale, pp. 98-99.

49. PSMFI, p. 7.

50. The rough copy was eventually acquired by the British Museum.

51. MMM, p. xviii.

52. London, 1969.

53. MMM, pp. 20, 64-65, 78-79, 127-28, 204.

54. Ibid., pp. 83, 85, 118, 204.

55. Ibid., p. 118.

56. See especially ibid., pp. 55-56, 140-41.

57. Ibid., p. 150.

58. Ibid., p. 225.

59. Diderot to CB, 18 Aug. 1771. (Leigh).

60. The most immediately noticeable difference is the location of paragraphs: in the first edition some of the paragraphs run to several pages in length; in the second edition, many new indentations have been added, and a number of the original footnotes have been assimilated into the text.

61. *Italian Tour,* p. 311.

62. PSMFI, pp. 26-27.

63. In correcting and expanding his work, he did not include any of the additions or corrections made by his German editors, nor did he make any references to their work.

64. The first complete French translation was that of Charles Brack, *De l'état présent de la musique en France et en Italie, dans les Pays Bas*, 3 vols., (Genoa, 1809-10). There is no complete version in Italian. The *Viaggio Musicale in Italia, 1770,* trans. Virginio Attenasio (Naples, 1921), is a translation from the French version, and, as the title suggests, the French portion of the journal is omitted.

65. *Carl Burney's der Musik Doctors Tagebuch einer musikalischen Reise durch Frankreich und Italien welche er unternommen hat um zu einer allgemeinen Geschichte der Musik Materialen zu sammeln. Aus dem Englischen übersetzt von C.D. Ebeling, Aufsehern der Handlungsakademie zu Hamburg* (Hamburg, 1772).

66. Ebeling to CB, 20 Aug. 1771 (Hamburg). The entire letter is printed in GDB, i, pp. 199-201.

67. Ebeling to CB, 27 July 1773 (Hamburg).

68. *Italian Tour*, p. 170. When Burney met Emanuel Bach in Hamburg in the middle of October the composer had already received a copy.

69. CB to James Gray, 25 June 1772 (Osborn).

70. "Ich habe ihrer nicht mehr machen mögen, damit man nicht galubte, ich wollte mich dem Verfasser oder den Lesern zum Lehrer aufdringen, da ich nur ihr Dollmetscher seyn soll." *Tagebuch*, i, pp. iv-v.

71. *Tagebuch*, i, pp. 29, 30, 31, 35, 54, 142, 156, 174, 237, 246, 250, and 259. Several of the notes in the Italian portion of the *Tour* merely refer the reader to a German account of the Italian cities. Ibid. 41, 53, 58, 69, 80, 83, 99, 141, 172, 193, 218, 248, 254, 291, and 295. The reader is advised to see Volkmann's *Nachrichten von Italie*.

72. *Tagebuch*, i, p. 203.

73. Burney's own note (PSMFI, p. 88) that the Germans call the organist Tarquinio Merula "Claudius Merulus" of Antwerp, for example, elicits only a parenthetical note from the translator that "Walter in the musical lexicon calls him Merula and gives Corregio as his place of birth." *Tagebuch*, ii, p. 59.

74. PSMFI, p. 195; *Tagebuch*, i, p. 139. PSMFI, pp. 120-23; *Tagebuch*, i, p. 83. PSMFI, p. 223; *Tagebuch*, i, p. 160. An important correction occurs in PSMFI, p. 269, *Tagebuch*, i, p. 195, where Burney's Signor Mosi is identified as Signor Masi. This identification has been overlooked by Scholes, (*Tours*, i, p. 204). Scholes repeats Burney's error, then solves the problem of identification by failing to index the name under any spelling. Poole in MMM renders the name as Mori, providing no further identification.

75. J.J.L. de la Lande, *Voyage en Italie*, 9 vols. (1796).

76. "Herr Burney scheint in diesen Anmerkungen gegen Herrn de la Lande fast den Engländer und der Tonkünstler zu sehr zu verrathen." *Tagebuch*, i, p. 255.

77. PSMFI, p. 349. Bode argued for the inclusion of dance, but he is not defending LaLande, but advancing the art as practiced by Noverre and Angiolini: "Er kann einem Schauspiele so viele Mannigfaltigkeit verschaffen, und wenn er in gehörigem Verhältnisse mit den übrigen Theilen desselben steht, diese so sehr heben, dass die Wirkung des Tanzes notwendig dabei ungemein gewinnen muss." *Tagebuch*, i, p. 256.

78. The translator is particularly insistent on the necessity of good acting in opera production. He complains about the breaking of the action by singers during their arias, and asserts that this break is necessitated only by the singer's vanity. He argues that, especially in the *opere serie*, the action should never be broken, and the singer should employ suitable gesture during even

the longest arias. According to the translator, in comic opera a break in the dramatic flow is less execrable, for

> "Im Komischen ist es ein anders, denn da ists erlaubt von er natürlichen Aktion zur Karrikatur überzugehen, und da ist auch die Musik nicht so mit Zierrathen überladen, und namentlich in der *Serva Padrona* am wenigsten." *Tagebuch,* i, p. 257.

The translator's use of the word *Schauspiel* several times in his note is misleading, for Burney never uses the two terms of theatre and opera interchangeably; he is explicit throughout his writings in stating that good spoken drama and good opera are very different in their construction and presentation. See Thomas Baumann, "Music and Drama in Germany: A Travelling Company and Its Repertory, 1767-1781," Ph.D. dissertation, University of California, Berkeley, 1977.

79. PSMFI, p. 376.
80. *Tagebuch,* i, p. 276.
81. PSMFI, p. 388.
82. *Tagebuch,* i, pp. 285-86. In the final extensive footnote to the journal, the translator expresses his complete confusion over Burney's note on the *Beat* (PSMFI, p. 388). He seems justified in his attack, since he claims that he was unable to find a German or English musician who could explain what Burney meant by this passage, and his meaning remains somewhat obscure today (see *Italian Tour,* p. 299). It is certain, however, that Burney was not confusing the *Tremulante* with the swell, as the German editor conjectures.
83. *Tagebuch,* i, p. 203. Ebeling notified Burney of his intention in his letter of 7 June 1772.
84. Ibid., i, p. vi. Burney's copy of the German translation, now housed in the British Museum, does not bear any notes by the author.
85. *Jenaische Zeitungen von gelehrten Sachen* (1772), p. 312. *Neue Bibliothek der schönen Wissenschaften und der freyen Künste* XIII (1772), p. 174. This notice says that the translation is being arranged by Bode, and does not mention Ebeling at all.
86. *Jenaische Zeitungen von Gelehrten Sachen* (27 Dec. 1773), pp. 893-95.
87. *"Vaghezza, chiarezza, e buona modulazione,"* which Burney renders as "Beauty, clearness and good modulation," and which Ebeling translates as *"Schönheit, Deutlichkeit, und gute Melodie."*
88. "Galuppis Definition einer guten Musik empfiehlt der Rec. allen Componisten, die so gern mit den Fittichen des Windes, oder dem Geklapper einer Klapperschlange den Ohren ihrer Zuhörer zu schmeicheln suchen, und glauben, jede Composition seh[r] originell, die abgeschmakt genug ist, um nichts singbares zu enthalten." *Jenaische Zeitungen* (27 Dec. 1773), p. 895.
89. "Mehr auszuziehn will uns der Raum nicht erlauben, wir hoffen aber, gegenwärtige Probe von dem Inhalt dieser schätzbaren Schrift, die uns ein ausserordentliches Verlangen nach Hn. B. Geschichte der Tonkunst macht soll hinreichend seyn, um jedem Kenner und Freund der Musik dieselbe zu empfehlen, und dass sie dieselben nicht allein lesen, sondern studiren werden." Ibid.
90. PSMFI, p. 317.
91. CB to Ebeling, Nov. 1771 (Hamburg). Abel had been in England since 1759, and Burney was very familiar with his work. "His taste is the most exquisite and refined, and his judgment and learning the most perfect that I have ever met united in one performer." He ranks C.P.E. Bach

as "the greatest writer for the Harpsichord now alive," and Hasse as the "best of the composers of opera songs, for grace, invention, and propriety."

92. CB to d'Holbach, 2 June 1772 (Osborn).

93. See Lonsdale, pp. 113, 114; and CB to d'Holbach, 2 June 1772 (Osborn); CB to Count Firman, 22 June 1772 (Osborn); CB to Sir James Gray, 25 June 1772 (Osborn); Gray to CB, 28 June 1772 (Osborn); Harris to CB, 30 June 1772 (Osborn); and Baretti to CB, 24 June 1772 (Osborn).

94. See Lonsdale, pp. 120-24. *Monthly Review* XLVIII (1773), pp. 34-44, 81-92, 321-35. Reviews also appeared in the *Annual Register* XVI (1773), pp. 166-88, 274-78; *London Magazine* XL (1773), p. 351; and *Gentlemen's Magazine* LXIII (1777), pp. 336-38.

95. *Gentlemen's Magazine* LXIII (1773), pp. 336-37. See also *London Magazine* XL (1773), p. 35; and *Annual Register* XVI (1773), pp. 166-88.

96. *Journal des scavans* (Sept. 1773), p. 626, and *Bibliothèque des sciences et des beaux arts* MDCCLXXIII (1773), pp. 208-9.

97. "Si nous ne pouvons décider du degré de perfection, dans lequel l'Auteur de ce Voyage posséde l'Art sur lequel il écrit, nous osons cependant assurer qu'on le trouvera un homme instruit dans les Sciences et les Beaux Arts en général, un Amateur distingué par le goût et par le zèle de l'Art qu'il a étudié, un Ecrivain agréable, libre, impartial, qui rend justice aux talents et aux vertus sans égard aux lieux, aux circonstances de leur naissance, et à tout ce qui n'est qu'accessoire." *Journal des beaux arts,* (Juillet, Août, Septembre 1773), p. 209.

98. *Neue Bibliothek der schönen Wissenschaften und der freyen Künste* XV (1773), p. 361.

99. CB to Ebeling, 20 June 1773 (Hamburg).

100. Ebeling to CB, 10 June 1773 (Hamburg).

101. A modern edition was published in Leipzig in 1968 by Phillip Reclam, Jr., but it follows Bode's text, though modifying spelling and punctuation.

102. PSMG, 1st ed., i, p. 24.

103. *Tagebuch,* iii, p. 271.

104. De Visme to CB, 30 Nov. 1772 (Osborn). Printed with notes, C.B. Oldman, "Charles Burney and Louis De Visme," *The Music Review* XXVII (1966), pp. 93-97.

105. *The Music Review* XXVII (1966), p. 96; *German Tour,* ii. 325.

106. J. Mumssen to CB, 16 Oct. 1772 (Osborn); cf. PSMG, ii, pp. 332-37. Burney also failed to acknowledge that his very detailed account of the Singschule of Dresden, which he says in the *Tour* was the result of investigation carried on during his residence in Dresden, was taken from information supplied in a letter by John Osborn, the British Envoy to Dresden. J. Osborn to CB, 20 Jan. 1773 (Osborn); c.f. PSMG, ii, 63-72.

107. See PSMG, ii, pp. 109-10.

108. Ibid., p. 250; see also p. 109.

109. CB to Ebeling, 15 July 1773 (Osborn). While preparing the translation, Ebeling sought permission to delete "political reasonings, which we believe to be not true enough, or to [*sic*] much Knewn in Germany, or thirdly those which we could not print without precluding your book the intrance [*sic*] in the Prussian or Wurtemberg Country."

110. CB to Ebeling, 15 July 1773 (Osborn).

322 Notes for Chapter 4

111. "Mir ist sein Urtheil oft partheiisch und oft als zu schnell niedergeschrieben vorgekommen; und ob ich gleich kein Musiker bin, und nach meiner besten Überzeugung nicht den geringsten Willen habe, partheiisch zu sein, so mag ich dennoch vielleicht manchen Lesern in den wenigen Noten so scheined. Diese bitte ich, zu merken, dass ich ein herzlicher Liebhaber der Musik und ein Deutscher bin, und dass ein gewisser Grad von Parteilichkeit fürs Vaterland—wenigstens verzeihlich ist." *Vorrede der Übersetzer*, n.p.

112. "Ist es ein Fehler, dass unsere Kritiker uns so viele Fehler Eurer guten Autoren zeigten, sobald sie über Deutschland schrieben? Männer wurden in Städte verwandelt und umgekehrt. Sogar Eure ausgezeichneten Autoren Home, Robertson, Harte etc. begehen enorme Irrtümer, wen sie über Deutschland schreiben. Wieviele Geschichten, Urteile und Bemerkungen sind offenbar falsch... Lasst irgend einen Engländer (den wir jetzt kennen) über Deutschland schreiben, und ich will mich hängen lassen, wenn ich nicht hundert Fehler finde." see also Ebeling to CB, 27 July 1773 (Hamburg).

113. *Tagebuch*, ii, p. 10. The most extensive deletions are in the 2d edition, I: 64-67; 75 footnote; 99-106 (five lengthy deletions); 111-13; 119-20; 160 footnote; 248; 285 footnote; 338-40. II: 1-3; 6-7; 17-23; 26-27; 37-38; 39-44; 52-54; 58-61; 64-65; 69; 79-80 footnote; 84-86; 101 footnote; 268-69; 333-36.

114. PSMG, i, p. 113; *Tagebuch*, ii, p. 83.

115. PSMG, ii, p. 39; *Tagebuch*, ii, p. 21.

116. PSMG, i, pp. 100, 106.

117. See GHM, ii, p. 951.

118. Ebeling to CB, 20 June 1773 (Hamburg).

119. *Tagebuch*, i, p. 49; ii, p. 271; notes, i, 23.

120. Ibid., iii, p. 49.

121. Ibid., ii, notes to 53.

122. Ibid., iii, pp. 41, 48 and 262.

123. PSMG, ii, p. 107; *Tagebuch*, iii, p. 72.

124. *Tagebuch*, iii, p. 91.

125. "Diese waren keine andre, als der durch seine medizinische Schriften allgemain bekannte herr Docter Unzer, seine ebenfalls durch schriften bekannte Ehegattin, und ihr Bruder, Herr Ziegler. Aber dergleichen lässt sich von einem Reisenden, der nur Musik in der Seele und zum Zweck hat, vergessen, ohne dass er deshalb Vorwürfe verdiene." Ibid., iii, p. 211.

126. Ibid., pp. 248, 255 n^2.

127. PSMG, ii, pp. 330-31; *Tagebuch*, iii, p. 268.

128. PSMG, i, p. 85; *Tagebuch*, ii, p. 66.

129. *Tagebuch*, ii, note to 66.

130. Ibid., iii, notes to 168.

131. PSMG, ii, p. 55.

132. *Tagebuch*, iii, notes to 2 n^2.

133. "Hat der Verfasser wirklich von Grauns deutschen Opern welche gesehen? Das wäre doch wohl notwendig; denn alle diese machte er, ehe er in italien gewesen war, Und sie haben soviel

Melodie, Ausdruck und Neuheit, als man in manchen Arien seiner neuern nicht finden würde." *Tagebuch,* iii, notes to 169.

134. *Tagebuch,* iii, notes to 171.

135. "Wenn doch ein Burney der Zweite im Jahr 1783 reisete, wie würden alsdann die Helden Burney's des Ersten, z.B. Haydn u.s.w. mitgenommen werden!" *Tagebuch,* iii, notes to 172.

136. Ibid., ii, notes to 174, 176.

137. PSMG, i, p. 37.

138. Ebeling to CB, 20 June 1773 (Hamburg).

139. "Über die Einfalt derer, welche die alte Musik darum verachten, weil sie alt ist." *Tagebuch,* ii, notes to 33.

140. Ibid., iii, p. 72.

141. Ibid., iii, p. 218.

142. Ibid., iii, notes to 151.

143. "Da steht denn endlich unser Debet und Credit; und wir armen Deutschen wüssten nunmehr, wie unser Sachen stünden, wofern wir nur die Hälfte, und vermutlich die überwiegende Hälfte unsrer zwo Cardinaltugenden, Geduld, üben, und nicht pedantischer Weise unsern unbeeidigten Buchhalter fragen wollen, ob er auch alles richtig aufgezählt habe.—Im Ernste, wenn man sich wieder besinnt, was man gelesen hat, und wieviel Gutes Herr Burney von der Originalität unsrer deutschen Tonmeister, von Hasse, Gluck, Bachs, Vanhall, Hofmann, Schwanberger, Benda, Müthel, Händel und andere mehr gesagt hat: so sollte man auf den Gedanken kommen, dass dieses Endurteil weniger aus einer kaltblütigen Überlegung der Gründe für und gegen eine ganze Nation, als vielmehr aus der mit Anmut getändelten, schönen Symmetrie der vier Worte Patience, Profundity, Prolixity und Pedantry, die alle so artig mit einem P. anfangen, entsprungen sei. Sollte diese Anmerkung jemandem ein harter Verwourf scheinen, den bitte ich, zu bedenken, dass sie bei einer Gelegenheit gemacht wird, da einer ganzen Nation, über eine Kunst, in der sie allen andern Nationen die achtungswürdigsten Meister geliefert hat, mit vier Worten und eben so cavallièrement ihr Urteil gesprochen wird, als ob ein junger Herr von seinem Schneider urteilte, der ihm ein Kleid nicht zu Danke gemacht hätte. Übrigens verkenne ich das viele Gute des Herrn Burney's keinesweges, besonders schätze ich sein lebhaft fühlendes Herz, das ihn selten anders, als bei Nationalvorurteilen, und wenn ihn die bösen Wege in Üble Laune gesetzt haben, zu verlassen pflege, recht sehr hoch!" *Tagebuch,* iii, pp. 279-80.

144. Bode overlooks Burney's final sentence in the journal, which notes, "they have alone the power to render even labour pleasing." PSMG, ii, p. 344.

145. CB to Fountaine, 3 Nov. 1773 (Berg).

146. Johann Friedrich Rechardt, *Brief eines aufmerksamen Reisenden die Musik betreffend,* 2 vols. (Frankfurt, 1774-76).

147. PSMG, i, pp. 64-81. See also GDB, i, pp. 251-53. The review in the *Allgemeinen deutschen Bibliothek,* which Scholes was unable to find, is contained in the *Anhang zu dem dreyzehnten bis vier und zwanzigsten Bande,* pp. 490-93. As Reichardt suggests, it is primarily concerned with correcting "errors."

148. Johann Nicolaus Forkel *Musikalisch-kritische Bibliothek* (Gotha, 1778), pp. 117-22.

149. "Kann jemand mehr dilettantische Ideen über das innerste Wesen der Kunst haben als unser Musikhistoriker, der schliesslich und endlich ein Doktor der Musik ist? Ist nicht ein einziges

dieser Beispiele genügend, um all die anderen Urteile des Autors über Dinge der Musik verdächtig werden zu lassen?" Ibid., p. 20.

150. " 'Was für eine Art von allgemeiner Geschichte der Musik,' fragt er, 'glauben unsere Leser erwarten zu können von einem Manne, der ein solches Urteil über musikalische Dinge fällt?' " Ibid., p. 20.

151. Osborn.

152. PSMG, ii, pp. 24-25.

153. Osborn.

154. PSMG, i, p. 75.

155. Ibid., i, p. 198.

156. Ibid., ii, p. 70.

157. Ebeling to CB, 20 June 1773 (Hamburg).

158. PSMG, 1st ed., p. 106; 2d ed., p. 107.

159. Ibid., 1st ed., ii, p. 91; 2d ed., ii, p. 92.

160. PSMG, i, p. 75.

161. Ibid., 1st ed., ii, p. 251; 2d ed., ii, p. 252.

162. One such footnote announces the return of Teuberinn (an opera singer) to the stage, revising a statement in the first edition which states that the continued exercise of her profession would be fatal to her because of bad health. PSMG, i, 323.

163. Ibid., ii, p. 273.

164. Ibid., ii, p. 319.

165. Other additions and alterations occur in PSMG i, p. 65, on the German language; i, p. 149 on Catholic schools; i, p. 181, a long citation from Montaigne; ii, p. 209, marriage of Madame Mara; ii, p. 329, note on the origin of the term *rosalia*.

166. See GHM, ii, p. 963.

167. Edward R. Reilly, *Quantz and his Versuch* (Philadelphia, 1971), p. 36. Burney himself noted a similar idea in his rough journal: "But I travel not only too fast to write but even to make *general* reflexions. Indeed they can never be made with fairness by persons who like meer birds of passage only fly over a kingdom without stopping to consider its constituent parts." MMM, p. 2.

168. GHM, ii, p. 963.

169. Frances Burney, *Diary and Letters of Madame d'Arblay,* ed. Austin Dobson, 6 vols. (London, 1904-5), iii, p. 73.

170. CB to FB, 2 Oct. 1786 (Osborn).

171. Newman, *The Sonata in the Classic Era,* p. 698.

172. CB to Ebeling, Nov. 1771 (Hamburg).

173. Notebook (Osborn).

Chapter 5

1. GHM, i, p. 16.
2. Ibid.
3. Ibid.
4. See Herbert M. Schueller, "The Quarrel of the Ancients and the Moderns," *Music and Letters* XLI (1960), pp. 113-30.
5. Lonsdale, pp. 172-88.
6. CB to TT, 30 Aug. 1773 (B.M.).
7. CB to TT, 28 Apr. 1773 (B.M.).
8. GHM, i, p. 17.
9. Ibid.
10. Ibid.
11. Notebook (Osborn).
12. GHM, i, p. 65, n^e.
13. Ibid., p. 59.
14. Ibid., p. 39.
15. Ibid., p. 82.
16. Ibid., p. 86; see also p. 98.
17. Ibid., p. 106. Of course, he can afford to declare his impartiality, secure in the knowledge that such facts do not exist.
18. Ibid., p. 87.
19. Ibid., p. 102-3.
20. Ibid., pp. 144-47.
21. Ibid., p. 145.
22. Osborn.
23. GHM, pp. 154-55.
24. Ibid., p. 149.
25. Ibid., p. 160.
26. PSMFI, p. 34. This passage is from his *Italian Tour*, and his view is manifestly the same in the *History*.
27. GHM, i, p. 387.
28. Ibid., p. 164.
29. See Lonsdale, pp. 160-61; 81. See also Arthur A. Moorefield, "James Bruce: Ethnomusicologist or Abyssinian Lyre?" *Journal of the American Musicological Society* XXVIII (1975), pp. 493-514. Moorefield substantiates the value of Bruce's information. Burney was also vindicated in his own day: "The French and English *scavans* gave their

general testimony to the truth of what Bruce has written about the Temple of Thebes..." CB to Mrs. Crewe, 8 Sept. 1800 (Berg).

30. GHM, i, p. 183.
31. Ibid., p. 184.
32. Ibid., p. 185.
33. Ibid., p. 191.
34. CB to Samuel Crisp, 31 May 1771 (Osborn).
35. For example, the meaning of "selah." GHM, i, p. 204.
36. Ibid., pp. 194-95.
37. Ibid., p. 201. Throughout this chapter, perhaps because of the "sacred" nature of the topic, Burney stays remarkably within the bounds of his subject. With the exception of a brief remark on the *improvisatore* of Italy, he does not draw in allusions to matters of contemporary music as he had done so successfully in the earlier chapters. GHM, i, p. 195 and n[e].
38. See section X of the "Dissertation," GHM, i, pp. 149-63.
39. GHM, i, p. 196.
40. Ibid.
41. C. "Medicina Musica."
42. Ibid.
43. C. "Farinelli."
44. CB to FB, 13 Dec. 1788 (Osborn).
45. GHM, i, p. 212.
46. Ibid., p. 214. The examples are taken from the works of Martini and Kircher.
47. Ibid., p. 215.
48. See Lonsdale, pp. 164-68.
49. CB to Samuel Crisp, 12 Mar. 1775 (Osborn). Not surprisingly, he finds opportunities for entertaining asides. In his discussion of the hymns of Bacchus, for example, he concludes: "...Our *Catches,* by the ingenuity of the musical composer, are perhaps fraught with more pleasantry, and are productive of more genuine mirth, than the Bacchanalian hymns of any other people of the globe." GHM, i, p. 246.
50. GHM, i, p. 255.
51. Ibid.
52. Ibid., p. 256.
53. Lonsdale, p. 166.
54. GHM, i, p. 283.
55. Herbert M. Schueller, "Correspondence Between Music and the Sister Arts According to Eighteenth-Century Aesthetic Theory," *Journal of Aesthetics* XIII (1953), pp. 334-59.
56. GHM, i, p. 279.

57. Ibid., p. 287.
58. Ibid., p. 303.
59. See Schueller, "Correspondence," pp. 334-59.
60. Ibid., p. 350.
61. Herbert N. Schueller, "Literature and Music as Sister Arts: An Aspect of Aesthetic Theory in Eighteenth-Century Britain," *Philological Quarterly* XXVI (1947), p. 199.
62. GHM, i, p. 303.
63. Ibid., p. 338.
64. Ibid., p. 104.
65. Ibid., p. 366.
66. See Lonsdale, pp. 150-55; p. 157; and Jamie Croy Kassler, "Burney's Sketch of a Plan for a Public Music-School," *Musical Quarterly* LVIII (1972), pp. 210-34; Scholes GDB, i, pp. 261-63.
67. John Bicknell, *Musical Travels through England. By Joel Collier, Organist*, 4th ed. (London, 1776; 1st ed. 1774), pp. i-iii.
68. Ibid., p. iv.
69. GHM, i, pp. 374-75. Earlier in his *History* he had occasion to remark that the Spartans of Greece, among the most militant of men, nevertheless continued to allow music, though it was not cultivated among them.

> Indeed, this is the case with respect to *Singers* in England; we love good singing, but will not be at the trouble or expence of establishing a school where our natives might be taught; which a little resembles the conduct of those men of pleasure, who not having the time or patience to *make love,* seek it where it can be purchased *ready made.*

Ibid., p. 309. n^q.
70. Lonsdale, pp. 155-56.
71. GHM, i, p. 320.
72. CB to Samuel Wesley, 28-30 Nov. 1799 (Osborn). See also CB to Arthur Young, 21 Sept. 1799 (B.M. Add. MS. 35127 f. 26).
73. GHM, i, p. 283.
74. Ibid., p. 307.
75. Ibid., 382.
76. Lonsdale, p. 239.
77. 25 [Sept. 1778], JRL Eng. MS. 543.6, quoted in Lonsdale, p. 246.
78. GHM, i, p. 411.
79. Ibid., p. 423.
80. Ibid., pp. 423-24.
81. Ibid., p. 419.

82. Ibid., p. 417.
83. Ibid., pp. 425 and 447.
84. Ibid., p. 425.
85. Ibid., pp. 423-47.
86. Ibid., pp. 437-38.
87. Ibid., p. 435.
88. Ibid., p. 443.
89. Ibid., pp. 447-56.
90. Ibid., p. 449.
91. Ibid., p. 457.
92. Ibid., pp. 466-67.
93. Ibid., p. 474.
94. Ibid., p. 479.
95. Ibid., p. 463. Despite his seemingly ludicrous arrangements of this kind, Burney was not indifferent to the musical content of the early samples of counterpoint. Examining a Welsh manuscript, dated 1100, Burney says "... whether the tune and their notation are coeval with the words, cannot early be proved; nor is the counterpoint, though far from correct or elegant, of so rude a kind as to fortify such an opinion." [Ibid., p. 484.] Of an example of descant taken from the writings of Franco of Cologne, Burney notes that though it may "neither please nor instruct the modern Contrapuntist, yet whoever compares it with the compositions of Hubald [sic], Odo and Guido, must regard it with wonder." Ibid., p. 515.
96. GHM, i, p. 490.
97. GHM, i, p. 506.
98. Ibid., p. 522.
99. Ibid., p. 526.
100. See, for example, GHM, i, pp. 532-34.
101. GHM, i, p. 532.
102. Ibid., p. 538.
103. Ibid., p. 540.
104. Ibid., p. 541.
105. Sir John Hawkins, *A General History of the Science and Practice of Music,* 2 vols. (New York, 1963), i, p. 218. Even in the most trivial of circumstances, Burney purposefully avoids mentioning Hawkins by name. When Burney records the mention of the *Speculum Musicae* in the writings of Mersenne, Du Cange, and Rousseau, he omits Hawkins, who also mentions the manuscript.
106. Hawkins, *History,* i, p. 217.
107. GHM, i, p. 550.
108. Ibid., p. 552.

Notes for Chapter 5   329

109. Ibid., p. 557.
110. TT to CB, 4 Nov. 1780 (B.M.).
111. Ibid.
112. Ibid., (italics added).
113. Lonsdale, p. 238.
114. Ibid.
115. Mason to CB.
116. GHM, i, p. 561.
117. Ibid., p. 567.
118. Ibid., pp. 571, 572-73, 576-77.
119. Ibid., p. 611; see also pp. 613-14.
120. Ibid., pp. 586-87.
121. Ibid., p. 574.
122. Ibid. See J.B. Beck, *La Melodie dei trouvadori* (Milan, 1939), pp. 44, 59-60. The copy in the Vatican is only one of several different melodies to this text.
123. These were common, even in historical anthologies, such as Crotch's *Specimens* for his musical lectures.
124. GHM, i, p. 590.
125. Ibid., p. 164.
126. Ibid., p. 616. He did not overlook the opportunity for a general criticism of the work: "Indeed, it was natural to expect assistance in this particular from the author of *Essai sur la Musique Ancienne et Modern;* but though he has inserted a dry and petulant critique, by a friend, upon the narrative which the Count de Caylus and the Abbe le Beuf have given of this old French poet-musician, no specimens either of his melodies or Counterpoint are inserted in that voluminous work; which seems so particularly intended to blazon the talents of French composers, that not a single specimen of music in parts by those of any other country has admission, except the celebrated canon of *Non nobis Domine* by our William Bird; which, by being inserted among French canons, without the author's name, may perhaps pass in the crowd for the production of a native of France."
127. Ibid., p. 617.
128. Ibid., p. 585. "It is wished, however, that some consummate judge of music and antiquity, of undisputable authority would kindly inform us, once and for all, what were so highly esteemed and so diligently cultivated."
129. Ibid., p. 609.
130. Ibid., p. 617.
131. Ibid., p. 621.
132. Ibid., p. 622.
133. Ibid., p. 631.
134. Ibid., p. 640.

135. Ibid., p. 642.
136. Ibid., p. 648.
137. Ibid., p. 650.
138. Ibid., p. 667.
139. Ibid.
140. *GHM*, i. 666.
141. Ibid., pp. 673-74; Hawkins, *History*, i, p. 254.
142. Lonsdale, p. 248, and CB to Oxford Cantab [1781]; CB to TT, 10 Nov. 1783 (B.M.), and TT to CB, 19 Dec. 1778 (B.M.).
143. GHM, i, p. 675.
144. Ibid., p. 701.
145. Ibid., p. 702.
146. Ibid., p. 695.
147. Ibid., p. 703.
148. Ibid., p. 705. The results of some of his labors survive in the form of his "Extracts" preserved in eleven volumes in the British Museum. A manuscript preface to the first volume relates his "Creed of Criticism:"

> The language in which Musical ideas are written, like every other Language, becomes obsolete and unintelligible in the process of Time. But though Melody soon becomes uncouth, old fashioned, and difficult to express, or execute; yet the Harmony and Conjecture of the Parts will never be lost if collected under one point of view, in a *Score;* a task which for want of Bars, our forefathers could with difficulty perform and how they were enabled to construct compositions in so many different parts, or of so complicated a kind as that in which many of them were written, without placing them under each other and marking the several *Tacts,* Times or Measures, is a problem of no easy solution to Modern Musicians. In all my researches after old Music I never met with a Score of any antiquity. At Rome indeed I purchased a manuscript in 1770, which was called the *Study di Palestrina* and consisted of a great number of +Chants+ in 4, 5 and 6 parts, many of them in his own hand written over each other irregularly Barred. This is the most ancient Music I ever saw, in Partition or Partitura. B.M. Add. MS. 11581.

149. GHM, i, p. 705.
150. Ibid., pp. 708-9. The plan is remarkable in its anticipation of modern music library procedures. It is obviously the effort of a man who has spent many hours rummaging through disorganized collections of music and books in the major libraries of Europe. His own extensive library may have been catalogued according to the plan published here; his auction sale catalogue lists a now-lost manuscript, *Dr. Burney's Folio Catalogue of his Music, on a superior plan.* His criteria for music librarians blend the skills of the custodian and the musician, requiring that one should be "a good Practical Musician, as well as theorist and scholar." It would undoubtedly gratify him to know how fully his scheme for a "National British Library of Music" has been realized, and what an important part his own library plays in its collection.
151. Ibid., pp. 714-16.

Notes for Chapter 6   331

152. Ibid., pp. 720-21.

Chapter 6

1. GHM, ii, p. 111.
2. TT to CB, *Country Clergyman*, p. 105.
3. GHM, ii, pp. 738-39.
4. Ibid., i, 731.
5. Ibid., i, p. 735.
6. Notebook (Osborn).
7. TT to CB, 8 Dec. 1781 (Osborn).
8. GHM, i, p. 750.
9. Ibid.
10. Ibid., p. 748-49.
11. *Country Clergyman*, p. 109.
12. GHM, i, p. 751.
13. Ibid., pp. 764-65.
14. Ibid., p. 762.
15. Ibid. One such case was a $^5_{3}^{4}$ chord in an example from Isaac, which "seems uncouth and unwarrantable to the Eye, yet it will not offend the Ear in this place."
16. Ibid.
17. Ibid., p. 745.
18. Ibid., p. 742.
19. Ibid., p. 738.
20. Ibid., p. 743.
21. B.M. Add. MS. 11589 f. 29, 30, 34, and 39. On Burney's application of ficta and other editorial practices, see Don Harran, "Burney and Ambros as Editors of Josquin's Music," in *Josquin des Prez: Proceedings of the International Josquin Festival-Conference*, ed. Edward Lowinsky. (New York, 1971), pp. 158-75.
22. GHM, i, pp. 739-44.
23. Ibid., p. 746.
24. Ibid., p. 752.
25. Ibid., p. 763.
26. Ibid., p. 738.
27. Ibid., p. 763.
28. Ibid., p. 766.
29. Ibid., p. 769.

30. "I can discover no variety of measure or subject; nor is the want of melody compensated by the richness of harmony, ingenuity of contrivance or learning of modulation." GHM, i, p. 770.
31. Ibid., p. 750.
32. Ibid., p. 759.
33. Ibid., p. 785.
34. Ibid., p. 786.
35. Ibid., p. 795.
36. Ibid., p. 785.
37. Thomas Morley, *A Plaine and Easie Introduction to Practicall Musicke* (London, 1597), p. 151. Sir John Hawkins, *A General History of the Science and Practice of Music,* 2 vols. (New York, 1963), i, p. 353.
38. Compare, for example, Hawkins on John Traverner, *History,* i, pp. 354-55, and GHM, i, pp. 786-90.
39. GHM, i, p. 794.
40. Ibid., pp. 795-96.
41. Ibid., p. 807.
42. Ibid., p. 808.
43. Ibid., pp. 362-63. Hawkins's work is obviously before him as he writes. Hawkins expressed surprise that Morley had omitted King Henry VIII from his list of musicians. There was, according to Hawkins, existing evidence of this monarch's understanding and skill in the art of music in his motet "Quam pulchra es," which Hawkins prints in its entirety. Burney in the first paragraph of his volume remarks that this composition is doubtless authentic, "as it is not too masterly, clear or unembarrassed for the production of a Royal Dilettanti." [Ibid., ii, p. 13.] Once again Hawkins's taste is directly challenged, with an assurance that almost forbids dissension.
44. GHM, ii, p. 36.
45. Ibid., p. 41.
46. Claude le Jeune he calls a master of harmony; GHM, ii, p. 47.
47. GHM, ii, p. 57.
48. William Mason, *Essays, Historical and Critical, on English Church Music* (London, 1782; 2d ed. 1795).
49. CB to Mrs. Stephen Allen, Apr. 1764 (Osborn).

> I will own to you however that tho I may have defended Psalmody I have had my Ears too much *Debauched* by refined modulations and elegant Execution, to relish those simple strains suited to Psalmody as to have much devotional fervor raised in me by either hearing or mentally joining in them; and if this be the case with me, I can easily conceive that you, so much more habituated to all the delicacy as well as practice in the Art must have more of what I have called this *debauchery* about you. But is that species of Music, certainly pleases and even piously affects Millions, to be laid aside merely because consummate judges of the Art cannot (as they certainly cannot) be affected by it? I think

certainly not, and therefore when treating on the subject contented myself with giving a few hints, which might tend to meliorate a Practise, which I am confident, while Protestantism remains, *ought* never to be set aside, because it never can be so without giving offence to an infinite majority of the best disposed Christians—

William Mason to CB, 28 June 1795 (Osborn). See also CB to FB, 9 June 1795 (Berg); CB to FB, 10 June 1794 (B.M.); CB to Mason, May 1778 (Osborn); CB to Mason, 8 June 1795 (Berg); Mason to CB, 27 May 1788 (Osborn); and Mason to CB 23 May 1795 (Osborn).

50. CB to Mason, 8 June 1795 (Berg). See also C. "Lawes" and "Mason."
51. *Monthly Review* XX (1796), p. 404.
52. Ibid., p. 405.
53. William Boyce *Cathedral Music, being a Collection in Score of the Most Valuable and Useful Compositions of that Service by Several English Masters of the Last Two Hundred Years*, 3 vols. (1760 to 1778).
54. All of the music discussed in the chapter is not in Boyce's collection.
55. GHM, ii, p. 61.
56. Hawkins, *History,* ii, p. 572.
57. GHM, ii, p. 65.
58. Ibid.
59. Ibid., pp. 67-68 and n^z.
60. Ibid., p. 82. As a result, most of Burney's text is given over to Byrd's secular songs and keyboard music.
61. Ibid., p. 87.
62. Ibid.
63. Ibid., p. 92 and n^c.
64. Ibid., p. 161.
65. CB to Ebeling, 30 Mar. 1772 (Osborn).
66. GHM, ii, p. 201.
67. Ibid.
68. Ibid.
69. Ibid.
70. Ibid., p. 211.
71. Ibid., pp. 210, 213, 230.
72. Ibid., pp. 230-32.
73. Ibid., p. 235.
74. Hawkins, *History,* i, p. 448.
75. GHM, ii, p. 242 (italics mine).
76. Ibid.

77. Ibid., pp. 252-53.
78. Ibid., p. 124.
79. Ibid., p. 128.
80. CB to TT, 10-12 Nov. 1783 (B.M.).
81. GHM, ii, p. 263.
82. Ibid., p. 290.
83. Ibid., p. 307.
84. Ibid., p. 342.
85. See Percy A. Scholes, *The Puritans and Music in England and New England* (London, 1934).
86. GHM, ii, p. 352.
87. Ibid., pp. 353-55.
88. See, for example, Harold Watkins Shaw, "Blow," *Groves V,* i (London, 1954), p. 772; Manfred F. Bukofzer, *Music in the Baroque Era* (New York, 1947), p. 188; Ernest Walker, *A History of Music in England,* 3rd ed. (Oxford, 1952) p. 293; Heathcote D. Statham, "Dr. Blow's Church Music and its Deformities," *The Musical Time* LXVII (1926), pp. 988-90, 1083-85; Harold Watkins Shaw, "Tradition and Convention in John Blow's Harmony," *Music and Letters* XXX (1949), pp. 136-45.
89. Shaw, *Groves V,* i, p. 772.
90. GHM, ii, p. 350.
91. Ibid.
92. Ibid., p. 357.
93. Ibid., p. 359 n[e].
94. Ibid., p. 352.
95. Ibid.
96. See points 1, 2, and 3 of the first plate, ibid., p. 353.
97. Hawkins, *History,* ii, p. 743.
98. CB to TT, 10-12 Nov. 1783 (B.M.)
99. GHM, ii, p. 384.
100. Ibid., p. 384 n[f].
101. Ibid., p. 411.
102. Ibid., p. 418.
103. Ibid., p. 419.
104. This style Burney found first in the music of Giacomo Carissimi and Alessandro Scarlatti.
105. GHM, ii, p. 419.
106. Ibid., p. 482.

107. "Having lately examined the chief works of his predecessors, and informed myself of the state in which he found our choral Music, I was the better able, in perusing his productions immediately after, to judge of the additions he had made to the common stock of melody, harmony, and modulation, during near twenty years that he presided over the first choir in the kingdom." Ibid.
108. Ibid.
109. Ibid., p. 483.
110. Ibid., p. 483 n^i.
111. Ibid., p. 482.
112. Ibid., p. 484 n^m.
113. Ibid., p. 483.
114. Ibid., p. 489.
115. Ibid., p. 491.
116. It is also the feature that most clearly distinguishes Burney's work from Hawkins's. His suggestions for correcting the faults evident in these compositions must surely have heightened his reader's respect for him as a musician as well as a critic, further emphasizing the difference in training between the rival historians.
117. GHM, ii, p. 494.
118. Burney's interest in the oratorio was stimulated by his knowledge of King George III's musical taste. In September, 1786, reporting to Fanny on his progress, he wrote, "I am now deep in my History of the *Oratorio,* his M----y's favourite Music and have brought it down to the death of the unfortunate Stradella..." CB to FB, 4 Sept. 1786 (Osborn).
119. GHM, ii, p. 578.
120. Ibid., p. 580.
121. Ibid.
122. Ibid., p. 581.
123. Ibid., p. 579.
124. Ibid., p. 586.
125. C. "Caldara."
126. *Italian Tour,* pp. 120-21.
127. See chap. 9, below.
128. C. "Handel."
129. For a complete list of the directors, see GDB, ii, pp. 62-63.
130. CB to Twining, 31 July 1784 (Berg).
131. Ibid.
132. Ibid.
133. Ibid.
134. *Memoirs,* ii, pp. 385-86.

135. Ibid., p. 386.
136. *Account,* p. 80. The footnote has been merged with the text. See Percy A. Scholes, "George the Third as Music Lover," *Musical Quarterly* XXVIII (1942), pp. 78-92.
137. Burney traces the establishment of the oratorio in England from Handel's *Esther,* and he particularly notes that Handel's *Deborah* was performed for the first time at the opera house, and was advertised as the *Opera of Deborah.* He further notes the establishment of oratorios as a regular feature at the opera house, observing that *Deborah* was revived and performed three times, "always by his Majesty's command and though in English and still life, always on the nights usually appropriated to the Italian opera." It was only later that Handel's works acquired a certain reverence as sacred works, and were restricted to Lenten performances. During Burney's youth they were manifestly dramatic works. GHM, ii, pp. 787-88.
138. CB to Lord Mornington, post-1776 (Osborn).
139. Ibid.
140. *Account,* p. 98.
141. GHM, ii, p. 546.
142. C. "Mattheson."
143. *Account,* p. 88.
144. GHM, ii, p. 505.
145. *Account,* n., p. 34.
146. Ibid., p. 39.
147. Ibid., p. 75.
148. Ibid.
149. Ibid., pp. 88-89.
150. GHM, ii, p. 127.
151. *Account,* p. 29.
152. Ibid., p. 37.
153. Ibid., p. 35.
154. Ibid., p. 39.
155. Ibid., p. 112.
156. Ibid., p. 86.
157. Ibid., p. 83.
158. Ibid., p. 76.
159. Ibid., p. 75.
160. MM, pp. 91-112.
161. Author anonymous, quoted by Robert Manson Myers, *Handel's Messiah: A Touchstone of Taste* (New York, 1948), p. 78.
162. Hawkins, *History,* ii, p. 890.

163. *Account,* p. 85.
164. Ibid., pp. 36, 82.
165. Ibid., p. 37.
166. Ibid.
167. Ibid., p. 49.
168. Stanley to CB, 21 Apr. 1784 (Coke).
169. CB to Sir Joseph Banks, 26 May 1784 (Yale).
170. *Italian Tour,* pp. 127-28.
171. Ibid.
172. *German Tour,* p. 114.
173. *Italian Tour,* pp. 115-16.
174. C. "Lotti."
175. *Account,* p. 79.
176. *Italian Tour,* p. 72. Later he wrote that this piece "excited hope and expectations that he would soon be ranked among composers of the first class; and we were not disappointed;..." C. "Monza."
177. *Italian Tour,* p. 73.
178. C. "Martini, Giovanni Batista San."
179. *Italian Tou..,* p. 117.
180. Ibid.
181. Ibid., p. 134.
182. C. "Santarelli."
183. Review of William Jackson of Exeter's *Observations on the Present State of Music in London* (1791) in *Monthly Review* VI (1791), pp. 196-202.
184. C. "Jomelli."
185. GHM, ii, p. 929.
186. Edward Olleson, "Church Music and Oratorio," *The New Oxford History of Music* (London, 1973), p. 326.
187. CB to Lord Mornington, post-1776 (Osborn).
188. C. "Rolle." Olleson calls Rolle's oratorios "Sacred drama,""Church Music and Oratorio,". 328.
189. GHM, ii, p. 582.
190. C. "Jomelli."
191. *German Tour,* p. 108.
192. Sven Hostrup Hansell, *Works for Solo Voice of Johann Adolph Hasse (1699-1783),* Detroit Studies in Bibliography No. 12 (Detroit, 1968). "The Solo Cantatas, Motets and Antiphons of Johann Adolf Hasse." PH.D. dissertation, University of Illinois, Urbana (1966).

193. *German Tour*, p. 96.
194. C. "Sachini."
195. GHM, ii, p. 941.
196. Ibid., p. 952.
197. Ibid.
198. C. "Durante."
199. Berg.
200. Notebook (Osborn).
201. CB to Latrobe, July 1803 (Osborn).

Chapter 7

1. GHM, i, p. 781.
2. Ibid., p. 782.
3. Ibid., p. 796.
4. Ibid., p. 773.
5. Joseph Kerman, *The Elizabethan Madrigal: A Comparative Study*, (Philadelphia, 1962), p. xvi.
6. GHM, ii. p. 89.
7. Edmund Horace Fellowes, *The English Madrigal Composers*, 2d ed., (London, 1948), p. 125.
8. Ibid., p. 126.
9. See Lonsdale, p. 190.
10. CB to TT, [Aug. 1773] (Osborn).
11. CB to Malone, 21 Nov. 1810 (Yale).
12. GHM, ii, p. 113.
13. Ibid., p. 166.
14. Marenzio's works appear in the earliest partbooks of the Madrigal Society. See J.G. Craufurd, "The Madrigal Society," *Proceedings of the RMA* LXXXII (1955-56), pp. 33-45.
15. Gesualdo's works were also in the repertory of the Madrigal Society.
16. GHM, ii, p. 178.
17. B.M. Add. MS. 11588.
18. Glen Watkins, *Gesualdo: The Man and His Music*, (Lodnon, 1973), p. 305.
19. B.M. Add. MS. 11588 f. 48.
20. GHM, ii, p. 180.
21. Ibid., p. 181.
22. Ibid., p. 180 n^i.

23. Ibid., p. 190.
24. Ibid., p. 191 n°.
25. Ibid., p. 191.
26. Our expectations are premised on a broad inclusive concept of music history available to us at the flip of Grout's *History of Music,* library shelves bulging with editions of the great masters, and music from antiquity to the present day, in score, neatly catalogued. Even when we undertake investigations of obscure composers and unknown repertoires, they are approached with a surety provided by the results of two hundred years of earlier historical writing.
27. GHM, ii, p. 258.
28. Ibid., p. 404.
29. Ibid., p. 329.
30. Ibid., p. 374.
31. Ibid., p. 117.
32. CB to TT, 10-12 Nov. 1783 (B.M.).
33. GHM, ii, pp. 280-81.
34. Ibid., p. 279.
35. Ibid., p. 316.
36. His most famous are *Jack and Jill* and *Peter White.*
37. GHM, ii, p. 328; see also ii, p. 414. Catches were composed throughout the century, encouraged by the activities of the Noblemen and Gentlemen's Catch Club, founded in 1761, which allowed professional musicians a limited membership by invitation, and held annual competitions to encourage catch compositions. The original Club consisted of eight members: three were earls, two were generals, and three were gentlemen. Of these, four, including all three earls, were subscribers to Burney's *History.* In light of the spirit of accommodation which prevails in much of his work, it is tempting to consider these circumstances as shaping forces in his criticism of this style. There is, however, no substantiating the charge through Burney's published or manuscript papers.
38. GHM, ii, p. 390.
39. C. "Purcell."
40. He does mention in the *Cyclopaedia* article "Cantata" that late in the century Sarti brought about a slight revival of the form. Perhaps the shift in his attention is due to changing conditions in London concert life. We are told that the cantata was "seldom cultivated" by 1789, having been replaced by opera scenes and single songs. Burney favored a revival of the cantata as "a little drama entire" because of its dramatic unity, and because a proper orchestra was seldom available for chamber performances of opera songs. GHM, ii, p. 638. Nevertheless, the cantata had lost its place in English music history, and thus lost its place in Burney's *History.*
41. It is in keeping with his denigration of French music throughout the *History* that he ignored such epochal achievements as the Parisian chanson, the accompanied Air, and the Ballet de Cour, even though the traces of such in printed form, were readily available in London.
42. GHM, ii. p. 983.

340   Notes for Chapter 7

43. C. "English Singing."
44. GHM, ii, p. 1004.
45. Ibid., p. 1015.
46. Ibid., p. 1017.
47. C. "English Singing."
48. CB to FB, 2 Nov. 1798 (Osborn).
49. CB to Mrs. John Hunter, n.d. (Osborn).
50. GHM, ii, p. 77.
51. Ibid.
52. Ibid.
53. Ibid., p. 78.
54. Ibid., p. 96.
55. Ibid.
56. Ibid.
57. Ibid., p. 97.
58. Ibid., p. 99.
59. Ibid., p. 462.
60. Ibid., p. 422.
61. Ibid., p. 423.
62. Ibid.
63. Most of his attention to keyboard music is directed to the resurgence of organ construction after the Reformation, a discussion which somewhat masks his slight treatment of the keyboard music of this period. Ibid., pp. 343-47.
64. C. "Frescobaldi."
65. Notebook (Osborn). In the essay which surveys the history of keyboard music in England, he wrote, "Till the publication of Handel's Harpsichord Lessons, Concertos and fugues for the organ, we had no Music of that kind in England."
66. The manuscript appears to consist entirely of music copies from prints. Folio 16 of the manuscript is in part an elaborate duplication of a title page:

Sonate
A
Violino e Basso
Composite Da
Francesco Geminiani
Opera IV
Stampate in Parigi 1739
transcribed nella Citti di
Chester MDCCVLIV
Dal Carlo Burney gioraneal 18 anni

B.M. Add. MS. 39957.

67. CB to TT, 14 Dec. 1781 (Osborn).
68. Notebook (Osborn).
69. Domenico Scarlatti was a significant force in English keyboard music. England's foremost virtuosi kept Scarlatti's sonatas in practice, including the leader of the "Scarlatti sect," Thomas Roseingrave. During Roseingrave's last years in the environs of London, Burney was a frequent visitor to his residence, in the home of one Mrs. Bray at Hampstead. Burney learned a good deal from the unstable musician about Scarlatti, and took full advantage of his "willingness to instruct young persons." It is unclear what specific influence Roseingrave may have exerted on Burney, other than as a lover of Scarlatti's style, but whatever the case, Burney's *Six Sonatas* from 1761 are among the most imitative of Scarlatti's techniques of all the music composed by members of the Scarlatti Sect. Roseingrave's music did not please Burney: the harmony was "intolerably harsh and ungrateful," and suffered from licentious and extravagant modulation. William S. Newman, *The Sonata in the Classic Era: The Second Volume of a History of the Sonata Idea* (Chapel Hill, 1963), p. 698.

    Ibid., p. 178.
71. *A.B.C. Dario Musico,* (London, 1780), p. 13.
72. Notebook (Osborn).
73. CB to TT, 14 Dec. 1781 (Osborn).
74. Osborn.
75. Notebook (Osborn).
76. CB to Ebeling, Nov. 1771 (Hamburg).
77. CB to TT, 10-12, Nov. 1783 (B.M.).
78. Osborn.
79. 19 Nov. 1775 (Osborn).
80. GHM, ii, p. 955.
81. Samuel Wesley, *Letters of Samuel Wesley to Mr. Jacobs,* Eliza Wesley, ed., (New York, n.d.), preface n.p.
82. C. "Palschau."
83. See Laurence Picken, "Bach Quotations from the Eighteenth Century," *Music and Letters* V (1944), pp. 83-95. See also Hans F. Redlich, "The Bach Revival in England," *Hinrichsen's Musical Yearbook* VII (London, 1952), 287-300.
84. *Account,* p. 41.
85. See Dragon Plamenac, "New Light on the Lost Years of Carl Phillip Emanuel Bach," *Musical Quarterly* XXXV (1949), p. 584.
86. Ibid., p. 577.
87. Characteristically, the editors of *The Bach Reader* (p. 265) quote Reichardt's revised opinion without reference to the first passage. Hans T. David and Arthur Mendel, eds., *The Bach Reader: A Life of Johann Sebastian Bach in Letters and Documents,* rev. ed., (New York, 1966).
88. CB to Wesley, 17 Oct. 1808 (Osborn).

89. GHM, i, p. 726.
90. PSMG, ii, pp. 80-81.
91. Ibid., p. 83.
92. GHM, ii, p. 952.
93. Ibid., p. 953.
94. Ibid., p. 1019.
95. Fashion has changed once again and Burney has been judged wanting for his failure to fully grasp the genius of Bach. It is perhaps because Burney shunned the profound and manifest contrapuntal genius displayed in Bach's works—the very quality most admired by modern musicians—that his remarks have been so ridiculed.
96. CB to TT, 14 Dec. 1781 (Osborn).
97. GHM, ii, p. 916.
98. The numerous sonatas of Rutini also go unmentioned.
99. GHM, ii, 953.
100. Wagenseil's keyboard music was first published in England in 1760. See Newman, p. 352-54.
101. C. "Wagenseil."
102. Notebook (Osborn).
103. Fanny says 1766, but Lonsdale has shown that the journey took place in 1765. See also Ronald R. Kidd, "The Emergence of Chamber Music with Obligato Keyboard in England," *Musicologica* XLIV (1972), pp. 122-124.
104. GHM, ii, p. 257.
105. Notebook (Osborn).
106. C. "Haydn."
107. CB to Charles Butler, 23 Aug. 1798 (Osborn).
108. These arrangements, long thought to be by Haydn, were reprinted several times. Hoboken finally identified them as Burney's from a notice in *The Public Advertiser*, 5.I. 1784. See Anthony van Hoboken, *Thematisch-bibliographisches Werkverzeichnis*, Bd. I (Mainz, 1957), p. 753.
109. CB to TT, c. 1783 (B.M.).
110. CB to Mrs. Chambers, 3 Nov. 1797 (*Journal of the Warburg and Courtauld Institute* III [1939], pp. 161-64).
111. *Monthly Review* VI (1791), pp. 196-202.
112. C. "Theme."
113. See catalogue of the music auction.
114. Berg.
115. In a letter to Lady Elizabeth Lowther, Burney remarked on Cramer's abilities as a performer and composer: "I have not seen Cramer's Exercises, but some of my family play them, and speak of their beauties and difficulties in the same manner as you do—I have no doubt but

that they are excellent. Cramer has a very powerful hand, much expression and refinement in his execution, and has pleased me extremely by some of his late compositions. and these Toccata must be excellent studies for the present stage of your musical acquirements." [post-9 Nov. 1807] (Osborn).

116. C. "Muthel."
117. Ibid.
118. Ibid.
119. CB to FB, 2 Oct. 1789 (formerly Hilles, now Yale).
120. Mason to CB, 6 Nov. 1790 (Osborn).
121. CB to FB, [13] Dec. [1790] (formerly Hilles, now Yale).
122. Lonsdale, p. 422.
123. GHM, ii, p. 283.
124. Ibid., p. 284.
125. Ibid., p. 285.
126. Ibid., p. 333.
127. Ibid., p. 322.
128. Ibid., p. 309.
129. Ibid., p. 380.
130. Ibid., p. 399.
131. Ibid.
132. Ibid., p. 403.
133. Ibid., p. 410. It is interesting to speculate as to what Burney may have learned of Viennese musical life from Matteis. Definite information is nonexistent, but it is known that he was employed at the Viennese court form 1700 to 1730, during the time in which Fux was a court composer of ballet.
134. Matteis was also the founder of a custom to which Burney and most others of his day adhered: the printing of music which he composed for his student's use. The practice, according to Burney, occasioned a revival of music engraving in England.
135. GHM, ii, p. 409.
136. Ibid., p. 410.
137. Ibid., p. 436.
138. Arthur Hutchings, *The Baroque Concerto,* 3d ed., (London, 1973), p. 348. The duration and intensity of the taste for Corelli in England, as opposed to the modern style of Haydn, Boccherini, and Giardini are amusingly captured in a Hogarthian-style print by Burney's nephew, Edward Francesco Burney. Edward's drawing, entitled *The Tye Wig School,* shows a group of extremely superannuated gentlemen amateurs playing Corelli's music, while Haydn, Boccherini, Pleyel, and even Beethoven scores are seen blazing in the fireplace, and ascending the chimney as so much rubbish. It is not to be overlooked that among the number of puns and visual jokes included in the print, Edward printed the part of the second violin in

lozenge-shaped notes, exaggerating both the antiquity of Corelli's music and the stupidity of those who would hear no other.

139. GHM, ii, p. 441.
140. Ibid., p. 716.
141. Ibid., p. 443.
142. Ibid., p. 442.
143. Ibid., p. 443.
144. Ibid., p. 444.
145. Ibid.
146. This awareness is reflected in his sarcastic comment that Haydn's fame must "be left to the determination of time, and the increased rage of depraved appetites for novelty." Ibid., p. 437.
147. They were issued by Welcker, Walsh, and Longman and Broderip, and were staple pieces with London violinists.
148. GHM, ii, p. 499.
149. PSMFI, 1st ed., p. 125.
150. GHM, ii, p. 453.
151. Ibid., p. 450.
152. Thomas Baltzar was recorded as being at Oxford in 1658, and he died in London in 1663. Gottfried Finger also performed in London. Possibly brought to England by these and other performers, the compositions of Dietrich Becker were also known to Burney. The music of all three failed to impress him.
153. GHM, ii, p. 462.
154. Ibid., p. 472.
155. Ibid., p. 976.
156. Ibid., p. 990.
157. Ibid., p. 991.
158. Ibid., p. 995.
159. Ibid., pp. 1007-8.
160. Ibid., p. 1013.
161. Ibid.
162. Ibid., p. 1015.
163. Notebook (Osborn).
164. William Smith and Charles Humphries, *A Bibliography of the Musical Works Published by the Firm of John Walsh During the Years 1721-1766,* (London, 1968), p. 314.
165. Published by Bremner in 1761.
166. C. "Kelly."

Notes for Chapter 7   345

167. GHM, ii, p. 945.
168. Ibid.
169. Ibid., 866.
170. C. "Vanhal."
171. CB to TT, 10-12 Nov. 1783 (B.M.).
172. GHM, ii, p. 455.
173. *German Tour*, p. 88.
174. Ibid., p. 100.
175. Ibid., p. 124.
176. H.C. Robbins Landon, *Haydn: Chronicle and Works. Volume III. Haydn in England 1791-1795*, (Indiana, 1976), p. 24. See also, Christopher Roscoe, "Haydn and London in the 1780's," *Music and Letters* XLIX (1968), pp. 203-12.
177. Roscoe, "Haydn and London," p. 205.
178. Notebook (Osborn).
179. Joseph Haydn, *The Collected Correspondence and London Notebooks of Joseph Haydn*, H.C. Robbins Landon, ed., (London, 1959), p. 128.
180. The relationship between Burney and Haydn has been related in great detail by Scholes, Rosemary Hughes, "Dr. Burney's Championship of Haydn," *Musical Quarterly* XXVII (1941), pp. 90-96, and most recently in the fifth volume of H.C. Robbins Landon's documentary biography, *Haydn: Chronicle and Works*. The record, though substantial, is still incomplete, but the many entries in Burney's diaries and essays, including the complete text of an expanded version of his review of Haydn's *Seven Last Words*, will have to await publication of the Burney papers.
181. GHM, ii, p. 958.
182. C. "Theme."
183. Berg 198788B folder 5.
184. GHM, ii, p. 1038.
185. Landon, *Haydn: Chronicle and Works*, p. 25.
186. Nicholas Temperly, "Beethoven in London Concert Life, 1800-1850," *The Music Review* XXIX (1960), p. 208.
187. C. "Mozart."
188. Burney learned of Crotch's remarks from an unknown partisan, possibly Salomon himself, in January and February, 1805.
189. Cecil B. Oldman, "On Burney and Mozart," *Mozart Jahrbuch* (1962-63), p. 80.
190. GHM, ii, 1038.
191. CB to Latrobe, [March 1805] (Osborn).
192. C. "German School of Music."
193. Landon, *Haydn: Chronicle and Works*, p. 26; *Memoirs*, iii, p. 334.

194. *Memoirs,* iii, loc. cit.
195. Temperly, "Beethoven," pp. 211-13.
196. In a paper read for the Ernest Bloch Lectures, University of California, Berkeley, 1977.
197. CB to Wesley, n.d. (Osborn).
198. GHM, ii, p. 87; C. "Morley."
199. Berg.

Chapter 8

1. GHM, ii, p. 506.
2. Ibid., p. 903.
3. Ibid., p. 675.
4. MM, ii, p. 43.
5. GHM, ii, p. 877.
6. He mentions specifically the London production of Paisiello's *Il Re Teodoro* (1787), the "unity of style" of which was destroyed by the additions of arias by Corri, Massingi and Storace. Ibid., p. 901.
7. Ibid., p. 799.
8. Ibid., p. 860.
9. Ibid., p. 543. Burney objected to the complete abandonment of dramatic unity. He requested that Samuel Hoole censure the practice in the preface to his translations of Metastasio's works. See CB to Samuel Hoole, 5 Feb. 1799 (Berg).
10. GHM, ii, p. 680.
11. Ibid., p. 676.
12. Ibid., p. 509.
13. C. "Lyric Poetry."
14. MM, ii, p. 253n.
15. C. "Lyric Poetry."
16. MM, i, p. 330.
17. C. "Metastasio."
18. MM, iii, pp. 316-24.
19. C. "Metastasio."
20. Ibid.
21. C. "Opera."
22. MM, iii, pp. 184-85.
23. Ibid., p. 183.
24. Ibid., ii, p. 331.

25. Ibid., p. 334.
26. Ibid.
27. GHM, ii, p. 508.
28. Ibid., p. 515.
29. Roger Fiske, *English Theatre Music in the Eighteenth Century,* (London, 1973), p. 66.
30. Burney was not alone in his view that the tasteful development of music resulted from the performers and composers striving to meet the expectations of a public audience: Abel, one of the proprietors of the famous Bach-Abel series of concerts (also a subscription series), suggested that had J.S. Bach and C.P.E. Bach been employed at one of the great capitals, "they would doubtless have simplified their style," keeping their invention within the bounds of taste. C. "Bach"; and GHM, ii, p. 955.
31. GHM, ii, p. 517 (italics added).
32. Ibid., p. 518.
33. Ibid., p. 519.
34. Ibid.
35. Modern facsimile ed. Adolf Sandberger, (Augsburg, 1927), p. 39.
36. To compensate, he gives extensive excerpts from Pietro della Valle's writings, which illuminate the musical practice of the time.
37. GHM, ii, p. 546.
38. Ibid.
39. Ibid., p. 553.
40. Ibid.
41. Ibid., p. 555.
42. Ibid., p. 608.
43. Ibid., pp. 612-15.
44. Ibid., pp. 607-8.
45. Ibid., p. 607.
46. Ibid., p. 609.
47. Ibid.
48. Ibid., p. 610.
49. Ibid.
50. Ibid., p. 615.
51. Ibid., p. 621.
52. Ibid., p. 625. See Frank Walker, pp. "Salvator Rosa and Music," *The Monthly Musical Record* LXXIX (1949), pp. 199-204; and Gloria Rose Donington, "The Cantatas of Carissimi," Ph.D. dissertation, Yale University, 1959.
53. GHM, ii, p. 624.

54. Ibid., p. 629.
55. Ibid., p. 628.
56. Ibid., p. 629.
57. Ibid., p. 631. Burney's manuscript contained thirty-five cantatas, but now appears to be lost. Of the few that can be identified (he does not title them), none belong to any single collection indexed by Edwin Hanley, "Alessandro Scarlatti's Cantate da Camera; A Bibliographical Study," Ph.D. dissertation, Yale University, 1963.
58. GHM, ii, p. 629.
59. Ibid., p. 618.
60. Ibid., p. 630.
61. Ibid., p. 463.
62. Ibid., pp. 466-67.
63. Ibid., p. 470.
64. Ibid., p. 472.
65. Ibid.
66. Ibid., p. 276.
67. Ibid., p. 271.
68. C. "Opera."
69. See chap. 7, above.
70. GHM, ii, p. 304.
71. Ibid., p. 389.
72. Ibid., p. 393.
73. The inclusion of Geminiani in this list of composers, and later Haydn, Kozeluch, Pleyel, indicates that in Burney's mind the dominance of the foreigners extended beyond opera, condemning English musicians to mediocrity in all forms. Ibid., p. 399 n^z.
74. Ibid., p. 399.
75. Ibid., p. 392.
76. Ibid., pp. 642-43.
77. Ibid.
78. Ibid., p. 659.
79. Amidst the somewhat confused narrative and polemics of this chapter, the first indication of Burney's concept of the history of opera in eighteenth-century England emerges: according to Burney, the arrival of the first great Italian castrato, Nicolino Grimaldi, establishes a new era in the annals of the lyric theatre. Burney pronounces him "the first truly great singer to sing on an English stage." Nicolini sang with English singers in multi-lingual performances, an absurdity which Burney points out, "for the honour of our nation," was also endured in Germany. Nicolini's arrival was not a brilliant beginning for Italian opera in England, as the music sung by the first Italian singers, particularly works by Bonocini, Francesco Mancini,

Francesco Conti, and others, was "neither dramatic, passionate, pathetic, nor graceful." Nevertheless Italian opera had gained a foothold. Ibid., p. 665.

80. Ibid., p. 670.
81. The chapter on Italian opera in Handel's England covers 253 pages, 161 of which chronicle the development of opera, (including all of Handel's operas), before Burney's arrival in London in 1745. Only 92 pages are devoted to opera after this time, although his arrival in London divided the period roughly in half. In order to provide the reader with a satisfactory view of musical life prior to 1745 he relies on a variety of resources, including a vast collection of clippings, reviews, programs and other documents collected by his son, Charles Burney, Jr. c.f. B.M. add. MS. 939, b. 1; 938, e-r; 939, 1.9; 936, 6.2; 938, a-d, d-e; and 936 g.
82. GHM, ii, p. 924.
83. Ibid., pp. 711-12.
84. Burney says of Handel's first opera for England, "no one of them requires us to mount up to the time in which it was composed so much as *Rinaldo,* which has not been only pillaged by others, but by himself." Ibid., p. 675.
85. C. "Accompaniment."
86. Ibid.
87. Notebook (Osborn). The change in style is better attributed to Leo than Vinci.
88. GHM, ii, p. 917.
89. C. "Naples."
90. C. "Vinci."
91. C. "Hasse."
92. PSMG, ii, p. 354.
93. Notebook (Osborn).
94. MMM, p. 176. Hasse was later deleted from the list, probably because he was not born in Italy.
95. PSMFI, p. 331.
96. A considerable portion of Matteis's obituary of Jommelli is given in the *History* and *Cyclopaedia* article.
97. Better known as *Astianatte* (Rome, 1741).
98. MM, ii, p. 376.
99. MMM, p. 177.
100. GHM, ii, p. 683.
101. Ibid., p. 697.
102. "Pena tiranna io sento al core" is also not censured for crowding the voice. Important imitations of the vocal melody do not appear in the orchestra in either aria. Ibid., p. 55f.
103. Ibid., p. 46.
104. *Account,* p. 49.

Notes for Chapter 8

105. Ibid.
106. GHM, ii, p. 713, n^z.
107. Ibid., p. 755.
108. Ibid., p. 713.
109. Ibid., p. 822.
110. Ibid., p. 796.
111. Other modern arias mentioned: Ibid., pp. 735, 754-55, 765, 773, 794-95, 806, 808-9, and 822.
112. *Account*, p. 21.
113. There are other indications that Burney is occasionally writing against his own instincts and taste in this chapter. His essay on Griselda (1772) by Handel's rival, Giovanni Bononcini seems to contradict Burney's own most dearly held beliefs.

    The melodies, in general, of this opera, are as graceful and elegant as any of the time, and though there is little ingenuity of design in the accompaniments, or science in the harmony and modulation, yet there is a clearness and facility of style, which are more likely to afford pleasure to the unlearned and greater part of an audience, than original and masterly composition, of which they knew nothing. In process of time, however, Handel taught us how to judge of these, and to despise inartificial composition, in which harmony is sacrificed to trite and frivolous melodies, consisting of rapid and inconnected passages of execution, which by frequent use are become as common and insipid as the flat and stale jokes of Swift's *Polite Conversation*. [*GHM, ii, p. 735.*]

    Certainly Burney recognized Handel as the superior composer, but this passage seems especially contrived to suit the admirers of Handel. Moreover, he does not mention Bononcini's recitatives, an oversight which may have been intentional: the *Cyclopaedia* article on Bononcini states that his recitatives were universally allowed to be the best of the time, a sentiment which would surely have riled the Handelians in 1789. GHM, ii, p. 735.
114. Notebook (Osborn).
115. C. "Handel."
116. Two parallel but distinct currents are evident throughout Burney's criticism of Handel's arias. On the one hand, arias that are brilliant and satisfying to the senses receive praise for the delight that they provide as a kind of "absolute music, distinct from any dramatic content; on the other hand, and to Burney more important, was music which was truly dramatic: the extraordinarily affective, pathetic arias and dramatic recitatives.
117. *Account*, pp. 61-63.
118. Ibid., p. 61.
119. The first extended musical example incorporated into the body of the text of the *History* is a short sample of accompanied recitative from Handel's *Teseo*, praised for its admirable expression. *GHM,,* ii, p. 687.
120. Ibid., p. 714.
121. Ibid., p. 842, (italics mine).
122. MM, iii, p. 344.
123. See GHM,, ii, pp. 673, 687, 694, 718, 721, and 810.

124. Ibid., p. 701.
125. Ibid., p. 136.
126. Ibid., p. 696.
127. Ibid., p. 744.
128. Ibid., p. 788.
129. Notebook (Osborn).
130. Ibid.
131. C. "Rinaldo."
132. GHM, ii, p. 927.
133. MM, iii, p. 326.
134. GHM,, ii, p. 674.
135. Ibid., p. 761.
136. Ibid., p. 786. See also pp. 682, 715, 721, and 770.
137. Ibid., p. 707.
138. Ibid., p. 715. See also p. 743.
139. Ibid., p. 724. The passage is in "Con un vezzo" in act II.
140. Ibid., p. 802. The aria is "Impara ingrata" from act I.
141. Ibid., p. 808.
142. Ibid., p. 743.
143. Ibid., p. 722.
144. Ibid., p. 709. See also p. 724.
145. Ibid., pp. 709, 802, 808, and 845.
146. Ibid., p. 781. Handel was not the only foreigner who supplied material for the English pillagers. Nicola Porpora's arrival in England supplied "much of the *new taste*, and new passages of the period." Ibid., p. 719.
147. Ibid., p. 868.
148. C. "Goldoni."
149. Ibid.
150. C. "Piccini."
151. Ibid.
152. C. "Finale."
153. When, in 1791, he had the opportunity to use the services of a friend traveling to Italy, he asked only for "any new or curious productions of Paisiello that are supposed not yet to have reached England." CB to J.C. Walker, 29 Sept. 1791 (City of Liverpool Public Library).
154. GHM, ii, p. 900.
155. Ibid., p. 860.

352 *Notes for Chapter 8*

156. Ibid.
157. C. "Cocchi."
158. GHM, ii, p. 813.
159. Ibid., p. 683.
160. Ibid., pp. 813-14.
161. Ibid., pp. 668-69, and 710-11, 831-37.
162. C. "Roulade."
163. GHM, ii, pp. 850-51. Professor Daniel Heartz has pointed out an error in this plate. This passage from *Sirbace* marked "close" is actually from the B♭ aria from *Enrico*. *Music in the Classical Era*, chap. III (in progress).
164. C. "Execution."
165. Ibid.
166. *Account*, p. 24.
167. Ibid.
168. GHM, ii, p. 752.
169. Something of the lavish manner in which a mid-eighteenth-century performer in England would have realized the outlines of an aria by Handel can be seen in a surviving copy of the embellishments which Gaetano Guadagni transcribed for seven arias from Handel's *Ottone* (1751 performance). Hellmuth Christian Wolff, *Original Vocal Improvisations*, Anthology of Music XLI (New York, 1972). Three of these arias, with their embellishments, have been published in the Anthology of Music series. The editor, Hellmuth Wolff, does not speculate as to why Guadagni transcribed these embellishments. The writers of an article in the *Handel-Jahrbuch* suggest that Guadagni wrote these embellishments for the use of another Italian singer, Francesca Cuzzoni, but admit that their attribution is "purely speculative" (James S. and Martin V. Hall, "Handel's Graces" in *Handel-Jahrbuch* IX [1957], pp. 25-43). This conclusion is suspect, especially if one considers that Cuzzoni at this time (1751) is described as old, poor, and almost deprived of voice by age and infirmities (GHM, ii, p. 737), while Guadagni is described as a "full and well toned counter-tenor"; but a "wild and careless singer" (GHM, ii, p. 875), with exceptional extemporaneous abilities. "The music he sung was the most simple imaginable; a few notes with frequent pauses, and opportunities of being liberated from the composer and the band were all he wanted. And in these seemingly extemporaneous effusions, he proved the inherent power of melody totally divorced from harmony..." (GHM, ii, pp. 876).
170. GHM, ii, p. 760.
171. Ibid., p. 544.
172. Ibid., p. 821.
173. Ibid., p. 806.
174. C. "Passage."
175. GHM, ii, p. 790.
176. Ibid., p. 797.
177. Ibid., p. 684.

178. Ibid., p. 847.
179. Ibid., p. 894.
180. C. "Sacchini."
181. Ibid.
182. Sacchini's *Evelina* (Paris, 1788) appears in the catalogue of Burney's library.
183. C. "Cimarosa."
184. Quoted in William C. Smith, *The Italian Opera and Contemporary Ballet in London 1789-1820* (London, 1955), p. 14.
185. PSMFI, p. 32.
186. Ibid., p. 19.
187. Ibid., p. viii.
188. Tosi remarks, "The voice of the scholar, whether it be di Petto or di Testa, should always come forth neat and clear without passing thro the Nose, or being choaked in the Throat; which are two most horrible Defects in a Singer, and past all Remedy if once grown in the Habit." Pier Francesco Tosi, *Observations on the Florid Song,* trans. Mr. Galliard (London, 1743), chap. I, #19 n.p.
189. PSMFI, p. 25.
190. Ibid., p. 27.
191. Ibid., p. 23.
192. Ibid., p. 28.
193. Thomas Busby, *A Complete Dictionary of Music,* 3rd. ed., (London, 1811). There has been considerable confusion about the meaning of this term. The several definitions given in *Groves V* in the articles "Portamento," "Port de voix," and "Ornaments" refer to very different concepts than those presented by Burney or Busby. The term had two distinct meanings in the eighteenth century: the earlier sense, as it is used by Burney, was one of bringing forth the voice; the latter sense was a type of ornament of a glide between two pitches—see Leopold Mozart, "Versuch einer grundlicher Violinschule" (Augsburg, 1756). See also E. Forman, *Practical Reflections on Figured Singing* (Champaign, 1968), and a translation with notes of Giovanni Battista Mancini, *Pensieri, e riflessoni, pratiche sopra il canto figurato* (Vienna, 1774).
194. Johann Joachim Quantz, *On Playing the Flute,* trans. Edward R. Reilly (London, 1966), p. 300.
195. C. "Cantare," in Tenducci's instructions to his scholars, number ix, is "Never to force the voice, in order to extend its compass *voce di petto,* upwards; but rather cultivate the *voce di testo,* in what is called *falsetto* in order to join it well and imperceptively to the *voce di petto* for fear of incurring the disagreeable habit of singing in the throat, or through the nose;— unpardonable faults in a singer." Similarity between this rule and Burney's definition of *Portamento* is the basis of this assumption.
196. Quantz, *Flute,* p. 334.
197. PSMG, i, p. 8.
198. GHM, ii, p. 498.

199. PSMFI, p. 32.

200. Jean-Jacques Rousseau, *Lettre sur la musique française* (Paris, 1753), p. 643; Strunk's translation has been slightly revised. C.f. chap. 4, n. 22, above.

201. Rousseau, *Lettre*, p. 650.

202. Ibid., p. 648.

203. Ibid., p. 652.

204. Ibid., pp. 640-41.

205. C. "Cantare."

206. PSMFI, p. 33.

207. Ibid., p. 31; he was quite wrong in this regard.

208. Ibid., p. 33.

209. Ibid., p. 31.

210. Originally produced in October, 1737, *Castor et Pollux* was revived in a different version in 1754 when it was placed in opposition to Pergolesi's *Le Serva padrona* by the advocates of the French national style; it was revised in 1764-65. It sustained a long run, with 28 representations in 1764, and 40 in 1765. It is thus possible that Burney heard it during either of his early two visits to Paris. Madame Arnould sang the role of Telaire, a *dessus* part, beginning in 1764, a role which she filled once again in the third revival of the opera in 1773. Although the *Catalogue* of Burney's library states that he owned a copy of the score dated 1735, the date is in error. The first edition of the score appeared in 1737, and an edition of the revised version was published in 1754. Burney's critical remarks are directed to the 1754 edition, which reflects the version he heard in 1764-65 in Paris. Reports of these productions are given in *Le Mercure de France* (Feb. 1764), and *L'Avant-Courer* (1764). GHM, ii, p. 967.

211. Ibid.

212. C. "Motivo": Burney writes, "The theme, subject, or two or three first bars of a composition... it expresses the primitive and original idea upon which a composer forms an air or movement, and arranges his design... The principal motivo or subject ought to be continually in the composer's mind, nor should he suffer it to be forgotten by the audience."

213. GHM, ii, p. 967.

214. C. "Rallentando." The italics are Burney's.

215. GHM, ii, p. 967.

216. This example was realized from Berard's symbols by Dr. Mary Cyr, and was included in her paper "French and Italian styles of signing: Rameau's writing for the voice." Read before the joint meeting of the Northern and Southern California chapters of the A.M.S., at Stanford University (6 Apr. 1974).

217. GHM,, ii, p. 967.

218. Among these were *Persée, Achille et Polixene, Atys, Phaëton, Roland,* and *Psyche.*

219. GHM, ii, p. 968.

220. C. "Phrase." For a sound, well-thought-out response to non-French critics of Rameau's rhythmic structure and phraseology, see Cuthbert Girdlestone, *Jean-Philippe Rameau: His Life and Work,* enlarged edition (New York, 1969), pp. 184-7.

221. CB to Ebeling, 30 Mar. 1772 (Hamburg).
222. Rousseau, *Lettre,* p. 639.
223. GHM, ii, p. 968.
224. Ibid.
225. C. "Liberté de Musique."
226. GHM, ii, p. 972.
227. Ibid.
228. C. "Monsigni."
229. See chap. 4.
230. GHM, ii, p. 972.
231. Ibid., p. 977.
232. C. "Monsigni."
233. GHM, ii, p. 87. C. "Morley."
234. "The Merope of Nasolini, composed originally in Italy for Ms. Billington—it is beautiful music—elegant, natural and new..." B.M. Add. MS. 48345.
235. It is clear elsewhere that Mozart's name should have joined Nasolini's on Burney's list; the omission is surely an oversight.
236. PSMG, i, pp. 293-94.
237. Ibid.
238. GHM,, ii, p. 972.
239. Burney's review of "Revolutions of the Italian Opera," [*Le rivoluzioni del teatro musicale italiano*], *Monthly Review,* LXXIX (1788), p. 660.
240. GHM, ii, p. 972.
241. Ibid.
242. MM, ii, p. 89.
243. GHM, ii, p. 844.
244. Elsewhere Gluck is referred to as the only good composer not formed on the Neapolitan School. C. "Vinci."
245. MM, ii, pp. 334-35.
246. C. "German School of Composition."
247. C. "Bach, John Christian."
248. Introduced into a pasticcio, *La Vendemmia,* by Giuseppe Gazzaniga, King's Theatre, Haymarket, 9 Apr. 1789.
249. Fiske, *English Theatre Music,* p. 506.
250. Quoted by C.B. Oldman in "Attwood's Dramatic Works," *Musical Times* CVII (1967), pp. 23-27.

251. Smith, *The Italian Opera,* p. 107.
252. Quoted by Otto Deutsch in *Mozart: A Documentary Biography* (Stanford, 1965), pp. 377-78.
253. Quoted by C.B. Oldman in "Dr. Burney and Mozart," *Mozart-Jahrbuch* (Salzburg, 1964), p. 76.
254. C. "Stilo."
255. See also CB to Crotch, 4 Nov. 1805 (Osborn).
256. Auction Catalogue, p. 20.
257. A full score was published in the first decade of the nineteenth century by Simrock at Bonn, Germany.
258. Berg.
259. CB to TT, 24 Feb. 1782 (Osborn).
260. CB to SBP, 14 DEc. 1783 (Osborn).
261. GHM, ii, p. 892.
262. CB to TT, Aug. 1783 (Osborn).
263. CB to TT, Dec. 1784 (Osborn).
264. Richard Mount-Edgcumbe, *Musical Reminiscences of the Earl of Mount Edgcumbe,* 4th. ed. (London, 1834), p. 45.
265. CB to Richard Bull, late Jan. 1785 (Osborn).
266. Smith, *The Italian Opera,* pp. 18-20. Bertoni's *Quinto Fabio* was also given once at Pacchierotti's benefit.
267. See Lonsdale, p. 360.
268. Smith, *The Italian Opera,* p. 22.
269. MM, iii, p. 328.
270. Ibid.
271. CB to CB, Jr., 9 Nov. 1801 (Berg).
272. CB to Lord Mornington, Jan.-Mar., 1807 (Osborn).

Chapter 9

1. See Lonsdale, pp. 209-19.
2. *Universal Magazine* LXXVII (1790), pp. 86-87.
3. *Harmonicon* X (1832), p. 216.
4. Lawrence Lipking, *The Ordering of the Arts in Eighteenth-Century England* (New Jersey, 1970), p. 322.
5. Lonsdale, p. 337.
6. Lipking, *The Ordering of the Arts,* p. 313.
7. GHM, ii, p. 1010.

8. Lipking, *The Ordering of the Arts*, p. 313.
9. Osborn. Several alternate readings have been omitted in favor of one continuous text.
10. *Account*, pp. 40-41.
11. C. "Handel."
12. Notebook (Osborn).
13. Lipking, *The Ordering of the Arts*, p. 285.
14. *Harmonicon* X (1832), p. 216.
15. For a partial listing of Burney's translations from Rousseau, see Thomas Webb Hunt, "The Dictionnaire de Musique of Jean-Jacques Rousseau," Ph.D. dissertation, North Texas State University (1967), pp. 561-62.
16. Christopher Welch, *Six Lectures on the Recorder,* Lecture III (London, 1911), p. 336.
17. William Chappell, *Popular Music of Olden Times,* (London, 1844), pp. i, ix.
18. Hawkins, *History*, ii, p. 798.
19. GHM, ii, p. 480.
20. Hawkins, *History*, ii, p. 784.
21. GHM,, ii, p. 487.
22. Compare Burney on Croft, GHM, ii, p. 481, and Hawkins, *History*, ii, p. 796; or Maurice Green, GHM, ii, pp. 488-89, and Hawkins, *History*, ii, pp. 800 and 879.
23. *Encyclopaedia Perthensis* XV (London, 1807), pp. 433-77. See notebook (Osborn).
24. *European Magazine* XVI (1789), pp. 104-5.
25. GHM, ii, p. 961.
26. Quoted in the *European Magazine* XVI (1789), p. 104.
27. Man kann nicht läugnen, dass Herr Burney die meisten Theile der alten Musik sehr gut, und mit Ordnung abgehandelt hat. Auch findet man einen Reichthum von Bemerkungen, nicht selten mit sehr gründlichen Urtheilen unterstüz, die Herrn Burney auf alle Weise als einen Mann zeigen, der eine sehr ausgebreitete Gelehrsamkeit besitz, und alles mögliche gelesen hat, was man zum Behuf einer solchen Arbeit, wie die allgemeine Geschichte unserer Kunst ist, nur immer lesen kann. Johann Nicolaus Forkel, *Musikalisch-kritsche Bibliothek,* 3 vols. (Gotha, 1778-79), p. 190.
28. Noch verdient bemerkt zu werden, dass der Verfasser am Schulss des zhenten Kapitels im 4. Band seine ehemaligen Urtheile über den mangel an Genie der Deutschen auf eine edele Art als unbegründet und ungereimt nicht nur förmlich widerrufen, sondern auch dieser Nation desfalls eine Ehrenerklärung getan hat. Diese Handlung macht nicht nur seiner Gerechtigkeits- und Wahrheitsliebe Ehre, sondern wird ihm auch als musikalischer Kunstrichter und Geschicht- schreiber bei seinen Lesern ein grösseres Mass von Zutrauen verschaffen, als er ehedem bei so einseitigen und unbergründeten Urtheilen erwarten konnte. Johann Nicolaus Forkel, *Allgemeine Litteratur der Musik* (Leipzig, 1792), p. 28.
29. *Allgemine Musikalische Zeitung,* 8 Dec. 1802, col. 198.
30. *Burney, Doctor* der *Musik,*—hat sich durch seine *musikalische Reisen* und sonderlich durch seine *Geschichte der Tonkunst* in ganz Europa bekannt gemacht. Zwar enthalten seine

Reisen einen Reichthum von richtigen und gediegenen Bemerkungen, und verrathen ungemein viel musikalische Kenntnisse: allein seine Urtheile sind zu *brittisch*, d.i. zu kühn, und oft ganz und gar unrichtig. *Ebeling*, der Uebersetzer dieser Reisen, und *Reichard* haben ihm diess aufs nachdrücklichste bewiesen, und seine Irrthümer, auch oft seine Verleumdungen grosser Männer mit deutschem Muthe gerügt. *Burney* reiste viel zu schnell und flüchtig, als dass er mit philosophischer Kälte hätte Beobachtungen anstellen können. Uns Deutschen lässt er bey weitem nicht die gehörige Gerechtigkeit widerfaher . Er räumt uns bloss *Kunstfertigkeit* und *Fleiss* ein, spircht uns aber das musikalische *Genie* ab—eine Verleumdung, welche durch die ganze Geschichte der Tonkunst, zur Ehre unsrere Nation widerlegt wird.

Seine *musikalische Geschichte,* woran er zwanzig Jahre lang sammelte und schrieb, enthält zwar einen schwelgenden Aufwant von Gelehrsamkeit, wozu derjenige leicht gelangen kann, der Geld genug hat; allein das Werk wimmelt von Irrthümern; sein Urteil ist nicht original, sondern meist französich und sein *äesthetisches Gefühl* will gar nicht veil sagen.

Eschenburgs Uebersetzung dieses Werks hat inzwischen viele von diesen auffallenden Fehlern hinweggewischt. Christian Friedrich Daniel Schubart, *Ideen zu einer Ästhetik der Tonkunst.* ed. *Ludwig Schubart* (Vienna, 1806), p. 258.

31. ...aber mit einer Eile, die notwendig seinen Untersuchungen und Erfahrungen als Geschichtsschreiber nachtheilig sein musste und ihn manches dunkel oder von der unrechten Seite kennen lernen liess. Ernst Ludwig Gerber, *Historisch Biographisches Lexicon der Tonkünstler,* 2 vols. (Leipzig 1790-[1792]), pp. 228-29.

32. Nicht zufrieden, dass er das, was er sagt, allezeit auf das gefälligste einkleidet, oder mit andern Worten: die trockensten Materien auf die angenehmste Weise vorzutragen weiss, so steht ihm auch seine muntere Laune und sein mit immer am rechten Ort zu Gebote, um den Leser auf den langen, öden und von Kunstanbaue leeren Stationen nicht einschlafen zu lassen. Ungleich anziehender aber muss dies Werk seinen Landsleuten sein, denen keine seiner Anspielungen, keiner seiner Seitenblicke verloren gehen kann, und die insbesondere seine ausführliche und vollständige Geschichte der London schen Operntheater sehr interessieren muss. Überhaupt hat er aber zur Geschichte der dramatischen Musik noch unendlich viel hinzugetan, was dem Hawkins noch fehlte, und wovon sich Printz garnichts ahnen lassen konnte, da vor der Erscheinung von Matthesons Patrioten und dessen Ehrenpfordte in keiner deutschen Schrift der Oper nur mit einem Worte gedacht wird. Glück für uns, dass in unserm Zeitalter soeben ein Forkel in Göttingen lebt, der einer solchen unübersehbaren Arbeit gewachsen ist, und uns die Hülfe der Ausländer in diesem Fache entbehrlich macht; sonst hätten wir Ursache, beide Hände nach einer Übersetzung der Burneyischen Werke auszustrecken. Ernst Ludwig Gerber, *Neues historisch-biographisches Lexicon der Tonkünstler,* 4 vols. (Leipzig, 1812-[1814]), No. 88 (31 Oct. 1804), p. 699.

33. *Journal des beaux arts* VI (1780), p. 96.

34. *Correspondance des amateurs musiciens* LXXXVIII (31 Oct. 1804), p. 699.

35. The records of Burney's nomination are in the archives of the institute, volume $2E_3$ p. 161. Lonsdale remarks that the honor was delayed for four years, until 28 April 1810, the date which appears on Burney's diploma. If there was such a delay, there is no mention of it in the official minutes or other records of the institute.

36. *Notice des travaux* (1811), p. 20.

37. Cote Rés. 605.

38. CB to Lady Banks [Nov. 1805] (Osborn).
39. Archives of the French Institute, 2E₅ pp. 51-56.
40. *Notice des travaux* (1814), p. 9.
41. *Annual Review and History of Literature* I (1802), pp. 859-66.
42. GHM, i, p. 301.
43. GHM, i, pp. 46-47.
44. MMM, p. 224.
45. C. "Arabian Music."
46. There is a large article on the organ in the *Cyclopaedia.*
47. MMM, p. 224.
48. GHM, ii, p. 8.
49. Ibid., p. 966.
50. "Taste," *Oxford English Dictionary* (Oxford, 1933).
51. MMM, p. 23.
52. Lipking, *The Ordering of the Arts*, p. 322.
53. *European Magazine* XX (1791), p. 118.
54. Ibid.
55. The notebooks in the Osborn Collection stand as impressive memorials to Burney's herculean labors in treating ancient music, to mention only one topic.
56. Jack Westrup, *Purcell,* The Great Composer Series (New York, 1962), p. 273.
57. Charles Cudworth, "Song and Part-Song Settings of Shakespeare's Lyrics, 1660-1960," *Shakespeare in Music,* ed. Phyllis Hartnold, (London, 1969), p. 61.
58. Joseph Kerman, *The Elizabethan Madrigal: A Comparative Study* (Philadelphia, 1962), p. 161.
59. GHM, ii, p. 955.
60. Edward Dent, *Mozart's Operas: A Critical Study* (London, 1973), p. 15.
61. Lipking, *The Ordering of the Arts,* p. 285.
62. Lipking also writes of "the improvement in Burney's opinion of Mozart," an attitude betraying his failure, despite his own warnings, to approach Burney on his own terms and in the context of his time. Lipking, *The Ordering of the Arts,* pp. 284-85.
63. Wilton Mason, "The Architecture of St. Marks Cathedral, and the Venetian Polychoral Style: A Clarification," in *Studies in Musicology; Essays in the History, Style, and Bibliography of Music in Memory of Glen Haydon,* ed. James Pruett (Chapel Hill, 1969), p. 178.

Bibliography

Manuscript Sources

An inventory of the Burney manuscripts is given in Lonsdale, pp. 495-97. The location of letters extant in manuscript is given in Joyce Hemlow's *Catalogue*.

Burney's Published Works

1766

The Cunning-Man, a Musical Entertainment, in Two Acts. As it is Performed at the Theatre Royal in Drury-Lane. Originally written and composed by M. J.J. Rouseau. London, 1766.

1769

An Essay towards a History of the Principal Comets that have appeared since the Year 1742. Including a particular Detail of the Return of the famous Comet of 1682 in 1759, according to the Calculation and Prediction of Dr. Halley. Compiled from the Observations of the most eminent Astronomers of this Century. With Remarks and Reflections upon the Present Comet. To which is prefixed, by way of Introduction, A Letter upon Comets. Addressed to a Lady, by the late M. de Maupertuis. Written in the Year 1742. London, 1769.

1771

The Present State of Music in France and Italy: or, The Journal of a Tour through those Countries, underaken to collect Materials for a General History of Music. By Charles Burney, Mus.D. London, 1771. Second edition, 1773.
Dr. Burney's Musical Tours in Europe. ed. P.A. Scholes. 2 vols. London, 1959. Vol. i: *An Eighteenth-Century Musical Tour in France and Italy.*
Music, Men, and Manners in France and Italy, 1770. ed. H. Edmund Poole. London, 1969.

Translations:

Carl Burney's der Musik Doctors Tagebuch einer Musikalischen Reise durch Frankreich und Italien welche er unternommen hat um zu einer allgemeinen Geschichte der Musik Materialen zu sammlen. Aus dem Englischen übersetzt von C.D. Ebeling, Aufsehern der Handlungsakademie zu Hamburg. Hamburg, 1772.

Rijk gestoffeerd verhaal van de eigenlijke Gesteldheid der hedendaagsche Toonkunst of sir Karel Burneys Dagboek van Zyne onlangs gedaane Reizen door Frankryk, Italien en Deutschland. Groningen, 1786.

De l'état présent de la Musique en France et en Italie, dans les Pays-Bas, en Hollande et en Allemagne, ou Journal des Voyages faits dans ces differents Pays avec l'intention d'y recueillir des matériaux pour servir à une Histoire générale de la Musique, par Ch. Burney, Professeur de Musique, Traduit de l'Anglais par Ch. Brack, de la Société Royale de Gottingue. 3 vols. Gênes, 1809-1810.

Viaggio musicale in Italia, 1770. Traduzione di Virginio Attanasio. [Milan,] 1921.

Lettera del defonto Signor Giuseppe Tartini alla Signora Maddalena Lombardini inserviente ad una importante Lezione per i Suonatori di Violino. With English title: *A Letter from the late Signor Tartini to Signora Maddalena Lombardini (now Signora Sirmen) Published as an Important Lesson to Performers on the Violin. Translated by Dr. Burney.* London, 1771. Second edition, 1779.

1773

The Present State of Music in Germany, the Netherlands, and the United Provinces. Or, The Journal of a Tour through those Countries, undertaken to collect Materials for a General History of Music. By Charles Burney, Mus. D., F.R.S. 2 vols. London, 1773. Second edition, corrected, 1775.

Dr. Burney's Musical Tours in Europe. ed. P.A. Scholes. 2 vols. London, 1959. Vol. ii: *An Eighteenth-Century Musical Tour in Central Europe and the Netherlands.*

Translations:

Carl Burney's der Musik Doctors Tagebuch seiner Musikalischen Reisen. Zweyter Band. Durch Flandern, die Niederlande und am Rhein bis Wien. Aus dem Englischen übersetzt; and *Dritter Band. Durch Böhmen, Sachsen, Brandenburg, Hamburg und Holland. Aus dem Englischen übersetzt. Mit einigen Zusätzen und Anmerkungen zum zweyten und dritten Bande.* Hamburg, 1773.

For the Dutch translation by J.W. Lustig, Groningen, 1786, and the French translation by Charles Brack, Gênes, 1810, see under "1771."

1776

A General History of Music, from the Earliest Ages to the Present Period. To which is prefixed, a Dissertation on the Music of the Ancients. By Charles Burney. Mus.D., F.R.S. Volume the First. London, 1776. Second edition, corrected and revised, 1789.

A General History of Music... by Charles Burney, with critical and historical notes by Frank Mercer. 2 vols. London, 1935. Reprinted, New York, 1957.

Translation:

Dr. Karl Burney's Abhandlung über die Musik der Alten... übersetzt, und mit einigen Anmerkungen begleitet von J.J. Eschenburg. Leipzig, 1781.

1779

Account of an Infant Musician [William Crotch]. *By Charles Burney, Doctor of Music, F.R.S. Read at the Royal Society, Feb. 18, 1779.* London, 1779.

Reprined in *Philosophical Transactions of the Royal Society for 1779,* lxix (Pt. I), 183-206.

1782

"Advice to the *Herald*": a poem in *The Morning Herald,* 12 March 1782.
A General History of Music. From the Earliest Ages to the Present Period. To Which is prefixed, a Dissertation on the Music of the Ancients. By Charles Burney. Mus. D., Volume the Second. London, 1782. Reprinted, with the original date, but with modern "s" throughout, by [? W. Byanes], in 1811 or 1812. Edited by Frank Mercer, London, 1935. Reprinted, New York, 1957.
A review, with Twining's assistance, of Francis Maxwell's *An Essay upon Tune,* in *Critical Review,* liv (Aug. 1782), 117-25.

1785

An Account of Mademoiselle Theresa Paradis, of Vienna, the Celebrated Blind Performer on the Piano Forte, including a *Cantata in German Written for Mademoiselle Paradis, by her blind friend M. Pfeffel, of Colmar, and set to music by her music-master, M. Leopold Kozeluch, of Vienna, 11th November 1784. Imitated by Dr. Burney.*
An Account of the Musical Performances in Westminster-Abbey, and the Pantheon, May 26th, 27th, 29th; and June the 3d, and 5th, 1784. In Commemoration of Handel. London, 1785.

Translation:

Dr. Karl Burney's Nachricht von Georg Friedrich Händel's Lebensumständen und der ihm zu London in Mai und Jun. 1784 angestellten Gedächtnissfeyer. Aus dem Englischen übersetzt von Johann Joachim Eschenburg. Berlin, 1785.

1785-1802

Book reviews, and contributions to the "Correspondence" section, in the *Monthly Review.* For a full list of Burney's articles, see B.C. Nangle, *The Monthly Review, First Series, 1749-1789, Indexes of Contributors and Articles.* Oxford, 1934; and *Second Series, 1790-1815.* Oxford, 1955.

1789

A General History of Music, from the Earliest Ages to the Present Period... Volume the Third and *Volume the Fourth.* London, 1789. Edited by Frank Mercer. London, 1935. Reprinted, New York, 1957.

Translation:

The introduction to volume iii was translated by J.J. Eschenburg in *Berliner Musik-Wochenblatt,* 1792, pp. 73-75 and 81-88.

1791

Verses on the Arrival in England of the Great Musician Haydn. London, 1791.

1796

Memoirs of the Life and Writings of the Abate Metastasio. In which are incorporated, Translations of his Principal Letters. By Charles Burney, Mus.D. F.R.S. 3 vols. London, 1796.

Didon abandonée; traduit de l'Italien...par Madlle. M. Grignon. Together with an extract from Memoirs of the Life and Writings of the Abate Metastasio: by Charles Burney. London, [?1810].

1799

Hymn for the Emperor. Translated by Dr. Burney. Composed by Doctor Haydn. London, 1799.

1802-1819

Articles on music and musicans contributed to *The Cyclopaedia; or, Universal Dictionary of Arts, Sciences, and Literature,* ed. Abraham Rees. 39 vols. London, 1802-19. 6 volumes of plates completed the work in 1820.

1803

A hymn, "Again the day returns of holy rest," *Gentleman's Magazine,* lxiii (Dec. 1803), 1140.

1808

"Memoirs and Character of the late Mrs. Ord," *Gentleman's Magazine,* lxxviii (July, 1808), 581-83.

Bibliography of Secondary Sources

Standard reference works, publications which were used merely to verify the accuracy of Burney's statements, and literature on aesthetics have not been included, unless they are cited in the text. The several hundred scores used in following Burney's survey of music history have not been cited.

ABC Dario Musico. Bath, 1780.

Allen, Warren Dwight. *Philosophies of Music History: A Study of General Histories of Music 1600-1960.* New York, 1962.

Allorto, Riccardo. "Il canto ambrosiano nelle lettre di G.B. Martini e di Charles Burney." *Studien zur Musikwissenschaft.* Festschrift für Erich Schenk, vol. 25. Köln, 1962.

Avison, Charles. *An Essay on Musical Expression.* 2d ed. London, 1753.

Balderston, K.C. "Dr. Johnson and Burney's History of Music." *Publications of the Modern Language Association* IL (1934): 966-68.

Barzun, Jacques. "Music into Words." *Lectures on the History and Art of Music: The Louis Charles Elson Memorial Lectures at the Library of Congress 1946-1963.* New York 1968.

Bayly, Anselm. *Alliance of Music, Poetry and Oratory.* London, 1789.

Bicknell, John. *Musical Travels Through England. By Joel Collier, Organist.* 4th ed. London, 1776.

Bingley, Rev. William. *Musical Biography; or Memoirs of the Lives and Writings of the Most Eminent Composers.* London, 1814.

Bouvier, Rene. *Farinelli: Le chanteur des rois.* Paris, 1943.

Boyce, William. *Cathedral Music, being a Collection in score of the Most Valuable and Useful Compositions of that Service by Several English Masters of the Last Two Hundred Years,* 3 vols. (1760-1778).

Brocklesby, Richard. *Reflections on Antient and Modern Musick, with the Application to the Cure of Diseases To which is subjoined, an Essay to Solve the Question, wherein consisted the Difference of Antient Musick from that of Modern Times.* London, 1749.

Brofsky, Howard. "Doctor Burney and Padre Martini: Writing a General History of Music," *Musical Quarterly* LXV (1979):313-45.
Brown, John. *A Dissertation on the Rise, Union, and Power, the Progress, Separations and Corruptions of Poetry and Music. To which is Prefixed, the Cure of Saul.* London, 1763.
Brown, John (painter). *Letters upon the Poetry and Music of the Italian Opera, Addressed to a Friend.* London, 1791.
Brown, Peter A. "The Earliest English Biography of Haydn." *Musical Quarterly* LIX (1973):339-54.
Bukofzer, Manfred F. *Music in the Baroque Era.* New York, 1947.
Burke, Edmund. *A Philosophical Enquiry Into the Origin of Our Ideas of the Sublime and Beautiful.* 2d ed. London, 1779.
Burney, Frances. *Diary and Letters of Madame d'Arblay.* edited by Austin Dobson. 6 vols. London, 1904-5.
_____. *The Early Diary of Frances Burney.* Edited by Annie Raine Ellis, Rev. ed., 2 vols., London, 1907.
_____. The Journals and Letters of Fanny Burney (Madame d'Arblay). Edited by Joyce Hemlow. Oxford, 1972.
_____. *Memoirs of Dr. Burney.* 3 vols. London, 1832.
Busby, Thomas. *A Complete Dictionary of Music.* 3d ed. London, 1811.
_____. *Concert Room and Orchestra Anecdotes of Music and Musicians, Ancient and Modern.* 3 vols. London, 1825.
_____. *A General History of Music from the Earliest Times to the Present.* 2 vols. London, 1819.
_____. *A Grammar of Music.* London, 1818.
Callcott, John Wall. *A Musical Grammar.* London, 1806.
Chenette, Louis F. "Music Theory in the British Isles during the Enlightenment." Ph.D. dissertation, Ohio State University, 1969.
Cole, Elizabeth. "Stafford Smith's Burney." *Music and Letters* XL (1959):35-38.
Collins, Arthur Simmons. *Authorship in the days of Johnson; being a study of the relation between author, patron, publisher and public. 1726-1780,* New York, 1929.
Cramer, Carl Friedrich, ed. *Magazin der Musik.* Hamburg, 1783-89.
Craufurd, J.G. "The Madrigal Society." *Proceedings of the RMA* 82nd Session (1955-56):33-45.
Croker, John Wilson. "Madame d'Arblay's Memoirs of Dr. Burney." *Quarterly Review* xlix (1833):91-125.
Crotch, William. *Substance of Several Courses of Lectures on Music.* London, 1831.
Cudworth, Charles. "Song and Part-Song Settings of Shakespeare's Lyrics, 1660-1960." *Shakespeare in Music.* Edited by Phyllis Hartnoll. London, 1964.
Darenberg, Karl H. *Studien zur englischen Musikaesthetik des 18 Jahrhunderts.* Band 6. Brittanica et Americana, Hamburg, 1960.
David, Hans T., and Mendel, Arthur, eds. *The Bach Reader: A Life of Johann Sebastian Bach in Letters and Documents.* Rev. ed. New York, 1966.
Dean, Winton. *Handel and the Opera Seria.* Berkeley, 1969.
_____. *Handel's Dramatic Oratorios and Masques.* London, 1959.
De Brosses, Charles. *Lettres sur l'Italie.* Paris, 1799.
Dent, Edward J. *Mozart's Operas: A Critical Study.* London, 1973.
Deutsch, Otto. *Mozart: A Documentary Biography.* Stanford, 1965.
Donington, Gloria (Rose). "The Cantatas of Carissimi." Ph.D. dissertation, Yale University, 1959.
Downes, Edward. "The Operas of Johann Christian Bach as a Reflection of the Dominant Trends in Opera Seria 1750-1780." 3 vols. Ph.D. dissertation, Harvard University, 1958.
Draper, John W. "Poetry and Music in Eighteenth Century Aesthetics." *Englische Studien,* 67 Band, 1 Heft (1930):69-85.

———. William Mason. *A Study in Eighteenth-Century Culture*. New York, 1927.
Eastcott, Richard. *Sketches of the Origin, Progress and Effects of Music*. London, 1793.
Edwards, Owain. "The Response to Corelli's Music in Eighteenth-Century England." *Studia Musicologica Norvegica* ii (1976):51-169.
Farmer, Henry George. *Music Making in the Olden Days, the Story of the Aberdeen Concerts 1748-1801*. London, n.d.
Fellowes, Edmund Horace. *The English Madrigal Composers*. 2d ed. London, 1948.
Fetis, Francois Joseph. *Biographie universelle des musiciens*. 2d ed. 8 vols. Paris, 1860-65.
Fiske, Roger. *English Theatre Music in the Eighteenth Century*. London, 1973.
Foreman, E. *Practical Reflections on Figured Singing* (Champaign, 1968), a translation with notes of Giovanni Battista Mancini, *Pensieri, e riflessioni, pratiche sopra il canto figurato* (Vienna, 1774).
Forkel, Johann Nicolaus. *Allgemeine Geschichte der Musik*. 2 vols. Leipzig, 1788-[1801].
———. *Allgemeine Litteratur der Musik*. Leipzig, 1792.
———. *Musikalisch-kritische Bibliothek*. 3 vols. Gotha, 1778-79.
———. *Musikalischer Almanach für Deutschland auf das Jahr 1782*. Leipzig, 1782.
Framery, Nicolas-Etienne and Guinguené, Pierre-Louis. *Encyclopedie méthodique. Musique*. 2 vols. Paris, 1791-[1818].
Garrick, David. *The Letters of David Garrick*. Edited by David M. Little. 3 vols. Cambridge, 1963.
Geiringer, Karl. *Haydn: A Creative Life in Music*. Berkeley, 1963.
Geminiani, Francesco. *Treatise on Good Taste and Rules for Playing in Good Taste*. London, 1747.
Gerard, Alexander. *An Essay on Genius*. London, 1774.
———. *An Essay on Taste*. 3d ed. Edinburgh, 1780.
Gerber, Ernst Ludwig. *Historisch-Biographisches Lexicon der Tonkünstler*. 2 vols. Leipzig, 1790-[1792].
———. *Neues historisch-biographisches Lexikon der Tonkünstler*. 4 vols. Leipzig, 1812-[1814].
Gerbert, Martin. *De cantu et sacra a prima ecclesiae aetate usque ad praesens tempus*. 2 vols. St. Blasien, 1774.
Girdlestone, Cuthbert. *Jean-Philippe Rameau: His Life and Work*. Rev. and enlarged. New York, 1969.
Goldschmidt, Hugo. *Die Musikaesthetik des 18 Jahrhunderts und ihre beziehungen zu sienum Kunstschaffen*. Zurich, 1915.
Grabo, Carrol. "A Bibliography of Musical Aesthetics and Criticsm in England 1700-1800." Seminar paper, University of California, Berkeley, 1964.
———. "The Practical Aesthetics of Thomas Busby's Music Reviews." *Journal of Aesthetics and Art Criticism* XXV (1966):37-45.
Grétry, André Ernest Modeste. *Mémoires ou essai sur la musique*. 3 vols. Paris, 1789.
Griffin, Sister Mary Ignatia. "The Trial of Midas the Second or Congress of Musicians by Dr. Charles Burney 1777." Ph.D. dissertation, Fordham University, 1962.
Hall, Martin V., and Hall, James S. "Handel's Graces." *Händel Jahrbuch* IX (1957):25-43.
Händel, Georg Friedrich. *Werke*. Leipzig, 1858-85.
Hanley, Edwin. "Alessandro Scarlatti's Cantate da Camara: A Bibliographical Study." Ph.D. dissertation, Yale University, 1963.
Hansell, Sven Hostrup. "The Solo Cantatas, Motets and Antiphons of Johann Adolf Hasse." Ph.D. dissertation, University of Illinois, Urbana, 1966.
———. *Works for Solo Voice of Johann Adolph Hasse (1699-1783)*. Detroit Studies in Bibliography, no. 12. Detroit, 1968.
Harris, James. *Three Treatises*. 3d ed. London, 1772.
Harrison, Frank Llewellyn. *Time, Place and Music. An Anthology of Ethnomusicological Observation c. 1550 to Ca. 1800*. Source Materials and Studies in Ethnomusicology, no. 1. Amsterdam, 1973.

Hawkins, Sir John. *An Account of the Institution and Progress of the Academy of Ancient Music.* London, 1770.

_____. *A General History of the Science and Practice of Music.* 2 vols. New York, 1963.

Haydn, Joseph. *The Collected Correspondence and London Notebooks of Joseph Haydn.* Compiled and translated by H.C. Robbins Landon. London, 1959.

_____. *Gesammelte Briefe und Aufzeichnungen.* Kassel, 1965.

Heger, Elisabeth. *Die anfänge der neueren Musikgeschichts-schreibung um 1770 bei Gerber, Burney um Hawkins.* Strassburg, 1930.

Helm, Ernest Eugene. *Music at the Court of Frederick the Great.* Norman, 1960.

Hemlow, Joyce. *The History of Fanny Burney.* London, 1958.

Heriot, Angus. *The Castrati in Opera.* London, 1956.

Highfill, Philip H. Jr.; Burnim, Kalman A.; and Langhans, Edward A. *A Biographical Dictionary of Actors, Actresses, Musicians, Dancers, Managers and other Stage Personnel in London 1660-1800.* 4 vols. Carbondale, 1973-

Hoboken, Anthony van. *Thematisch-bibliographisches Werkverzeichnis.* Bd. I. Mainz, 1957.

Hogarth, George. *Musical History, Biography and Criticism.* 2d ed. London, 1838.

Hughes, Rosemary. "Dr. Burney's Championship of Haydn." *Musical Quarterly* XXVII (1941): 90-96.

_____. *Haydn.* London, 1962.

Hunt, Thomas W. "The Dictionnaire de Musique of Jean-Jacques Rousseau." Ph.D. dissertation, North Texas State University, 1969.

Hutchings, Arthur. *The Baroque Concerto.* 3d ed. London, 1973.

Jackson, William of Exeter. *Observations on the Present State of Music in London.* London, 1791.

Jacob, Hildebrand. *Of the Sister Arts; An Essay.* London, 1734.

Johnson, Samuel. *A Dictionary of the English Language.* 2 vols. London, 1756.

Jones, Edward. *Musical and Poetical Relics of the Welsh Bards.* London, 1784.

Kames, Lord Henry Home. *Elements of Criticism.* New York, 1830.

Kassler, Jamie Croy. "British Writings on Music, 1760-1830: A Systematic Essay toward a Philosophy of Selected Theoretical Writings." 2 vols. Ph.D. dissertaton, Columbia University, 1971.

_____. "Burney's Sketch of a Plan for a Public Music School." *Musical Quarterly* LVIII (1972):210-34.

_____. "The Systematic Writings on Music of William Jones." *JAMS* XXVI (1973):92-107.

Kausch, Johann Joseph. *Johann Joseph Kausch's Abhandlung über den Einfluss der Töne und ins besondere der Musik auf die Seele; nebst einenn Anhange über den unmittelbaren Zweck der Schönen Künste.* Breshau, 1782.

Kelly, Michael. *Reminiscences.* Edited by Roger Fiske. London, 1975.

Kerman, Joseph. *The Elizabethan Madrigal: A Comparative Study.* Philadelphia, 1962.

Kidd, Ronald R. "The Emergence of Chamber Music with Obligato Keyboard in England." *Acta Musicologica* XLIV (1972): 122-44.

Kirkpatrick, Ralph. *Domenico Scarlatti.* Princeton, 1953.

Kivy, Peter. "Mainwaring's 'Handel': Its Relation to English Aesthetics." *JAMS* XVII (1964):170-78.

Kollmann, August Friedrich Christopher. *An Essay on Musical Harmony, According to the Nature of that Science and the Principles of the Greatest Musical Authors.* London, 1796.

_____. *An Essay on Practical Musical Composition, According to the Nature of that Science and the Principles of the Greatest Musical Authors.* London, 1799.

La Borde, Jean Benjamin de. *Essai sur la musique ancienne et moderne.* 4 vols. Paris, 1780.

La Lande, Joseph Jérome le François de. *Voyage en Italie.* 9 vols. Paris, 1769.

Landon, H.C. Robbins. *Haydn: Chronicle and Works. Volume III. Haydn in England 1791-1795.* Indiana, 1976.

――――. *The Collected Correspondence and London Notebooks of Joseph Haydn.* London, 1959.
Larsen, Jens Peter. *Handel's Messiah: Origins. Composition Sources.* Copenhagen, 1957.
Launay, Denise, ed. *La Querelle des Bouffons.* 3 vols. Genève, 1973.
Leigh, R.A. "Les Amitiés français du Dr. Burney." *Revue de Literature Comparée* XXV (1951):161-94.
Lipking, Lawrence. *The Ordering of the Arts in Eighteenth-Century England.* New Jersey, 1970.
Lonsdale, Roger. "Dr. Burney and the Integrity of Boswell's Quotations." *Papers of the Bibliographical Society of America* LIII (1959):327-331.
――――. "Dr. Burney, John Weaver and the *Spectator.*" *Famed for Dance: Essays on the Theory and Practice of Theatrical Dancing in England, 1660-1740.* New York, 1960.
――――. "William Bewley and the *Monthly Review:* a Problem of Attribution." *Papers of the Bibliographical Society of America* LV (1961):309-18.
Lovell, Percy. "Ancient Music in Eighteenth-Century England." *Music and Letters* LX (1979):401-415.
Lynch, James J. *Box, Pit and Gallery: Stage and Society in Johnson's London.* Berkeley, 1953.
Marsh, John. "A Comparison Between the Ancient and Modern Styles of Music." *Monthly Magazine* II, part I (1796):981-986.
Martini, Giambattista. *Piano generale per una storia della musica do Carlos Burney con un catalogo della sua biblioteca musicale.* Bologna, 1972.
Mason, Wilton. "The Architecture of St. Marks Cathedral, and the Venetian Polychoral Style: A Clarification." *Studies in Musicology; Essays in the History, Style and Bibliography of Music in Memory of Glen Haydon.* Edited by James Pruett, Chapel Hill, 1969.
Matthew, James E. "The Antient Concerts 1776-1848." *Proceedings of the RMA* XXXIII (1907):55-80.
Mee, John H. *The Oldest Music Room in Europe: A Record of Eighteenth Century Enterprise at Oxford.* London, 1911.
Mount-Edgcumbe, Richard. *Musical Reminiscences of the Earl of Mount Edgcumbe.* 4th ed. London, 1834.
Myers, Robert Manson. *Handel's Messiah: A Touchstone of Taste.* New York, 1948.
Monteverdi, Claudio. *Monteverdis Orfeo; facsimile des erstdrucks der Musik...herausgegeben von Adolf Sandberger.* Augsburg, 1927.
Moorefield, Arthur A. "James Bruce: Ethnomusicologist or Abyssinian Lyre?" *JAMS* XXVIII (1975):493-514.
Morley, Thomas. *A Plaine and Easie Introduction to Practicall Musike.* London, 1597.
Nangle, Benjamin Christie. *The Monthly Review, First Series 1749-1789; Indexes of Contributors and Articles.* Oxford, 1937. *Second Series 1790-1815.* Oxford, 1955.
Newman, William S. *The Sonata in the Classic Era: The Second Volume of A History of the Sonata Idea.* Chapel Hill, 1963.
North, Roger. *Memoirs of Music.* Edited by Edward Rimbault. London, 1846.
Oldman, Cecil B. "Charles Burney and Louis DeVisme." *Music Review* XXVII (1961):93-97.
――――. "Dr. Burney and Mozart." *Mozart Jahrbuch* (1962-63):75-81.
――――. "Dr. Burney and Mozart Addenda and Corrigenda." *Mozart-Jahrbuch* (1964):104-10.
――――. "Haydn's Quarrel with the Professionals in 1788." *Musik und Verlag* (1968):459.
Olleson, Edward. "Church Music and Oratorio." In *The Age of Enlightenment, 1745-1790.* Vol. VII, pp. 228-335. The New Oxford History of Music (1973).
Parke, W.T. *Musical Memoirs; Comprising an Account of the General State of Music in England from...1784 to the Year 1830.* London, 1830.
Petty, Fred C. "Italian Opera in London, 1760-1800." Ph.D. dissertation, Yale University, 1971.
Picken, Laurence. "Bach Quotations from the Eighteenth Century." *Music and Letters* V (1944):83-95.

Plamenac, Dragan. "New Light on the Last Years of Carl Phillip Emanuel Bach." *Musical Quarterly* XXXV (1949):565-87.
Quantz, Johann Joachim. *On Playing the Flute.* Translated by Edward R. Reilly. London, 1966.
Raeburn, Michael. "Dr. Burney, Mozart and Crotch." *Musical Times* XCVII (1956):514-20.
Redlich, Hans F. "The Bach Revival in England." *Hinrichsen's Musical Yearbook* VII (1952):287-300.
Reichardt, Johann Friedrich. *Briefe eines aufmerksamen Reisenden die Musik betreffend.* 2 vols. Frankfurt and Leipzig, 1774-[1776].
_____. *Musikalischer Almanach.* Berlin, 1796.
_____. *Musikalisches Kunstmagazin.* 2 vols. Berlin, 1782-91.
Reilly, Edward R. *Quantz and his Versuch.* Philadelphia, 1971.
Rogerson, Brewster. "Ut Musica Piesis. The Parallel of Music and Poetry in Eighteenth Century Criticism." Ph.D. dissertation, Princeton University, 1945.
Roscoe, Christopher. "Haydn and London in the 1780's." *Music and Letters* X (1968):203-12.
Rosen, David. "Musical Aesthetics in Eighteenth-Century Britian: A Bibliography." Seminar Paper, University of California, Berkeley, 1963.
Rousseau, Jean-Jacques. *Dictionnaire de musique.* Paris, 1768.
_____. "Essai sur l'origine des langues, où il est parlé de la mélodie, et de l'imitation musicale." *Project concernant de nouveaux signes pour la musique.* Geneva, 1781.
_____. "Lettre à M. Burney sur la musique avec fragmens d'observations sur l'Alceste italien de M. de le chevalier Gluck." *Traités sur la musique.* Geneva, 1781.
_____. *Lettre sur la musique française.* Paris, 1753.
Routh, Francis. *Early English Organ Music from the Middle Ages to 1837.* New York, 1973.
Rowen Ruth H. "Some Eighteenth Century Classifications of Musical Style." *Musical Quarterly* XXXIII (1947):90-101.
Sadie, Stanley. "Concert Life in Eighteenth Century England." *Proceedings of the RMA* LXXXV (1959):17-30.
Sainsbury, John S. *A Dictionary of Musicians from the Earliest Times.* 2 vols. London, 1825.
Scholes, Percy A. "George the Third as Music Lover." *Musical Quarterly* XXVIII (1942):78-92.
_____. *The Great Dr. Burney.* 2 vols. London, 1948.
_____. *Life of Sir John Hawkins.* London, 1953.
_____. *The Puritans and Music in England and New England.* London, 1934.
Schubart, Christian Friedrich Daniel. *Ideen zu einer Asthetik des Tonkunst.* Edited by Ludwig Schubart. Vienna, 1806.
Schueller, Herbert M. "Correspondences between Music and the Sister Arts according to Eighteenth Century Aesthetic Theory." *Journal of Aesthetics and Art Criticism* XIII (1953):334-59.
_____. "Imitation and Expression in British Music Criticism." *Musical Quarterly* LXXIV (1948):550-561.
_____. "Literature and Music as Sister Arts: an Aspect of Aesthetic Theory in Eighteenth-Century Britain." *Philological Quarterly* XXVI (1947):193-205.
_____. "The Pleasures of Music: Speculation in British Music Criticism 1750-1800." *Journal of Aesthetics and Art Criticism* VIII (1950):155-71.
_____. "The Quarrel of the Ancients and the Moderns." *Music and Letters* XLI (1960):313-30.
_____. "The Use and Decorum of Music as Described in British Literature, 1700-1780." *Journal of the History of Ideas* XIII (1952):74.
Shaw, Harold Watkins. "Blow." *Grove's V* I (1954):772.
_____. "Tradition and Convention in John Blow's Harmony." *Music and Letters* XXX (1949):136-45.
Shield, William. *Introduction to Harmony.* London, 1790.

Smith, William, and Humphries, Charles. *A Bibliography of the Musical Works Published by the Firm of John Walsh during the Years 1721-1766.* London, 1968.

Smith, William C. *The Italian Opera and Contemporary Ballet in London 1789-1820.* London, 1955.

Southgate, T.L. "Music at the Public Pleasure Gardens of the Eighteenth Century." *Proceedings of the RMA* XXXVIII (1911-12):141-58.

Statham, Heathcote. "Dr. Blow's Church Music and its Deformities." *Musical Times* LXVII (1926):988-90; 1083-85.

Stefani, Gino. "Musica sacra, societa negli scritti di Ch. Burney." *Nouova rivista musicale italiana* V (1971):22-39.

Strunk, Oliver. *Source Readings in Music History: From Classical Antiquity through the Romantic Era.* New York, 1950.

Temperly, Nicholas. "Beethoven in London Concert Life 1800-1850." *Music Review* XXIX (1960):207-14.

Tosi, Pier Francesco. *Observations on the Florid Song.* Translated by Mr. Galliard. London, 1743.

Twining, Thomas. *Aristotle's Treatise on Poetry: Translated with Notes and Two Dissertations on Poetical and Musical Imitation.* 2d ed. 2 vols. London, 1812.

_____. *Recreations and Studies of a Country Clergyman of the Eighteenth Century.* Edited by Richard Twining. London, 1882.

Ullrich, Hermann. "Musica Theresia Paradis in London." *Music and Letters* XLIII (1962):16-24.

Walker, Ernest. *A History of Music in England.* 3d ed. Revised and enlarged by J.A. Westrup. Oxford, 1952.

Walker, Frank. "Salvator Rosa and Music." *Monthly Musical Record* LXXIX (1949):199-205.

Watkins, Glenn. *Gesualdo: The Man and His Music.* London, 1973.

Webb, Daniel. *Observations on the Correspondence between Poetry and Music.* London, 1769.

Welch, Christopher. *Six Lectures on the Recorder.* London, 1911.

Wesley, Samuel. *Letters of Samuel Wesley to Mr. Jacobs.* Edited by Eliza Wesley. New York, n.d.

_____. "Reminiscences." British Museum. Add. MS. 27593.

Westrup, Jack. *Purcell.* The Great Composer Series. New York, 1962.

Winesanker, M. "Musico-Dramatic Criticism of English Comic Opera 1750-1800." *JAMS* (1949):87-96.

Wolff, Hellmuth Christian. *Original Vocal Improvisations.* Anthology of Music XLI New York, 1972.

Young, Percy M. *The Bachs: 1500-1850.* New York, 1970.

_____. *A History of British Music.* London, 1967.

Index

To lend order to the rich diversity of spelling used by Burney (Jomelli, Piccini, Schwindl, Schwindle, Schwindel), proper names, though retained in the text in Burney's spellings, are indexed under a single common form.

Abel, Karl Friedrich, 78, 93, 197, 208, 210, 212, 218, 320-21n.91, 347n.30
Academy of Ancient Music, 136, 175
Addison, Joseph, 11-12, 67, 234
Admeto (Handel), 242, 245
The Adopted Child (Attwood), 277
Agricola, Johann Friedrich, 91
"Ah, crudel" (Handel), 245
"Ah, speitato! e non te muove" (Handel), 240
Alberti bass, 191
Alberti, Domenico, 190, 192, 197, 200
Alceste (Gluck), 274, 275
Alcina (Handel), 240
Alembert, Jean le Rond d', 68, 263
Algarotti, Francesco, 236
Allegri, Gregorio, 75
"All we like sheep have gone astray" (Handel), 157
Alta Trinita, 121
Amadigi (Handel), 239, 242
Ancient music, 52, 55, 64; arrangements of, 98-99; attitude toward, 99-100; inferior to modern, 95-97, 100; loss of interest in, 108; reluctance to treat, 95-96; skepticism about, 104; treatment of, 95-101; Greek, 95-101, 103-8; Roman, 106
Andromaca (Jommelli), 238
"And the glory of the Lord" (Handel), 158
"And with His stripes" (Handel), 163
Anfossi, Pasquale, 237, 272
"Anima infida" (Handel), 240
Annibali, Domenico, 258
Annual Congress of Musicians, 136, 164
"Aria del Tasso" (Tartini), 208
Aristotle, 106
Armide (Gluck), 275
Armide (Sacchini), 281
Armino (Handel), 258
Arnaud, François, 70

Arne, Thomas, 7, 14, 22, 190, 191, 231, 234, 246; changes English song style, 182-84; operas, 246
Arnold, Samuel, 184, 235, 241, 286
Arnould, Madelaine-Sophie, 263, 265
Artaserse (Vinci), 229
Artaxerxes (Arne), 234
Artaxerxes, 281
Arteaga, Stefano, 293
Arthur, Aux Couteaux, 144
Ashwell, Thomas, 132
Astarto (Bononcini), 245
Aston, Hugh, 132
Atalanta (Handel), 245
Athalia (Handel), 97, 245
Attilio Regolo (Jommelli), 238
Attwood, Thomas, 277, 278
l'Augier, 190
Avison, Charles, 17-19, 210, 211, 215
Ayrton, William, 285

Babbi, Gregorio, 244
Bach-Abel Concerts, 211-13
Bach, Carl Philipp Emanuel, 23, 29, 41-42, 78, 83, 87, 91, 92, 164, 190, 191, 192, 199, 304, 320-21n.91, 347n.30; church music of, 165-66; compared with Handel, 195-96; view of Handel, 195-96; influence of, 198; keyboard music of, 193, 198, 200; Müthel and, 201
Bach, Johann Christoph, 90, 93, 111, 207, 210, 212, 218, 276
Bach, Johann Sebastian, 25, 28, 77, 164, 167, 198, 201, 203, 288, 303, 342n.95, 347n.30; Credo by, 196; evaluation of, 194-98; fugues of, 190; keyboard music of, 194-97; sacred music of, 167-68
Bai, Tommaso, 75
Banchieri, Andriano, 189
Banti-Giorgi, Brigida, 5, 281, 307n.9

Baretti, Giuseppe, 71
Barrington, Daines, 278
Barthélemon, François Hippolyte, 5, 12, 13
Barzun, Jacques, 19
Bassani, Giovanni Battista, 164
Bates, Joah, 154, 155, 289
"Batti, Batti" (Mozart), 277
Bassiron, Philippe, 132
Beethoven, Ludwig van, 46, 203, 215, 305; instrumental music of, 216-18; keyboard music of, 200, 201
Beggar's Opera, The (Gay), 30
La bella pescatrice (Guglielmi), 281
"Belta poi che l'assenti" (Gesualdo), 175
Benda, Franz, 84, 86
Benda, Georg, 86, 198
Berard, Jean Baptiste, 265
Berlin school, 83, 85, 86, 88-89
Bernacchi, Antonio, 244
Bertie, Willoughby, 214
Bewley, William, 5, 66, 79, 214, 283
Bianchi, Francesco, 260, 277, 307n.9
Biber, Heinrich Ignatz Franz, 209
Bibiena. *See* Galliari
Bible, 102-3
Bickham, George, 181
Bicknell, John, 106-8
Billington, Elizabeth, 281
Blainville, Charles Henri de, 56, 62, 231
Blow, John, 21-22, 51, 140, 143, 170, 189, 291-92, 303; his "crudities," 141-43
Boccaccio, Giovanni, 121
Boccherini, Luigi, 206, 208, 212, 213, 218
Bode, Johann Christoph, 77, 80, 87, 90, 93, 293; translation of the *Italian Tour*, 76-77; translation of the *German Tour*, 81-87; response to by CB, 88-89
Boesset, Jean-Baptiste, 144
Bonnet-Bourdelot, Pierre, 58
Bonnet, Jacques, 56, 58
Bononcini, Giovanni, 229, 245; compared to Handel, 289, 350n.113
Bontempi, Giovanni, 57-58
Bossler, Heinrich, 293
Bourdelot, Pierre, 58
Bow, earliest use of, 118
Boyce, William, 9, 51, 136, 137, 143, 149, 165, 245, 288, 291
Brack, Charles, 296
Bremner, Robert, 213
Breton, Joachim le, 296
Brossard, Sébastian de, 58, 315-16n.60
Brown, John, 61-62, 105
Browne, Richard, 102
Bruce, James, 101-2, 325-26n.29
Brumel, Antoine, 26, 132
Le bûcheron (Philidor), 74

Bull, John, 188, 190
La buona figliuola (Piccinni), 246
La buona figliuola maritata (Piccinni), 246
Burial Service (Morley), 137
Burney, Charles, achievement compared to Hawkins, 283-85; autobiography of, 2-5; biographies of, 1-2; influence of society upon, 1-2, 11, 12, 285-86, 287; library of, 314n.22; literary estate of, 2-4; as patron, 202-3; personal attributes of, 7; reliability as a critic, 12, 13, 14; reputation of, 293-95, 296-97; struggle for social gain of, 6, 11; veracity of, 154-56
  WORKS: LITERARY
    An Account of the Commemoration of Handel, 154-56, 160, 162, 287-89; German reaction to, 195-96;
    A General History of Music, "Essay on Musical Criticism," 300, 301; French translation of, 296; genesis of, 49-56; models for, 56-64; contemporary assessments of, 284-85; portions of directed against Hawkins, 114-15; progressive view of history in, 53, 55, 142, 145, 204; shortage of space in, 234-35; triumph of, over Hawkins's *History,* 108-9. *See also* Burney, Works: Plan for a General History of Music;
    Lettera del defonto signor Giuseppe Tartini alla signora Maddalena Lombardini, 208;
    Memoirs of Metastasio, 223;
    Plan for a General History of Music, 49-56, 297-302; translations of, 313n.6; versions of, 313n.8;
    "Plan for a Public Music School," 106-8;
    Rees's *Cyclopaedia,* articles for, 290;
    The Tours, influence of on CB, 93-94; parody of, by Collier, 106-8; *The Present State of Music in Germany, the Netherlands, and the United Provinces,* 75, 78-93, 90, 193-94, 196, 213; apology for remarks made in, 92-94; compared with Italian, 90; plan for, 78-79; read to queen by FB, 92-93; reviews of, English, 79-80; reviews of, German, by Reichardt, 87; reviews of, German, by Forkel, 87-88; second edition of, 81, 91; translation of, 80-90; *The Present State of Music in France and Italy,* 65-78; English editions of, 65, 66-74; Baretti's corrections of, 71; German translation of, 75-78; Italian reception of, 71-72; plan for French translation of, 70; reviews of, English, 66-68; reviews of, German, 77-78;

reviews of, Italian, 317-18n.41; second edition of, 73-74; translations of, 74-78, 319n.64; use of other sources in, 318n.43; versions of, 71-74
WORKS: MUSIC
23, 24, 199, 211; "Constancy," 32, 38; *Four Patriotic Songs,* 184; *A Midsummer Night's Dream,* 232; *La Musica che si canta annualmente nelle funzioni della settimana santa nella cappella pontifica,* 75, 77; *Preludes, Fugues and Interludes for the Organ* (1787), 22; *Robin Hood,* 182; *Six Cornet Pieces* (1751), 22; *Six Sonatas for the Harpsichord* (1766), 40, 191-92; *Six Sonatas for two Violins... Opera Prima* (1748), 22; *A Second Number of Two Sonatas for the Harpsichord and Forte Piano* (1772), 40; *XII Canzonetti a due voci in canone* (1790), 22
Burney, Charles Rousseau, 185, 200, 201, 202, 294
Burney, Esther, 200, 202
Burney, Frances, 49-50, 203, 302; account of appearance at Windsor, 10; biography of CB, 1-6; editorial work, 2-5; publishers notes on *Commemoration,* 155; reading of *German Tour* at court, 92-93; view of her father's career, 3-5
Burton, Avery, 132
Busby, Thomas, 37, 38, 261, 292
"But who may abide" (Handel), 160
"By man came also the Resurrection"(Handel), 159
Byrd, William, 51, 126, 136, 137, 159, 185-88, 190, 288

Caccini, Giulio, 225
La caduta de' gigianti (Gluck), 238
Caffarelli. *See* Majorano, Gaetano
Caldara, Antonio, 153, 164
Callcott, John Wall, 217
Calvin, Jean, 134
Calvisius, Sethus, 57
Calzabigi, Ranieri di, 275
Camerata, 225
Campioni, Carlo Antonio, 192, 208
Cannabich, Christian, 192, 216
Canon, 180-81
Cantata, 228-30, 339n.40
Capriccio, 42
Carestini, Anna, 244, 255
Carissimi, Giacomo, 58, 143, 153, 226, 233, 288
Carse, Alan, 9
Cassiaux, Dom. Phil. Jos., 316n.60
Castor et Pollux (Rameau), 263-69, 354n.210

Catalani, Angelica, 281
Catch, 180-81, 339n.37
Catch as Catch Can (Hilton), 181
Cathedral service, 141
Cathedral Music (Boyce), 136, 143
Cavalieri, Emilio de', 152
Cavalli, Pier Francesco, 157, 226, 228-29, 231
"Cease Myne Eyes" (Morley), 172
Cerone, Domenico Pietro, 56-57
Cesti, Marc' Antonio, 226, 228, 229
Chamber music, defined, 171
Chant, 110
Chant, Ambrosian, 111
Chapel, Royal, 141
Chappell, William, charges CB of plagiarism, 291
Charles I, King of England, 205
Charles II, King of England, 141, 180, 205, 206
Chastellux, François-Jean de, 224
Chaucer, 122
Cherubini, Luigi, 260, 272, 280
Child, William, 141, 180, 291
"Ch'io mi scordi di te" (Mozart), 277
"Chi per pieta mi dice" (Jommelli), 165
Choice Collection of Lessons for the Harpsichord or Spinet (Purcell), 189
Choron, Alexandre, 296
Church music, 76-77, 113-14, 125, 127, 137, 162-63, 164, 167; defined, 163; cathedral service in, 136-37; difficulty in studying, 125; propriety in, 148-52, 164; CB's standard of evaluation of, 125; early Christian, 110-13; uniformity in style of, 138; Flemish, 139; Netherlands, 139-40; fifteenth century, 126-31; Renaissance, 126-34; CB's apology for, 132; seventeenth-century English, 140-44; seventeenth-century French, 144-45; eighteenth-century English, 145-52; eighteenth-century French, 168; eighteenth-century German, 167; Spanish, 139. *See also* polyphony, sacred music, chant, mass, motet and country of origin
Cibber, Colley, 233
Cimadoro, Giovanni Battista, 5
Cimarosa, Domenico, 237, 247, 260, 272, 278
Clari, Giovanni Carlo Maria, 164, 288
Clayton, Thomas, 234
Clementi, Muzio, 5, 200
La clemenza di Tito (Mozart), 278, 279, 280
Clio and Euterpe, 182-83
Cocchi, Gioacchino, 184, 247
Coleman, Charles, 178, 180
Coleman, Edward, 180
Colista, Matteo, 77
Collier, Joel. *See* Bicknell, John
Colonna, Giovanni Paola, 164, 168, 288

"Comfort ye my people" (Handel), 158
Comus (Lawes), 232
Concert of Ancient Music, 136, 154
Concert Spirituel, 209, 260, 261
Les contes Moraux (Grétry), 261-62
Conti, Giovachino, 258
Cook, Henry, 180
Coperario (John Cooper), 180
Corelli, Arcangelo, 27, 40, 58, 127, 129, 143, 205, 210, 212, 218, 229, 240, 288, 290, 343-44n.138; assessment of, 206-8; influence on Croft, 145; plagiarism of by Bononcini, 245
Così fan tutte (Mozart), 278
Counterpoint, CB's attitude toward, 22-26, 94
Couperin, François, 28, 188
Courtenay, John, 184
Couteaux, *See* Arthur
Cramer, William, 200, 202, 342-43n.115
Creation, The (Haydn), 168-69
Crescentini, Giralomo, 280
Crisp, Samuel, 8, 66-68, 79, 104
Critical vocabulary, 20-45
  barbarism, 21
  caricato, 35
  character, 27
  chargé, 35
  chiarezza, 35
  clarity, 35-36
  clearness, 35, 236-37
  contrast, 36, 159-60
  contrivance, 25-26
  easy, 29, 30
  effects, 35
  elegance, 31
  expression, 17, 34
  extraneous (modulation), 38-40
  feeling, 31-32
  fire, 35
  force, 35
  genius, 28-29, 43
  gothic, 25
  grace, 21
  harmony, 37-42
  imagination, 27
  invention, 27
  laboured, 26
  licence, 21
  melody, 36-37
  natural, 30
  pathos, 32
  simplicity, 30-31
  spirit, 35
  sublime, 34-35
  taste, 17-19, 42-45
  transparency, 36
Criticism, approach to, 17-28; attitude of CB toward, 11-15; creed of, 330; of living musicians, 12
Croft, William, 51, 145-48, 149, 164, 170, 290

Crosdill, John 5
Crotch, William, 12, 203, 216-17
"Crudel perche finora" (Mozart), 277
"Crudel, tu non farai" (Handel), 239
La Cythère assiégée (Gluck), 275
Cuzzoni, Francesca, 244

Dance, 280
Dante, 121
Dard, M., 316n.60
David, 51, 102-3, 299
De beata virgine (Josquin), 26
Defesch, Willem, 246
"Deh respirar lasciatemi" (Vinci), 229
"Deh vieni" (Mozart), 277
Delcambre, Mlle. (singer), 261
Demofoonte (Hasse), 238
Dent, Edward, 304
Des Prez, Josquin, 26, 29, 126-31, 132, 134, 163, 170, 284; CB's enthusiasm for, 126-27, 131; inventor of the true choral style, 126; model of excellence, 131
Devisme, Louis, 81, 87, 93, 295
Diana ed Endimione (Pescetti), 255
Dibdin, Charles, 184
Diderot, Denis, 68-69, 73
Diderot, Mlle., 69, 73
Dioclesian (Purcell), 233
Ditters von Dittersdorf, Karl, 213, 216, 304
Divisions, as hallmark of style, 248-59
Don Giovanni (Mozart), 277, 279
Doni, Giovanni Battista, 225
Dowland, John, 179
Dragon of Wantley, The (Lampe), 245
Duckles, Vincent, 50
Duni, Egidio Romualdo, 272, 273
Durante, Francesco, 164, 168, 236, 237
Dussek, Jan Ladislav, 200-202

Early music, arrangements of, 113, 117-20, 328n.95
Ebeling, Christoph Daniel, 37, 60, 81-83, 90, 91, 93, 94, 138, 167, 193, 276, 293, 294; translates the *Italian Tour,* 74-79; reaction to the *German Tour,* 80-82
Eckard, Johann Gottfried, 78, 192
Egyptian music, 101-102
Eichner, Ernst, 78, 192, 200
Elizabethan music, 172-74, 185-88
Eloi, Eloi (Harrington), 14
Encyclopédists, 65, 68, 93, 297
English music, 184-85; medieval, 121-23; renaissance, sacred, 132-38; renaissance, secular vocal, 172-74; seventeenth-century instrumental, 204-6; eighteenth-century, 210-12; song, 171-72, 182-85
English school, 181-82
Ercole amante (Cavalli), 231
Erismena (Cavalli), 226

Index 375

Ernelinde (Philidor), 74
Ernst, Franz Anton, 198
Eschenburg, Johann Joachim, 195, 196, 293
Esther (Handel), 157
Ethnic music. See national music
Euridice (Peri and Caccini), 225-26
"Even so in Christ" (Handel), 159
"Every Valley" (Handel), 161
Eximeno, Antonio, 25, 36

Fancy, 185-88, 204
Faramondo (Handel), 255
Farinelli (Carlo Broschi), 48, 102-3, 244, 248-54, 255, 258-59
Farnaby, Giles, 190
Fasch, Johann Friedrich, 167
Fasch, Karl Friedrich Christian, 198
Faustina (Hasse, née Bordoni), 244
Favart, Charles, 262
Fayrfax Manuscript, 171
Fayrfax, Robert, 132
Fellowes, Edmund H., 172, 179
Fel, Marie, 262
Ferrarese del Bene, Adriana, 280
Fevin, Antoine, 132
Il filosofo di campagna (Galuppi), 247
Filtz, Anton, 192, 206
Fioroni, Giovanni Andrea, 111
Fischer, Johann Christian, 78, 92, 210
Fiske, Roger, 277
Fitzwilliam Virginal Book, 185-88
Flavius (Handel), 245
Fleischer, Friedrich, 84, 198
Folk music. See national music
"For as in Adam all die" (Handel), 159
Forkel, Johann Nikolaus, 80, 196, 295, 299; assessment of CB's work, 293-94; attacks on German Tour, 87-88; plagiarisms of CB, 89, 292-93; response to, by CB, 88-89
Forty Select Anthems (Greene), 148
"Fortz chauza es tot to major dan," 117-20
"For unto us a child is born" (Handel), 158, 160
Fountaine, Brig, 87, 276
"Frà l'orror" (Handel), 240
Framery, Nicholas Étienne, 70-71, 317n.39
Frederick the Great, King of Prussia, 83, 85
French music, 74; CB acknowledges prejudice, 300; CB's attack in the Italian Tour, 66-71; medieval, 118; Renaissance, 132; Renaissance, sacred, 138-39; seventeenth-century instrumental, 209; seventeenth-century secular vocal, 182; eighteenth-century instrumental, 209
Frescobaldi, Girolamo, 189, 190, 195, 204, 288
Fux, Johann Joseph, 164, 167

Gabrieli, Andrea, 189
Gafurius, Franchino, 111
Galliari (Bibiena), Andorno, 244

Galliari (Bibiena), Bernardo, 244
Galuppi, Baldassare, 32, 35, 60, 73, 77-78, 167, 197, 236, 237, 242, 255, 273; church music, 163-64; comic operas of, 246-47
Garrick, David, 71
Gasparini, Francesco, 288
Gassmann, Florian Leopold, 90, 164
Geminiani, Francesco, 13, 27, 190-91, 212, 218, 233, 288; instrumental music of assessed, 210; taste for French music, 67
Genius, lack of, in Germans 80-81; relationship to cultivation, 90
George II, King of England, 8
George III, King of England, 92, 286, 289, 335n.118; CB recommends music as cure for, 103; intervention in writing Account, 154-56; preference for Handel, 286
George IV, King of England, 45
Gerard, Alexander, 44
Gerber, Ernst Ludwig, 294-95
Gerbert, Martin, 56, 63-64, 91, 116
German music, 78-79, 89-90; Bode's defense of, 86; CB's awareness of, 78; compared to Italian, 94; medieval, 123; Renaissance, 138; seventeenth century, 144; seventeenth-century instrumental, 209; seventeenth-century secular vocal, 182; eighteenth-century instrumental, 209-18
Gesualdo, Carlo, 174-76, 303
Giacomelli, Geminiano, 308n.61
Giardini, Felice de, 14, 107, 184, 199, 208, 210, 211, 218
Gibbons, Orlando, 136, 140, 181, 189, 204
Giornovichi, Giovanni, 5
Gladwin, John, 13
Gli equivoci nel sembiante (Scarlatti, A.), 229
Gli schiavi per amore (Paisiello), 247
"Glory to God" (Handel), 159
Gluck, Christoph Willibald, 86, 87, 90, 92, 231, 237, 272, 277, 303; assessment of, 274-76; compared with Hasse, 274; London performance of Orfeo, 222
Goldwin, John, 291
Gossec, François Joseph, 296
Grassineau, James, 315-16n.60
Graun, Johann Gottlieb, 85
Graun, Karl Heinrich, 85, 164, 167, 276
Gray, James, 74
Greene, Maurice, 51, 148-52, 164, 165, 246, 290
Grétry, André Ernst Modeste, 273, 296
Greville, Fulke, 7-8, 9
Grimaldi, Nicola, 248-52
Guadagni, Gaetano, 258, 352n.169
Guglielmi, Pietro Alessandro, 237, 278, 281
Guido d'Arezzo, 51, 113, 114
Gui, Pierre, 68

Halde, Jean Baptiste du, 54
"Hallelujah Chorus" (Handel), 160

Hanboys, John, 122-23
Handel, George Frideric, 13, 27, 28, 35, 67, 73, 86, 87, 90, 92, 103, 153, 165, 167, 189, 192, 203, 210, 212, 218, 229, 233, 234, 244, 246, 255, 276, 277, 282, 301, 305; accompaniments of arias by, 238-44; adapts style to suit singers, 256-57; arias of, 350n.116; compared with Bach, 195-96; compared with Bononcini, 350n.113; compared to Hasse, 243-44; compared with Purcell, 143; dominance of, 162; effect on English music of, 304; errors of text setting by, 157-59; evaluations of, by CB, 287-89; extensive treatment of in GHM, 234-35; fugues of, 190; and George II, 7-9; Hawkins's criticism of, 160-61; instrumental music of, 210; instrumental music of, in opera, 242-43; keyboard music of, 190-91; merits compared with vices, 243; modernism of, 240; operas of, 238-43; oratorios of, 154-162; oratorio choruses of, 35; organ music of, 198; overtures of, 242; plagiarisms of, 245; songs of, 184; treatment of, in CB's works, 286-89
Handelians, influence of, 154-56, 243-44, 286-90; jealous of Haydn, 169
Harrington, Henry, 14
Hasse, Johann Adolph, 25, 37, 63, 73, 86, 87, 90, 91, 92, 103, 113, 152, 164, 167, 197, 236, 240, 244, 273, 275, 276, 277; compared with Gluck, 274; compared with Handel, 243-44, 289; Neapolitan style of, 237; sacred music of, 166-67
Hässler, Johann Wilhelm, 215
Have Mercy Upon Me O God (Humfrey), 141
Hawkins, Sir John, 108, 123, 126, 143, 172, 179, 188, 295, 297, 304, 328n.105, 332n.43; achievement of, compared with CB, 283-85; Blow, evaluation of, 143; claims for superiority of early music, 126; critical response to his work, 284-85; assessment of Gesualdo's madrigals, 175; *History* impeding CB's work, 110-12, 121; *History* vanquished by CB's, 108-9; influence, 114-16, 117, 133-34; manner of writing history, 133-34; plagiarisms of by CB, 290-93
Haydn, Franz Joseph, 4, 5, 29, 37, 41, 46, 78, 85, 92, 143, 164, 201, 202, 212, 217-18, 219, 245, 278, 297, 304, 305; CB's advocacy, of, 214; effort to bring to England for opera, 280; instrumental music of, 208, 209, 213-15; keyboard music of, 198-99; oratorios of, 168-69; masses of, 276; string quartets of, 214
Hebrew music, 103
"He comes, he comes to end our woes" (Handel), 154
"He shall feed His flock" (Handel), 161

"He trusteth in God" (Handel), 155
"He was despised and rejected of men" (Handel), 157-58, 161
Hemlow, Joyce, 6
Henry VIII, King of England, 332n.43
Hiller, Johann Adam, 31, 78, 84
Hilton, John, 179
"His yoke is easy" (Handel), 158
Hoffmann, Heinrich Anton, 86, 213
Holbach, Baron Paul Thyry d', 69-70, 78
Holtzbauer, Ignatz, 192, 216
Hook, James, 202
Huber, Pancrace, 213
Hucbald, 114
Humfrey, Pelham, 140, 141, 143, 181
Hummel, Johann Nepomuk, 202, 203, 215

Idalide (Sarti), 281
Idomeneo (Mozart), 279
"I know that my Redeemer liveth" (Handel), 161
Imitation, of nature in music, 100; literal, censured, 157
Indian Queen (Purcell), 233
Ingegnesi, Angelo, 222-23
In Josquinum a prato (Ducis), 127
Institut de France, 296-97
Instrumental music (chamber and orchestral), 203-19, 298-99; influence of performer on, 206; Renaissance, 203-4
Interregnum, 141
Iphigénie en Tauride (Gluck), 274
Isaac, Heinrich, 132
Isacco figura del Redentore (Jommelli), 165
Israel in Egypt (Handel), 159
Italian music, compared with German, 90, 94; medieval, 118-19; seventeenth-century, 144. *See also* cantata, madrigal, mass, motet, oratorio and opera

Jackson, William, 200, 215, 216, 278
James I, King of England, 205
Jelyotte, Pierre, 262
Jenkins, John, 180, 204
Johnson, Robert, 134
Johnson, Samuel, 116; definitions of, 7, 21, 26, 29, 31, 32, 34, 35; hard words of, 42; literary estate of, 3
Jommelli, Niccolò, 27, 32, 73, 91, 161, 164, 197, 236, 273, 275-76, 277; operas of, 237-38; overtures of, 212; sacred music of, 165-66
Jozzi, Giuseppe, 191
Julius Caesar (Handel), 241

Kasar, William, 132
Keeble, John, 28
Keiser, Reinhard, 230
Kelly, Earl of, 212, 278

Kelly, Michael, 277
Kelway, Joseph, 28
Kerman, Joseph, 172, 303
Keyboard music, 185-203; eighteenth century, 190-203; eighteenth-century German, 198-203; eighteenth-century Italian, 197; Renaissance 185-88
King's Band, 9, 286
King's Band of Music in Ireland, 10
Kircher, Athanasius, 57
Kirnberger, Johann Philipp, 23
Klopstock, Friedrich, 80
Knox, John, 134
Kollmann, A.F.C., 23, 195
Koželuck, Leopold Anton, 200, 216
Krebs, Johann Ludwig, 77
Kunzen, Friederich, 293

La Borde, Jean Benjamin, 118, 137, 144-45, 168, 189, 209, 293, 315n.60, 329n.126
Lalande, J.J. de la, 76
Lampe, Johann Friedrich, 245, 246
Lampugnani, Giovanni Battista, 255
Landon, H.C. Robbins, 215
Lanier, Nicolaus, 178, 179
La Rue, Pierre, 132
"Lasciami sola a piangere" (Scarlatti, A.), 229
Lasso, Orlando di, 126, 139, 178
Latilla, Gaetano, 237
Latrobe, Christian Ignatius, 216, 276, 293
Lawes, Henry, 51, 178, 179, 232
Lawes, William, 51, 179, 205
Le Clair, Jean Marie, 209
Legrenzi, Giovanni, 206
Leo, Leonardo, 164, 236, 237, 244
Library, plan for, 330n.150
Libretto, 221-24
"Lift up your heads, o' ye gates" (Handel), 159
Linley, Thomas, Jr., 73, 231
Lipking, Lawrence, 286, 287, 289, 302, 305
La locanda (Paisiello), 281
Lonsdale, Roger, 1, 2, 5, 284, 295, 303
Lotario (Handel), 245
Lotti, Antonio, 163, 164
Louis XIV, King of France, 206
Lucchese, Andrea, 91
Luigi. *See* Rossi
Lully, Jean-Baptiste, 56, 58, 67, 85, 263, 274, 275, 301; Handel's plagarism of, 245; model for Purcell, 233; operas of, 231, 269
Lupi, Johannes (?), 178
Lupus, 178
Luther, Martin, 134
Lyric poetry, 223-24

Machaut, Guillaume de, 118
"Mad Bess" (Purcell), 97, 182
Madrigals, 174-78; of Gesualdo, 174-75; of Marenzio, 174; of Monteverdi, 176-77; uniformity of style of, 174
Madrigal Society, 175
Mainwaring, John, 193
Majo, Ciccio di, 237
Majorana, Gaetano, 244
Malcolm, Alexander, 58-59
Malone, Edmond, 14, 174
Mancini, Giambatista, 113
Manna, Gennaro, 237, 238
Mannheim school, 211-12, 218
Manzoli, Giovanni, 281
Mara, Gertrude, 281
Marbeck, John, 132
Marcello, Benedetto, 288
Marchand, Louis, 28
Marchesi, Luigi, 44
Marchetto da Padua, 113-14
Le maréchal ferrant (Philidor), 73
Marenzio, Luca, 137, 174, 175
Margarita, Francesca, 248-51
Marpurg, Friedrich Wilhelm, 23, 56, 57, 60, 78, 84, 90, 91, 185, 196, 230, 276, 306, 315n.42, 315n.43
Martini. *See* Sammartini
Martini, Giambattista (Padre), 56, 60-61, 62-63, 71, 93, 102, 111, 136, 167
Mason, William, 49-50, 52, 117, 135-36, 148, 202
Mass, 126-29
Il matrimonio segreto (Cimarosa), 260
Mattei, Saverio, 238
Matteis, Nicola, 206, 343n.133, 343n.134
Mattheson, Johann, 60, 78, 84, 86, 157, 276, 295, 315n.41
Mercer, Frank, 21
Mersenne, Marin, 57
Merula, 238
Messiah (Handel), 155, 157-162
Metastasio, Pietro Antonio, 3, 14, 114, 222-24, 229, 244, 275, 281-82, 297; collaboration with Hasse, 237; Jommelli, and, 238
Micheli, Romano, 26
Mingotti, Regina (Valentini), 255, 281
Minuet, 76-77
Miserere à 5 (Josquin), 127
Miserere à 5 (Jommelli), 165
Misericordias Domini (Josquin), 127-28
Missa di dadi (Josquin), 127, 130
Modes, church, 110-11
La Molinara (Paisiello), 281
Mondonville, Jean-Joseph, 209
Monsigny, Pierre-Alexandre, 272, 273
Monte, Philippe de, 178
Monteverdi, Claudio, 22, 176, 225-26
Monticello, Angelo Maria (singer), 255
Monza, Carlo, 163
Morales, Cristóbal de, 139

Index

Morelet, André, 32
Morichelli, Bosello Anna, 5
Morley, Thomas, 51, 115, 136, 137-38, 172, 218, 290, 313n.13
Mornington, Garrett Wellesley, First Earl of, 165-66
"Moro lasso" (Gesualdo), 175
La morte di Mitridate (Nasolini), 273-74
Mortellari, Michele, 30
Moscovita (singer), 255
Motet, 126-27
Mount-Edgcumbe, Richard Edgcumbe, Earl of, 278, 281
Mouton, Jean, 26, 132
Mozart, Wolfgang Amadeus, 46, 81, 201, 202, 203, 214, 217-18, 219, 245, 304, 305; comic operas of, 247; instrumental music of, 215-18; keyboard music of, 200; masses of, 167, 169; operas of, 276, 277-80; piano music of, 199-200
Mumssen, J., 81
Muris, Jean de, 115-16
Music, healing power of, 102-3; invention of, 101
Musica ficta, 127, 130
Musical Offering (Bach), 195
Musica sacra (Croft), 145-47
Musica transalpina, 172
Müthel, Johann Gottfried, 84, 86, 198, 200-201
Muzio scevola (Bononcini), 245
"My Flocks feed" (Weelkes), 174
Myslivecek, Joseph, 276

Nardini, Pietro, 73
Nares, James, 191
Nasolini, Sebastiano, 273-75, 355n.243
National music, 52, 54-55, 117, 297-98
Naumann, Johann Amadeus, 276
Neapolitan school, 132, 167, 243-38, 244, 282
Neefe, Christian Gottlob, 84
Newman, William, 93, 191
Nicolini. *See* Grimaldi, Nicola (singer)
Noel (Caurroy), 139
Non nobis Domine (Byrd), 139, 181
"Non piu andrai" (Mozart), 277
"Non vi piacque ingiusti Dei" (Handel), 255
Norman, John, 132
North, Roger, 59, 204
Notation, 112-13
Le nozze di Figaro (Mozart), 277

Ockeghem, Johannes, 126
Ode of Pindar, 98-99
Odo de Clugny, 114
O God, Thou Art my God (Purcell), 40
"Oh! Oh! Master Moor" (Lampe), 245
Old music, CB's intolerance of, 86
Olimpiade (Jommelli), 238

O Lord Rebuke Me Not (Croft), 147
Omnes penitus, 122
Opera, 76-77, 221-22; audience as legislator of, 225; balance of elements in, 222-26; comic, in England, 246-47; comic, French, 272-73, 317n.20; in England, decline in, 280-81; in England, early attempts, 233; in England, of Handel, 234-35, 238-46; in England, native English, 245-46; in England, opponents of, 233-34; in England, seventeenth century, 231-34; in France, 97, 98, 301; in France, seventeenth century, 227, 231; in France, eighteenth century, 260-73; in Germany, seventeenth century, 230-31; in Germany, eighteenth century, 276-80; Italian, 73; Italian, seventeenth century, 225-30; Italian, Neapolitan, 236-38; principles for criticism of, 221-25; resources for writing history of, 234-35; role of singers in creating, 247-59, 352n.169; role of singers in creation of French, 260-72
Oratorio, 144, 152-53, 336n.137; chorus in, 156-57; classical, 162-70; German, 166; Handel's compared with modern, 153-54; standard of, 156-57
O'Reilly, Robert May, 278
Orfeo (Gluck), 274, 275
Orfeo (Monteverdi), 225-26
Orfeo (Rossi), 231
Organ music, 189, 195-96
Organum, 113
Orlando (Handel), 243
Orontea (Cesti), 226
Orpheus Britannicus (Purcell), 181
O Sing Unto the Lord (Handel), 161
Out of the Deep (Croft), 145
"O worship the Lord" (Handel), 161

Pacchierotti, Gaspare, 202, 255, 280, 281; taste of, 43-44
Paisiello, Giovanni, 5, 31, 46, 231, 236, 237, 238, 245, 260, 272, 273, 275-76, 278, 281, 311n.73; comic operas of, 246-47
Palestrina, Giovanni Pierluigi da, 12, 75, 126, 136, 137, 138, 139-40, 143, 163, 169, 175, 288
Pammelia, 25, 181
Pantheon Opera, 280-81
Paride ed Elena (Gluck), 275
Parnasso in Festa (Handel), 245
Parody mass, 131
Parsons, Robert, 134
Parsons, William, 203
Pasche, William, 132
Pasticcio, 222
Il pastor fido (Handel), 259
Pathetic style, 32-34, 311n.79
Patronage, CB's attitude toward, 6, 10; CB's struggle to gain, 7-11; influence of, 286-89

Pepusch, Johann, 111, 188
Pérez, David, 132, 164, 166, 237, 273
Performance, attributes of good, 44
Pergolesi, Giovanni Battista, 27, 40, 152, 164, 243-35, 236, 237, 238, 241, 244, 273, 293
Peri, Jacopo, 225
"Per salvarti" (Handel), 245
Persée (Lully), 245
Pescetti, Giovanni Battista, 191, 255, 310n.61
Petrarch, 121
Pevernage, Andries, 178
Philidor, François, 73-74, 272, 273
Philip V, King of Spain, 103
Philips, Peter, 185
Phrase, in music, 37, 269-72
Piccinni, Niccolò, 27, 32, 73, 197, 231, 236, 237, 238, 272, 273, 275-76; comic operas of, 247-47
Piozzi, Gabriele Mario, 184
Plagiarism, by CB of Hawkins, 290-92; by opera composers, 245-46; from CB's work by Germans, 292-93; from CB's work in England, 292; from CB's work in France, 292
Playford, John, 178-79
Pleyel, Ignatz, 208, 214, 216, 218, 277
Plutarch, 96
Polyphony, before 1450, 118, 123-24
Poole, H. Edmund, 72
Porpora, Nicola, 236, 237, 240, 242, 244, 351n.146; compared with Handel, 289
Porter, John, 291-92
Power, Lionel, 132
Praetorius, Michael, 57, 189
Printz, Wolfgang, 57, 295
Professional Concert, 214
Psalmody, metrical, 15, 134-36, 332-33n.49
Pucitta, Vincenzo, 278
Purcell, Henry, 22, 40, 51, 136, 140, 143, 145, 153, 164, 165, 170, 182, 189, 288, 290, 291-92; catches of, 181-82; instrumental music of, 205, 210; operas of, 233; style compared with Handel's, 233
Pythagorus, 99

Quantz, Johann Joachim, 86, 261
Quarrel of the Ancients and Moderns, 96
Queen's Band of Music, 10
Querelle des bouffons, 231

Raguenet, François, 58
Rameau, Jean-Philippe, 231, 263-69, 274, 275, 284, 300, 301
Recitative, 221, 222, 227-28, 241-42
Reichardt, Johann Friedrich, 80, 84, 198, 294; assessment of Bach, 196; attack on CB's *German Tour,* 87; CB's response to, 88-89; plagiarism of, 292
Reilly, Edward, 91

Renaissance music, attributes of, 140; phrasing in, 172; uniformity of style of, 134
Reynolds, Sir Joshua, 116
Ricciarelli, Signor (singer), 255
Richard Coeur de Lion (Grétry), 273
Rinaldo (Handel), 245
Rinaldo di Capua, 237, 244
Rodio, Rocco, 189
Rogers, Benjamin, 180
Rolle, Johann Heinrich, 164, 166
Romanina, La (singer), 244
Roman school, 174; in Renaissance, 132, 139-40
Rore, Cipriano de, 139, 178
Rosamond (Addison), 234
Rosa, Salvatore, 229
Roseingrave, Thomas, 13, 341n.69
Roselli, Agrippino, 5
Rosen, Charles, 217
Rossi, Luigi, 58, 226, 230, 231
Rousseau, Jean-Jacques, 28, 31, 32, 35, 38, 40, 43, 52, 58, 68, 70, 98, 201, 218, 236, 261, 274, 295, 297, 298, 299, 300; influence of, 62-63, 66-68, 221, 281-82, 301; opera, criticism of, 221, 261-72; unity of melody, 235-36; works of, basis for *Cyclopedia* article, 290
Royal Consort (Lawes, W.), 205

Sacadus, 105
Sacchini, Antonio, 27, 73, 164, 184, 197, 231, 236, 237, 272, 273, 275-76, 281, 305; sacred music of, 167; operas of, 260
Sack, Johann Philipp, 77
Sacred music, history of, incomplete, 162. *See also* church music
St. Germain, Count, 210
Sala, Nicola, 237
Salieri, Antonio, 272
Salomon, Johann Peter, 5, 215, 217-18
Salve Regina (Hasse), 31, 166
Sammartini, Giovanni Battista, 163, 192, 208, 210
Sammartini, Giuseppe, 192, 208
Sarti, Giuseppe, 236, 273, 275-76, 278, 281
Saul, 102-3
Saul (Handel), 245
Savile, Jeremy, 180
Scarlatti, Alessandro, 58, 164, 229, 237, 240, 242, 288; contribution of, 230
Scarlatti, Domenico, 13, 25, 41, 188, 190, 192, 197, 341n.69; influence on CB's compositions, 38-40, 191-92; keyboard music, 191, 193, 200
Scena for Tenducci (Mozart), 278
Scheibe, Johann Adolph, 78
Scheidemann, Heinrich, 189
Scheidt, Samuel, 144, 189

Schein, Johann Hermann, 144
Schlick, Arnolt, 189
Schobert, Johann, 78, 192, 198, 200, 305
Scholes, Percy, 1, 72, 89, 295, 297
Schubart, (Christian Friedrich) Daniel, 80, 294-95
Schultz, Johann, 198
Schuster, Joseph, 277
Schütz, Heinrich, 144
Schwanberg, Johann Gottfried, 86
Schweizer, Anton, 84
Schwindl, Friedrich, 78, 208
Science of music, 53-54
"Scoglio d'immota fronte" (Handel), 241
Select Musicall Ayres and Dialogues (Playford), 178, 179
Semiramide (Bianchi), 5, 307n.9
"Se nel ben" (Stradella), 152
Senesino, Francesco, 241, 248-52
"Se Poma Filli" (Pergolesi), 153
Serva Pedrona (Pergolesi), 153
"S'estinto è l'idol mio" (Handel), 239
Seven Last Words, The (Handel), 215
Shakespeare, William, 174, 231-32
Shaw, Watkin, 141, 142
Shepherd, John, 132, 133-34
Shield, William, 38, 42, 184, 195
Simpson, Christopher, 180, 204
"Since by man came death" (Handel), 159
Singer, French, in opera, 260-272; history of, in England, 234, 247-259, 280-81; role in creating opera, 247-59; technique of, 261, 162-63; training of, 327n.69
Sing Unto the Lord (Croft), 148
"Sing ye to the Lord" (Handel), 157, 159
Siroe (Hasse), 238
Siroe (Handel), 239-40, 255
Sister-arts, 76, 222-26, 227, 238
"Si tornerò" (Handel), 255
Smith, John Christopher, 190, 246
Smith, Stafford, 122
"A Song from Thibaut, King of Navarre", 171
"Song on the Victory at Agincourt", 122
"Song unto God" (Croft), 147
Le sorcier (Philidor), 74
"Sorge infausta una procella" (Handel), 161-62, 239
"Sovengati o bella" (Handel), 245
Spem in alium (Tallis), 136
Spenser, Edmund, 174
Stabat Mater (Pergolesi), 40
Stamitz, Johann, 91, 192, 208, 209, 211, 212, 216, 218
Stanley, John, 10, 13, 28, 145, 149; on *Messiah*, 162
Steffani, Agostino, 164, 229, 288
Steibelt, Daniel, 199, 200
Sterkel, Johann Franz, 277

Stile, Sir Francis, 97
Stillingfleet, Benjamin, 30
Stölzel, Gottfried Heinrich, 167
Storace, Anna Selina (Nancy), 277, 278
Storace, Stephen, 277, 278
Strada, Anna Maria del Po, 258
Stradella, Alessandro, 137, 143, 229; model for Purcell, 233; oratorios of, 152-53
Suard, Jean Baptiste, 68-70
Sulzer, Johann, 293
Sweelinck, Jan Pieterszoon, 189
"Sweet Echo Sweetest Nymphe" (Lawes, H.), 232
Symphony, 211-18

Tallis, Thomas, 51, 126, 136, 288
Tartini, Giuseppe, 30, 73, 77, 208, 210, 218, 313n.12
Tate, Miss, 201
Taverner, John, 132
Te Deum (Purcell), 143
Telemann, Georg Phillip, 164, 167
Tempest (Arne), 231
Teseo (Handel), 245
Tesi-Tramontini, Vittoria, 244
Text setting, 158-59
Thrale, Hester Lynch, 10, 110, 116
Timotheus, 108
"Ti pentirai crudel" (Handel), 239
Toccate d'intavolature di cimbalo et organo (Frescobaldi), 189
Toeschi, Carlo Giuseppe, 216
Tom Jones (Philidor), 74
Tomkins, Thomas, 189
Torelli, Giuseppe, 206
Trabaci, Giovanni Maria, 189
Traetta, Tommaso, 237
Le trame per amore (Paisiello), 31
Trento, Vittorio, 278
"Tristes apprêts, pales flambeaux" (Rameau), 265
"Tu se' morta" (Monteverdi), 226
Twining, Thomas, 50, 52, 54, 55, 96, 99, 105, 108, 110, 116, 121-22, 126, 127, 140, 154-55, 174, 190, 192, 197, 213, 232, 280, 290
Tye, Christopher, 133

Unity of melody, 35

Valenti, Urbani, 248-51
Vanhall, Johann Baptist, 86, 197, 201, 212-13, 214, 218, 304; instrumental music of, 208, 212, 216
Vento, Matthia, 184
Verdelot, Philippe, 178
Verdonck, Corneille, 178
Viennese classical school, 217-18
La villanella rapita (Bianchi), 277

Vinci, Leonardo, 29, 85, 103, 152, 229, 236-37, 240, 241, 244, 260, 273, 275, 276
Vingt-quatre violons du roi, 206
Viol, 204-5
Violin, 205, 208
Viotti, Giovanni Battista, 5
"Vi ricorda a boshi ombrosi" (Monteverdi), 226
Visconti, Guido (singer), 255
Vitry, Phillipe de, 115-16
Vocal music, medieval, 117; secular, 171-85
Vogler, Georg Joseph, 170
Voltaire, François-Marie Arouet de, 209, 231
Vossius, Isaac, 97

Waelrant, Hubert, 178
Wagenseil, Georg Christoph, 78, 198
Walker, Joseph Cooper, 14
Walpole, Robert, 8
Walsh, John, 191
Walther, Johann Gottfried, 57, 59, 189, 209, 291-92
Wanhal. *See* Vanhall, Johann Baptist
Watkins, Glenn, 175
"The Waves of the Sea" (Handel), 161
The Ways of Zion do Mourn (Wise), 142
Webb, William, 179
Weelkes, Thomas, 174
Weerbecke, Gaspar van, 132

Welch, Christopher, 290
Well-Tempered Clavier (Bach), 195
Wert, Giaches de, 178
Wesley, Eliza, 194-95
Wesley, Samuel, 194-95, 218
Westrup, Jack Allan, 303
"Where the Banners of Glory are Streaming" (Attwood), 277
White, Matthew, 136
White, Robert, 136
Willaert, Adrian, 159
Wilson, John, 179
Winter, Peter, 296
Wise Michael, 140, 141, 142, 143, 170
Wolf, Ernst Wilhelm, 84, 164
Worgan, John, 12-14, 28
Wright, Sir James, 71

Xerse (Cavalli), 231

Yaniewicz, Felix, 5

Zanetti, Francesco, 192, 208
Zarlino, Gioseffo, 159, 178
Zauberflöte, Die (Mozart), 278
Zémire et Azor (Grétry), 273
Zeno, Apostolo, 222, 244